Training in Organizations

Needs Assessment, Development, and Evaluation

Fourth Edition

Related Titles

Psychological Testing

Psychological Testing, 5th edition
Kaplan and Saccuzzo

Groups

Group Processes, Group Action
Baron, Kerr, and Nelson

Group Dynamics, 3rd edition
Forsyth

Intergroup Relations
Brewer and Miller

Psychology Applied to Work

Industrial/Organizational Psychology, 3rd edition
Aamodt

Psychology Applied to Work, 5th edition
Muchinsky

Statistics

Comprehending Behavioral Statistics, 2nd edition
Hurlburt

Essentials of Statistics for the Behavioral Sciences, 3rd edition
Gravetter and Wallnau

Training in Organizations

Needs Assessment, Development, and Evaluation

Fourth Edition

Irwin L. Goldstein
University of Maryland

J. Kevin Ford
Michigan State University

WADSWORTH

™

THOMSON LEARNING

Australia • Canada • Mexico • Singapore • Spain • United Kingdom • United States

WADSWORTH

★ ™

THOMSON LEARNING

Publisher: *Vicki Knight*
Acquisitions Editor: *Marianne Taflinger*
Marketing Team: *Joanne Terhaar,*
 Justine Ferguson, and Margaret Parks
Editorial Assistant: *Stacy Green*
Project Editor: *Mary Anne Shahidi*
Production Service: *Lachina Publishing*
 Services
Manuscript Editor: *Kathleen Deselle*

Permissions Editor: *Sue Ewing*
Interior Design: *Adriane Bosworth*
Cover Design: *Denise Davidson*
Cover Illustration: *© Dave Cutler/SIS*
Interior Illustration: *Lachina Publishing*
 Services
Print Buyer: *Vena Dyer*
Typesetting: *Lachina Publishing Services*
Printing and Binding: *Webcom*

For more information about our products, contact us at:
WADSWORTH
10 Davis Drive
Belmont, CA 94002-3098 USA
1-800-423-0563 (Thomson Learning Academic Resource Center)
www.wadsworth.com

Printed in Canada.
10   9   8   7   6   5   4   3   2   1

Library of Congress Cataloging-in-Publication Data

Goldstein, Irwin L. [date]
    Training in organizations : needs assessment, development, and evaluation / Irwin L. Goldstein, J. Kevin Ford.—4th ed.
        p. cm.
    Includes bibliographical references and indexes.
    ISBN 0-534-34554-9
    1. Employees—Training of. 2. Employees—Training of—Evaluation 3. Organizational learning. 4. Assessment centers (Personnel Management procedure) I. Ford, J. Kevin (John Kevin) II. Title.

HF5549.5.T7 G543 2001
658.3'12404—dc21   2001026061

My wife Micki and I dedicate this book to the value-added part of our lives, our grandchildren Miriam, Benjamin, Zachery, and Ethan.
      Irv Goldstein

I dedicate this book to Duke and Mattie Ford, my parents, the best trainers and facilitators one could ever ask for.
      Kevin Ford

Brief Contents

Contents

— clearing.

Chapter 2 A Systematic Approach to Training   22

Chapter 3 The Needs Assessment Phase   34

PART 2   Evaluation

P A R T 3 *Instructional Approaches*

Chapter 7 *Training Delivery: Traditional Instructional Approaches and Emerging Learning Technologies*   *220*

Chapter 8   A Variety of Training Interventions and Learning Experiences   271

Chapter 9   Learning Systems   328

Preface

Training in Organizations was originally published in 1974. Irv Goldstein welcomes with great pleasure Kevin Ford as his partner. This fourth edition is written at a very exciting time when organizations are facing a very competitive environment both domestically and internationally. Technology is revolutionizing both organizations and training systems themselves. It is a time when organizations are moving from an industrial society to a knowledge society. In this environment, there is increasing concern about how to utilize training systems to develop a continuous learning philosophy. Trainers are grappling with how to work with teams, how to develop leaders, and how to respect diversity as well as worrying about how to alleviate individual skill gaps. This dynamic, fast-moving, and complex environment makes it an especially exciting time to revise *Training in Organizations*.

We have written our book for undergraduate and graduate students as well as for researchers and practitioners who are impacted by this changing environment. We continue to believe that needs assessment, design and development of a learning environment, and thoughtful evaluation of instruction efforts form critical foundations for working with training systems in organizational settings. In this book, we work toward considering these perspectives on needs assessment, learning environments, and evaluation within the context of the dynamic changes facing organizations today. We also introduce many of the new training systems, such as virtual reality training and web-based instruction, that themselves have arisen as a result of the changing work and technology environments. Our goal is to capture the excitement of the many research and systems issues that abound both when training is introduced and considered and when new trainees enter the world of the work organization through training programs.

Part 1 emphasizes the needs assessment and learning processes that form the foundation for training programs. Chapter 1 has been rewritten to reflect training issues in the context of a competitive and dynamic working environment. We include information on developments that will affect training policy, such as major changes in the demographics of the working population, the influence of a shift from manufacturing to service markets, the effects of increasing technology in the workplace, and the dynamics of global environments. We also discuss how training is changing in this environment, including topics such as what we know about trainers and training methods and the changes brought about in training systems by the emerging delivery technologies. We note the increasing emphasis on accountability, which in part stems from the current competitive business environment. Following this introductory material, Chapter 2 presents a training systems model that provides the overarching framework that is the structure behind the book. Chapter 2 gives the reader an overview of all the interacting components of needs assessment, design, development, and evaluation of training programs. In a sense, this chapter provides a summary of many of the topics that follow and how they all fit together in a systems framework.

Chapter 3 describes the needs assessment process, including the organizational, task, and person analyses, which in turn provide inputs for the consideration and design of training programs. In the third edition, this chapter was totally rewritten and a new model encompassing the entire needs assessment process was introduced. The model focuses on how needs assessment, as a part of training systems, fits into an organization. This model presents all the components for a needs assessment model, including issues such as organization support and requirements analysis, which describes the decisions that need to be considered before the actual needs assessment begins. For this edition, the model has been refined to include further work. Also, the chapter continues to include a variety of workshop materials and scales that are useful for people who actually conduct needs analyses. Chapter 4 describes the learning environment, including material related to the preconditions of learning, significant issues in learning and instruction, the variables that support transfer, and factors that determine a quality training environment. In the last edition, most of this material was rewritten in order to incorporate the recent work on cognition and instructional theory as it relates to training. Thus, for the first time, concepts like automaticity, advanced organizers, and novice versus expert learners were presented and their relevance to training issues explored. In this edition, there are further extensive revisions to this chapter. A new model is presented that organizes all of the material in the chapter for the reader and provides an overview of the important learning/training components. There is a new section on building effective instruction that takes the reader from the design of training objectives to a plan of instruction. Also, the section on trainee issues is completely updated with new material to reflect a growing research literature on topics such as trainee readiness and trainee motivation to learn. We have added a new section on conditions of transfer, which is very important to both trainers and organizations.

Part 2 focuses on the evaluation process. For us, evaluation is the systematic collection of descriptive and judgmental information necessary to make effective training decisions related to the selection, adoption, value, and modification of various instructional activities. The objectives of instructional programs reflect numerous goals ranging from trainee progress to organizational goals. From this perspective, evaluation is an information-gathering technique that cannot possibly result in decisions that categorize programs as good or bad. Rather, evaluation should capture the dynamic flavor of the training program. The necessary information will then be available to revise training programs to achieve multiple instructional objectives. Chapter 5 on criteria and Chapter 6 on evaluation models were both heavily revised to integrate issues that are common to both chapters, such as the philosophy of evaluation and values. Chapter 5 specifically focuses on the establishment of criteria that are used to measure the multiple objectives of training programs. The major addition to this chapter is a section on the growing research literature concerning the relationships between reactions, learning, behavior, and results. In addition, a new section reflects the development by Kraiger, Ford, and Salas of a more conceptually based classification scheme of learning. This is probably the first new complete conceptual classification scheme concerning criteria since Kirkpatrick originally introduced his model of reactions, learning, behavior, and results. Chapter 6 presents materials about the various evaluation models that are available to provide information for intelligent revisions of training programs. This includes material on different models of the evaluation process, such as considerations about utility, content validity, and individual difference models. The general flavor of many of the designs that have been developed reflects a positive attitude about the use of models that best fit the constraints of the environment. We present a number of new examples of the innovative use of experimental designs.

Part 3 provides information about instructional and training delivery approaches. All the chapters in this section have been thoroughly rewritten and updated. We eliminated discussions of training systems which might have had historical interest but are no longer being utilized in work organizations. We also added sections on most of the new approaches being used while continuing to update materials on approaches that have been included in previous editions. Chapter 7 presents some of the variety of approaches, including rewritten sections on classical lecture and discussion approaches, case studies, and role playing. This is followed by a new section on self-directed learning programs ranging from workbooks to programmed instruction. The chapter closes with a new section on emerging training delivery systems stemming from advances in technology such as distance learning, CD-ROM, web-based instruction, intelligent tutors, and virtual reality training. Chapter 8 is also totally reorganized and rewritten and focuses on training interventions and learning experiences for developing employees, teams, and leaders. It begins with a section on building employee capabilities using techniques such as orientation programs, newcomer socialization, and on-the-job training. The following section focuses on building team effectiveness and has materials on topics such as cross training, team self-management, and adventure and action learning. The last section of Chapter 8 describes techniques for developing leaders, including business simulations, behavior role modeling, assessment centers, diversity training, and global leadership.

We have titled the final chapter of our book "Learning Systems," and our new focus here is on training from a broader, more macro perspective. This approach recognizes that learning is not a discrete event but an everyday experience that occurs within an organizational culture. As organizations view continuous learning as the key to a competitive advantage, training is seen as one component in a larger orientation toward continuous improvement. Thus, in this chapter, we present new materials on training and learning, including sections on total quality and corporate universities as well as the characteristics and challenges of becoming a learning organization. We complete the chapter with updated sections on societal concerns, including increased workforce readiness, ensuring fairness and enhancing opportunities at work, and retraining workers given changing markets. Some of the topics covered in these sections on societal concerns include facilitating school-to-work transition, the glass ceiling, the Americans with Disabilities Act, and training displaced workers.

This book comes at a time when work organizations and training organizations within them are in a rapid state of flux. We hope this fourth edition contributes to an understanding of these issues.

INFORMATION ABOUT INFOTRAC COLLEGE EDITION

A FREE four-month subscription to this extensive on-line library is enclosed with every new copy of this book. This gives you and your students instant access to over 900,000 news and research articles, updated daily and spanning four years. This easy-to-use database features thousands of full-length articles (not abstracts) from hundreds of journals and popular sources. InfoTrac is a cost-free way to expand your library and keep courses up to date. It provides an effective teaching tool that gives students opportunities to research a large variety of topics.

Some of the specific journals and popular magazines that have relevant information on training topics are *Training and Development, HR Focus, Personnel Journal, Personnel Psychology, Human Relations, Workforce, Working Woman, Executive Female, Across the Board,* and many more.

Almost all of the major topics in the Table of Contents are covered in Info-Trac's extensive database. When the general topic "learning" is searched, over 250 references with specific articles are found. Of course, some of those articles might be related to learning in contexts other than training. However, when more specific topics are listed, the information is typically highly correlated with the topics in the text. The following topics and number of citations provide a good illustration of the usefulness of this search engine: employee trainers—over 60 citations; workforce readiness and training—over 130 citations; learning organizations—over 28 citations; management training—over 90 citations; team training—over 25 citations. At the end of each chapter, we list InfoTrac terms relevant to that chapter's material.

ACKNOWLEDGMENTS

In closing, we would both like to say that this text is a result of the efforts of many generous people. We are both indebted to all the authors and researchers who took time from their busy schedules to graciously share their articles, data, ideas, and manuscripts. Those of you who are fortunate enough to be involved in the Society for Industrial and Organizational Psychology know how we feel when we say that our members' generosity in sharing ideas and helping each other is overwhelming. We are especially indebted to the faculty and graduate students of the Industrial-Organizational Psychology programs at the University of Maryland and Michigan State University. We also thank the following reviewers for their helpful comments and suggestions: E. Sam Cox, Central Missouri State University; Philip K. Duncan, West Chester University; Donald Hantula, Temple University; Dennis R. McGough, University of New Haven; Stephanie B. Narvell, Wilmington College; Karen Proudford, Morgan State University; Daniel Sachau, Minnesota State University–Mankato; Debra Steele-Johnson, Wright State University; and David J. Whitney, California State University–Long Beach. We especially thank Marianne Taflinger of Wadsworth who spent vast amounts of energy working with both of us so that this edition actually came to fruition. We are very appreciative of the terrific professional staff at the Wadsworth Group who worked with us every step of the way.

A note from Irv: I also want to express my appreciation to Greg Geoffroy and Dan Mote, respectively Provost and President of the University of Maryland at College Park. They believe that administrators should continue to be active scholars, and, as a result, my efforts and time to complete this manuscript were strongly supported. I also want to warmly thank the staff in the College of Behavioral and Social Science for graciously taking on assignments to allow me time to work on this revision. I am indebted to my two close friends and colleagues, Ben Schneider and Shelly Zedeck, who insist that this academic administrator continues to be an active organizational psychologist. This book is most of all the result of a loving and caring environment designed by my wife, Micki, who gave up many days of family time so that I could continue on projects like this book. My daughter and son, Beth and Harold, were in grade school when the first edition was published, and now they have their own wonderful families and careers. I am very lucky in having a son as a colleague. I am also very fortunate that all of my family understands what support is, and they specialize in love.

A note from Kevin: I want to express my deep appreciation to Irv Goldstein who offered me the opportunity to work with him on this revision to the training book. I have used the earlier editions of this textbook in my graduate and undergraduate courses at Michigan State University. But there is much more to the story than that simple fact. Irv was my guide and mentor relevant to my entry into the field of industrial and organizational (I/O) psychology. Irv taught the first class that I took in I/O psychology when I was an undergraduate student at the University of Maryland. He took pity on this "wet behind the ears" undergraduate who timidly asked if there were any opportunities to gain some research experience. He challenged me in research on a training and performance evaluation project, encouraged me to attend the Ohio State University for graduate school (where he had previously been a faculty member), and supported me in my pursuit of research on improving training and development in work organizations. Thanks, Irv—it is an opportunity of a lifetime to work with you. In addition, I want to thank my graduate school mentor, Rich Klimoski, for helping me to become a better thinker. I greatly appreciate the support of my colleagues at Michigan State University, especially Neal Schmitt, who has always been there to help. Karen Milner deserves many thanks for the terrific research she did on various topics for this book. Her work was always top notch and led to a much better product. The opportunity to work on this revision is in great part a function of my wife, companion, and "stay at home" mom, Melanie, who has been there as my best friend. She picked up the slack when work called or crises loomed. She also helped out in reading and editing parts of this book. Irv talks of his children being in grade school when the first edition was published. In full-circle fashion, this fourth edition is being published with a new family of children. The Ford family includes four children from eight years to one year old—Katie, Tynan, Megyn, and Reilly. Thanks for "forcing" Dad to stop working and start playing in the sandbox, pushing you on the swing set, and in general reminding him to enjoy life each day.

About the Authors

 **Irwin L. Goldstein** (Ph.D., University of Maryland, 1964) is a professor of psychology and dean of the College of Behavioral and Social Sciences at the University of Maryland. His research career has focused on issues facing individuals as they enter work organizations. He is especially interested in how individuals learn about organizations, how they are selected, and how they are trained. Irv is the author of the three previous editions of *Training in Organizations.* He also wrote the training chapter in the *Handbook of Industrial and Organizational Psychology* and edited the 1989 Frontiers Series volume on *Training and Development in Organizations.*

In 1995, Irv received the Swanson award for research excellence from the American Society for Training and Development, and in 1992, he received the Distinguished Service Award from the Society for Industrial and Organizational Psychology. He was also honored by being elected to serve as president of the Society for Industrial and Organizational Psychology. Irv has been elected to fellow status by the American Psychological Association, the American Psychological Society, and the Human Factors Society. He has also served as associate editor of the *Journal of Applied Psychology* and *Human Factors,* and as series editor for the Frontiers Book Series of the Society of Industrial and Organizational Psychology. Currently, he is president of the Society of Industrial and Organizational Psychology Foundation.

 **J. Kevin Ford** (Ph.D., Ohio State University, 1983) is a professor of psychology at Michigan State University. His major research interest involves improving training effectiveness through efforts to advance our understanding of training needs assessment, design, evaluation, and transfer. Kevin also concentrates on building continuous learning and improvement orientations within organizations. He has

published more than 50 articles, chapters, and books. He was the lead author of the book *Improving Training Effectiveness in Work Organizations* and wrote the chapter on employee training for the recent *Encyclopedia of Psychology.*

Kevin is an active consultant on training, teamwork, and organizational development issues in both the private industry and the public sector. His most recent consulting work has been in the areas of leadership development, continuous quality improvement, transformational change, and training evaluation. He is a fellow of the American Psychological Association and the American Psychological Society. He has served on the editorial board of *Personnel Psychology, Academy of Management Journal,* and *Training Research Journal,* and currently serves on the board of *Human Performance.*

Information on the Internet

A wealth of information relevant to training systems can be found on the Internet. The number of organizations with sites on the World Wide Web that have information related to training is enormous. Here is a partial list of some of the sites:

American Society for Training and Development (www.astd.org)
This is probably the largest organization of training practitioners and researchers, and its Web site is a virtual storehouse of information. You will often find a discussion session going with a leader in the learning and training area, along with a chat room to discuss current training issues. In addition, the site contains information on e-learning, research on various topics, and a store of training books and materials that can be purchased. ASTD also publishes *Training and Development,* a practitioner-based journal containing useful training information. The Web site provides information about the journal, including executive summaries from the most current issue.

Ericae.net (www.ericae.net)
This is a clearinghouse for information on educational assessment, evaluation, and research methodology. It includes a library of over 400 books and articles that address educational measurement, evaluation, and learning theory. Although its focus is on education, many of the topics are interrelated to topics in training systems, such as accountability, instruction and learning, evaluation design and methods, and program evaluation. In addition, it offers a database of more than 1 million abstracts and articles on the same type of topics, as well as a comprehensive list of on-line journals maintained by the American Education Research Association Special Interest Group on Communication among Researchers. The on-line journal *Practical Assessment, Research and Evaluation* is also available.

University of Wisconsin Distance Education Clearinghouse
(www.uwex.edu/disted)
The University of Wisconsin-Extension Service has a long history in distance
education, and its Web site offers a wealth of materials related to training
issues. For example, it maintains a section on articles, bibliographies, journals,
and electronic mailing lists. Topics covered in the article section include up-
to-date materials on distance learning, e-learning, and instructional design.
Similar topics are included in the bibliographies. One recent bibliography
described on the Web site was devoted to evaluation issues, such as the difficulties of finding statistically significant differences. It also has cross-listings
for other Web sites that contain training information.

Learnativity (www.learnativity.com)
This is another site with loads of information about human resources and
training. It is organized around groupings. For example, the first group,
"Reading," lists articles, books, magazines, and trade journals that have materials on relevant topics. The second grouping is "Themes," where you can look
up particular topics such as adult learning, cognitive skills, learning styles, or
simulations. For each of these topics, Learnativity lists Web sites, books, and
other resources that have materials related to the themes.

Knowledge Transfer Center (www.t2ed.com)
This Web site is a joint effort between Westinghouse and the U.S. Department of Energy to make available to the general public tools, training courses,
manuals, and other materials funded by the Energy Department. Materials
that can be downloaded include training needs analysis instruments, transfer
of training measures, and technical training materials.

THE TRAINING CONTEXT

Throughout our lives learning experiences are a potent source of stimulation. This text emphasizes the systematic modes of instruction designed to produce environments that shape behavior to satisfy stated objectives. From this point of view, *training* is defined as the systematic acquisition of skills, rules, concepts, or attitudes that result in improved performance in another environment. Therefore, training programs are planned to produce, for example, a more considerate supervisor, a more competent technician in the workplace, or leaders of complex organizations. In some cases, such as on-the-job training, the instructional environment is almost identical to the actual job environment. In other instances, such as a classroom lecture on electronics theory for technicians, the learning environment is further removed from the job situation. However, in both circumstances effective training stems from a learning atmosphere systematically designed to produce changes in the working environment.

As stated in the preface, the purpose of this book is to present the interacting components of training systems, including materials related to the ways in which training needs are assessed and the training effort is evaluated. Information is also presented about different types of training programs and their effectiveness. In addition, we explore issues that intersect between training and societal concerns, such as training and the hard-core unemployed, training and fair employment practices, and training and the aging worker. This chapter provides background information concerning the scope of training in our society and the status of the training enterprise.

Scope of the Instructional Process

Training programs are an enormous business in terms of both the amount of effort expended and the money spent. For example, consider the following examples:

1. The American Society for Training and Development (Bassi & Van Buren, 1998) in its state of the industry report estimated that $55 billion was spent by employers on formal training. The survey, known as the Human Performance Practices Survey (HPPS), is based on a random sample of 540 organizations with 50 or more employees.

2. In another survey (Ralphs & Stephan, 1986) of Fortune 500 firms, it was found that 91% of the firms provided training for middle management, 75% for sales training, 56% for secretarial training, 51% for executive development, and 44% for technical training.

3. One study after another points to the important role that training has in the workplace. One study of 1000 firms found that a 10% increase in the educational attainment of a company's workforce resulted in an 8.6% increase in productivity. A 10% increase in value of capital stock such as tools and buildings only resulted in a 3.4% increase in productivity (National Center on Educational Quality of the Workforce, 1995). Yet another study found that retraining workers for new jobs is more cost effective than releasing them and hiring new ones (Cascio, 1994). And, of course, those data don't even mention the increase in morale for the workforce in that type of climate.

4. Corporations find themselves required to participate in some training activities because many people entering the workforce lack basic skills. Thus, Motorola Corporation spends an average of $1350 per person per year to teach six basic skill courses so that the worker can reach a level at which he or she can be retrained for jobs, and Polaroid Corporation spent $700,000 at its Cambridge, Massachusetts, facility to teach basic English and mathematics to its employees (Cascio, 1994). One estimate is that half of the Fortune 500 firms are becoming "educators of the last resort" (*Time, 1988*, p. 56).

5. Training itself has become a very large business. In the competition for employees and organizations, almost every city and state has become involved in job training. Thus, Minnesota has set aside $7.5 million for skills training partnerships between companies and community colleges. One fifth of that sum is set aside to provide basic training to allow people to move from welfare back to work (Leonhardt, 1997). Observers such as the American Society for Training and Development even note that Wall Street has discovered the potential

for training companies, and capital is starting to flow into them from investment banks and other funding sources (Gallagan, 1997). In their Annual Review Chapter covering the period since 1992, Salas and Cannon-Bowers (in press) note that there has been an explosion of training-related research in the last decade.

6. When training systems are well designed, they can have an impact on a huge number of different kinds of activities. Thus, banks are concerned with how to train customers to use ATMs. Systems have been designed to enable university quarterbacks to use large-scale video displays as an interactive teaching tool where quarterbacks learn to recognize defenses and actually respond to game type situations (Walker & Fisk, 1995). And Motorola Corporation considers learning such an embedded part of its culture that it has developed Motorola University. Part of its focus is to develop long-term learning interventions, which the company will need to deal with market pressures that are 10 to 15 years away (Koonce, 1997).

7. The Ritz-Carlton Hotel, L. L. C., manages thirty-six luxury hotels worldwide. In 1998, it had about 17,000 employees and sales of more than $1 billion. In 1999 it became the first and only service company to twice receive the Malcom Baldridge National Quality award in the service category. One aspect of the evaluation cited the hotel for using training as a key to employee retention and the company's customer-focused culture. Every first-year manager at Ritz-Carlton received between 250 and 310 hours of training. The training programs are designed to align with its strategic plan and organizational objectives.

WHAT DO WE KNOW ABOUT TRAINERS?

Examining the scope of activities for professionals involved in training and development provides further insights into the ever-increasing emphasis on instructional systems. The extent of growth in this area is evidenced by the number of people belonging to professional societies. For example, the American Society for Training and Development had 15 members in 1943, 5000 members in 1967, 9500 in 1972, 20,000 in 1980, 29,000 in 1991, and more than 41,000 in 2000. This does not include the many people involved in training activities who may be members of other societies such as the Society for Industrial and Organizational Psychology, the American Psychological Association, the American Psychological Society, the American Educational Research Association, the American Academy of Management, the National Society for Performance and Instruction, or the Society for Human Resource Management.

Pinto and Walker (1978) surveyed American Society for Training and Development members to determine which activities were a significant part of their work. Based on almost 3000 responses, these authors performed a factor analysis, a technique used to determine the common dimensions among the job activities. Table 1.1 presents the activities identified in the survey. The authors note that, to meet needs for specific learning and behavior changes, program design and development were the most significant parts of the training practitioners' work.

An important area of concern for training developers is ethical consideration. Lowman (1991) quotes from a personal communication from London about ethical concerns of students attending a training-and-development course. They are as follows:

- *Voluntary consent:* Trainers should not implicitly coerce unwilling or skeptical participants into self-revealing or physical activities.
- *Discrimination:* Age, sex, race, or handicaps should not be used as barriers to determine who receives training.
- *Cost effectiveness:* Training activities should be based on demonstrated utility, should show a demonstrated benefit vis-à-vis costs, and should not be undertaken simply to spend a training budget.
- *Accurate portrayal:* Claims for the benefits of training need to be accurate; training should be consistent across time and trainers; training materials should be appropriately depicted.
- *Competency in training:* Teaching methods that do not work, such as talking down to audiences, should be avoided.
- *Values:* Trainers should believe in the value of what they teach (pp. 208–209).

A good way of summarizing this material is to note that training is a people-to-people activity. Thus, honesty and respect for the individual go a long way.

What Do We Know about Types of Training and Training Methods?

The American Society for Training and Development Human Performance Practices Survey (HPPS) of 540 organizations provides lots of good information about types of training and training methods. Bassi and Van Buren (1998) present the amount of training time by course type for each of the organizations in the survey (see Table 1.2). Of these types of efforts, the most expensive for organizations is technical skills training, which focuses on procedures

TABLE

1.1   TRAINING AND DEVELOPMENT PRACTITIONER ROLES

a. *Needs Analysis and Diagnosis*
    Construct questionnaires and conduct interviews for needs analysis, evaluate
    feedback, etc.

b. *Determine Appropriate Training Approach*
    Evaluate the alternatives of "ready-made" courses or materials, use of programmed
    instruction, videotape, computer managed and other structured techniques versus a
    more process-oriented organization development/team-building approach.

c. *Program Design and Development*
    Design program content and structure, apply learning theory, establish objectives,
    evaluate and select instructional methods.

d. *Develop Material Resources (Make)*
    Prepare scripts, slides, manuals, artwork, copy, programmed learning, and other
    instructional materials.

e. *Manage Internal Resources (Borrow)*
    Obtain and evaluate internal instructors/program resource persons, train others how to
    train, supervise their work.

f. *Manage External Resources (Buy)*
    Hire, supervise, and evaluate external instructors/program resource persons; obtain and
    evaluate outside consultants and vendors.

g. *Individual Development Planning and Counseling*
    Counsel with individuals regarding career development needs and plans; arrange for
    and maintain records of participation in programs, administer tuition reimbursement,
    maintain training resource library, keep abreast of EEO.

h. *Job/Performance-Related Training*
    Assist managers and others in on-the-job training and development; analyze job skill
    and knowledge requirements, determine performance problems.

i. *Conduct Classroom Training*
    Conduct programs, operate audio-visual equipment, lecture, lead discussion, revise
    materials based on feedback, arrange program logistics.

j. *Group and Organization Development*
    Apply techniques such as team-building, intergroup meetings, behavior modeling, role-
    playing simulation, laboratory education, discussions, cases, issues.

k. *Training Research*
    Present and interpret statistics and data relating to training; communicate through
    reports, proposals, speeches, and articles; design data collection.

l. *Manage Working Relationships with Managers and Clients*
    Establish and maintain good relations with managers as clients, counsel with them and
    explain recommendations for training and development.

m. *Manage the Training and Development Function*
    Prepare budgets, organize, staff, make formal presentations of plans, maintain informa-
    tion on costs, supervise the work of others, project future needs, etc.

n. *Professional Self Development*
    Attend seminars/conferences, and keep abreast of training and development concepts,
    theories, and techniques; keep abreast of activities in other organizations.

Source: From "What Do Training and Development Professionals Really Do?" by P. R. Pinto and J. W. Walker, in *Training
and Development Journal,* July 1978, *28,* pp. 58–64. Copyright 1978 by the American Society for Training and Development,
Inc. Reprinted by permission.

TABLE

1.2   TRAINING TIME BY COURSE TYPE

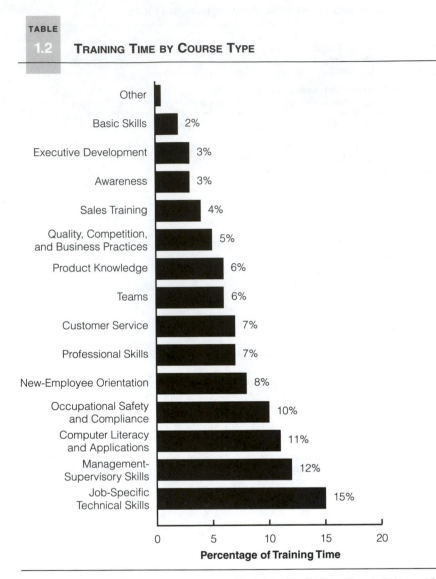

Source: From "The 1998 ASTD State of the Industry Report," by L. J. Bassi and M. E. Van Buren. In *Training and Development Journal, 52*(1), pp. 21–43. Copyright 1998 by the American Society for Training and Development, Inc. Reprinted by permission.

to create products. Technical skills training accounts for 30% of the budget. Professional skills training, which focuses on specialized knowledge such as accounting, computer science, and information systems management, accounts for another 19% of the budget. In contrast, basic skills and new employee training receive the least percentage of training dollars at about 2%.

These data and other surveys also make it clear that most training dollars are spent on high-level professional and technical skill and management development. Robert Reich (1991), who recently served as U.S. Secretary of Labor, noted less than 8% of U.S. firms provided remedial programs for their workers. A study by Olson (1994) produced data that were consistent with these perceptions. Taking data from the National Household Education Survey, he found in the 1990s that about 25% of the employed U.S. workforce participated in some form of training during any 12-month period. However, that training was unevenly distributed in the workforce and mainly assisted the more skilled workers in the upper portions of the wage distribution. Further, the HPPS found that employees with a college education are three to four times more likely to receive training than employees with less than a high school education. These data reinforce the concerns expressed by Reich, who feels that the future workplace will need the abilities of all our workers in order to have the skilled workforce required by modern technology.

The HPPS also provides information about the most commonly used training methods. These results (see Table 1.3) show that the most popular approach to training is the use of videotapes followed by the use of workbooks and business books.

One of the most fascinating parts of the survey result is that despite the fact that new learning technologies continue to be introduced every day, in 1996 84% of all training was still classroom-based and instructor-led. These firms were projecting that by 2000 classroom-based instruction would drop to 61% of all courses. They were also projecting a corresponding rise in the use of learning technologies from 6% in 1996 to a projected 22% in 2000 (Bassi & Van Buren, 1999).

At this point, even though face-to-face classroom contact still represents the majority of training delivery systems, there are a number of other emerging delivery technologies. These include the following systems, which will be discussed in further detail in later chapters:

1. Distance learning where training is delivered across multiple sites at one time;
2. Virtual reality training where trainees can view a 3D world of the kinds of situations they might face on the job;
3. Computer-based training (CBT) where trainees can respond to training materials on CD-ROMs;
4. Intelligent tutoring systems where training can be customized to meet individual training needs through extensive testing and branching of training materials; and
5. Web-based training, which allows for more self-instruction and learner control because instruction is sorted and transmitted as requested by trainees from remote sites and accessed by the web.

TABLE 1.3   USE OF DELIVERY METHODS

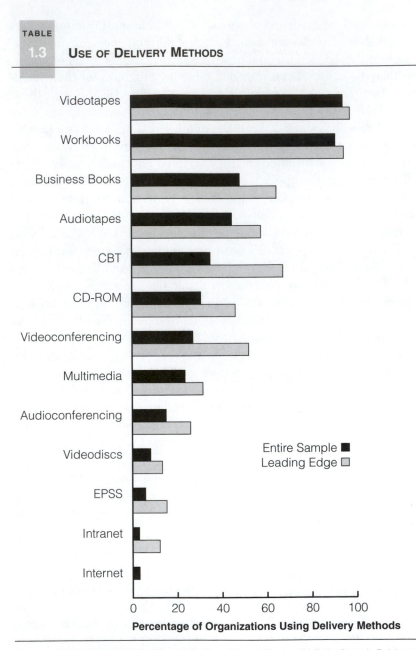

Percentage of Organizations Using Delivery Methods

Source: From "The 1998 ASTD State of the Industry Report," by L. J. Bassi and M. E. Van Buren. In *Training and Development Journal, 52*(1), pp. 21–43. Copyright 1998 by the American Society for Training and Development, Inc. Reprinted by permission.

Although these emerging technologies offer significant potential for improving teaching and learning, they also complicate training design considerably (Hannafin, Hannafin, Hooper, Rieber, & Kini, 1996). The challenge is to develop training designs that utilize the potential advantages of the new

TABLE 1.4	TRAINING EXPENDITURES BY WORK ORGANIZATIONS	
	Training Expenditures as a Percent of Payroll	**Training Expenditures per Employee**
Leading-Edge Firms N=32	4.39%	$1956
All Firms in Survey N=500	1.81%	$649

Source: Adapted from "Sharpening the Leading Edge," by L. J. Bassi and M. E. Van Buren. In *Training and Development Journal, 53*(1), pp. 23–33. Copyright 1999 by the American Society for Training and Development, Inc. Reprinted by permission.

technologies rather than only providing another means of training delivery. How technological capabilities are used is more critical than the capabilities themselves. Designers must be aware of the cognitive demands their training systems place on learners. The training design must thoughtfully apply techniques that support, not interfere, with learner efforts. As noted by Krendl (Krendl, Hare, Reid, & Warren, 1996), it is far easier to create something with great cosmetic appeal than develop an integrated learning system that is consistent with available research and theory. An integrated learning system is defined as a set of instructional events whose major features, from needs assessment to training design and evaluation, facilitate learner efforts toward accomplishing training objectives. One goal of this book is to contribute information toward the design of integrated learning systems.

The 1998 survey also differentiates between leading-edge companies, which include companies identified in various competitions such as "best places to work in America." This resulted in 32 of the 500 companies surveyed being chosen as leading-edge firms. It is interesting to examine the differences between leading-edge firms and the average of all 500 firms in terms of dollars spent on training per employee and training as a percent of payroll. As apparent from the information in Table 1.4, the leading-edge firms were much more committed to the use of training as a personnel practice to advance their organizations.

TRAINING CHALLENGES

The increased emphasis on professional activities presented in Table 1.1 has resulted in the development of many professionals who are capable of designing programs that meet instructional objectives based on clearly specified needs. The types of instructional goals that organizations hope training programs can achieve vary widely but could include producing quality goods in a shorter time, reducing accidents with a corresponding decrease in insurance premiums, implementing a management system that is more service-oriented toward its customers, and increasing health-oriented approaches to lifestyles as a way of reducing absenteeism due to illness and stress. The potential number of goals is unlimited. Although training is not a panacea for all societal ills, well-conceived training programs have and do achieve many beneficial results. There is an increasing number of thoughtfully developed programs. This text will present many examples of training programs that work.

Unfortunately, some programs are not based on appropriate needs assessment, and many organizations do not collect the information to determine the usefulness of their own instructional programs. Their techniques remain unevaluated, except for the high esteem with which they may be regarded by their developers. For example, the survey by Ralphs and Stephan (1986) of the Fortune 500 firms provides information about evaluation methods, which are presented in Table 1.5. These results indicate that most evaluations (86%) consist of trainee reactions that are written at the end of the course. Relatively few efforts are made to collect information concerning performance changes by means of follow-up on the job, which is when both the trainee and the organization could discover whether the programs are achieving the desired results and when the evaluation could provide clues to the modifications necessary to enable the program to work. Saari et al.'s (1988) survey of over 600 firms found similar results. For example, these companies reported that executive MBA programs were the most expensive management-training approach

TABLE 1.5 HOW OFTEN ARE THE FOLLOWING EVALUATION METHODS USED IN YOUR COMPANY?

Almost Always 5	4	3	2	Almost Never 1		
					5 Only	4 and 5
A. Course evaluation form filled out by learner at end of course					73%	86%
B. Course evaluation form filled out by instructor at end of course					12%	23%
C. Evaluation by boss, peers, or subordinate					8%	23%
D. Follow-up evaluation by participants					7%	16%
E. Follow-up questionnaire by participants					5%	14%
F. Use of pre- or post-tests					6%	15%
G. Use of business data records					5%	12%

(averaging about $14,000 for each participant). Yet, 42% of the companies reported that they did not conduct any evaluations of their effectiveness. Similarly, only 27% of the companies surveyed had a formal procedure designed to conduct needs assessments in order to determine the specific training and education needs of their managers. Given recent advances in the development of needs assessment and evaluation, which will be emphasized in this text, we now have many approaches for conducting both phases of the process that hopefully will lead to fewer of these types of issues.

Many more outstanding efforts in the training area have appeared during the last decade than at any time before. As the next section indicates, this is a particularly critical time. Competition is very intense, and companies operate in a highly technical and global environment. The workforce is becoming even more diverse in terms of its cultural values with the entry of more women, minorities, and older persons. In addition, greater variation exists in the educational skills of entry-level workers.

Training systems are viewed by both organizations and individuals as a positive step in providing skills and opportunities. For all of us to benefit the most, training systems need to be more carefully designed and more carefully evaluated to ensure that they are meeting the expectations of both the organizations and the individual trainees. We hope that this text will serve as a source for information and techniques necessary to design and evaluate training programs.

THE CHANGING WORKPLACE AND WORKFORCE

Changes that have implications for the use of training systems in the future workplace are described in this section. In the following section, the training implications of these changes in the workplace are discussed. In describing both the future workplace and training implications, articles written by Goldstein and Gilliam (1990) and Goldstein and Goldstein (1990) provide many of the initial thoughts. Table 1.6 summarizes many of these ideas.

Changes in Demographics of Entry-Level Persons in the Workforce

Based on the past trends of labor force activity, it is possible to project, with relative accuracy, future trends in labor force participation. Individuals entering the labor force in the early part of the 21st century have already been born. For the last dozen years, projections indicate the degree of workforce participation will have a serious impact on human resource management in a way never experienced before (Cascio & Zammuto, 1987). In brief, the analyses

TABLE
1.6   COMPARISON OF JOB AND LABOR MARKET TRENDS IN THE 1990S

	Job-Market Needs	Labor-Market Description
Industry	Service-oriented	Manufacturing-oriented
Employment	24 million additional jobs—10 million of them don't exist yet	16 million additional workers
Demographics	Younger, skilled, literate	Diverse, older, unskilled, semi-literate
Education	Greater education required	Fewer high-school and college graduates
Job Level	More advanced job opportunities available	Fewer workforce entrants to fill advanced jobs
Job Type	Cognitive and complex jobs	Procedural and predictable jobs
Management	More skilled leaders	More traditional leaders

Source: From "The Challenge of Training in the Nineties," by S. L. Cohen. In *Training and Development Journal*, July 1991, *45*, pp. 29–35. Copyright 1991 by the American Society for Training and Development, Inc. Reprinted by permission.

projected the following changes will occur (Braddock, 1999; Cascio & Zammuto, 1987; Fullerton, 1999; Offerman & Gowing, 1990):

1. The workforce will grow more slowly in the upcoming decade because new entrants—that is, individuals primarily between the ages of 16 and 24—will decrease substantially. As a result, the number of individuals comprising the entry pool will be smaller, and data indicate that a number of these people will enter the workforce with inadequate basic skills. These factors led some commentators to project that the entry pool of selectees for industry would be dismal at best (Cascio & Zammuto, 1987). As it turns out, these analysts may have actually underestimated the situation. The competition for highly skilled workers, especially with information technology expertise, has turned so intense that local newspapers print dozens of pages of recruiting advertisements, and workers often find recruitment messages on their answering machines. A good example of this problem was identified in a study conducted by Virginia Tech University. The report estimated that 346,000 computer programmer and system analyst jobs are vacant in U.S. companies with more than 100 employees (Chandrasekaran, 1998). Congress allows the Immigration and Naturalization Service (INS) to give out a certain number of visas for foreign skilled professionals. For the fiscal year ending in September 2000, the INS had the authority to give out 115,000 visas, but before the fiscal year was half completed, it had used up all of its visas (*Washington Post*, 2000). As

one sign of the increased need, Congress was being pressured by high technology firms to increase the number of visas allotted.

2. The proportion of the entry-level workforce that is white will decline, and the proportion of minority populations will increase significantly. Cox and Blake (1994) point out that behind these statistics are vastly different ages and fertility rates for people of different racial and ethnic groups. Thus, in the United States, the average white female is 33 years old and has (or will have) 1.7 children. Corresponding figures for African Americans are 28 and 2.4 and for Mexican Americans, 26 and 2.9. Immigration also continues to play a role in the growth of the U.S. labor force. It is estimated that the Hispanic labor force will expand nearly four times faster than the rest of the labor force, growing to 12.7% of the labor force by 2008 as compared with a 10.4% share in 1998. The Hispanic labor force had a 6.1% share in 1980.

3. The composition of the workforce will also change to include more older workers and more women. Data indicate that individuals between the ages of 45 and 64 years old will increase by at least 25% in the coming decades. It is estimated that the 50-to-59-year-old age group will jump from about 15% of the workforce in 2000 to 21% of the workforce in 2010. Further, with social security benefits being delayed and requirements to retire at certain ages being declared illegal, people are likely to continue working longer. Thayer (1997), in summing up these effects, observed that the traditional retirement age between 45 and 64 is changing to a new definition of the older worker as encompassing those aged 50 to above 70. There are also expectations that women will continue to enter the workforce in increasing numbers and that already they are filling approximately two-thirds of the new jobs created this decade. The Bureau of Labor Statistics indicates that women, non-white males, and new immigrants will account for 80% of the growth of the labor force, and women will constitute 47% of the labor force in the first decade of the new millennium. The complexity of the changes stemming from diversity in the workforce is made very apparent by issues facing women in the workforce. These include difficulties in obtaining higher level jobs and in charges involving sexual harassment, resulting in massive lawsuits both in public and private sector employment (Melton & Grimsley, 1998).

Increasing Job Complexity

There is a rush toward more highly technological, sophisticated systems. Industry has utilized the technology opportunities to establish advanced manufacturing techniques that permit the tailoring of products to the needs of a customer by simply reprogramming the machine (Wall & Jackson, 1995).

Experts agree that programmable automation will have its greatest impact on semiskilled and unskilled jobs where job loss is likely to be significant. On the other hand, the increases in technology require a highly trained workforce to design and operate the systems. Thayer (1997) notes that this results in placing a great deal more responsibility on the individual worker and often enlarges and enhances the job. This becomes especially true when the job requires teams of workers to coordinate their activities in order to accomplish their purpose. In these cases, team members not only need to know their own job but also know the job of other team members.

Drucker (1995) believes that we are moving from an industrial to a knowledge society. In an industrial society, the workers do not own their own tools. But in a knowledge society, workers carry their knowledge both in their head and in their computer, and they can transport it from job to job. However, even for skilled employees, the rapid change in technological developments requires a continuous learning philosophy. Also, organizations are rediscovering that humans are their critical resource and that a commitment to training and continuous learning is crucial for them to remain competitive. As reported by Bassi and Van Buren (1998), this has driven some organizations to outsource some of the training activities and depend on other companies to do everything from designing training programs to actually providing the training for their employees. Smaller organizations (with fewer than 500 employees) typically spend more than 50% of their training budget on outside suppliers. Obviously, in this rapidly changing and dynamic environment, all organizations are struggling to keep their employees at the very top of the knowledge economy. On the other hand, as will be discussed later, persons with a skill gap will find the job market daunting, to say the least.

A related issue is the education of the workforce. In 1998, about one quarter of the share of jobs required at least an associate college degree. It is estimated (Braddock, 1999) that occupations requiring an associate degree will account for 40% of the job growth from 1998 to 2008.

The complexity of these issues was made clear in a report from a commission established by Congress titled the Commission for the Advancement of Women and Minorities in Science, Engineering, and Technology Development (Chea, 2000). The commission notes that the nationwide shortage of qualified high-tech workers will create serious economic disturbances unless the country is able to expand its pool of workers by including more women, minorities, and people with disabilities. They note that these groups are vastly underrepresented in science and engineering schools.

Shifts from Manufacturing to Service Jobs

There is a shift in our economy from a manufacturing to a service orientation. In 1995, three quarters of the workforce was employed in the service sector (Howard, 1995), and it is estimated that from 1998 to 2008, 90% of the growth

of jobs will be in the service sector (Fullerton, 1999). These jobs are characterized by an increase in the importance of people work, that is, working with
customers and clients rather than interacting primarily with co-workers and
things (Klein & Hall, 1988). Entry-level service-oriented jobs are also characterized by lower pay levels than the manufacturing sector. Displaced manufacturing sector workers unfortunately have discovered that they are expected
to learn new interpersonal skills for service-oriented jobs that pay less than
what they previously earned. Interestingly, in some cases technological
advances are also having an impact on service-oriented jobs (for example, the
use of on-line stock market trading).

Organizations are discovering that the increase in service-sector jobs also
has important implications for training. In service jobs, people-to-people
interaction is critical, and people need to be trained for those skills. We are all
discovering that teaching interpersonal skills creates the same kinds of challenges as teaching employees how to work with products coming off the
assembly line. This is especially the case given the diversity of the workforce
and the need for people to work with others who may come from backgrounds
with different value systems.

Organizations and Global Markets

Finally, a look at the future of jobs and organizations makes increasingly fluid
world market arrangements appear quite likely. Many novel strategies are
being explored. For example, companies send projects involving data-entry
jobs to other countries because the advantages of low wages and surplus workers outweigh the disadvantages of long-distance electronic data transmission.
Most consumers are now aware that it is not unusual for manufacturers to produce products (for example, automobiles) that are partially manufactured in
the home country and partially manufactured in a different country. Sometimes, these involve arrangements between liaison teams directing the overall
efforts between different employees, in different organizations, and in different countries, all contributing to the production of a single final product. The
implications for the whole human resource function are enormous. It means
that companies not only have to worry about how they train their own citizens
but also about training people all across the globe.

IMPLICATIONS FOR FUTURE
WORKPLACE TRAINING SYSTEMS

A number of important training implications stem from the preceding analyses of the changing workplace. These issues are covered only briefly in this
section because they are addressed in relevant places in other chapters.

The Problem of Youth with a Skill Gap

The analyses of demographic information concerning people entering the workforce compel the consideration of some harsh realities. First, fewer people will be available to enter the workforce. Yet, the analyses indicate that the demand for workers will remain high, especially given the development of service-sector and high-technology jobs. Second, the demographics indicate that many of the individuals who will be available to enter the workforce will be underskilled and undereducated youth. Significant numbers of these individuals will also be members of culturally diverse groups that society has not successfully integrated into the workforce. Although many members of minority groups have overcome adversity and have successfully entered professional and technical careers, it is also the case that many of the hard-core unemployed are members of minority groups. In the future, however, society will desperately need their talent in the workplace, but the issues involving training and development programs are extremely complex. For example, many of these programs are successful to the degree to which the organization itself is willing to make a commitment rather than assuming all the necessary change must come from the entry-level trainee. In addition, organizations are facing difficult choices concerning the need to develop basic entry-level programs, such as literacy training, or to arrange partnerships with beleaguered and underfunded school systems. These concerns are discussed further in Chapter 9.

Changes in Technology

The kinds of issues stemming from rapidly changing technologies involve a whole set of individual, organizational, and societal factors. All descriptions of personnel requirements for future work organizations emphasize the need for more complex cognitive skills. For example, executives at a plant in Michigan describe their expectations of their workers:

> They want their new employees to be able to work in teams, to rotate through various jobs, to understand how their tasks fit into the entire process, to spot problems in production, to trouble shoot, articulate the problems to others, suggest improvements and write detail charts and memos that serve as a road map in the assembly of the car. (Vobejda, 1987, p. A14)

The implications for training system design are obvious. A report by a commission of the U.S. Department of Labor (1991) notes that a strong back and weak mind will not permit the United States to compete in today's marketplace. The commission reports that it is not simply a matter of literacy skills but the need for complex thinking skills. Included in the required skills are the abilities to assess information, understand work systems, deal with new technologies as the workplace changes, and develop interpersonal skills. Of course, these changes are in addition to the three "Rs" of reading, writing, and arithmetic. The report also notes that unless students learn these skills by the time they leave high school, they face a bleak employment picture. The fast-moving advances in technology and resulting competition make this a necessity. Paradoxically, the increases in technology and machine responsibility increase the demands on the human being. As noted by Howell and Cooke (1989), increasingly "smart" machines thereby also increase the cognitive complexity for the human being. Instead of simple procedural and predictable tasks, the human becomes responsible for inferences, diagnoses, judgment, and decision making, often under severe time pressure. Adding to the complexity of these issues is the rapid technical obsolescence of individuals who previously had advanced training. Thus, estimates are that an engineer's education has a half-life of five years, meaning that half of what is learned in school is obsolete five years after graduation. Because individuals are also likely to respond to many job changes, as a result of technology shifts, understanding types of abilities and how transfer of learning can occur across jobs will be important.

Concern for Maximizing Individual Worker Potential

One implication of the decreasing size of the workforce is that it will become increasingly necessary to maximize the potential of the individual worker. This means that the future of work organizations will become more dependent on their ability to effectively use many members of society, often by providing training and giving workers more opportunities for self-directed learning experiences. Despite evidence that indicates the importance of work in the lives of most individuals, a number of difficult realities have existed within the world of work. Many researchers conclude that a contributing factor that has resulted in lost opportunities for qualified individuals is the cycle of discrimination plaguing minorities, women, and older workers. As a result of these lost opportunities, increased litigation has focused on organizational decisions involving training opportunities and their lack of availability to members of minority groups, women, older workers, and, more recently, handicapped workers. The HPPS (Bassi & Van Buren, 1998) found that women, minorities, and younger and older people (people less than 25 or more than 55 years old) were less likely to receive training than men, whites, and prime age workers. Training programs that discriminate in providing equal opportunity for promotional and job opportunities are being struck down by the courts. This is especially the case when completing these training opportunities is required for advancement. Much of the tensions here come about because individuals view training as instrumental in helping them achieve advanced opportunities, and thus they are concerned when they feel programs are not made available. Some believe that as organizations have a greater need for workers, these difficulties will diminish; others are not as confident. As noted earlier, many firms are turning to immigration as a way of gaining skilled workers, and, as found in the HPPS, organizations are spending very little of their training budget helping entry-level workers. These are very complex issues that will be discussed further in the text. From any perspective, however, these topics clearly have important implications for future training systems.

Managerial Training Implications of a Competitive Environment

The training implications of all the preceding issues are enormous, especially for managers who will be working with people. Rothwell and Kolb (1999) note that there is an increased emphasis on using training as a tool for coping with, managing, and anticipating the rapid market changes occurring in work organizations today. These issues make it obvious why the training business is a growth industry. Managers need to provide on-the-job training to integrate unskilled youth into the workforce, while working with job incumbents and other managers who previously may not have been a traditional part of the workforce. Supervisors need to perform these activities at a time when jobs have become increasingly complex and national and international competition more intense. In addition, the increase in service-sector jobs requires managers to work more with people rather than with objects from an assembly line. All this makes training in areas such as interpersonal skills even more important in the future workplace. Moreover, the rapid changes in a knowledge society fueled by technological developments also call for training systems that promote and deliver high-quality just-in-time training (Rothwell & Kolb, 1999).

For the manager, the training implications for being able to manage such emphases are enormous. Managers are expected to understand and manage the processes for achieving quality as well as learning to manage team efforts, which are likely to be emphasized as a way of achieving success. Added to this is the fact that organizations are operating in a more complex environment. Downsizing, for example, has affected almost everyone in the United States. Thayer (1997) notes that more than five million jobs were lost in the 1980s and the count rose in the 1990s. There are many explanations for downsizing, but, in part, it is a response of organizations that are trying to be more flexible, responsive, and competitive. It is also important to note that a lot of the job growth is in small companies where training is less affordable, so again there is an emphasis on hiring highly skilled workers who have the desire to maintain their abilities through continuous learning. Thayer also notes that the political climate is having an impact on training programs. Thus, for example, part of the decision process involving welfare systems are programs to return people to the world of work. These types of programs have important societal as well as political implications. The success of these programs in finding jobs for individuals as well as providing training remain relatively unknown at this time.

In discussing the training implications of these complex environments, Ronen notes that the manager given an assignment in a different country must possess the "patience of a diplomat, the zeal of a missionary, and the linguistic skill of a U.N. interpreter" (1989, p. 418). Ronen is correct, but the issue is just as complicated for managers working in their own countries because the workplace will need to incorporate individuals who come from environments with very diverse cultures and values. These issues are also discussed further in this text.

Accountability

The amount of emphasis concerning evaluation methodology, including information about criterion development, evaluation designs, values and ethics, and problems of performance evaluations in organizations, has exploded. Many organizations are recognizing the important needs that have increased the use of training systems, and they are becoming increasingly concerned about training program evaluation as a way of determining whether their goals are being met. Indeed, many organizations are trying to benchmark their programs against companies with the very best practices. This has led some associations such as the American Society for Training and Development to develop forums where they select real-life case studies of the very best practices (Overmyer-Day & Benson, 1996). The criteria for selection include responses to the following questions.

1. How has this practice shown measurable results and success departmentally and organizationally?
2. What can forum members learn from this practice?
3. How will the practice transfer to other organizations?
4. Does the practice reflect a current trend or issues that are of interest to the forum as a whole?

These are excellent questions and with the increased emphasis on quality, training programs are likely to be even more carefully scrutinized to determine the degree to which they are achieving such goals as increased quality service, quality products, or both. The tremendous costs of instructional programs have also resulted in questions about their effectiveness. In many cases during the past several decades, a fads approach to instructional design was dominant. This approach emphasized the use of the newest training technique. Indeed, we still regularly receive calls inquiring about the newest training techniques. Campbell (1971) discerned the following pattern to the fads approach:

1. A new technique appears with a group of followers who announce its success.

2. Another group develops modifications of the technique.
3. A few empirical studies appear supporting the technique.
4. There is a backlash. Critics question the usefulness of the new technique but rarely produce any data.
5. The technique survives until a new technique appears. Then, the whole procedure is repeated.

When there are no empirical data to evaluate techniques, the cycle of fads continues. Evaluation needs to be thought of as a tool to provide information rather than as a technique to determine passing and failing. A systematic examination of training literature indicates the occurrence of many more efforts at assessing the impact of training and some emphasis on determining which techniques might be best for which behaviors in which situations. The emphasis on accountability will make it more likely that organizations will insist correctly on understanding the impact of the programs they sponsor. In addition, the organization's need to control costs in order to compete in today's market economy puts added emphasis on training being tied to cost reduction and demonstrating added value.

TRAINING AS A SUBSYSTEM

A text that considers only the technical aspects of needs assessment and evaluation design overlooks much of the dynamics concerning training systems. It is unrealistic to think of training systems as if they were in a vacuum. Training programs exist within organizations. In some instances training analysts have thoughtfully considered the organizational environment before deciding what type of program might work.

Organizations are very complex systems, and training programs are but one subsystem. Thus, changes in the selection system, which can result in people with higher or lower job-relevant skills and abilities, will have a dramatic effect on the level of training required. Changes in jobs as new technologies develop can have similar effects. More effective training programs can also affect all other systems in the work organization. The dynamics of training systems must include the realization that one of the first places to which many new employees are sent is a training program. Similarly, when individuals change positions as a result of a career change or promotion, many enter a training program. It is as important to understand the effects of training experiences as part of the socialization process in entering organizations as it is to evaluate specific training outcomes. Our goal in this text is to provide some understanding of the dynamics of training systems as well as information related to systematic development and evaluation of training programs.

The next chapter presents an instructional model that outlines the various factors to be considered in the design of systematic programs. The description of these interacting components should clearly indicate that no easy technique or gadget can be used in the development of well-conceived programs. Instructional materials have a profound effect on everyone's life. A great deal of knowledge is presently available and should be used in the development of new programs. A wonderful side benefit is that such efforts can contribute even more information to our existing knowledge about what works in developing productive training programs.

InfoTrac College Edition

For additional readings, go to http: www.infotrac-college.com/wadsworth and enter a search term related to your interest. The following key terms will pull up several related articles.

Changing Workplace	Sex Distribution (Demography)
Employee Training	Technology Assessment
Job Complexity	Training Ethics
Management Training	Workplace Literacy

A SYSTEMATIC APPROACH TO TRAINING

Workplace training is a systematic approach to learning and development to improve individual, team, or organizational effectiveness. A systematic approach refers to the idea that the training is intentional. It is being conducted to meet a perceived need. Learning and development concerns the building of expertise as a function of these systematic training efforts. Learning outcomes can include changes in knowledge, skills, or attitudes (KSAs). Improvement is measured by the extent to which the learning that results from training leads to meaningful changes in the work environment. Therefore, a critical issue is the extent to which the KSAs are transferred to the job and improve individual effectiveness. Finally, employee training can also be viewed from a broader, more macro perspective, as a mechanism for enhancing work team and organizational effectiveness. In this way, training is seen as integral to facilitating larger scale organizational change and development issues (see Ford, in press).

This chapter presents the overarching framework that is the structure behind the book. The framework focuses on understanding the components of assessing, designing, and evaluating training. In addition, the book emphasizes what we know about the factors that impact learning and transfer so that more effective training efforts can be developed and implemented. In each chapter, we stress the need for training to be based on a systematic and organized framework. Trainers must carefully plan and develop activities to meet the needs of the individual employees, teams, departments, and or organizational functions. One well-established framework for organizing the important steps of training is the instructional design model based in the instructional technology area.

Whereas the term *technology* commonly refers to the development of hardware, *instructional technology* refers to the systematic development of programs in training and education. The systems approach to instruction emphasizes the specification of instructional objectives, precisely controlled learning experiences to achieve these objectives, criteria for performance, and evaluative information. Other characteristics of instructional technology include the following:

1. The systems approach uses feedback to continually modify instructional processes. From this perspective, training programs are never totally finished products; rather, they are modified as information becomes available as to whether the program is meeting its stated objectives.
2. The instructional-systems approach recognizes the complex interaction among the components of the system. For example, one particular medium, like web-based training, might be effective in achieving a set of knowledge acquisition objectives, whereas another medium, such as work simulators, might be preferable for achieving a set of skill acquisition objectives. Similar interactions could involve learning variables and specific individual characteristics of the learner. The systems view stresses a concern with the total system rather than with the objectives of any single component.
3. Systematic analysis provides a frame of reference for planning and remaining on target. In this framework information should be collected to determine whether and how programs are meeting their goals.
4. The systems view treats training as one of a set of interacting systems. Training programs interact with and are directly affected by a larger system involving corporate policies (for example, selection and management philosophy).

The various components of the training or instructional-systems approach are not new. Evaluation was a byword years before systems approaches were in vogue. Thus, the systems approach cannot be considered a magic wand for all the problems that were unsolved before its inception. If training designers were convinced that their programs worked, a systems approach would be unlikely to convince them that their programs could be enhanced by evaluation and examination. However, the systems approach does provide a model that emphasizes important components and their interactions, and good evidence exists that this model is an important impetus for the establishment of clear objectives and useful evaluation procedures. As such, it is an effective tool that enables designers of training programs (as well as authors of books like this one) to examine the total training process.

Figure 2.1 presents one model of an instructional system. Most of the components of this model (for example, derive instructional objectives and develop criteria) are considered important to any training system, although what might be emphasized could change for different programs. The chapters

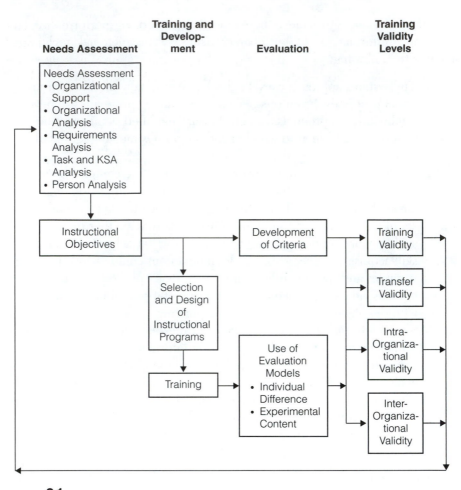

FIGURE **2.1**

An instructional system. There are many other instructional-system models for military, business, and educational systems.

that follow discuss material related to each of these model components. This chapter provides an overview of the system and discusses the relationships among the components.

ASSESSMENT PHASE

Assessment of Training Needs

The assessment phase provides the information necessary to design the training program. An examination of the model indicates that the training and evaluation phases depend on input from this needs assessment phase. Sometimes programs do not achieve their full potential because trainers are more interested in conducting the training program than in assessing the needs of their organizations. Trainers are sometimes sold a particular approach, such as the use of CD-ROM technology or a team training module, before they have determined the training needs of their organization and whether the techniques will be useful in meeting those needs. The needs assessment phase consists of organizational support and analysis systems, including a requirements analysis that helps the analyst determine what data needs to be collected and from whom. Needs assessment also includes the development of task and KSA analysis and a person analysis, which is used to determine what gaps actually exist in the workforce concerning needed knowledge, skills, and abilities. This chapter provides an overview of these topics, which will be discussed in full detail in Chapter 3.

Organizational support.   In many ways, a needs assessment must be thought of as an intervention into an organization. That is, you are going to be entering the lives of people in an organization, and, to some extent, you are going to disrupt their patterns of behavior while you collect information to help design the training program. When the needs assessment is carefully designed and supported by the organization, the disruption is minimized and cooperation is much more likely. Thus, the analyst needs to take steps to work effectively with all parties and gain the trust and support of the participants in the needs assessment. Establishing liaison teams and work groups that help facilitate the process becomes a necessary part of the needs assessment. We consider establishing organizational support (and maintaining it throughout the entire project) as the first step in the needs assessment process because a failure to do so makes accomplishing a needs assessment a very difficult, if not impossible chore. As such, this is the first major topic covered in Chapter 3.

Organizational analysis.   Following the establishment of organizational support, the next step in the needs assessment is an organizational analysis, which begins with an examination of the short- and long-term goals of the organization, as well as of the trends that are likely to affect these goals. As described in Chapter 1, organizations are in a very fluid state in an increasingly competitive environment. Thus, there is a certain degree of uncertainty about people and human resource issues, and organizational analysts need to ask questions like the following (Schuler, 1994):

Is there a sufficient supply of people?

How do you attract, retain, and motivate an increasingly diverse workforce?

How do you compete for individuals with the right skills, knowledge, abilities, and attitudes?

How do your employees have to behave in order for the company to be competitive both domestically and internationally?

Organizational analyses often require that upper-level management examine their own expectations concerning their training programs. Training designed to produce proficient sales personnel would typically be structured differently from programs designed to train sales personnel who are capable of moving up the corporate ladder to managerial positions. When organizational analysis is ignored, planning difficulties can abound. Some corporations have spent considerable sums of money retraining personnel because the original training programs and decisions on performance capabilities were based on a system that soon became obsolete. In addition, it is becoming increasingly clear that organizations must ensure that there is a positive climate for trainees to transfer what they have learned in the training program onto the job. Thus, supervisors must ensure that trainees are supported and have the opportunity to use their learned behavior. Otherwise, what is learned in training can rapidly disappear. Another aspect of organizational analysis focuses on training programs and supporting systems—for example, selection, human-factors engineering, and work procedures. Some types of problems might best be resolved by changes in selection standards or redesign of the work environment, not necessarily by training changes.

Requirements analysis.   While organizational support and organizational analysis issues are being examined, information for a requirements analysis should also be collected. It is in this phase that the analyst focuses on questions such as What jobs are being examined? Who has information about the jobs? What types of systems, such as job observations, interviews, and surveys, are going to be used to collect information? The analyst even has to ask very basic questions such as What is the target job? For example, in today's dynamic environment, the same job might be performed in several countries, and significant aspects of the job could differ depending on where it is being performed. Actually, it would not be unusual for important job components to change even if the job is performed in different geographical regions of the same country. Or, the job could differ if it is performed during the winter or summer or day or night. If the training program is going to provide people with expertise to perform these jobs, then the requirements analysis has to identify how this information is going to be collected and how much information needs to be collected to ensure that the data are indeed representative and reliable.

Task and knowledge, skill, and ability analysis.   The next part of the needs assessment program is a careful analysis of the job to be performed by trainees upon completion of the training program. Often this process begins with specifying the tasks required on the job. Then the tasks are used to ask what skills, knowledge, and attitudes (KSAs) are required to perform those tasks on the job.

For example, a brief description of an airline reservation clerk's job might indicate that the clerk makes and confirms reservations, determines seat availability, and so on. Thus, a task for the airline reservation clerk might be "inspects availability board to determine seats available for passengers on standby status." Then it is possible to determine what KSAs are required to perform those tasks. For example, to perform the task concerning airline seat availability, the reservation clerk might have to have the knowledge of seating plans for the different types of aircraft used by that carrier and the skill in calling up that information on a computer system. In addition to determining the KSAs, the analyst often asks questions such as which KSAs are most critical to job performance or which should be learned before coming to the job, which in training, or which are not learned until actually on the job.

Person analysis.   Here the emphasis is not on determining which tasks or KSAs are necessary but on assessing how well the employee actually performs the KSAs required by the job. To perform person analysis, deriving measures of job performance known as *criteria* becomes necessary. (This will be discussed further in the evaluation section of this book.) A very important aspect of person analysis is to determine which necessary KSAs have already been learned by the prospective trainees so that precious training time is not wasted repeating what has already been acquired. For employees already on the job, a critical aspect becomes determining the current knowledge and skill level and comparing this to standards for performing the job. In today's environment, these standards can change rapidly, and one aspect of the person analysis is to determine whether training of the present workforce can fill that gap or whether other interventions, such as new hiring strategies or some combination of these strategies, need to be used.

Deriving Instructional Objectives

From information obtained in the assessment of instructional needs, a blueprint emerges that describes the objectives to be achieved by the trainee upon completion of the training program. These objectives provide the input for the design of the training program as well as for the measures of success (criteria) that will be used to judge the program's adequacy. One approach to establishing instructional objectives is known as *specification of the behavioral objectives* (Mager, 1984). Mager notes the statement "to develop a critical understanding of the importance of effective management" (1984, p. 24) does not begin to express what the learner will be doing when he or she has mastery of the objective. However, the following does give a good idea of what is to be achieved:

> Given all available engineering data regarding a proposed product, be able to write a product profile. The profile must describe and define all of the commercial

characteristics of the product appropriate to its introduction to the market, including descriptions of at least three major product uses. (Mager, 1984, p. 25)

Another way of looking at instructional objectives is to ask what, given a particular task and the specification of the KSAs necessary to perform the task, are the effective behaviors that will tell you that the task is being performed correctly? Asking what ineffective behaviors are being exhibited when a task is performed incorrectly can also provide useful information for developing objectives.

Well-written instructional objectives, which are based on tasks and KSAs, specify what the trainee can accomplish when successfully completing the instructional program. They also indicate the conditions under which the performance must be maintained and the standards by which the trainee will be evaluated (Mager, 1984). Thus, objectives communicate the goals of the program to both the learner and the training designer. From these goals the designers can determine the appropriate learning environment and the criteria for examining the achievement of the objectives. Chapter 3 examines the assessment phase, which includes organizational support, requirements and task analyses, and person analyses. Training objectives and instructional design issues are discussed in Chapter 4.

TRAINING AND DEVELOPMENT PHASE

Choosing a Training Environment

Once the tasks, KSAs, and objectives have been specified, the next step is to design the learning environment to achieve the objectives. This is a delicate process that requires a blend of learning principles and media selection, based on the tasks that the trainee is eventually expected to perform. Learning is typically defined as a relatively permanent change in knowledge, skill, or attitude produced by some type of experience. As applied psychologists, we are concerned with both learning and acquisition and also with training transfer, which is the degree to which trainees effectively use what they have learned on the job. In addition, we are learning about the characteristics of the trainee and work environment that support effective transfer back to the job. While written a long time ago (in 1960), Gilbert accurately described the temptations that often lead to a poor training environment. At that time, the remarks were most appropriate for a teaching machine, which provides programmed instruction (see Chapter 7 for a discussion of programmed instruction). Today, they are probably more appropriate for some of the advanced informational technology systems such as CD-ROM, distance learning, and intelligent tutoring systems. In any case Gilbert's remarks are just as relevant today.

If you don't have a gadget called a teaching machine, don't get one. Don't buy one; don't borrow one; don't steal one. If you have such a gadget, get rid of it. Don't give it away, for someone else might use it. This is a most practical rule, based on empirical facts from considerable observation. If you begin with a device of any kind, you will try to develop the teaching program to fit that device. (1960, p. 478)

It is important to consider the tasks that are performed and the KSAs necessary to perform those tasks and ask what type of training program will produce the best results. Flight trainers often choose simulators that create the characteristics of flight in order to teach pilots; however, a simulator is not usually considered appropriate to teach members of the U.S. State Department a foreign language so that they can represent us throughout the world. The analysis of job tasks and performance requirements, and the matching of these behaviors to those produced by the training environment, is at this time as much an art as a technology. Thus, we are very interested in how a learner moves from the status of being a novice to becoming an expert. In addition, we are interested in the aspects of the learning environment that support maintenance of long-term learning retention and the adaptability of trained responses to new tasks and situations. It is clear that we have learned a great deal about various aspects of the training environment, such as the characteristics of successful trainees as well as the kinds of learning variables that support learning in training.

Trainee Characteristics

Certain trainee characteristics are important preconditions for learning. Thus, there is an extensive literature on trainee readiness and the degree to which the person is ready to benefit from the actual training program. Also, there is evidence that there are differences in the amount of motivation to learn among different trainees and that this relates to how successful the trainee is in the training program.

Learning Principles

In training environments, the instructional process involves the acquisition of skills, concepts, and attitudes that are transferred to a second setting (usually to a job situation). The acquisition phase emphasizes learning new KSAs. Job performance focuses on transfer of learning from the training program to the job setting. Both theoretical and empirical sources of information are available to aid in the design of environments to improve worker performance. Theorists have progressed to a stage of development at which it is clear that the choice of the proper learning variable or level of that variable should be carefully selected.

Contextual Factors

There is also a growing literature on a number of contextual factors that help spell out whether the training program will be successful. For example, Kozlowski and Hults (1987) found that organizations that supported updating activities and provided incentives for participating had engineers who took more training. Similarly, Quiñones (1997) describes work showing that when organizations provide information to trainees that is not accurate, it can be very disruptive to training efforts. In addition, Rouillier and Goldstein (1993) have helped define organizational consequences that make it either more or less likely that trainees will actually transfer what they have learned in training back to the work organization. Chapter 4 presents information on trainee characteristics, learning principles, and contextual factors.

EVALUATION PHASE

Because the development of a training program involves an assessment of needs and a careful design of the training environment, the trainee is expected to perform his or her job at acceptable levels. However, careful examination of the training process discloses numerous pitfalls. The assessment of instructional need might have omitted important job components, or the job itself might have changed since the program was designed, or perhaps the training program was well designed but not well delivered. In today's rapidly changing environment, it is becoming increasingly important to ensure that training meets the organization's needs.

Unfortunately, as described in Chapter 1, some programs are not evaluated. As noted by Salas and Cannon-Bowers (in press), training evaluation is "easier said than done" (p. 30). Indeed, the word *evaluation* raises all sorts of emotional defense reactions. In many cases the difficulties seem related to a failure to understand that the design of training programs is an effort that must be massaged and treated until the required results are produced. An experience of one of the authors may illuminate this problem.

> A community agency was offering a program for previously unemployed individuals to help them obtain jobs. A colleague and I were invited to visit and offer suggestions about improvements to the program. Our questions about the program's success were answered by reference to the excellent curricula and the high attendance rate of the participants. A frank discussion ensued related to the program's objectives, with particular emphasis on the criteria being utilized to measure its adequacy—that is, how successful the participants were in obtaining and holding jobs. This discussion led to the revelation that the success level was simply unknown because such data had never been collected. Of course, it is possible that the program was working successfully, but the information to make such a

judgment was unavailable. Thus, there was no way to determine the effectiveness of the program or to provide information that could lead to improvements. Basically, unless there is information about the effectiveness of the programs in helping trainees to find jobs, it is not possible to know whether it made sense to revise or where to place the efforts when revisions were necessary.

The evaluation process centers around two procedures. The first is designing measures of success (criteria) and the other is the use of evaluating designs to help specify what changes have occurred during the training and transfer process. The criteria are based on the behavioral objectives, which were determined by the assessment of instructional need. Criteria must be established for both the evaluation of trainees at the conclusion of the training program and the evaluation of on-the-job performance (referred to as transfer validity in the model). One classification for this purpose suggests that several different measures are necessary, including reaction of participants, learning of participants in training, behavior changes on the job, and final results of the total program (Kirkpatrick, 1994). These issues are discussed in Chapter 5.

Besides criterion development, the evaluation phase must also focus on the necessary design to assess the training program. As indicated in Figure 2.1, a number of different designs can be used to evaluate training programs, and to some extent the choices depend on what you know about your training program and what constraints exist in collecting the information. In the last column of the diagram, a number of potential goals are listed:

1. *Training validity:* Did trainees learn during training?
2. *Transfer validity:* Is what has been learned in training transferred as enhanced performance in the work organization?
3. *Intraorganizational validity:* Is the performance of a new group of trainees in the same organization that developed the training program consistent with the performance of the original training group?
4. *Interorganizational validity:* Has the analyst attempted to determine whether a training program validated in one organization can be used successfully in another organization?

As discussed in Chapter 6, these questions often result in different evaluation models or, at the very least, different forms of the same evaluation model. For example, an experimental design model could use control groups (people not attending training) as a way of accounting for extraneous effects. Some startled trainers have discovered that their control group performed as well as trainees enrolled in an elaborately designed training program. This sometimes occurred because the control groups could not be permitted to do the job without training. Thus, they either had on-the-job training or were instructed through a program that existed before the implementation of the new instructional system. Of course, such a result might lead to a particular set of decisions based on the cost effectiveness of the different approaches.

Besides experimental designs, other approaches to evaluation provide varying degrees of information. Chapter 6 stresses that the rigor of the design affects the quality and quantity of information available for evaluation. There are situations in which it is not possible to use the most rigorous design because of cost or because of the particular setting. In these cases it is important to use the best design available and to recognize those factors that affect the validity of the information.

Information may become available at many different stages in the evaluation process. For example, an effective monitoring program might show that the training program has not been implemented as originally planned. In other instances, decisions might await data that isn't available until the trainee has transferred back to the job. As indicated by the feedback loops in the model (see Figure 2.1), the information derived from the evaluation process is used to reassess the instructional need, thus creating input for the next stage of development. The development of training programs must be viewed as an evolving process.

INSTRUCTIONAL TECHNIQUES AND TRAINING METHODS

For training to occur, decisions must be made regarding the selection of instructional techniques and training methods. Chapter 7 presents some of the vast variety of approaches to instruction that exist from the use of the traditional classroom, including lecture and discussion, case studies and role playing, to self-directed learning programs, ranging from workbooks to programmed instruction. Chapter 7 also includes a section on work simulations. These materials are followed by a discussion of what makes up effective instruction. The chapter closes with a section on emerging training technologies, discussing new technological approaches to instruction, including distance learning, CD-ROM, web-based instruction, intelligent tutors, and virtual reality training.

Chapter 8 focuses on training interventions and learning experiences for developing employees, teams, and leaders. It has a section on building employee capabilities using techniques such as orientation programs, newcomer socialization, and on-the-job training. The next section emphasizes building team effectiveness, and it has materials on topics such as cross training, team self-management, and adventure and action learning. The last section of Chapter 8 describes techniques for developing leaders, including business simulations, behavior modeling, assessment centers, diversity training, and global leadership.

We have titled the final chapter of our book Learning Systems. In this chapter, we examine training from a broader, more macro perspective. This macro perspective recognizes that learning is not a discrete event but is an everyday experience that occurs within an organizational culture. As organizations view continuous learning as the key to competitive advantage, training is seen as one component in a larger orientation toward continuous improvement. We also focus on integrating materials that we introduced in earlier chapters such as societal issues and their implications for training systems. Thus, in Chapter 9 we present materials on the learning organization as well as training and societal concerns such as workforce readiness, ensuring fairness and opportunities at work, and retraining workers given changing market forces.

The instructional design approach presented in this chapter (see Figure 2.1) presents a somewhat linear steplike approach to the development of training systems. We think following these steps helps in the design of effective instructional systems. It also helps the authors (and we hope the readers) organize the material that follows. But it is also important to realize that often projects do not follow all of the steps in the instructional design process. Sometimes, a needs assessment has been accomplished somewhat earlier, and the organization then decides at a later time that it needs a new training program. Perhaps the needs assessment does not have all of the information required, but the organization does not want to begin all over again. We would hope that in these situations the approach would be to thoughtfully adapt models and systems that permit modifications that will lead to well-designed training programs. This might include an approach where critical information is reassessed by the use of a focus group to determine whether the information is still useful. Or perhaps specific data sets are collected to augment information that already exists. Similarly, there are instances where full evaluations are not possible at that time. It is still possible to collect the best information available and be aware of the limitations in interpreting your results. Interested readers concerned about this topic will enjoy an article by Dipboye (1997) that describes some of the organizational barriers to implementing a rational model of training such as the one presented in Figure 2.1.

Our text begins the description of the training design process with Chapter 3 on needs assessment.

INFOTRAC COLLEGE EDITION

For additional readings, go to http: www.infotrac-college.com/wadsworth and enter a search term related to your interest. The following key terms will pull up several related articles.

Instructional Design	Training Evaluation
Learning Principles	Training Systems

THE NEEDS ASSESSMENT PHASE

Training programs are designed to achieve goals that meet instructional needs. There is always the temptation to begin training without a thorough analysis of these needs; however, a reexamination of the instructional model introduced in Chapter 2 will emphasize the danger of beginning any program without a complete assessment of tasks, behaviors, and environment. The model shows that the objectives, criteria, and design of the program all stem from these analyses. Goals and objectives are the key steps in determining a training environment, and unless they are specified, there is no way to measure success. Organizations are becoming aware that understanding their training needs is a critical component of strategic planning. Understanding the capabilities of people in the organization is part of the road map you need as part of the planning process. Cascio (1994) states:

> As both economic conditions and technological developments change rapidly, the ability to adapt to these changes becomes the essence of future competitiveness. Adaptation involves three processes: (1) identifying the areas needing change; (2) planning and implementing the actions necessary to make a change; and (3) evaluating the effectiveness of the changes. (p. 1)

Understanding the capabilities of the workforce is a critical part of identifying the areas needing change. It is not possible to make a strategic change unless you understand whether your present workforce can support the change, or whether they need further training, or whether you require a combination of training and new personnel. In any case, you need to start with the needs assessment. A "let's do it in our heads" approach or a "we know it all already" approach simply does not work in today's dynamic world. The problems are made obvious by a report of the U.S. Merit Systems Protection Board (1995), which did an assessment of federal government agencies. The board found that more than half its respondents did not feel they did a good job assessing their organization's present training needs and less than 33% thought that their assessments provided an accurate picture for the future.

Carefully described objectives that set forth required behavior are needed to plan effective training programs; moreover, there should be a direct relationship between these objectives and the type of instruction. Physicians diagnose illness using X-ray film and laboratory tests before they attempt to prescribe a cure through medication, surgery, or other techniques. The training analyst also makes a diagnosis using needs assessment techniques to determine if a cure is necessary and which cure is most likely to produce the desired result. A training needs assessment is the diagnostic X-ray film for the training analyst. Figure 3.1 presents a model of the components of the needs assessment process. Most of this chapter will be devoted to a discussion of these components. However, because many of the various parts described in Figure 3.1 are dependent on each other, a short description of each component will be helpful before beginning a more thorough discussion.

The first column, organizational support, signifies that a needs assessment is an intervention into the lives of employees and will require the time and effort of many people in order to be successful. Thus, it is critical that the analyst

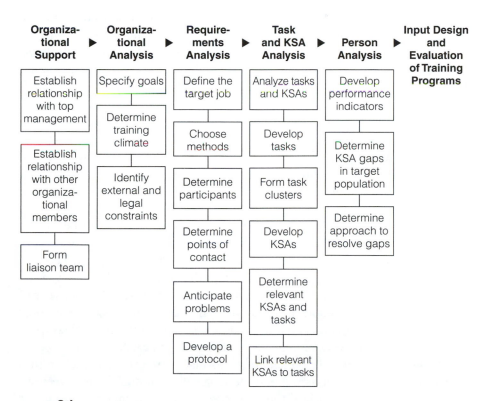

FIGURE **3.1**

A model of the needs assessment process.

work carefully with all parties to gain the trust and support necessary for a careful effort. Often this requires establishing liaison teams and work groups to facilitate the entire process. We consider this as the necessary first step in working with the organization.

As this is being accomplished, an organizational analysis (see the second column) can be conducted to codify the important factors that can impact the effectiveness of training programs that operate within an organizational context. Training managers must clearly understand the strategic direction of their organization. To design training systems that do not fit into the organization's goals and plans would not make sense. For example, failing to develop training programs for a major technology shift in operations is not a way for the training department to endear itself to top management. In addition, the context is extremely important. Few people would want to design a training program that would violate safety and health regulations or a program that might result in charges of employment discrimination or sexual harassment. Similarly, it does not make sense to design a training program that is unacceptable to current supervisors.

The third column, requirements analysis, describes the steps that must be considered before collecting information concerning the tasks and knowledge, skill, and abilities (KSAs) required to perform the job. It begins with determining the target job being examined. Although that might seem self-evident, jobs that have the same label might vary dramatically when performed in different locations or under different conditions. For example, the job of a firefighter is very different for fires in large high-rise buildings versus fires on the docks of San Francisco Bay. If the training is going to be designed for both components of the job, the analyst has to ensure that all are included in the assessment. Defining the target jobs also helps determine what methods will be used in the assessment and who will need to participate in order to successfully describe the job.

The next stage in training needs assessment consists of the collection of the important tasks and KSAs necessary to perform the job. These components will be the input for the actual design of the training program. The fifth column, person analysis, recognizes the fact that it is critical to analyze the workforce to determine which of these competencies need to be the focus of training efforts. For example, it is possible to find that your present workforce needs training on KSAs related to computer programming, whereas new people coming into the workforce need training on KSAs related to quality control. This requires the development of performance indicators and a determination of where the KSA gaps are in the target population. The next sections of this chapter discuss each of these needs assessment components, but it is always important to remember that there is a strong interaction between each of the parts. Thus, if the wrong target job is selected in the requirements analysis, the wrong KSAs will likely be chosen as the focus of training efforts.

Another purpose of Figure 3.1 is to provide both the authors and the reader a road map of the various components of the training needs assessment. We hope you will use it as you read this chapter and that it helps specify the important components of the needs assessment process for you.

ORGANIZATIONAL SUPPORT
FOR THE NEEDS ASSESSMENT PROCESS

The needs assessment process can be thought of as a type of organizational intervention. An *intervention,* such as a needs assessment or training program, is a procedure that interrupts organizational members' daily routines and patterns of work behavior. A carefully designed training needs assessment helps to ensure that the disruption is minimal. The success of needs assessment largely depends on the extent of the support offered by the organization and its members. Thus, as presented in Figure 3.1, gaining the support of the organization is a critical first step in the needs assessment process.

The needs assessment process will be effective only if the assessor can gain the trust of all parties or organizational stakeholders. The process underlying appropriate analysis suggests an interactive system. To design effective training systems, the training organization needs the information from the working organization. Just as important, the training department must also gain the cooperation of the working organization in order to have appropriate support for the training system. This suggests an interactive give-and-take relationship to work out the necessary goals and relationships. It also means that organizational conflicts must be resolved before the instructional program is designed and implemented. Glaser and Taylor (1973) report on case studies that examined the factors determining the success of applied research. One interesting finding is that successful interventions are characterized by highly motivated people who develop, early in the program, a two-way communication network. The projects had early and active contacts with all pertinent parties. In many cases, this resolved many conflicts. One particular vignette from these case studies focuses on this issue:

> When a group of people or a team are truly involved and participating . . . they look ahead and conceive of their role in time and space in such a manner that includes what they see themselves doing in relation to the project. They usually attempt to interject their own pet theories and questions. . . . At the very least there's usually a rather heated discussion to work out the details, whether they be of an administrative nature or concern the ideas embodied in the design. (p. 142)

A critical issue in these case studies was the behavior of the person heading the team. Successful investigators negotiated differences, cleared up misunderstandings, and strongly discouraged their group members from adopting a "we versus they" attitude. The less successful studies were more insular and were characterized as having "tunnel vision." This point cannot be overemphasized. A lack of trust in the analyst or the procedure being followed can have dire consequences. An example of the problems that can be created comes from a recent experience of one of the authors of this book. These issues were especially illuminating because everyone told about the incident responded with similar types of experiences.

> I was invited by an organization's top management to design a needs assessment package that would be used to establish rating scales for performance appraisal. As part of that process, I requested that the first meeting be with a union-management committee, which I had heard about from top management. The committee had representatives from all parts of the organization. The hostility in the atmosphere at the meeting was made apparent by such questions as "What are you trying to sell us?"; "Did you ever do this type of work before?"; "Are you trying to stick us with a system you developed for someone else?" Finally, after several hours of "conversation," I learned that this committee had, at the request of top management, developed an earlier plan for the project. After countless hours of volunteer time, they submitted a report. On the same day their report was submitted, they were informed that an outside consultant had been asked to perform the same activity. Unfortunately for me, I was the chosen consultant. I decided not even to try to begin the project. Instead, we arranged for meetings between top management, the committee, and our research team to work out everyone's feelings and to establish appropriate roles for each group. Eventually, the project proceeded with everyone's cooperation. Months later, members of the committee noted that, if we had not met with them and if we had not resolved these difficulties, no one in the organization would have cooperated during the needs assessment; they had intended to subvert the entire needs assessment process. I have no doubt that they would have accomplished their purpose.

The temptation for the training analyst in these types of situations is to ignore the conflict and hope it will go away. However, conflicts do not usually disappear; they usually become more troublesome. Perhaps, more seriously, some intervention programs exacerbate the conflict, and the program itself is blamed for the failure. In many cases, the solution to these types of problems is not training programs but conflict-resolution procedures, which must first be used to resolve such difficulties. This example illustrates the importance of establishing the trust of organizational members. Distrust will, at best, result in inaccurate information concerning the job in question. Besides the questionable quality of the information gathered, the ease with which the information is gathered will also be affected. It is highly improbable that participants who mistrust the process will go out of their way to facilitate the needs assessment procedure. Thus, gaining the trust of the organizational members is an important first step for the assessor. Some of the aspects involved in establishing these relations suggested in Figure 3.1 are discussed next.

Establishing a Relationship with Top-Level Management

At the beginning of the process, establishing communication with the relevant top administrator in the organization is necessary. French and Bell (1999) point out the importance of this contact. They state that if top leadership does not clearly understand the goals and strategies of the needs assessment, then the procedure may become vulnerable to the natural ups and downs that accompany any organizational intervention. First, it is necessary to agree on why the needs assessment is being done (that is, to design a new training program, to improve an existing training program, to determine the validity of an existing training program, and so on). Second, the analyst must determine who the other people are in the organization whose cooperation must be obtained. Third, the assessor must establish what expectations are being held by top management. These points are important whether the analyst is an outside consultant or a member of the in-house training staff. Thus, it would not make sense for either an in-house or outside consultant to design a plan for the training department without understanding the organization's future goals, nor would it make sense to proceed with a needs assessment unless it was first determined whose cooperation was needed. Some expectations that might need clarification are the role of the analyst within the organization, the participation of organizational members involved in the assessment procedure, the type of results that can be expected, and the type of actions that can be implemented.

In some instances, top management may have expectations concerning issues that they wish to have resolved. For example, they might be interested in the number of dissatisfied employees in their organization. This type of outcome is not usually one of the products of a needs assessment for training and development. If different expectations exist, then they must be negotiated at the outset of the assessment process. Besides delineating top management's expectations, it is important for the analyst to explain his or her own expectations. In this regard, some items that should be discussed might include the following:

1. The discussion should establish whether the organization is ready to lend support, time, and effort toward the successful completion of the needs assessment.
2. Information should be exchanged concerning the methods or procedures by which the analyst will operate, the probable time span of the assessment, and the cost of the process.
3. Information on types of outcomes that can result from the process should be presented so that different expectations can be resolved.
4. Issues concerning the confidentiality of the results for any individual member of the organization should be resolved.

Establishing a Relationship with Members of the Organization

Bennis (1969) emphasizes that it is extremely important to gain a "hierarchical umbrella of acceptance" if the needs assessment process is to succeed. This means that it is critical to involve, advise, and inform all key people in the organization about the procedure and to obtain the commitment of these individuals to the assessment process. The term *key people* in this case refers to all those people who are affected by the needs assessment. These range from top-level managers to first-level managers to the actual job incumbents. One way to achieve this "umbrella of acceptance" is to set up a liaison team. The liaison team consists of a small number of people from the organization who serve as the primary contact between the assessor and the organization. The needs assessment process can benefit in several ways through the formation of a liaison team.

First, a liaison team can aid an assessor by functioning as a communication pipeline to members of the organization. Members of liaison teams often have access to data that is very useful for the analyst, such as the attitudes and feelings of fellow employees. Information can flow in both directions along this pipeline. That is, liaison team members can be a source of communication about concerns involving the needs assessment. For example, an analyst may discover concerns regarding how the needs assessment participants are being chosen. In addition, liaison team members will undoubtedly have discussions with other employees concerning their experiences with the assessor. If these discussions reveal to employees that the assessor is honest, candid, and professional, then further support for the assessment process may be gained.

The team can help with many important tasks. For example, the team can make suggestions concerning the characteristics of individuals who should participate, prepare memos to participants explaining the process, and set up meetings with participants. This type of participation results in a sharing of the process, which helps establish the trust necessary to accomplish a successful needs assessment. Thus, the liaison team functions by increasing participation and involvement of organizational members in the assessment procedure and by gaining the support of other employees for the entire process.

Because members of a liaison team serve these important functions, the team members should be chosen with care. Obviously, it will be necessary to enlist the aid of various organizational representatives in helping to choose team members. The following criteria can help you create an effective liaison team:

1. Ensure that the various components of the organization are represented. In different organizations, this can include representative components from such stakeholder groups as the training department, union representation, management, and job incumbents from the affected units.

2. Choose members who are recognized leaders of their respective units; they should have good information concerning their units and be able to communicate effectively with the people in their units.
3. Choose members who are generally in tune with the idea of helping by being a problem solver for the organization.

ORGANIZATIONAL ANALYSIS

People concerned with training face a serious problem. That is, the individuals who participate in training programs must learn something in one environment (training) and then use their acquired KSAs in another environment (on the job). Thus, the trainee will enter a new environment subject to the effects of all the interaction components that represent organizations today.

Organizational analysis refers to an examination of systemwide components of the organization that may affect a training program beyond those ordinarily considered in task and person analyses. Task and person analyses are more specific, focusing on job tasks and the required employee characteristics (KSAs). Organizational analysis has a much broader scope. It is concerned with the systemwide components of an organization, including an examination of organizational goals, resources of the organization, transfer climate for training, and internal and external constraints present in the environment.

The actual components of an organizational analysis depend on the type of program being instituted and the characteristics of the organization. To be perfectly candid, only recently have industrial-organizational psychologists begun to realize the importance of these issues. For example, little attention has been given to understanding the strategic plans of the organization and the implications of such plans for training efforts. Clearly, if an organizational goal is to pursue quality enhancement, training efforts need to be consistent with that objective. The procedures and issues for accomplishing these types of organizational analyses are not completely understood. Also, the scope of the organizational analysis probably depends on a number of variables, including who is to be trained, what type of training is contemplated, the size of the organization, and so on. However, examining some of the concerns and making suggestions about some of the procedures that can be used to collect the necessary information is possible. The following broad categories should be considered.

Specifying Goals

When organizational goals are not clear, designing or implementing training programs is difficult. As a result, specifying criteria that would be used in the evaluation process is also not possible. Sometimes, training programs are judged to be failures because of organizational system constraints. For example, the statements "start training at the top" and "I wish my boss had been exposed to this training program" indicate real differences between the approach or values of the training program and those of upper-level supervisors. However, it is too late to compare the goals of upper-level supervision with those of the training program after the instructional program has been instituted. Many of the activities previously described in determining the organizational support for the intervention provide critical information about these issues. Training programs that are in conflict with the goals of the organization are likely to produce confused and dissatisfied workers.

A classic study by Fleishman, Harris, and Burtt (1955) was probably the first study to suggest the difficulties that arise when the training program and the working environment promote different values. These researchers designed a training program to increase the amount of consideration (friendship, mutual trust) in supervisors. The initial results, collected at the end of the training program, indicated success (as shown by the training scores). However, a follow-up of the program showed that the consideration factor was not maintained on the job. The researchers discovered that the day-to-day social climate, influenced by the supervisors, was not sympathetic to the new values. This study suggests that the climate on the job is a critical component in determining whether the knowledge and skills gained in the training program will be used on the job. The Fleishman study also makes clear why experimental designs that enable researchers to study the effects of learning in training and its transfer onto the job are so important. These designs will be examined in Chapter 6 as a part of the study of the evaluation processes.

London (1991) presents a variety of situations concerning whether clear goals exist and the implications for policy decisions such as whether to train.

Situation 1. Goals are clear and options to achieve the goal are available. An example of this is when an organization chooses a new technology and knows that training is needed. If the training program has been developed and is available either within the organization (or a relevant one can be purchased), all of the attention would typically turn to training the individuals and evaluating the program to ensure that the training has occurred.

Situation 2. Goals are clear but options to achieve the goal are not available. For example, new technology might be introduced, but training programs might not be available. Perhaps, a series of complaints makes it clear that bank tellers need instruction in how to serve customers differently because of the implementation of new technology. The specific type of training program might not be available in the organization and a relevant one might not be available from a training vendor. Or often, organizations wish to have their own customized programs to meet specific needs. In this case, the effort needs to begin right at the needs assessment stage to determine what types of KSAs need to be learned, and then the training environment has to be designed. Once that is accomplished, this situation reverts to one where the goals are clear and the attention is on training the individuals.

Situation 3. Goals are unclear or in the process of change. This could occur when two firms are merging and the responsibilities for the emerging product line are not clear. Or perhaps as organization is trying to develop over some period of time a global multinational corporate culture or is considering change brought about by outside forces. For example, police organizations often spend considerable training on skill requirements (such as operating a police vehicle or utilizing firearms) or information requirements (knowing the law regarding a felony versus a misdemeanor). However, when public safety organizations become involved in the specification of goals with community associations as part of the strategic move to a community policing philosophy, they often discover the need to attend to other objectives—such as presentation skills and improved interpersonal relationships with the public regardless of race, color, or creed. In these cases, it requires a reanalysis to determine the goals and the vision. In the case of becoming a multinational firm, for example, teams of individuals might need to ask a whole series of questions like Is it possible to grow your own managers to participate in the multinational firm, or do you have to buy them from other organizations? This could result in further analysis such as whether it is possible to have a fast-track program for high-potential homegrown managers. Then, depending on the analysis, you will move toward a process similar to that in situation 1 or 2.

Besides the importance of specifying goals, Ostroff and Ford (1989) add another important idea. They point out that there are various levels of analysis, such as the individual worker, the work group, and the organization. They indicate that it is important to consider the goals from each operational level. For example, they note that the goals of the unit or department might be used to determine what training is needed. However, at an individual level, the worker might perceive that a training program does not have the potential to help in achieving his or her goals. Thus, the training might not turn out to be useful because the individual is not motivated to learn the material. Or, as in the Fleishman study, there might be a serious conflict between individual, unit, or organizational goals. The point that Ostroff and Ford make is that it is necessary to determine what level of analysis needs to be examined. Also, it is critical not to generalize from one level to another without having the appropriate data.

Determining the Organizational Training Climate

As complex as the specification of systemwide organizational objectives appears to be, the determination of objectives alone will not do the job. People who participate in training are faced with a problem; they are required to learn something in one environment (training situation) and use the learning in another environment (on the job). This suggests that another critical aspect of organizational analysis is an examination of the components of the organization that may affect a trainee arriving with newly learned skills. Thus, training programs are often judged to be a failure because of organizational constraints that were not originally intended to be addressed by the instructional program. As an example, a trainee will have difficulty overcoming a situation where he or she arrives with a set of behaviors that are not consistent with the way the manager prefers to have the job performed. Also, training programs are not likely to be successful when managers are forced to maintain production standards while the employee is sent to a training program.

As noted earlier, Fleishman, Harris, and Burtt (1955) originally found that there might be difficulties when the values of the training program and the job environment were not the same. Recently, a few authors have made similar suggestions. Michalak (1981) warns us that trainers put too much effort into the portion of training dealing with the acquisition of skill and not enough in what happens afterward. Similarly, Marx (in press) stresses the identification of high-risk situations that the trainee would face and the need for coping skills in those situations. Russell, Terborg, and Powers (1985) evaluated co-worker and supervisory practices to determine whether these personnel were using similar methods as those taught in training. The belief was that if these individuals were behaving in a manner consistent with the training, then trainees will be "reminded" to use such behavior on the job. The results of the study indicate that organizational support is significantly related to organizational performance.

The preceding issues specify the importance of organizational climate in transfer of training. However, compared with task and KSA analysis, work in this area is at an early stage. As noted by Goldstein and Thayer (1987), a conceptual model specifying the type of concerns that should be examined is sorely lacking. Rouillier and Goldstein (1993) have worked on research that has identified transfer climate components and classified the components based on an organizational behavior model developed by Luthans and Kreitner (1985). Two major components of transfer climate, situational cues and consequences, were predicted to influence the extent to which transfer would occur. Table 3.1 presents some of the types of items included in each of these categories.

Rouillier and Goldstein (1993) conducted a study investigating their model with a large franchise that owns and operates 102 fast-food restaurants. Surveys were developed that individually measured the transfer climate (situational cues and consequences) of each of the 102 organizational units and the transfer behavior of trainees assigned to the unit. The trainees were assistant managers who completed a nine-week training program and then were assigned on a random basis to one of the 102 organizational units. They found

| TABLE 3.1 | SOME EXAMPLES OF ORGANIZATIONAL ITEMS FOR THE ASSESSMENT OF TRANSFER CLIMATE |

Situational Cues	Consequences
Existing managers make sure that new managers have the opportunity to use their training immediately.	Existing managers let new managers know they are doing a good job when they use their training.
Existing managers have new managers share their training experience and learning with co-workers on the job.	Existing managers refuse to accept statements or actions from new managers that are different from those learned in training.
The equipment used in training is similar to the equipment found on the job.	More experienced workers ridicule the use of techniques taught in training (reverse scored).
Existing managers assign an experienced co-worker to help trainees as needed back on the job.	Existing managers do not notice new managers who are using their training (reverse scored).
Existing managers ease the pressure of work for a short time so new managers have a chance to practice new skills.	New managers who successfully use their training are likely to receive a salary increase.
Training aids are available on the job to support what new managers have learned in training.	New managers who use their training are given preference for new assignments.

Source: From "The Relationship Between Organizational Transfer Climate and Positive Transfer of Training," by J. Z. Rouillier and I. L. Goldstein, 1993, *Human Resource Development Quarterly, 4*, pp. 377–390. Copyright © 1993 by Jossey-Bass, Inc. Reprinted by permission by Jossey-Bass, Inc., a subsidiary of John Wiley & Sons, Inc.

that trainees assigned to units that had a more positive transfer climate in terms of influencing trainees to use what they've learned (situational cues) and rewarding trainees for doing so (consequences) demonstrated more transfer behavior onto the job. Also, as expected, trainees who had learned more in training performed better on the job, but the interaction between transfer climate and learning was not significant. This provided evidence that the degree of positive transfer climate affected the degree to which learned behavior was transferred onto the job independent of the amount of knowledge and skills gained as a function of attending the training program. The investigators concluded that transfer climate was a potentially powerful tool that organizations should consider to facilitate training transfer.

Since the time of the Rouillier and Goldstein study, Tracey, Tannenbaum, and Kavanagh (1995) replicated most of the study and found the climate transfer measure substantially predicted supervisory ratings of 104 manager trainees in 52 stores of a supermarket chain. In addition, Tracey added another set of items that measured "a continuous learning culture" and also found similar results with that measure. In addition, Ford, Quiñones, Sego, and Sorra (1992) surveyed USAF airmen four months after they had completed technical training and found that they had been given different opportunities to perform the tasks for which they had been trained. Ford and his collaborators also found that these opportunities were related to their supervisors' attitudes toward the trainee and the degree of work-group support received once on the job. Interestingly, the opportunity to perform the tasks for which they had been trained is also a component of the transfer climate measure that Rouillier and Goldstein used. Thus, there appears to be the development of a literature that points to transfer climate in the organization as a component of the degree to which trainees transfer their learning. Thayer and Teachout (1995) have added an important addition to this conceptualization. They note that there are two aspects that facilitate positive transfer. One aspect is the positive transfer climate previously discussed. The other is transfer-enhancing activities that occur during the training itself. This is a very good point, and these activities that occur during training itself will be covered in Chapter 4 on the learning environment.

Identifying External and Legal Constraints

The preceding sections on organizational analysis have identified issues related to specifying organizational goals and establishing a positive transfer climate. In this section we examine the importance of the interacting constraints impacting an organization and their effects on training programs. External constraints have become a very serious problem in the design of training programs.

Ledvinka and Scarpello (1991) describe how the legal environment has changed; Figure 3.2 illustrates some of those changes. Ledvinka and Scarpello note that regulation was originally organized by industry. Thus, the Interstate Commerce Commission (ICC) regulates the trucking industry and the Food and Drug Administration (FDA) regulates the drug industry. Each industry and sector of the economy, listed at the top of the figure, has a regulatory agency specifically tied to it. That type of regulation is known as vertical regulation. More recently, horizontal regulation has been established in industries or sectors of the economy. The Occupational Safety and Health Administration (OSHA) is concerned with one activity, job safety, in all industries, and the Equal Employment Opportunity Commission (EEOC) was created to solve issues related to employment discrimination. Thus, the older vertical agencies, such as the FDA, were created to solve problems specific to an industry, whereas the newer horizontal agencies were established to solve social problems. As a result, the horizontal agencies have as their constituents the groups concerned with those problems, such as civil rights groups. They are less concerned with the specific mission of the organizations they regulate. The regulations established by the horizontal agencies have had a dramatic effect on practice and research involving human resources in work organizations.

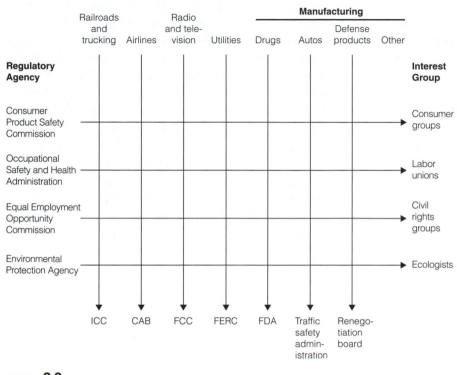

FIGURE 3.2

Horizontal and vertical regulation.

Source: From "The Cost of Government Regulation of Business," by M. L. Weidenbaum. Hearings Before the Subcommittee on Economic Growth and Stabilization of the Joint Economic Commission, 95th Congress, 2d Session, April 11 and 13, 1978, p. 39.

Specific aspects related to employment discrimination and training are covered in Chapter 9, but a personal example should make the point clearer. The first author of this book was asked to design a career-development program to replace an organization's original effort. The original procedure had been found by the courts to discriminate by not making training opportunities available for minorities. Yet, completing the training program was required to be eligible for consideration for promotion. Thus, the court's decision turned out to be a stimulus for the design of a new training effort.

Fair employment practice guidelines have important implications for the needs assessment process, the design of programs, the evaluation of programs, the selection of participants, and even the type of records that must be maintained. Fair employment practices are only an illustration of the factors that must be considered. In other cases, the constraint might be new federal or state safety or environmental requirements that affect the objectives of training programs. Note that Table 1.2 indicates that a considerable amount of company time is spent on occupational safety and compliance. Much of this is related to federal and state regulations. It would be counterproductive to design a training program to teach ways to implement new technology that is in violation of safety and health regulations. Nor would it usually be advisable for a local police agency to teach techniques that were in violation of state or federal regulations. Although the emphasis here has been on legal regulations, external constraints affecting training programs could easily include other factors. Thus, the culture of different countries makes some job behaviors unacceptable in different places, and training programs teaching those job behaviors must account for that fact. The U.S. State Department runs its own school that in addition to language training spends considerable time on cultural issues for employees who will be relocated to different countries.

Resource Analysis

It is difficult to establish working objectives without determining the human and physical resources that are available. This analysis should include a description of the layout of the establishment, the type of equipment available, and the financial resources. More important, human resource needs must include personnel planning that projects future requirements. Too often, organizations respond to personnel needs only in a crisis situation—for example, when they realize they are losing 5% of their workforce through retirement. Few organizations plan for change within the organization. For example, there is a tremendous increase in the number of computer-controlled machine tools and computer-aided design machines being used by industry. It was estimated that investment in this type of equipment grew about 15% annually from 1983 to 1989 (Office of Technology Assessment, 1990) and has continued to grow since. At the same time, the use of this technology has dramatic implications for training programs. If an organization is planning to implement such technology, it would need to do a resource estimate to determine whether it had the people capable of being trained to use the technology.

Schuler (1994) describes the Barden Corporation in Danbury, Connecticut. The company, which manufactures precision bearings, recognized that it would have to continually install numerical control (CNC) machines. It recognized this as a major people-related issue and created an ad hoc committee representing both technical skills and industrial relations. Schuler described the outcome as follows:

> The committee concluded that CNC machinists would have to be developed in-house and it blocked in the technical competencies (machining, trigonometry, basic computer programming, etc.) that would be required. The training unit

TABLE 3.2	DATA REQUIRED FOR PERSON RESOURCE INVENTORY

1. Number of employees in the job classification
2. Number of employees needed in the job classification
3. Age of each employee in the job classification
4. Level of skill required by the job of each employee
5. Level of knowledge required by the job of each employee
6. Attitude of each employee toward job and company
7. Level of job performance, quality and quantity, of each employee
8. Level of skills and knowledge of each employee for other jobs
9. Potential replacements for this job outside company
10. Potential replacements for this job within company
11. Training time required for potential replacements
12. Training time required for a novice
13. Rate of absenteeism from this job
14. Turnover in this job for specified period of time
15. Job specification for the job

Source: From *Training in Business and Industry,* by W. McGehee and P. W. Thayer. Copyright © 1961 by John Wiley & Sons, Inc. Reproduced by permission.

then put together a specific course of training including the hours involved, identified instructors, worked out a full apprenticeship program with the State Department of Labor, and assisted in identifying employees with acceptable minimum qualifications. (p. 15)

This was followed by a team of line managers chaired by the human resource manager working on the people-related business issues of skill shortages. The team identified the strategic steps to be taken and turned the operational aspects over to the training department. This kind of solution represents a strategic way of looking at the resource issues. Table 3.2 lists some of the important resource questions that should be asked. Also, recent advances in computerized databases make it much easier to maintain information concerning human resources. Kavanagh, Gueutal, and Tannenbaum (1990) provide valuable insights about the advantages of such systems.

REQUIREMENTS ANALYSIS

Performing a requirements analysis is another critical preliminary step in the needs assessment process. The steps in this process are presented in Figure 3.1.

A *requirements analysis* is basically an examination of the details that must be made clear in order for the assessment procedure to function properly. The requirements analysis consists of many specifications that must be completed prior to the collection of tasks and KSAs in order for the assessment procedure to function properly. For example, during this process, it is determined whether a job might be performed differently in different offices or locations. In that case, the needs assessment would have to account for those circumstances. The points that must be addressed in the requirements analysis include the following topics.

Understanding the Job in the Context of the Organization

The first goal of the requirements analysis is to understand the organization so that decisions concerning how the phases of the needs assessment should be conducted can be determined. The best way to accomplish that purpose is to analyze information concerning the organization from available multiple sources. As noted previously, this certainly includes communicating with management and members of the liaison team. Besides the information obtained from participants of the organization, the assessor can use other sources of information. These additional sources of information can be organized into two major categories—previous needs assessment analyses and other documentary materials.

Previous analyses.   Information on previous needs assessment of many series of jobs is available from government sources and often from other work organizations. One useful source is O*NET 98, which is a relational database sponsored by the U.S. Department of Labor's Employment and Training Administration (1998), representing a collaborative project joining public and private interests. O*NET 98 has data describing over 1100 occupations, and users are able to locate occupations through skill requirements or key word. It uses electronic links to permit utilization of other classification systems and it includes labor market information. Other information is available in military and educational technical reports through the National Technical Information Service (for military documents) and the ERIC Clearinghouse on Educational Media and Technology (for educational documents). It is also worth inquiring of other organizations who have similar jobs whether they have needs assessment materials available. Sometimes these organizations are willing to share information concerning tasks and KSAs, especially with the understanding that any new information gathered would be available to them.

Documentary materials.   Besides specific job analysis materials, there is also a substantial literature describing training programs and other aspects of organizations. It includes catalogs and descriptions prepared by the organization itself; technical literature prepared by trade associations, labor unions, and professional societies; pamphlets and books prepared by federal, state, and municipal departments in the appropriate field (health, education, or labor); and books and pamphlets generally related to the subject. Previous needs assessment and documentary materials provide useful introductions. However, they are not substitutes for the analyses that must be performed when a training program is designed. Often, analyses of previous jobs do not describe the conditions in the target organization. Sometimes, careful examination shows that only the names of the tasks or the job are the same. Even if earlier job analyses were performed on the targeted job, it may not indicate how the job is currently performed. On the other hand, if there was actually a needs assessment performed on the job in question, that information should be checked for its accuracy and used to the extent that it is helpful. Thus, these sources provide information that is useful in the initial examination of the job and sometimes reduce the required effort, but the final analysis must be performed with the organization on the jobs of immediate concern.

Defining the Target Job

As presented in Figure 3.1, one of the most critical objectives of the requirements analysis is to identify precisely the job being analyzed. This seemingly simple activity can actually be difficult. The use of a standard job title or generic job name often turns out to be misleading because it can mask a variety of different jobs. For example, the title of administrative aide in hospital management groups often includes a wide variety of different jobs, such as executive secretary, laboratory assistant, or personnel analyst. In many of these types of instances, it is necessary to determine whether all these activities are to be included in the analysis or whether the intention is to examine particular activities. Similarly, the same job might vary considerably depending on a number of factors, including where or when it is performed. Thus, the same job might be performed differently in various geographical locations or on different work shifts. All these factors need to be determined before the job analysis begins because the determination of which activities will be targeted affects decisions such as which sites are visited and which individuals are chosen to participate.

Choosing the Methods for Conducting a Needs Assessment

It is helpful to think of the needs assessment process as taking accurate, multiple photographs of a job. If the purpose of the needs assessment is to provide information for the design of training programs, it is necessary to know what is actually done on the job in order to design relevant instruction. Sometimes, needs assessment procedures focus on likely future changes that may occur in the job and what new training programs may be needed. Given the rapidly changing character of jobs, this is likely to become more and more important. Later in the chapter, those types of approaches will be discussed. However, even in those instances, it is usually first necessary to collect information about the job as it presently exists in order to have a reference point for experts to use in considering future changes. Because the needs assessment process must be accurate, it is important to develop a method of collecting needs assessment information in a manner that least biases the quality and accuracy of the information. Therefore, focusing attention on the methodology for collecting needs assessment information is necessary.

Learning to select a needs assessment strategy that produces high-quality information requires effort. There are a number of different methods for collecting task and KSA information. Each method has unique characteristics that can affect both the kind and quality of the information obtained. For example, an interview is dependent on the interviewer's skills and biases, whereas a mail questionnaire can be subject to sampling biases that occur if a substantial number of participants do not return the survey. Steadham (1980) has developed a list of the advantages and disadvantages of some of the needs assessment methods, which is presented in Table 3.3 on pages 54 and 55. An assessor should consider the following steps in planning which methods to use in the needs assessment process:

1. An assessor should be aware of the potential problems associated with each of the various methods and designs used in the needs assessment process. Prior knowledge of these potential problems allows the assessor to avoid as many difficulties as possible in planning a needs assessment strategy. For example, it is possible to train interviewers to avoid biases that can contaminate the information being collected.
2. An assessor should use more than one methodology when collecting needs assessment information. Each method has different strengths. One way to take advantage of these strengths is to use multiple methods. An assessor should select two or more methods in such a way that the advantages of one offset the disadvantages of another. Table 3.3 shows some of these techniques and their various strengths.
3. Respondents should represent cross samples of the organization with relevant information about the job. Multiple perspectives would reveal whether there are alternative viewpoints of the job. For example, it is possible to obtain information from supervisors and top-level management as well as experienced job incumbents. If there are differences in viewpoints, the best approach for the training analyst is to first determine why there are discrepancies rather than simply proceeding with the design of the training program. By using these relevant multiple sources of information, assessors can obtain a complete picture of the target job for which they will be designing training programs.

4. It is important to design systems that permit the documentation of the information obtained during the needs assessment process. The collection of materials often comes from many different sources and methods over a period of time. For both practical and legal reasons, document all information obtained in an organized fashion. This is one point that an assessor does not want to learn the hard way. Trying to explain to an opposing attorney or a judge that you really performed a carefully designed needs assessment but you just don't have the documentation is a very unpleasant experience.

In conclusion, a general theme in conducting needs assessment is to never do something once when twice will do. This includes multiple methods to collect needs assessment information and using multiple sources of information (for example, supervisors, incumbents, upper-level management). It is also important to avoid having only one person conduct interviews, job observations, or job panels. Multiple methods essentially provide replication, which is a strength in the use of these types of methods. Obviously, this can be carried to extremes and collecting this information is costly. But some care to ensure that the information is accurate and reliable goes a long way when you have to defend your analyses.

Determining the Participants in the Needs Assessment Process

Another step of the requirements analysis is to determine who in the organization will participate in the assessment process. Within organizational constraints, one goal is to try to involve as many relevant organizational members as possible. These constraints can include restrictions such as the budget allotted to the needs assessment, time pressures, and scheduling conflicts. The reasoning behind the idea of involving the maximum number of participants is twofold. First, as mentioned previously, increased involvement and participation in the process builds support. If organizational members believe that their training program was designed with their help and input, they are more likely to lend support for such a program once it is implemented. Second, it is critical to collect information concerning multiple perspectives. Thus, it is important to have a sample that is both representative and large enough to form a complete, accurate picture of the job. In this sense, the photograph analogy of a job analysis can be extended: Multiple photographs covering multiple perspectives provide the most accurate picture, making it much more likely that the job analyst has an accurate picture of the job. Several other important points are as follows:

1. One logical way to involve many participants is to have different individuals included in the various stages of the assessment procedure. These stages are described in the next section on the collection of task

TABLE 3.3

ADVANTAGES AND DISADVANTAGES OF NINE BASIC NEEDS ASSESSMENT TECHNIQUES

Advantages	Disadvantages
Observation	
• Can be as technical as time-motion studies or as functionally or behaviorally specific as observing a new board or staff member interacting during a meeting.	• Requires a highly skilled observer with both process and content knowledge (unlike an interviewer who needs, for the most part, only process skill).
• May be as unstructured as walking through an agency's offices on the lookout for evidence of communication barriers.	• Carries limitations that derive from being able to collect data only within the work setting (the other side of the first advantage listed in the preceding column).
• Can be used normatively to distinguish between effective and ineffective behaviors, organizational structures, and/or process.	• Holds potential for respondents to perceive the observation activity as "spying."
• Minimizes interruption of routine work flow or group activity.	
• Generates in situ data, highly relevant to the situation where response to identified training needs/interests will impact.	
• (When combined with a feedback step) provides for important comparison checks between inferences of the observer and the respondent.	
Questionnaires	
• May be in the form of surveys or polls of a random or stratified sample of respondents, or an enumeration of an entire "population."	• Make little provision for free expression of unanticipated responses.
• Can use a variety of question formats: open-ended, projective, forced-choice, priority-ranking.	• Require substantial time (and technical skills, especially in survey model) for development of effective instruments.
• Can take alternative forms such as Q-sorts, or slip-sorts, rating scales, either pre-designed or self-generated by respondent(s)	• Are of limited utility in getting at causes of problems or possible solutions.
• May be self-administered (by mail) under controlled or uncontrolled conditions, or may require the presence of an interpreter or assistant.	• Suffer low return rates (mailed), grudging responses, or unintended and/or inappropriate respondents.
• Can reach a large number of people in a short time.	
• Are relatively inexpensive.	
• Give opportunity of expression without fear of embarrassment.	
• Yield data easily summarized and reported.	
Key Consultation	
• Secures information from those persons who, by virtue of their formal or informal standing, are in a good position to know what the training needs of a particular group are:	• Carries a built-in bias, since it is based on views of those who tend to see training needs from their own individual or organizational perspective.
a. board chairman	• May result in only a partial picture of training needs due to the typically non-representative nature (in a statistical sense) of a key informant group.
b. related service providers	
c. members of professional associations	
d. individuals from the service population	
• Once identified, data can be gathered from these consultants by using techniques such as interviews, group discussions, questionnaires.	
• Is relatively simple and inexpensive to conduct.	
• Permits input and interaction of a number of individuals, each with his or her own perspectives of the needs of the area, discipline, group, etc.	
• Establishes and strengthens lines of communication between participants in the process.	
Print Media	
• Can include professional journals, legislative news/notes, industry "rags," trade magazines, in-house publications.	• Can be a problem when it comes to the data analysis and synthesis into a useable form (use of clipping service or key consultants can make this type of data more useable).
• Is an excellent source of information for uncovering and clarifying normative needs.	
• Provides information that is current, if not forward-looking.	
• Is readily available and is apt to have already been reviewed by the client group.	

(Continued)

	Advantages	Disadvantages
Interviews • Can be formal or casual, structured or unstructured, or somewhere in between. • May be used with a sample of a particular group (board, staff, committee) or conducted with everyone concerned. • Can be done in person, by phone, at the work site, or away from it.	• Are adept at revealing feelings, causes of and possible solutions to problems which the client is facing (or anticipates); provide maximum opportunity for the client to represent himself spontaneously on his own terms (especially when conducted in an open-ended, non-directive manner).	• Are usually time consuming. • Can be difficult to analyze and quantify results (especially from unstructured formats). • Unless the interviewer is skilled, the client(s) feel self-conscious, suspicious, etc. • Rely for success on a skillful interviewer who can generate data without making client(s) feel self-conscious, suspicious, etc.
Group Discussion • Resembles face-to-face interview technique, e.g., structured or unstructured, formal or informal, or somewhere in between. • Can be focused on job (role) analysis, group problem analysis, group goal setting, or any number of group tasks or themes, e.g., "leadership training needs of the board." • Uses one or several of the familiar group facilitating techniques: brainstorming, nominal group process, force-fields, consensus rankings, organizational mirroring, simulation, and sculpting.	• Permits on-the-spot synthesis of different viewpoints. • Builds support for the particular service response that is ultimately decided on. • Decreases client's "dependence response" toward the service provider since data analysis is (or can be) a shared function. • Helps participants to become better problem analysts, better listeners, etc.	• Is time consuming (therefore initially expensive) both for the consultant and the agency. • Can produce data that are difficult to synthesize and quantify (more a problem with the less structured techniques).
Tests • Are a hybridized form of questionnaire. • Can be very functionally oriented (like observations) to test a board, staff, or committee member's proficiency. • May be used to sample learned ideas and facts. • Can be administered with or without the presence of an assistant.	• Can be especially helpful in determining whether the cause of a recognized problem is a deficiency in knowledge or skill, or by elimination, attitude. • Results are easily quantifiable and comparable.	• The availability of a relatively small number of tests that are validated for a specific situation. • Do not indicate if measured knowledge and skills are actually being used in the on-the-job or "back home group" situation.
Records, Reports • Can consist of organizational charts, planning documents, policy manuals, audits and budget reports. • Employee records (grievance, turnover, accidents, etc.) • Includes minutes of meetings, weekly, monthly program reports, memoranda, agency service records, program evaluation studies.	• Provide excellent clues to trouble spots. • Provide objective evidence of the results of problems within the agency or group. • Can be collected with a minimum of effort and interruption of work flow since it already exists at the work site.	• Causes of problems or possible solutions often do not show up. • Carries perspective that generally reflects the past situation rather than the current one (or recent changes). • Need a skilled data analyst if clear patterns and trends are to emerge from such technical and diffuse raw data.
Work Samples • Are similar to observation but in written form. • Can be products generated in the course of the organization's work, e.g., ad layouts, program proposals, market analyses, letters, training designs. • Written responses to a hypothetical but relevant case study provided by the consultant.	• Carry most of the advantages of records and reports data. • Are the organization's data (its own output).	• Case study method will take time away from actual work of the organization. • Need specialized content analysts. • Analyst's assessment of strengths/weaknesses disclosed by samples can be challenged as "too subjective."

Source: From "Learning to Select a Needs Assessment Strategy," by S. V. Steadham. In *Training and Development Journal*, January 1980, *30*, pp. 56–61. Copyright © 1980 by the American Society for Training and Development, Inc. Reprinted by permission.

and KSA information but can include job observations, interviews, panels, and surveys. If this method is followed, the sample of involved individuals builds, with more and more individuals participating and supplying information as the assessment process proceeds. This building process of sample size has a logical progression. Many analysts start with job observations to gain a perspective about the job, switch to panels to obtain descriptions of the tasks and KSAs necessary for the job, and conclude with surveys to collect statistical information such as the importance of the tasks or KSAs.

2. It is important to remember that the number of participants, panels, and other techniques depend on the characteristics of the job. Thus, if the job is very different in four geographical sites, one panel for all four sites would probably not work. In this instance, it would be the same as conducting one panel for each of four different jobs, which would not give the analyst the multiple perspectives that are necessary.

3. The choice of exactly which groups of people in the organization should participate is complicated. The major criterion is which groups of individuals are most capable of providing the information. Many analysts have discovered that it is best to use job incumbents in the collection of task statements. The reason for this is that job incumbents find it easy to provide the assessor with information about what tasks they actually perform on the job, whereas supervisors might not have the level of detail to provide that kind of information. Supervisors, on the other hand, can often supply information describing the KSAs that are required on the job because they often think in terms of the abilities of the individuals they supervise.

4. Another issue is exactly which individuals should be selected for participation. The selection of individuals should be representative of the groups of job incumbents or supervisors who either perform or supervise the job. The optimum situation exists when individuals from the organization are selected in a random fashion so that there are no systematic biases operating as to who is selected. Using that type of procedure, the participants are most likely to be representative of the populations being assessed. If the job is found to vary in particular systematic fashions, then the selection should be made randomly within each of those classifications. This is often referred to as random selection within a stratified classification. Besides selecting a representative sample, it is also important to include groups of individuals within the organization who are small in number and thus might not be represented in the usual selection process. Categories of such classification could consist of facets such as minority status and gender. In those instances, it usually makes sense to overrepresent those groups to ensure that the sample size is large enough to be representative of

their views of the job. This gives the analyst an opportunity to analyze the needs assessment data to determine whether there are differences in the way the job is viewed by members of these groups.

5. A final issue in the selection of the participants is who selects the individuals. The analyst should select the individuals using a consistent strategy such as random stratified sampling. As noted earlier, this makes it more likely that the sample will truly be representative. Another choice is that the analyst can select the individuals according to a set of criteria such as those who are good job performers. That is also an acceptable strategy although it is necessary to be careful that the sample is representative. We do not favor having supervisors or members of the organization make the choice unless there is a clear set of guidelines. Otherwise, supervisors might tend to select particular kinds of individuals, which would result in a nonrepresentative sample such as job incumbents who are not needed at work that day. Also, trust is particularly enhanced when it is possible to announce to a panel that the analyst, not their organization, selected them. That type of announcement plus assurances that their individual responses will never be seen by anyone in the organization usually results in a situation where it is possible to collect information in a positive atmosphere.

Determining the Points of Contact in the Organization

Another step in the requirements analysis is to determine points of contact in the organization and the responsibilities of these contacts. It may be that all the organizational contacts are members of the liaison team; but then again, particular needs may require the help of other individuals. It is also important to make sure that the assessor and the organization are in agreement about these roles and responsibilities. This information should be specified so that harmful miscommunication can be avoided. Many an analyst has found some visits resulted in a wasted effort because important groups were not involved in the arrangements. For example, one of the authors of this book was sent by the corporate human resource director to conduct focus groups at a manufacturing plant only to find out that the end-of-the-month rush to fulfill orders at the plant made it difficult to pull workers off the line to participate in the focus groups. The plant human resource manager and the plant manager were not very happy to see the consultant walk through the door at that busy time.

Anticipating Problems to Be Resolved

Another major step in the needs assessment is to anticipate and plan to resolve problems and issues that can affect the process. This step is also part of the organizational analysis in which the internal and external organizational constraints, which can affect the success of the training program, are determined. However, in this stage of the analysis, the purpose is to determine what factors could be disruptive to the assessment process. Examples of the types of issues that can affect the needs assessment procedure are possible organizational strikes, changes in personnel policy or management, or vacations. Vacation patterns differ from organization to organization, so that critical people simply may not be available. The assessor needs to learn about these patterns and take precautions to avoid problems that could affect the needs assessment. Thus, recognizing particular issues during the panels and explaining their relationship to the needs assessment are possible.

For example, one of us was recently involved in a needs assessment in a telecommunications firm where a department reorganization was being considered. During the process, it was uncovered that job incumbents were concerned that the purpose of the needs assessment was secretly a way to redefine a job so that particular job classes could be eliminated. That was not the case, for the purpose of the needs assessment was the design of training programs. That problem was resolved by having the analyst and management discuss the issue at the beginning of each panel discussion. Obviously, these types of organizational issues can have a serious effect on the quality of the information obtained. The levels of cooperation and commitment on the part of the job incumbents is directly dependent on both being aware of the issues and being candid in dealing with the organization's concerns.

Developing a Protocol

Based on the information obtained in the requirements analysis, a protocol or a script for the assessor to follow in conducting the assessment panels or interviews can be developed. The protocol presents the standardized steps to be followed in collecting the needs assessment information. An outline of a protocol can be found in Table 3.4. The standard protocol includes an introduction, background information on what a job analysis is, and a description of what will be done in the information-gathering session. It also includes guidelines for the analyst on the appropriate steps to be followed and standardizes these steps so that all people involved in the project conduct their information-gathering sessions in a similar manner. Only an outline of a protocol is presented in Table 3.4 because the information in the script depends on the exact situation of the particular needs assessment.

In conclusion, the key to a successful analysis is advanced thought and planning regarding the needs assessment process. It is necessary to consider the variety of methods that can provide useful information and to determine which questions need to be asked. For the needs assessment to be successful, this planning process must be conducted before the task and KSA analysis begins.

TABLE 3.4	OUTLINE OF A SAMPLE NEEDS ASSESSMENT PROTOCOL

1. Introduce needs assessment team and other participants.
2. Present brief history of project.
3. Explain the general purpose of today's activities.
4. Provide opportunity for questions.
5. Provide background outlining needs assessment process.
    a. Indicate what needs assessment does.
    b. Indicate the various procedures that will be used during the needs assessment phases.
    c. Indicate the types of outcomes that stem from needs assessment.
    d. Indicate the general time lines for the project.
6. Provide specific information on how participants are selected.
7. Provide information on confidentiality of individual data.
8. Provide specific information on what will be done today.
9. Conduct activities.
10. After conducting activities, indicate how information will be used in the next step.
11. Answer questions and thank participants.

TASK AND KNOWLEDGE, SKILL, AND ABILITY ANALYSIS

A task analysis results in a statement of the activities or work operations performed on the job and the conditions under which the job is performed. It is not a description of the worker but a description of the job. On the other hand, the KSAs describe the knowledge, skills, and abilities necessary to perform these tasks.

Developing Task Statements

As presented in Figure 3.1, task and KSA analysis is used to determine the required content of a training program. A task analysis results in a statement of the critical activities or work operations performed on the job and the conditions under which the job is performed. Some examples of task statements from a variety of different jobs can be found in Table 3.5. The first phase in the task analysis is to specify all tasks performed on the job. The collection of this type of information requires the use of a number of the techniques described in previous sections, including interviewing panels of job experts (known as subject matter experts, or SMEs) and observing the job being performed. The rules for the specification of tasks have been evolving for a num-

TABLE
3.5   **EXAMPLES OF TASKS FROM A VARIETY OF JOBS**

1. Call job candidates to provide feedback and keep them informed during the preemployment selection process.

2. Monitor the implementation/practice of personnel procedures to ensure that provisions of the labor contract (for example, regarding required training, salary schedule) are maintained.

3. Interpret letters from the highway department concerning driver's license revocation in order to verbally advise citizens on the appropriate course of action.

4. Observe and evaluate the performance of job incumbents for the purposes of salary review.

5. Evaluate workloads, priorities, and activity schedules to determine staffing requirements and assignments for area of responsibility.

6. Inspect hospital facilities to determine compliance with government rules and regulations pertaining to health practices.

7. Maintain written records and logs of contacts with customers in order to provide documentation concerning steps taken to resolve their service problem.

8. Provide verbal feedback to first-line supervisors to assist them in critiquing their own performance after incidents in order to help them develop more effective ways of handling future situations.

Note: We thank many of our colleagues in the field of industrial-organizational psychology for the use of some of the materials presented in Tables 3.5–3.10, 3.12, and 3.13. In many cases, it is difficult to determine which iteration produced the actual materials included in the tables. Some of the colleagues involved in projects that resulted in the development of these materials include Wiley Boyles, Wayne Cascio, Joyce Hogan, Frank Landy, Bill Macey, Doris Maye, Jim Outtz, Erich Prien, Paul Sackett, Neal Schmitt, Ben Schneider, Joe Schneider, John Veres, and Shelly Zedeck. We gratefully acknowledge their contributions. All rights for the use of these materials remain the privilege of the researchers who used and developed them.

ber of years. The following summary is a synthesis of the work of a number of individuals (Prien, Goldstein, & Macey, 1987; Goldstein, Braverman, & Goldstein, 1991; Goldstein, Zedeck, & Schneider, 1993):

1. Use a terse, direct style, avoiding long involved sentences that can confuse the organization. The task statements should be neutral in tone and not refer to either outstanding or poor performance; this is a description of the tasks, not the capabilities of the individual necessary to perform the task. The language should be consistent both in form and level with the language of the people who perform the job.

2. Each sentence should begin with a functional verb that identifies the primary job operation. It is important for the word to describe the type of work to be accomplished. For example, a task statement that says "presents information for the use of supervisors in . . ." does not tell us much about the task. We have no idea whether a report has been written, a conversation is occurring, or a speech is being made. Certainly, the KSAs involved in writing a report for the use of supervisors would be different than the KSAs in giving a speech. Without

that information, determining what training needs to be designed is difficult.

3. The statement should describe *what* the worker does, *how* the worker does it, and to *whom/what* and *why* the worker does it. The *why* aspect often becomes a critical part of the task because it forms the foundation for understanding what KSAs may be required. Thus, if a manager has the task of conducting a performance appraisal in order to provide information for advising the job incumbent on needed performance improvement, KSAs needed might include assessing job performance and providing feedback to the individual. However, if the purpose of the performance appraisal is to provide a written recommendation to upper-level management on the pro-motability of the individual, the KSAs might include assessing job performance but might not include providing feedback to the individual.

The following illustration stems from the job of a secretary:

WHAT?
Sort

TO WHOM/WHAT?
correspondence, forms, and reports

WHY?
in order to facilitate filing them

HOW?
alphabetically

The next example comes from the job of a supervisor:

WHAT?
Inform

TO WHOM/WHAT?
next shift supervisor

WHY?
of departmental status

HOW?
through written reports

Note by examining these tasks and the tasks listed in Table 3.5 that the development of task statements is not limited by the particular type of job.

4. Determining whether multiple tasks should be included in one statement; do not include separate tasks in the same statement unless they are always performed together. If multiple tasks are likely to lead to very different KSAs or very different estimates of the importance of the task, you should consider keeping them separate. Otherwise, latter parts of the job analysis will be adversely affected. For example, if there are several tasks and they differ in importance for job performance, it will be difficult for the SMEs to assign an importance rating.

5. The tasks should be stated completely, but they should not be so detailed that it becomes a time-and-motion study. For example, a task could be "slides fingertips over machine edges to detect ragged edges and burrs." However, it would not be useful for the identification of tasks to say that the worker raises his or her hand onto table, places

fingers on part, presses fingers on part, moves fingers to the right six inches, and so on. Rather, each statement should refer to a whole task that makes sense. Usually, breaking down tasks into a sequence of activities is useful when the task is being taught in the training program. However, that step does not occur until the total task domain is identified and it is determined which KSAs need to be taught to perform those tasks. Similarly, avoid listing trivial tasks.

Determining Task Clusters

After a full task set is developed from the job analysis, another useful procedure is the development of *task clusters*. Table 3.6 illustrates an example of a task cluster for the job of a customer service representative.

The purpose of clustering is to help organize the task information and to help in the editing of tasks. As such, clustering is usually done following the collection of the complete task set from the job observations, panels, and interviews. It usually involves the following steps:

1. Develop definitions of task clusters that describe job functions. For the job of the customer service representative, the cluster and its definition are for interacting with the customer. Some other clusters, depending on the actual job tasks, might include interacting with technicians or vendors who solve the customer's difficulties and keeping records and logs so that customer information is recorded and maintained.

2. Once a set of task cluster definitions are developed, the next step is to have a group of subject matter experts (SMEs) independently sort each task into one of the clusters. The SMEs can be job incumbents or supervisors. Analysts who are involved in conducting the job analyses can also participate in this sorting process. In any case, if the analysts are involved in this process, the outcomes should be checked by job incumbents and supervisors.

3. Establish a rule that defines agreement on whether a task is successfully clustered. For example, if ten people are performing the clustering, a rule might be that seven of ten people must agree on where the task should be clustered.

4. Plan to rework the task cluster definitions. When disagreement occurs on the placement of a task, it usually provides very useful information concerning the development of either the task or the cluster. Usually, disagreement occurs for the following reasons:

   a. The task has more than one work component in it, and different judges focus on different parts of the task.

TABLE 3.6	EXAMPLE OF A TASK CLUSTER FOR THE JOB OF A CUSTOMER SERVICE REPRESENTATIVE

Task cluster title and definition: Interaction with the customer—the tasks involving communication by telephone between the customer service representative and the customer to determine what service difficulties have occurred.

1. Determine what difficulties the customer is having in order to complete a service report.
2. Ask the customer for relevant information in order to provide all information needed by the vendor to service the customer.
3. Call the customer to determine whether the problem has been resolved by the promised date and time.
4. Provide the customer with information so that he or she can follow up the call at a later time to obtain status information.
5. Provide instructions to the customer concerning basic self-checks that can be used to resolve the customer's difficulty.
6. Provide information to the customer about services that are available to resolve the problem.
7. Inform the customer about possible service charges that may be billed to the customer in order to service the customer's equipment.

Note: Please see note for Table 3.5.

b. The task is ambiguous, and different judges interpret the task differently.
c. The purpose of the task is not clear, and thus different judges place the task in a different cluster.
d. The clusters themselves are too broad or poorly defined.

This clustering process usually leads to very useful reediting of the tasks and the cluster definitions, which typically results in tasks becoming much clearer.

This procedure for organizing clusters is typically known as a *rational clustering exercise.* There are other procedures for clustering, using statistical techniques. However, there seems to be some question whether factor analytic techniques lead to useful task clusters. Cranny and Doherty (1988) have discovered that the clusters that emerge from such analyses are frequently not interpretable as important job dimensions. Even more serious, SMEs have found that the job dimensions that they deem important may not emerge as factors. At this point, there are no definitive answers to these questions. In any case, although there may still be some questions on the appropriate techniques to use in developing clusters, most researchers agree that it is a useful procedure for the reasons just specified and because the clusters can then be used to provide input for the development of KSAs, which is discussed next.

Knowledge, Skills, and Abilities and Psychological Fidelity

Whereas task analysis provides a critical foundation for any training needs assessment, a task-based system cannot usually provide the entire foundation for a training system. If training is provided on the exact tasks that exist on the job, the training system would have very high *physical fidelity*. However, in most cases, the goal in training systems design cannot be perfect physical fidelity. The reason for most training systems is that you cannot train an individual on the exact tasks that constitute the job. In some cases, such as flying an airplane, it is simply too dangerous, whereas in other cases the representation of the exact task is too overwhelming for the trainee to learn. Thus, in almost all situations, the task is some simulation of the actual tasks on the job. This includes simulations for learning management techniques such as role playing or learning to fly an airplane in a simulator. The goal is usually to choose simulated tasks that permit the calling forth of the skills and abilities that need to be learned. Of course, it is also necessary to specify the knowledge that needs to be learned in order to perform the tasks. This type of training environment is one that has high *psychological fidelity* in the sense that it sets the stage for the KSAs that need to be learned to be called forth by the simulated tasks. In that sense, the training program is content valid to the extent that it is designed so that the appropriate critical tasks are simulated and thus give the opportunity for the relevant KSAs to be demonstrated. This relationship between tasks and KSAs is shown in Figure 3.3. The section of the diagram that models that relationship is shaded; to the degree the training program represents that area, it has psychological fidelity. Too often, trainees are being asked to memorize huge amounts of material for jobs when they are never expected to know the material or don't have to memorize it as part of their job function. In that instance, the problem could have occurred for two reasons: A needs assessment was not properly done to determine what needed to be learned to perform the job, or the training designer did not pay attention to the needs assessment that was available. Thus, the purpose of the needs assessment is to obtain information concerning the critical tasks required to perform on the job and the KSAs necessary to perform those tasks. The next step is the development of KSAs called forth by simulated tasks that give the training program psychological fidelity.

Developing Knowledge, Skill, and Ability Analysis

The organizational analysis and the task analysis provide a picture of the task and the environmental setting. However, as previously noted, the task analysis provides a specification of the required job operations but does not provide information concerning the KSAs required to perform the tasks. The key issue

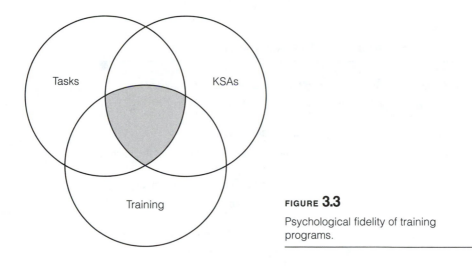

FIGURE **3.3**

Psychological fidelity of training programs.

is determining the human capabilities necessary to effectively perform the job. After these capabilities are specified, then it is possible to analyze the performance of the target population to determine whether training is necessary. There are several different systems for specifying human capabilities. One system advocated by Goldstein and Prien (for example, Prien, 1977; Goldstein, Macey, & Prien, 1981; Prien, Goldstein, & Macey, 1987) emphasizes the KSAs necessary to effectively perform the tasks developed in the task analysis. Prien defines these categories as follows:

> *Knowledge* (K) is the foundation on which abilities and skills are built. Knowledge refers to an organized body of knowledge, usually of a factual or procedural nature, which, if applied, makes adequate job performance possible. It should be noted that possession of knowledge does not ensure that it will be used.
>
> *Skill* (S) refers to the capability to perform job operations with ease and precision. Most often skills refer to psychomotor-type activities. The specification of a skill implies a performance standard that is usually required for effective job operations.
>
> *Ability* (A) usually refers to cognitive capabilities necessary to perform a job function. Most often abilities require the application of some knowledge base.

Examples of KSA characteristics are presented in Table 3.7 for a variety of jobs. The description involves judgments about what KSAs people need to perform particular tasks. Often, people who directly supervise the job being analyzed serve as effective SMEs to provide this information because they think about what a job incumbent needs to know or what skills and abilities are needed to perform the tasks. This is in contrast to the collection of task

TABLE
3.7 **EXAMPLES OF KSAS FOR A VARIETY OF JOBS**

1. Ability to recognize the strengths and weaknesses of subordinates.
2. Ability to recognize cues in performance of individuals that indicate the need for professional counseling.
3. Ability to organize facts and materials for presentations.
4. Ability to pass on information to subordinates verbally so that the information is understood.
5. Ability to communicate in writing accurately, concisely, and clearly.
6. Ability to organize incoming information for verbal transmission on the radio or telephone.
7. Ability to recognize the usefulness of information made available by others.
8. Skill in transcribing numbers from one document to another.
9. Skill in writing numbers and letters legibly.
10. Skill in adjusting volume and temperature of water spray.
11. Knowledge of map formats and symbols used in reading maps.
12. Knowledge of authority limitations to exceed budget.
13. Knowledge of federal and state laws regarding employee access to company records.

Note: Please see note for Table 3.5.

information where the job incumbents themselves often know exactly what tasks they perform on the job. Thus, one procedure to collect KSA information is to present one of the task clusters (such as that shown in Table 3.6) and ask members of a panel the following types of questions:

1. Describe the characteristics of good and poor employees on (tasks in cluster).
2. Think of someone you know who is better than anyone else at (tasks in cluster). What is the reason he or she does it so well?
3. What does a person need to know in order to (tasks in cluster)?
4. Try to recall concrete examples of effective or ineffective performance in performing (tasks in cluster). Then recall causes or reasons for effective or ineffective performance of (tasks in cluster).
5. If you are going to hire people to perform (tasks in cluster), what kind of KSAs would you want them to have?
6. What do you expect people to learn in training that would make them effective at (tasks in cluster)?

The KSAs shown in Table 3.7 are a sample of KSAs that stem from a variety of jobs. Some other relevant KSAs that stem from the task cluster for a customer service representative presented in Table 3.6 are offered in Table 3.8.

TABLE 3.8	KSAs FROM THE TASK CLUSTER TITLED CUSTOMER SERVICE REPRESENTATIVE

1. Ability to explain technical information to the customer in a way that he or she understands.

2. Ability to guide the conversation with the customer in order to obtain the necessary information needed by the vendor to service the customer.

3. Ability to resolve customer problems without having to refer them to the supervisor.

4. Ability to communicate with people from a broad variety of backgrounds.

5. Ability to reflect the company's public service image when speaking with others.

6. Knowledge of the services that can legally be provided by the company.

Note: Please see note for Table 3.5.

Some of the guidelines for the development of such KSA statements include the following:

1. Maintain a reasonable balance between generality and specificity. Exactly how general or specific the KSA statement should be will depend on its intended use. When the information is being used to design a training program, it must be specific enough to indicate what must be learned in training.

2. Avoid simply restating a task or duty statement. Such an approach is redundant and usually provides very little new information about the job. Ask what KSAs are necessary to perform the task. For example, a task might be "analyze hiring patterns to determine whether company practices are consistent with fair employment practice guidelines." Clearly, one of the knowledge components for this task will involve "knowledge concerning federal, state, and local guidelines on fair employment practices." Another component might involve "ability to use statistical procedures appropriate to perform these analyses." Both the knowledge and ability components would have implications in the design of any training program to teach individuals to perform the required task.

3. Avoid the error of including trivial information when writing KSAs. For example, for a supervisor's job, "knowledge of how to order personal office supplies" might be trivial. Usually, it is possible to avoid many trivial items by emphasizing the development of KSAs only for those tasks that have been identified in the task analysis as important for the performance of job operations. However, because the omission of key KSAs is a serious error, borderline examples should be included. At later stages in the process, these KSAs will be eliminated if SMEs judge them to be not important.

4. Ask for knowledge and skills and abilities in order to obtain as much information as possible to determine what is needed to perform the tasks. For example, having knowledge about how to hit a golf ball is very important if you want to play golf; yet we are all familiar with people who can tell you how to hit the ball but still cannot hit it. Thus, it pays to attempt to delineate all the various KSAs; although at times, deciding what should be listed as a knowledge or skill or ability becomes difficult. In those instances, make sure that the item appears in at least one of the categories.

Determining Relevant Task and KSA Characteristics

Once the tasks and KSAs are specified, obtaining further information about them is important. For example, it is necessary to know which tasks are important and frequently performed. Similarly, it is necessary to determine which KSAs are important or are difficult to learn. Designing a training program around KSAs that are unimportant or easy to learn would not make much sense. This step typically uses a *survey format* that permits the collection of greater amounts of information than can occur in the job observations, interviews, and panels used in the original collection of tasks and KSAs. The survey format makes it possible to collect data from experienced job incumbents or supervisors across large enough samples to ensure confidence in indicators such as the importance of the task. Also, by checking items such as different geographical locations or different units in the organization, determining whether the job is viewed the same way across the organization is possible. An added benefit is that it permits the analyst to involve more of the organization.

The exact questions asked on the survey vary depending on the purpose. For tasks, it is typically necessary to have information concerning the importance of the task and the frequency with which it is performed. Table 3.9 provides an example of an importance scale for tasks. Similar scales for the importance of KSAs can be designed. It may also be important in the design of training to know whether general familiarity or full recall of the knowledge is required for job performance. Table 3.10 presents a recall-level scale. Clearly, the training program would be different for each recall level of knowledge. Which scales are most useful depends on the questions that the particular needs assessment is designed to answer. Some of the questions for which scales can be designed include the following:

FOR TASKS
1. Is the task performed?
2. How frequently is the task performed compared with other tasks?
3. How important is the task for effective performance on the job?

TABLE 3.9	A SAMPLE IMPORTANCE SCALE FOR TASKS

IMPORTANCE *How important is this task to effective performance in your position?*

1 = Not important (Improper task performance results in *no* error or consequences for people, things, or places.)

2 = Slightly Important (Improper task performance may result in *slightly serious* consequences for people or *slightly serious* damages to things and places.)

3 = Important (Improper task performance may result in *moderate* consequences for people or *moderate* damages to things and places.)

4 = Very Important (Improper task performance may result in *serious* consequences for people or *extensive* damages to things and places.)

5 = Crucial (Improper task performance may result in *very serious* consequences for people or *very extensive* damages to things and places.

Note: Please see note for Table 3.5.

TABLE 3.10	EXAMPLE OF RECALL-LEVEL SCALE FOR KNOWLEDGE

RECALL-LEVEL REQUIRED DAY 1 — *What level of recall do you need at the time of appointment to apply this knowledge on the job?*

1 = General familiarity — A person must be aware of general principles and be able to efficiently locate pertinent details in source documents and/or seek guidance from others.

2 = Working knowledge — A person must be able to apply general principles and specific details from memory in typically encountered occurrences, but refer to source documents or seek guidance from others for applying specifics in unusual occurrences.

3 = Full recall — A person must be able to apply both general principles and specific details in a wide variety of occurrences from memory without referring to source documents or seeking guidance from others.

Note: Please see note for Table 3.5.

FOR KSAs

1. How important is the KSA for performing the job?
2. How difficult is it to learn the KSA?
3. Where do you expect the KSA to be acquired (before selection, in training, on the job, and so on)?

An example of a page of a questionnaire asking how important KSAs are and whether the job incumbent will need them on day 1 of work is given in Table 3.11 (some data analysis is provided as well). The KSAs presented in the table are for the position of radio operators whose job is to communicate with state troopers by radio in order to provide for the safety of both the trooper and the public.

The data collected can be analyzed to determine average responses, variability, and degree of agreement between different panel members. The analyst can set cutoffs for the determination of which tasks and KSAs should be used in further analyses. Thus, on the scale shown in Table 3.11, a value of 3 and above is associated with tasks that are judged important. Therefore, it might be decided that all KSAs that earn an average value of 3 and above are included in the next stage of the needs assessment process. Also, it should be clear that the type of information collected in these analyses is useful for decisions that extend beyond the training program. For example, it is possible to develop questions related to what KSAs individuals need before being selected for the job. Thus, the second column indicates the percentage of subject matter experts who indicated that a KSA is needed the first day on the job.

As mentioned previously, researchers sometimes discover that different groups of panel members (such as supervisors and employees) do not always agree on what characteristics (for example, tasks) are required to perform the job. In those instances, it would be important to resolve the disagreement before training programs are designed. At the present time, there are not much data about whether different groups within the organization are likely to consistently judge tasks and KSAs differently. One study by Schmitt and Cohen (1989) found very few differences between middle-level managers who were men and women or whites and nonwhites in their judgments concerning tasks. One difference they did find was that nonwhite job incumbents more frequently reported they did not perform a task as compared with their white colleagues. Another study by Landy and Vasey (1991) studied patrol officers with varying experience and found they tended to perform different jobs. Those officers with more than eleven years of experience tend to spend less of their time in traffic activities and more in noncriminal activities than their less experienced colleagues. In addition, researchers (Ford, Smith, Sego, & Quiñones, 1993) have discovered that personal characteristics have an effect on ratings of training needs among aerospace ground equipment mechanics in the U.S. Air Force. They measured self-efficacy, which is the belief or confidence that an individual has that he or she can perform a task. They found that high self-efficacy individuals were more likely to rate training needs as higher. It appears that those individuals who are confident in their skills have gained them through formal training and other job-related experiences. Their confi-

TABLE 3.11   **SAMPLE QUESTIONNAIRE FOR KSAs OF RADIO OPERATORS**

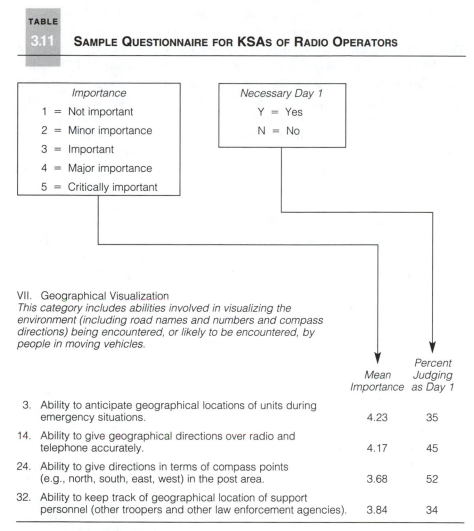

		Importance
1	=	Not important
2	=	Minor importance
3	=	Important
4	=	Major importance
5	=	Critically important

Necessary Day 1	
Y	= Yes
N	= No

VII. Geographical Visualization
This category includes abilities involved in visualizing the environment (including road names and numbers and compass directions) being encountered, or likely to be encountered, by people in moving vehicles.

		Mean Importance	*Percent Judging as Day 1*
3.	Ability to anticipate geographical locations of units during emergency situations.	4.23	35
14.	Ability to give geographical directions over radio and telephone accurately.	4.17	45
24.	Ability to give directions in terms of compass points (e.g., north, south, east, west) in the post area.	3.68	52
32.	Ability to keep track of geographical location of support personnel (other troopers and other law enforcement agencies).	3.84	34

Note: Please see note for Table 3.5.

dence in part comes from this training, and they believe strongly in the value of training as compared with low-efficacy individuals. They express this in higher ratings of recommended formal-training emphasis. On the other hand, Ford and his colleagues also measured the individual's cognitive ability and found no relationship to ratings of formal-training emphasis. The point is that, depending on who you choose to help describe the job, you might get different descriptions. These studies reemphasize the point that the samples involved in job analyses must be chosen carefully.

The usefulness of this type of job analysis data in helping to make judgments about training programs was demonstrated in a study by Mumford, Weeks, Harding, and Fleishman (1987). These investigators used a measure of task learning time, called the occupational learning difficulty (OLD) index, which are scales used by job analysts to describe the learning time for 600 tasks in forty-eight occupational specialties. They found that the OLD judgments by the job analysts accurately predict a number of important training program characteristics. Thus, when the OLD index indicates that the tasks take more time to learn, the training program for that occupation tends to be longer and have more instructional units. In addition, the programs tend to have smaller faculty-student ratios and more experienced instructors. Essentially, this study confirmed that this type of job analysis judgment is related to a large number of independent indicators describing the training course. As such, these investigators note that you can use this kind of information about learning difficulty of tasks to help make judgments for new training efforts to determine course length, allocation of time for training, or both.

Linking Knowledge, Skills, and Abilities to Tasks

At this point, the analyst has determined which KSAs and tasks are needed for the job. The next step in developing the needs assessment information base is to determine which KSAs are important for which tasks. To be maximally effective, the training program must be designed to help trainees learn the necessary KSAs to perform the tasks important to the job. The actual tasks used in training might be simulations of real job tasks as long as they can provide the environment necessary for learning the KSAs. Thus, it is critical to develop information on what KSAs are important to perform the critical job tasks. To be maximally efficient in this step, analysts usually consider only the tasks and KSAs that have met the various criteria, such as a 3 on the importance scale. An example set of instructions for performing the linking process between the KSAs and tasks is presented in Table 3.12. In this set of instructions, each individual KSA is linked to each individual task. Usually, the only tasks and KSAs being linked are those that have survived the various criteria, such as being rated as important. Even so, the number of remaining KSAs and tasks sometimes turns out to be quite large. In those cases, some analysts have the individual KSAs first linked to the task cluster (such as the cluster found in Table 3.6). After it is determined which KSAs are linked to which cluster, it is possible to have the SMEs link the KSAs to tasks in the cluster as a way of establishing relevant KSA to task links. This is an easier process because specific links between individual KSAs and individual tasks are established for only those KSAs that were first linked to the cluster.

Some examples of links that might occur for several different jobs are presented in Table 3.13. By looking at the required KSA and noting what types of

TABLE
3.12 AN EXAMPLE OF KSA–TASK LINKAGE INSTRUCTIONS

2 = Essential

This knowledge or ability is essential to the performance of this task. Without this knowledge or ability, you would not be able to perform this task.

1 = Helpful

This knowledge or ability is helpful in performing this task. This task could be performed without this knowledge or ability, although it would be more difficult or time-consuming.

0 = Not Relevant

This knowledge or ability is not needed to perform this task. Having this knowledge or ability would make no difference in the performance of this task.

Note: Please see note for Table 3.5.

TABLE
3.13 EXAMPLE OF KSA–TASK LINKS FROM VARIOUS JOBS

Job of Police Radio Operator

KSA   Knowledge of map formats and symbols used in reading maps.

Task Links   Searches maps for geographical information in order to respond to requests from the general public.

Receives information from troopers by phone, such as request for assistance to relay to the closest available trooper.

Receives information from the public by telephone, concerning items such as speeders or accidents, to relay to the trooper responsible for that geographical area.

Job of Customer Service Representative

KSA   Ability to explain technical information to the customer in a way that he or she understands.

Task Links   Provides instructions to the customer concerning basic self-checks that can be used to resolve the customer's difficulty.

Provides information to the customer about services that are available to resolve the problem.

Job of a Manager in a Production Plant

KSA   Ability to select, organize, and present pertinent information in logical order.

Task Links   Explains written directives to train subordinates in departmental policies and procedures.

Responds to questions and problems at community meetings in order to resolve community concerns.

Note: Please see note for Table 3.5.

tasks they are linked to, it is possible to design the training program around simulations of the tasks that actually require that KSA on the job. For example, in the job of customer service representative, the training designer would know from the linkage data that he or she must build training sequences to help the trainee learn to explain technical information concerning basic self-checks and to provide customers information about available services. Thus, at the conclusion of the linkage process, the training analyst has information concerning all the required KSAs and for which tasks they are needed. The analyst can also have information on which KSAs are most important, most difficult to learn, and so on. This provides a road map for the design of training programs that helps ensure that the training program will be job-relevant.

Competencies

One issue that always arises in examining the job analysis information is what degree of specificity is necessary. The approach described provides detailed information about the KSA–task relationships that can be used for the design of training programs targeted at specific audiences. It is also possible to organize these specific KSA–task links into broader, more general clusters. In part, this question is driven by organizations that wish to develop more holistic approaches that emphasize characteristics desired across individuals and jobs within an organization. This more holistic approach in organizations has been called *competency modeling* (DuBois, 1999). It often involves the identification of the knowledge and skills consistently used by exemplary performers across the organization. Thus, Intel (Meister, 1994) has identified six core values that form the basis for competencies that it wants every employee to have. An example of a core value is taking risks and challenging the status quo or striving to work as a team and having mutual respect for one another. We discuss competencies and some of the various approaches to developing them at the beginning of Chapter 8, which focuses on developing employees, teams, and leaders. The question of which methodology (cluster of KSAs or competency identification) is most appropriate is probably not an either/or question. It makes sense for organizations to develop core values that they as a total organization stand behind. In this age of global competition, this is one way for organizations to distinguish themselves from each other. However, it is just as likely that after core values are established, more specific training programs are needed. It is a positive step for a company to have core values of treating each other well and with respect, but it is also likely that management training courses would still need to teach individuals how to work with and address a critical inventory issue or the problem of a customer who is complaining about not receiving appropriate treatment.

PERSON ANALYSIS

The final step in determining training needs focuses on whether the individual employees need training and exactly what training is required. At this stage of the needs assessment, the training designer has already accomplished an organizational analysis that permits understanding of where the training systems fit in the work environment and what facilitators and inhibitors exist. Also, the task analysis has determined what important tasks are performed, and the KSA analysis has established which KSAs are important for task performance. The KSA analysis provides considerable information for the person analysis, including data indicating whether the KSA should be learned before entering the job, on the job, during training, and so on. However, in the person analysis, the emphasis is not in determining which KSAs are necessary but rather in assessing how well the actual employees perform the KSAs required by the job. Person analysis asks two questions:

Who within the organization needs training?

What kind of instruction do they need?

This can be directed at a specific training effort or a program of training for advancement in the organization.

Developing Performance Indicators

To actually perform a person analysis, it becomes necessary to develop measures of criteria that are indicators of performance. This will be discussed in Chapter 5. Many of these criteria are very important for a number of purposes in the design of training programs. We can use the criteria to assess performance before training, immediately after training, and on the job. The important point is that the criteria can also be used to determine the capabilities of the people on the job so that training is designed for the particular KSAs needed by those employees. For example, employees who receive performance appraisal ratings indicating that they need improvement might be candidates for a training program. It is also the case that negative performance appraisals are not greeted with enthusiasm either by the receiver or by the person who gives the information. Some observers think there might be less resistance to this type of performance appraisal if it is used as a basis to provide learning experiences helpful to the employee; however, this depends on how the whole process is viewed and managed by the organization. There is no solid body of research data on this issue.

Another way of approaching the problem is to have employees perform self-assessments of their abilities for training purposes. Unfortunately, in a review of 55 studies in which self-evaluation of ability was compared with measures of performance, Mabe and West (1982) did not find strong relationships between the two measures. Interestingly enough, Mabe and West did find some conditions that maximize the relationship: when the employee expected the self-evaluation to be compared with other evaluations, when the employee had previous experience performing self-evaluation, and when there were guarantees of anonymity. A clear warning on the difficulties researchers are likely to encounter in the use of self-assessments is provided by the work of McEnery and McEnery (1987). They found that self and supervisory needs assessment performed by hospital employees were not related. They also discovered that supervisors tend to project their own needs when they were asked to identify the needs for their subordinates.

Another study, which involves educators participating in an assessment center for high school principals, adds some very important information to the consideration of assessment of training skills (Noe & Schmitt, 1986). In this study, one variable of interest was employee acceptance of assessment of their skills. Noe and Schmitt found that trainees who reacted positively to the needs assessment procedure indicating their skill needs were being met were more likely to be satisfied with the training program content. This type of consideration is important because it not only asks whether we can assess trainee skills in order to determine appropriate training placement but also whether it is possible to determine which variables affect the trainees' willingness to participate and learn from training. In this regard, Noe and Schmitt also found that trainees who had the strongest commitment to job involvement were also the people who were more likely to acquire the key behaviors in the training program. In addition, those employees committed to career planning were the individuals who were more likely to apply training content to their work behavior, resulting in actual on-the-job improvement. These latter points are important for issues concerning motivation and learning (they will be discussed in more detail in Chapter 4).

Determining KSA Gaps and Developing Approaches to Resolve Them

An instructional program must be based on the characteristics of the group that will be placed in the training environment. If the program is intended for those people already on the job, the data from the performance, task, and person analyses provide the required information for an analysis of the target population. However, if the target population is a new job or a new group of employees, the analyses are incomplete. Observers have commented on the differences in values between those students entering school and work situations today and those of preceding generations. Such differences must be considered in program design. For example, particular errors may occur on a job due to difficulties related to computer analysis ability. However, entering trainees may have the prerequisite skills in computer techniques and need less emphasis in that particular area. Thus, the organization may need different training programs for employees and those coming to the job. Unfortunately, it is sometimes difficult to analyze the incoming target population because they are not presently employed. Potential solutions might consist of examining employees who have recently been hired or consulting with similar organizations that have recently hired trainees. The latter procedure must be performed carefully because differences between firms can change the characteristics of the entering population. Thus, two corporations with the same characteristics but differing locales (for example, rural versus urban) may attract employees with significantly different characteristics. It is necessary to match the characteristics of the target population to the requirements for successful performance.

SUMMARIZING THE NEEDS ASSESSMENT PHASE

The results of task, KSA, and person analyses provide critical input concerning such items as present level of performance, importance of tasks and KSAs, frequency of occurrence, opportunity to learn, difficulty in learning on the job, and so on. These responses can be organized into composite indices that reflect the different judgments provided for the task and KSA statements. For example, one index can reflect the following logic in the development of training content: The most important tasks to consider are those given the highest priority in the job and for which it is difficult to acquire proficiency. Similarly, the content to be included in the training curriculum can be identified with reference to a composite index identifying the KSAs important for full job performance and for which there is a minimum opportunity to learn on the job. The composite indices are thus evaluated to determine the content and priorities of the training curriculum.

Besides providing input for the design of new instructional programs, the thoughtful application of job-analysis procedures can provide useful input relevant to a variety of training development and evaluation questions. Some of the other potential applications include

1. *Examination of previously designed training programs:* It is possible to compare the emphasis of training programs presently being used with the needs assessment information. This type of comparison could determine whether the emphasis in training is being placed on tasks and KSAs that are important and that are not easily learned on the job.

2. *Design of trainee assessment instruments:* Needs assessment information provides valuable information on the capabilities of trainees to perform the job appropriately. As such, the needs assessment procedures can provide input to design performance-appraisal instruments to assess the capabilities of trainees at the end of training and on the job. It is also possible to design performance-appraisal instruments to determine which employees might need further training.

3. *Input to the interaction between selection systems and training systems:* The determination of the task and person element domains can provide input into the selection system by specifying the KSAs required to perform the various job tasks. The degree to which the selection system can identify and hire persons with various KSAs affects the design of the training system. For example, training programs might not need to emphasize those KSAs already in the repertoire of the trainee. Often this results in a training program that is not only more interesting but also less time-consuming.

It is important to emphasize that the choice of a particular methodology should be based on an analysis of the particular application requiring job information. Further, even the choice of questions within a particular methodology depends on the application. Thus, in some cases, criticality of performance information is important; in other cases, opportunity to learn or information related to where learning takes place is the key issue. In other instances, a whole variety of questions must be addressed. The critical point is this: Thoughtful planning that considers the variety of methods and applications makes it much more likely that a useful needs assessment will be designed that will more likely lead to a useful training program.

EXAMPLES OF NEEDS ASSESSMENT METHODS AND TECHNIQUES

Content-Oriented Job Analysis

The job analysis system described in the preceding pages, using both a task and KSA approach, emphasizes job content, which is then used to serve as the input for training. For that reason, a good term to describe the approach is *content-oriented job analysis* (Goldstein, Macey, & Prien, 1981; Prien, Goldstein, and Macey (1985). These authors describe a case study where the job analysis purpose was to determine what should be included in the training program. The setting for the study was a regional bank with a large central organization and many branch offices. Branch offices ranged in size from three employees to full-service operations of several hundred employees. The focus of the study included a broad range of jobs across the locations of bank operations. The management purpose for conducting the job analysis was to examine and evaluate job content to identify opportunities for on-the-job training through selective job-assignment rotation and to differentiate job components requiring classroom training because of few opportunities to learn on the job. These authors indicate that they went through the following phases to complete their study.

Phase 1. They developed a structure, or framework, for organizing and describing the content-domain data acquired through the application of various data collection procedures. This was achieved through an examination of available training records and materials and direct observation of the work setting and process. The information acquired at this stage provided a general understanding of business operations, terminology, and so on. The outcome of this research phase was a broad framework within which information acquired in later phases of the project could be placed.

Phase 2. The second phase of the job analysis involved a series of interviews with individuals who would qualify as SMEs, drawn from the entire organization. The purpose of these interviews was to collect information about the tasks employees perform and the duty-based KSAs required to perform those tasks. These researchers often found that it was easiest to obtain KSAs by supplying the SMEs with tasks and asking them what KSAs were required to perform those tasks. The result of these interviews was a set of descriptors in the task and element domain. These task and job element (KSA) statements were then evaluated for ambiguity, clarity, and accuracy by the researchers and training representatives to ensure that all content domain was represented.

Phase 3. In this phase of the project, SMEs (including job incumbents, supervisors, and members of management) who represented the organization provided further information about the job-content domains. To meet the requirements of identifying training needs, SMEs completed structured questionnaires comprising the task and job element statements by providing ratings representing a number of judgments. The two judgments relevant to this illustration are importance (ratings of the criticality of KSAs for full job performance) and opportunity to learn on the job (ratings of the opportunities to acquire KSAs on the job).

Phase 4. The fourth phase of the needs assessment strategy comprised the data analyses necessary to define the content of the job domain relevant for training purposes. The various components of the job were determined, and importance and opportunity-to-learn indices were computed. For purposes of illustration, a few knowledge and ability items for the construct of customer relations are presented in Table 3.14. The two jobs identified are work done in branch operations and auditing and staff services. Examination of the data in the table reveals that, in general, importance and opportunity-to-learn-on-the-job judgments are quite different for the two job examples. It is possible

TABLE
3.14   **CUSTOMER RELATIONS KSAs**

	Group 1— Branch Operations		Group 2— Auditing/Staff Services	
	Importance[1]	Opportunity to Learn on Job[1]	Importance[1]	Opportunity to Learn on Job[1]
Knowledge of bank security investment policies	1.3	1.1	1.1	.6
Knowledge of standard accounting principles and procedures	2.5	1.9	4.1	2.7
Ability to identify key individuals in client organizations	4.1	3.4	.0	.0
Ability to identify areas of inquiry from bank customers that require specialized assistance from individuals outside the bank	3.3	3.1	.3	.1
Ability to explain bank policy and procedure to customers dissatisfied with bank performance	4.8	4.5	.3	.1
Ability to recognize necessity of change in audit procedure from that originally identified in audit program	1.4	1.5	3.4	3.0

[1] The higher the number, the greater the importance and the greater the opportunity to learn.
Source: From "Multi-Method Job Analysis: Methodology and Applications," by E. P. Prien, I. L. Goldstein, and W. H. Macey. Unpublished paper. Memphis, TN: Performance Management Associates, 1985.

to compare the data displays for all KSAs and tasks and for all job groups simultaneously on various judgments (for example, criticality). An analysis of all tasks provided the answers to issues related to training content, where training was to be obtained (on the job versus in the classroom), and, for on-the-job training, what assignment would be most appropriate.

Strategic Job Analysis and Strategic Training

As described in Chapter 1, we have entered a period of intense competition involving a global marketplace. Also characterizing this era is a time when jobs are changing and organizations are struggling with strategic planning to focus on the future and what it means for their human resources. An area of growing concern is the question of future objectives. As the marketplace evolves, training programs are being considered for jobs that may not even exist. Jackson and her colleagues (Jackson, Schuler, & Rivero, 1989) examined data from 267 organizations and found that high-innovation organizations put more emphasis on training for promotion, transfer, and future company needs. Most interestingly, these same organizations did not use performance appraisals to identify training needs. Jackson et al. speculated that perhaps that was because with innovation occurring the skills needed in one's present position might not be all that related to what was needed in a new position. This idea was supported by the fact that managers in the high-innovative companies were reported to have more diverse skills. These views do emphasize the importance of establishing a relationship between the future strategic objectives of the organization and the future requirements for their executives.

To accomplish this, techniques will need to be developed that permit SMEs to describe explicitly future requirements for their organization. Essentially, a task and KSA analysis of future job requirements is needed. Schneider and Konz (1989) describe one possible strategy that they have titled *strategic job analysis*. Their procedure uses similar strategies to those described earlier—obtain tasks, task clusters, and linked KSAs. They also had the job incumbents rate the importance of the task clusters developed by the job-analysis procedures. The task clusters and a very brief description (the actual clusters used had the complete set of tasks presented) are as follows:

1. *Goals:* Sets goals with subordinates.
2. *Plans:* Plans and schedules.
3. *Informs:* Informs and advises subordinates.
4. *Monitors:* Monitors results and updates management.
5. *Supervises:* Supervises staff and resources.
6. *Feedback:* Gives feedback and counsels staff.
7. *Appraises:* Appraises subordinate performance.
8. *Trains:* Trains and develops subordinates.
9. *Staffs:* Staffs the unit (recruits, selects, and terminates).
10. *Customers:* Handles customers.

Then, they used SME panels from upper-level management to develop information on how the job will change and how that will affect the tasks as well as the KSAs required. Some of the changes that managers predicted included computerization of the job, with resulting changes in report preparation procedures, work group size, competencies required, and personal contact. They also described changes in increased state and federal regulations governing the business, such as increased financial services laws. Based on that discussion, the SMEs rated the clusters, and that data is presented in Table 3.15.

TABLE
3.15   TASK CLUSTER IMPORTANCE FOR PRESENT JOB AND FUTURE JOB

Task Cluster	Importance[1]	
	Present Job Mean	Future Job Mean
Goals	4.39	4.80
Plans	3.62	2.66
Informs	3.82	3.77
Monitors	3.18	2.56
Supervises	3.54	3.04
Feedback	4.24	4.73
Appraises	4.53	5.00
Trains	3.64	4.17
Staffs	3.87	4.75
Customers	3.45	2.17

[1] Five-point scale used (1–5) where 1 = not at all important, 2 = slightly, 3 = moderately, 4 = very, 5 = extremely important.
Source: Adapted from "Strategic Job Analysis," by B. Schneider and A. M. Konz. In *Human Resources Management*, Spring 1989, *28*, pp. 51–63. Copyright 1989 by John Wiley & Sons, Inc. Reprinted by permission.

Interestingly, the SMEs indicated a much greater range of importance for the task clusters of the future (from 2.17 to 5.00), as compared with the incumbents' present ratings of importance (from 3.18 to 4.53). They also believed that the clusters titled *goals, feedback, appraises, trains,* and *staffs* would be more important in the future, whereas *plans, monitors, supervises,* and *customers* would be less important. Most interesting is the discussion reported by Schneider and Konz (1989). For example, the reason the SMEs believe that *monitors* will be less important is that a set of tasks will be automated and done by computer. These researchers also collected information about how that might change the KSA requirements and therefore the training programs of the future.

Most of the issues in this chapter refer to the design of an individual training program. So, for example, we discuss how to collect needs assessment information and translate that into training programs. However, it is also important to recognize that the organization makes many strategic decisions about its entire company and where to train, where to select, where to downsize, and where to grow. This is especially true in this fast-moving economic environment where, as discussed in Chapter 1, issues of global competition, development of technologies, and changing organizations are rampant. Ford, Major, Seaton, and Felber (1993) note that it is critical for the organization as a whole to have a training plan that identifies who needs training, what type of training is needed, how training will be delivered, and when it will be delivered. They indicate that this planning process has several stages:

1. Scanning of information to assess training needs
2. Interpretation of the information to determine the right mix of training to meet the needs of the organization
3. Implementation of the training plan

It is clear that, given the rapid changes and developments across organizations, many companies are developing a continuous learning philosophy in order to compete. A critical aspect of this movement is to more closely link in a strategic way training plans with the business goals and plans of the company. Ford et al. found in their surveys of organizations that companies are using information about training and development needs as part of their focus on strategic planning. These types of organizations have training directors involved in the strategic planning of organizations. As they note from their studies, "Indeed, the significance of training's centrality has emerged as the study's most robust finding" (p. 357).

CONCLUSIONS

In this chapter we described the various components of needs assessment, including organizational analysis, task and KSA analysis, and person analysis. The needs assessment provides all the critical input for both the design of the training environment and the evaluation of the actual training program. The needs assessment may provide information indicating that training is not the intervention that is needed or that a number of other programs (for example, conflict resolution between different organizational units) has to be accomplished before training can be considered.

The process of going from task analysis to systematic identification of the behaviors to be learned remains one of the most difficult phases in the design of training programs. In this regard, some dramatic advances in cognitive psychology have strong implications for instructional design. Also, some of these advances have implications for the design of needs assessment procedures. However, before discussing how this may affect the collection of needs assessment information, it is necessary to understand some of the changes resulting from research in cognitive and educational psychology. This will be discussed in the next chapter.

The other aspect of training that follows from the analyses discussed in this chapter is the evaluation process. The criteria and methods for evaluating programs cannot be added conveniently onto the end of the project without disrupting the training program. In addition, some of the data must be collected before and during the training program, as well as some time after the employee has completed training. The evaluation design is an integral part of the entire program but is often a neglected function. This will be discussed in Chapters 5 and 6.

InfoTrac College Edition

For additional readings, go to http: www.infotrac-college.com/wadsworth and enter a search term related to your interest. The following key terms will pull up several related articles.

Competency Modeling	Organizational Support
Job Analysis	Task Analysis
Needs Assessment	

THE LEARNING ENVIRONMENT

CHAPTER

4

The learning environment refers to the dynamics of the training process with particular emphasis on those components that support learning in the training setting and then once back on the job. The basic foundation for instructional training programs is learning. Training procedures are based on the belief that it is possible to design an environment in which learning can take place. The close relationship between learning and instruction is suggested by most learning definitions: "Learning is a relatively permanent change in knowledge or skill produced by experience" (Weiss, 1990, p. 172).

This definition implies that the change is relatively permanent, but it does not assume that all changes lead to improvements in behavior. Although most learning does lead to improvements, there is clear evidence that people can acquire behavioral tendencies toward drugs or racial hatred that might be dysfunctional. Also, learning is an inferred process that is not directly observable. In some cases, learning becomes immediately observable through performance; in other cases, a considerable period of time passes before learning becomes apparent. This is demonstrated by the effects of alcohol and other drugs on behavior. For example, driving performance in a car is negatively affected by use of alcohol. However, that does not mean an individual has forgotten how to drive a car. When the effects of alcohol have worn off, the performance level returns to normal, without any extra training on how to drive a car. Therefore, an understanding of the learning environment requires an appreciation for what is meant by both the acquisition phase during training and the application phase in the transfer setting.

In particular, it is recognized that learning is a complex and multidimensional construct (Kraiger, Ford, & Salas, 1993). It consists of cognitive changes in a trainee's knowledge base and the way the trainee organizes and integrates the new material into his or her existing framework. Learning also can involve skill changes in terms of how well a trainee can enact new behaviors and ways of performing. Learning can even be indicated through changes in the attitudes

85

and motivation of the trainee to engage in learning and improving performance relevant to what has been trained.

The transfer of training is also a complex and dynamic construct that refers to the extent to which the trainee applies the knowledge and skills to the job and adapts or customizes what has been trained to meet the trainee's specific needs on the job. The application and customization of the training must have an impact on job performance if the training is to be considered to have some utility.

Clearly, the major concern for training is how to facilitate learning and transfer. There are three critical issues relevant to the learning environment and the factors that impact learning and transfer outcomes. The first issue concerns the development of an effective instructional design. Effective training involves the process of taking training needs assessment information and transforming it into training content. Instructional design includes (1) the development of training objectives of what is to be learned during the training program, (2) the creation of a plan of instruction that details how and in what sequence the training content will be delivered, and (3) the incorporation of learning principles into the design of the program to maximize the chances that learning will occur.

The second issue involves an understanding of the trainee factors that can influence the effectiveness of the training design. As noted by Campbell (1989), trainees do not just fall out of the sky but have long and varied experiences within an organization that creates certain attitudes and behaviors relevant to specific training activities. Thus, trainees must be ready to learn the material to be presented. Readiness includes having the prerequisites (level of knowledge, skills, and abilities) necessary to gain from the way the instruction is designed. In addition, trainees must be motivated to learn the content to be covered in the training program. The level of motivation a trainee brings to a training program is clearly related to its success.

The third issue concerns an understanding of the factors that can impact the extent to which the learning that occurs during training is transferred to improved job performance. In order to transfer the knowledge and skills from training to the job, trainees must be given the opportunity to apply them to the job setting. There must also be a climate within the organization that demonstrates to the trainee that the knowledge and skills gained are valued. Finally, the supervisor of the trainee must show support for the knowledge and skills gained in training, provide the resources needed for successful transfer, and minimize obstacles or constraints to the successful transfer of the training to the job.

Figure 4.1 presents our model for organizing the large literature on learning and transfer. The model depicts the linkages of instructional design, trainee factors, and work characteristics to learning and transfer outcomes. Working backwards in the model, learning outcomes that occur during train-

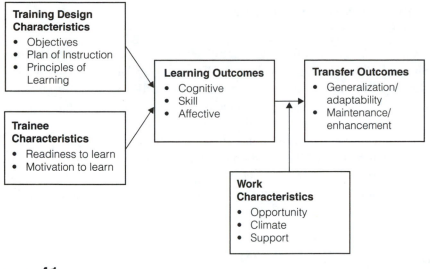

FIGURE 4.1

A model of characteristics affecting learning and transfer outcomes.

Source: Adapted from "Transfer of Training: A Review and Directions for Future Research," by T. T. Baldwin and J. K. Ford. In *Personnel Psychology*, 1988, *41*, pp. 63–105. Copyright © 1988 by Personnel Psychology, Inc. Reprinted by permission.

ing are seen as having direct effects on transfer outcomes. That is, for trained knowledge and skills to transfer, training material must be learned and retained by the trainee. Work environmental characteristics are viewed as having an influence on transfer by impacting the extent to which the learning that occurs during training is used on the job to improve performance. For example, a well-learned skill may not be applied or maintained on the job due to limited opportunity to apply the skill and the lack of supervisory support. Learning outcomes are presented in the model as being directly affected by the readiness and motivation of trainees to learn and the quality of the instructional design. Trainee and instructional design characteristics have an indirect effect on transfer outcomes through their impact on the learning outcomes that occur during the delivery of the training program.

The model in Figure 4.1 provides the framework for Chapter 4. In the first section, the factors relevant to effective instructional design are presented. The second section of this chapter focuses on the impact of trainee characteristics on learning outcomes. The final section examines the impact of learning outcomes and work environment characteristics on training transfer. In each section, relevant theories are described, empirical research summarized, and interventions that have been tested for improving learning and transfer evaluated. The chapter concludes with a discussion of the characteristics of an effective learning environment and future research needs.

INSTRUCTIONAL DESIGN

Instructional design is defined as a set of events that affect trainees so that learning is facilitated (Gagné, Briggs, & Wager, 1992). Thus, design refers to the development and arrangement of a set of activities so as to support the internal learning processes of the trainees. Instructional and cognitive theorists have started asking very serious questions about what is to be learned and what are the conditions for learning. Thus, the first step in designing a training program is to answer the question of what is to be learned to meet a critical need (Campbell, 1988). The second step is to build an effective instructional program that systematically moves a trainee toward meeting the learning goals of the training.

WHAT IS TO BE LEARNED?

As Glaser (1990) postulates, it was first necessary to put learning aside and begin to understand human performance. In other words, it is first critical to unravel what makes up competent performance so that an answer can be given to the central question of what is to be learned. This focus on understanding human performance and learning has led to major advances in areas such as our knowledge of the organization of memory and information processing requirements. Three theoretically driven approaches that have implications for addressing the question of what is to be learned include the work on identifying (1) learning outcomes, (2) stages of learning, and (3) expert–novice differences.

Learning Outcomes

One important aspect of learning outcomes is that it focuses on the behavior to be learned and suggests that different approaches might be used to support learning for different behaviors. One good illustration of the emphasis on what is to be learned is presented by work on instructional systems by Gagné and his colleagues (e.g., Gagné, Briggs, & Wager, 1992). They describe a set of categories of learning outcomes to organize human performance. The learning outcomes are as follows:

1. *Intellectual skills.* These skills include concepts, rules, and procedures. Sometimes this is referred to as *procedural knowledge.* The rules for mathematical computations are a good example of intellectual skills.
2. *Cognitive strategies.* This refers to the idea that learners bring to a new task not only intellectual skills and verbal information but also an understanding of how and when to use this information. In a sense,

the cognitive strategies form a type of strategic knowledge that enables the learner to know when and how to choose intellectual skills and verbal information.

3. *Verbal information.* This category is also sometimes called *declarative information,* and it refers to the ability of the individual to declare or state something. An example could be to state the various kinds of statistical programs and their uses.

4. *Attitudes.* Trainee preferences for particular activities often reflect differences in attitudes. People learn to have these preferences. They note that the number of different commercial messages by which we are bombarded is evidence of the common belief that attitudes are learned.

5. *Motor skills.* This skill refers to one of the more obvious examples of human performance. Examples of motor skills include writing, swimming, using tools, and the like.

Thus, Gagné and his colleagues have developed a set of learning categories that permits them to analyze tasks and code behavior into one of the learning outcomes. The five categories make it clear that there are different kinds of human performance that one might be interested in developing in a trainee. The categorization of learning outcomes also suggests that there is a different set of learning conditions for each category to develop effective and efficient instruction. They have examined each of the outcomes and determined the conditions of learning and instructional events that best support that learning outcome. This system is presented in Table 4.1. The behavioral learning outcomes (intellectual skill, cognitive strategy, and so on) are presented across the top of the table. Down the side of the table are a series of events that are considered important to the instructional system, such as gaining the learner's attention, providing feedback, and so on. The body of the table indicates how each instructional event is manipulated for each learning outcome.

Thus, for the event presenting stimulus material, you would present examples of concepts or rules for intellectual skill development, whereas you would present novel problems for the development of cognitive strategies. As more and more is learned about various ways to support learning performance, it is clear that such systems are very important in helping us design effective training environments.

Stages of Learning

One important aspect of cognitive instructional approaches is the idea that learning involves a series of stages and that different types of learning might be important during each stage. Anderson's ACT* model (Anderson, 1987, 1996) emphasizes that the major learning mechanism involves a series of stages. The

TABLE 4.1 Instructional Events and the Conditions of Learning They Imply for Five Types of Learned Capabilities

	Type of Capability				
Instructional Event	Intellectual Skill	Cognitive Strategy	Information	Attitude	Motor Skill
1. Gaining attention	Introduce stimulus change; variations in sensory mode				
2. Informing learner of objective	Provide description and example of the performance to be expected.	Clarify the general nature of the solution expected.	Indicate the kind of verbal question to be answered.	Provide example of the kind of action choice aimed for.	Provide a demonstration of the performance to be expected.
3. Stimulating recall of prerequisites	Stimulate recall of subordinate concepts and rules.	Stimulate recall of task strategies and associated intellectual skills.	Stimulate recall of context of organized information.	Stimulate recall of relevant information, skills, and human model identification.	Stimulate recall of executive subroutine and part-skills.
4. Presenting the stimulus material	Present examples of concept or rule.	Present novel problems.	Present information in propositional form.	Present human model, demonstrating choice of personal action.	Provide external stimuli for performance, including tools or implements.
5. Providing learning guidance	Provide verbal cues to proper combining sequence.	Provide prompts and hints to novel solution.	Provide verbal links to a larger meaningful context.	Provide for observation of model's choice of action, and of reinforcement received by model.	Provide practice with feedback of performance achievement.
6. Eliciting the performance	Ask learner to apply rule or concept to new examples.	Ask for problem solution.	Ask for information in paraphrase, or in learner's own words.	Ask learner to indicate choices of action in real or simulated situations.	Ask for execution of the performance.
7. Providing feedback	Confirm correctness of rule or concept application.	Confirm originality of problem solution.	Confirm correctness of statement of information.	Provide direct or vicarious reinforcement of action choice.	Provide feedback on degree of accuracy and timing of performance.
8. Assessing performance	Learner demonstrates application of concept or rule.	Learner originates a novel solution.	Learner restates information in paraphrased form.	Learner makes desired choice of personal action in real or simulated situation.	Learner executes performance of total skill.
9. Enhancing retention and transfer	Provide spaced reviews including a variety of examples.	Provide occasions for a variety of novel problem solutions.	Provide verbal links to additional complexes of information.	Provide additional varied situations for selected choice of action.	Learner continues skill practice.

Source: From *Principles of Instructional Design,* Fourth Edition, by R. M. Gagné, L. J. Briggs, and W. W. Wager. Copyright © 1992. Reprinted with permission of Wadsworth, an imprint of the Wadsworth Group, a division of Thomson Learning.

first stage, *declarative* learning, involves obtaining factual knowledge about a task without having learned the conditions of applicability. Thus, in this stage, the person learns facts and instructions, and there is a heavy reliance on memory. Because it is necessary to keep the learning in memory, the learner often uses much verbalization to retain the material. The second stage is *knowledge compilation,* which is the transition process where the learner turns declarative knowledge, which comes from texts or teachers' instructions, into *proceduralized knowledge.* In other words, it is the transition when learners go from knowing "what" into knowing "how" and when to apply knowledge.

Anderson's theory assumes that effective knowledge of procedures can only occur by actually being required to use the declarative knowledge. This knowledge-compilation stage is characterized by accelerated performance and less verbalization. As the person gains a high degree of knowledge compilation, it results in automaticity of previously acquired declarative knowledge, freeing the memory for the processing of new knowledge. The final stage, proceduralization, involves the application and use of knowledge to do something such as solving a complex arithmetic problem or playing the piano. Anderson's group has designed complex computer-tutoring programs for a number of complex skills such as programming (Anderson, 1990).

An example of the potential impact of these ideas for training systems is illustrated by the work of Kanfer and Ackerman (1989). These investigators conducted research using U.S. Air Force trainees who learned an air traffic control simulation task. The trainees learned to accept or land planes on specified runways, based on a series of rules such as weather conditions and amount of fuel. In the first phase, trainees acquired a basic understanding of the tasks, based on lectures and observations. This is the declarative knowledge phase, and as previously indicated, it has a very high attentional demand. In the second phase, knowledge compilation, the trainee is involved in task practice, trying out methods and using the knowledge gained. As learning continues, the attentional demands of the task are reduced. In the third phase, proceduralization, the learner is automating the skill. Here the task is being performed rapidly with minimum attention devoted to the assignment.

Kanfer and Ackerman (1989) conducted a series of experiments where they implemented various goal-setting interventions. The results essentially indicated that outcome goals, such as specifying how well you should perform, only had a beneficial result late in the learning process. This confirmed the investigators' hypotheses that outcome goal setting would only be helpful when some of the tasks were being performed more automatically, thus reducing the attentional demands. Earlier in the process, the attentional demands are too high for the goal setting to have an impact. This is an important study that illustrates how our understanding of stages of the learning process, specified by instructional theorists, might interact with other factors such as motivational variables like goal setting.

Expert-Novice Differences

Much of the work in learning has begun to focus on understanding cognitive strategies in the learning process, especially in relation to understanding the differences between experts and novices. The belief here is that understanding these differences can yield a fertile set of concepts and principles that can be applied to the training field. Ford and Kraiger (1995) note that the analysis of differences between experts and novices indicates that there are a number of specific mental characteristics demonstrated by experts that are not as well developed in novices. Each of these concepts will be discussed next.

Automatized skills and proceduralized knowledge.   As noted by Ford and Kraiger, highly competent individuals "know" the proper response procedures automatically and can perform them efficiently within a variety of task contexts. Thus, novices may have gained declarative knowledge but experts have, through the process of proceduralization, built their knowledge into a complex system where they can apply it to unique settings and situations. Competent individuals, through the use of continued practice and with appropriate experiences, build this to a level of automaticity where essentially there is rapid performance without much effort. Thus, as described in the section on automaticity later in this chapter, persons are able to perform tasks without conscious monitoring, and this permits individuals to focus on yet additional tasks requiring their attention.

Mental models.   Another distinction between experts and novices is the development of mental models used by individuals when performing a task. Glaser (1990) notes in his description of the structure of knowledge for problem solving that as competence is attained, elements of knowledge become increasingly interconnected, resulting in the learner having access to coherent chunks of information. The beginner's knowledge is spotty with isolated pieces and definitions. As the learner becomes more of an expert, the pieces become more structured and more integrated with past knowledge. Then, the learner has access from memory to larger and larger units. The true expert's memory retrieval system is based on the structured content of stored information, and these organizing structures of knowledge are known as *schemata*. The schemata enable experts to grasp the problem and bypass many steps while novices are trying to figure out the surface features.

These observations are supported by research performed by Gitomer (1988), who studied novice and expert mental models in an electronic troubleshooting task. The study examined the patterns of errors and verbal reports from the participants. Gitomer found that experts were guided by mental models that were much more consistent with the true functional properties of the troubleshooting task. Also, the experts' declarative knowledge was more complete and well organized, and they were also better at selecting strategies (procedural knowledge). The study implies that it might be possible to isolate the deficiencies of a trainee's mental model such as whether a trainee is having difficulty because of a lack of knowing what to do (procedural) or a lack of access to knowledge (declarative).

Another example of this type of work is a study of students learning a computer software statistical program called SPSS[x] (Kraiger, Salas, & Cannon-Bowers, 1995). They applied a technique called Pathfinder to provide a visual representation of the differences in the way trained (more expert) and untrained (novice) students viewed the same concepts relevant to the statistical program. Figure 4.2 compares novice and expert Pathfinder solutions for software programming. An examination of Figure 4.2 reveals that novices could not distinguish among the various concepts, whereas trained individuals had begun to categorize similar concepts together in their mental framework or schemata. While providing a dramatic example of differences between experts and novices, such research can also help to identify what would be appropriate training content. For example, the results show that training content should emphasize and clarify issues on creating data files and the use of error messages as these are linked to many concepts, whereas the issue of efficiency is not closely linked to other concepts in the expert model and therefore might not need to receive as much emphasis.

Another area of emphasis for cognitive psychologists examining mental models is the use of strategies to organize and retain information. In many of the situations involving complex cognitive tasks, there is a high demand on memory systems. Yet, a learner involved in short-term memory situations will find it difficult to temporarily retain more than seven items of information. The emphasis here has been on research to explore various cognitive schemes to enhance memory systems, such as organizing the material into chunks through mnemonic schemes or analogy systems. Similar principles are being developed and studied for use in storing information for the purposes of long-term memory. This line of work is consistent with classical learning theory that indicates the more meaningful the material, the more easily it is retained. It is important to properly organize the material and to establish principles to retain information, even if the material appears to be meaningless. Music students are aided in their retention of the musical notes corresponding to the lines and spaces of the staff through the use of coding schemes that organize the information. For example, the lines of the treble staff are the first letters of *Every Good Boy Does Fine*, and the spaces spell FACE. It is also important to realize that mnemonic schemes are but one way to organize materials. In a fascinating study, Bennett (1983) examined the memorizing strategies used by servers in remembering drink orders. The study found that the servers were much better at a memory task involving remembering drink orders than students. In addition, the highly accurate memories of the best servers resulted from vivid perceptual interactions at the time of ordering.

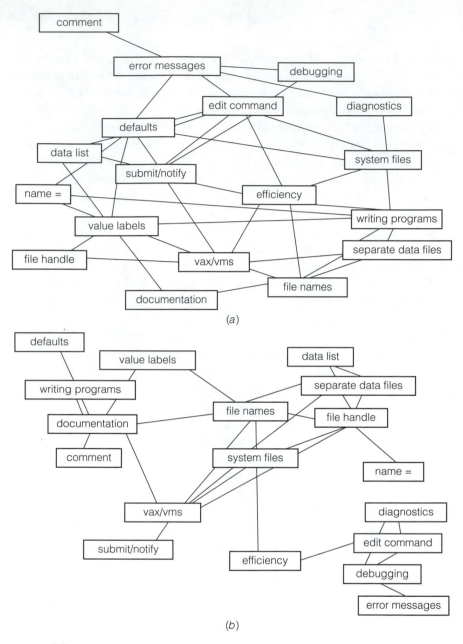

FIGURE 4.2

Comparison of (a) novice and (b) expert Pathfinder solutions for SPPS[x] programming.

Source: From "The Application of Cognitive Constructs and Principles to the Instructional Systems Model of Training: Implications for Needs Assessment, Design, and Transfer," by J. K. Ford and K. Kraiger. In C. L. Cooper and I. T. Robertson (Eds.), *International Review of Industrial and Organizational Psychology.* Copyright © 1995 John Wiley, Ltd. Reprinted by permission.

Metacognition and self-regulation.   Ford and Kraiger (1995) note that a third area of work describing differences between experts and novices is the ability to enact cognitive strategies of planning, monitoring, and revising behavior. Planning involves the learner's analysis of the learning situation and the determination of what strategy is likely to lead to successful acquisition of trained knowledge and skills. Monitoring consists of learners' active attempts to track the allocation of attention, as well as their assessment of how well they are comprehending the material. Revision involves learners' active assessment of their success in skill acquisition and the likelihood of successfully transferring the learned skills to the job. This self-evaluation component also includes the ability to correct ineffective learning strategies. Experts are more aware of these cognitive processes and are more effective in planning, monitoring, and evaluating their learning strategies concurrently with learning a new task (Ford & Schmidt, 2000). As described by Glaser (1990), "experts rapidly check their work, accurately judge its difficulty, apportion their time, assess their progress, and predict the outcomes of their activities" (p. 32).

A number of instructional programs have been designed to investigate these skills. For example, Brown and Palincsar (1989) designed a program for reading comprehension. Students participating in their program acquired knowledge and learning strategies that enabled them to work independently and yet monitor their own behavior. The program involved reciprocal teaching: Students took turns leading the group in the use of strategies that had previously been modeled by the instructor. The procedure included instruction and practice in executive strategies (questioning, summarizing, clarifying, and predicting), the use of an expert teacher model to initially demonstrate skills, and a setting where each student contributed to others' learning. Finally, the method also taught what is called a *zone of proximal development* where students are instructed to perform within their competence range while being helped to realize higher potential performance levels.

More recently, researchers have contended that increasing a learner's metacognitive processing during training will promote deeper processing of information by assisting him or her to integrate material and identify interrelationships among training concepts. In support of this idea, Volet (1991) found that by the end of a computer programming course, college students who were taught metacognitive activities (how to monitor and evaluate one's self) received better grades than the control group. They were also better at applying their knowledge to solve new problems. In addition, Ford, Smith, Weissbein, Gully, and Salas (1998) found that trainees who initiated more metacognitive activity not only learned more but were also better able to handle a more complex transfer task.

Implications of Cognitive Learning Approaches for Training Needs Assessment

The emphasis on learning outcomes, stages of learning, and the work on novices and experts is leading to different models of the needs assessment process. Ford and Kraiger (1995), while accepting the needs assessment model of developing task–KSA clusters as part of the input to training, contend that the approach is not enough. Rather, they argue for a more holistic approach for developing expertise in a particular job. As they state it, "a cognitive or instructional based perspective adds a dynamic learning component to task analysis through the asking of different types of questions about the linkages of tasks and knowledge and skills to a job. It focuses attention to the tasks that need to be taught to allow for the systematic development of knowledge and skills for retention and generalization" (p. 11). Howell and Cooke (1989) make a similar point by noting that it might be necessary to analyze the kinds of tasks and KSAs described in Chapter 3 in terms of their cognitive requirements.

The examination of cognitive requirements embedded within tasks and KSAs has been called *cognitive task analysis* or work analysis (Vicente, 1999). With a cognitive task analysis approach, a variety of procedures (e.g., protocol analysis in which experts talk about how they are completing a task as they perform it) are used to reveal the thought processes experts employ to achieve superior performance. The focus is not on what tasks are performed or what knowledge and skills are needed to perform a task. Instead, the focus is on identifying how tasks are accomplished. This includes the mental aspects of behavior—the goals, strategies, and decisions that underlie performance on a task (DuBois, Shalin, Levi, & Borman, 1998). Thus, rather than looking at tasks and KSAs as separate entities, a cognitive task analysis approach attempts to link tasks and KSAs based on the flow from the goals of the people completing a task to the various actions a person might take in performing the task. An examination of differences between experts and novices in terms of goals and actions can help identify areas for training and development to transform novices toward expertise.

One example of a type of cognitive task analysis has been conducted by the U.S. Air Force (Hall, Gott, & Pokony, 1995). The Precursor, Action, Results, Interpretation (PARI) methodology is an effort to understand the cognitive task requirements for complex and novel situations. Again, this relates to the appearance of increased technologically sophisticated work centers where it is necessary to perform well in dynamic environments. The PARI procedure includes problem-solving situations where experts use their knowledge to respond to problems. As they choose solutions, the experts are probed for the reasons behind their actions and their interpretations of the results of their actions. The probes become part of an interview that uses an instructor expert who poses a problem to a second expert who is naive with respect to the problem's source. The second expert generates a solution step by step, and the instructor expert provides the results of each step. Because the first expert does not know the source of the problem, the protocol produces very rich instructional material, including the relevant knowledge base and problem-solving strategies.

The authors indicate that the cognitive task analysis develops the psychological underpinnings for the type of task and KSA analyses described in Chapter 3. They would not argue that the task and KSA analysis is unnecessary but rather that the cognitive approach adds the underlying psychological processes and knowledge structures necessary for instruction. They argue their procedures are especially useful in producing knowledge that is usually tacit, such as goals, strategies, and assumptions. Their methodology reveals the difference between such knowledge as how a device works versus strategic knowledge that focuses on how to decide what to do and when. For example, they describe a situation where a particular device failed when a test was being run. The expert:

1. Focused on the components that were active when the test failed, thus avoiding the examination of a large number of irrelevant parts;
2. Determined that the testing equipment was more likely to go bad than the piece of equipment being analyzed, thus picking the unit with the highest probability of failure; and
3. Determined that one piece of equipment was much more difficult to troubleshoot, thus deciding to rule out the easier components first.

Each reason was directly tied to the knowledge of the equipment but involved considerably more knowledge than just how the equipment operated. Interestingly, when novices and experts were compared, they did not seem to differ substantially in their knowledge of troubleshooting procedures (for example, taking measurements or checking connections). However, novices could not formulate the type of strategies just described. Novices tended to not have hypotheses concerning the problem nor expectations concerning what result would occur from the use of their strategies. Often, they tended to focus on the use of outside sources for their strategies, such as deciding to perform a particular operation or test because a book or computer program instructs the learner to try this action. However, the novice learners are uncertain about what they will learn from the test.

While cognitive task analysis is still relatively new, researchers have begun exploring the implications for training program design. In one recent study, a troubleshooting course for technicians designed from a traditional task analysis was compared with a new troubleshooting course developed from information gathered through a cognitive task analysis (Schaafstal, Schraagen, & Van Berlo, 2000). Both the new and traditional training course on trouble-

FIGURE **4.3**

Reproduced by permission of PUNCH.

"I'm not learning anything. I'm developing cognitive skills."

shooting were designed to improve the skills of relatively novice technicians on the identification of equipment malfunctions and the appropriate steps for taking corrective action and solving the malfunction. The new training program developed from the cognitive task analysis was based on the observation of expert technician performance as well as an understanding of expert to novice differences. The new course design had a number of differences from the traditional course. For example, trainees were provided a more structured, explicitly discussed hierarchical approach to dealing with malfunctions that was more in line with how experts approach a troubleshooting task. Results indicated that there were a number of positive results in comparison to the program based on the traditional needs assessment process. In particular, technicians trained in the new troubleshooting course solved twice as many malfunctions, in less time, then those trained the traditional way. The new training was also completed in less time (33% reduction of time) than the traditional training program. Future research will likely provide very interesting examples of how these systems can be used both as a needs assessment technique and input to the design of training systems. As noted in Figure 4.3, the world of learning and training is certainly changing.

BUILDING EFFECTIVE INSTRUCTION

An earlier section provided different approaches for identifying what is to be learned during an instructional event. The cognitive and instructional psychology literatures have highlighted how advances are redirecting efforts toward better understanding the learner within an instructional context. As noted by Gagné (1995/1996), "the series of events we call instruction are designed to activate, support, and maintain a number of internal events that are the processes of learning" (p. 27). Gagné reminds us that instruction can be well designed when we consider it in terms of the planning processes to support trainee learning. This support can be related to "helping events" that facilitate learning or the elaborate aspects of practice or cues that help retrieval or feedback that confirms learning has taken place. This has led researchers to begin the task of developing instructional theories, relying on both theoretical and experimental analysis in the laboratory and applied problems taken from instructional settings. These researchers asked questions about the kinds of knowledge necessary to learn to read an instructional manual or to learn a new language (including computer languages). Theories have been developed about how the learner organizes and integrates information and how information is stored.

As defined by Gagné and Dick (1983), "theories of instruction attempt to relate specified events comprising instruction to learning processes and learning outcomes, drawing upon knowledge generated by learning research and theory" (p. 264). They also note that these theories are often prescriptive in that they identify conditions of instruction that will optimize learning, retention, and transfer. It is everyone's hope that such instructional theories become the underlying foundation for instructional design procedures that support learning activities. Effective instruction requires an organized approach to training from needs assessment to the development of training objectives to the creation of a plan of instruction (POI) and the incorporation of learning principles to maximize learning potential during training.

From Training Objectives to a Plan of Instruction

Training objectives constitute the formal description of what a trainee should be able to do once training is completed. Identifying a comprehensive set of training objectives provides a road map for training program design that focuses on operationalizing in very specific terms what is to be learned in the training program. Well-written objectives provide the basis for the development of the POI. Objectives convey the training goals, provide a framework for developing course content, and provide a basis for assessing trainee achievement.

A well-written training objective includes three characteristics (Mager, 1984). First, a training objective includes the capability or desired terminal behavior. The stating of a desired behavior begins with a verb that describes an observable action, such as *take the temperature of a patient*. Table 4.2 presents words that can be used to convey capabilities or desired terminal behaviors relevant to each of the five learning outcomes proposed by Gagné and his colleagues.

| TABLE 4.2 | STANDARD VERBS TO DESCRIBE HUMAN CAPABILITIES, WITH EXAMPLES OF PHRASES INCORPORATING ACTION VERBS | | |

Capability	Capability Verb	Example (action verb in italics)
Intellectual Skill		
Discrimination	discriminates	discriminates by *matching* French sounds of *u* and *ou*
Concrete Concept	identifies	identifies by *naming* the root, leaf, and stem of representative plants
Defined Concept	classifies	classifies by *using a definition,* the concept family
Rule	demonstrates	demonstrates by *solving* verbally stated examples, the addition of positive and negative numbers
Higher-Order Rule (Problem Solving)	generates	generates by *synthesizing* applicable rules, a paragraph describing a person's actions in a situation of fear
Cognitive Strategy	adopts	adopts a strategy of imagining a U.S. map, to recall the states, in *writing* a list
Verbal Information	states	states *orally* the major issues in the presidential campaign of 1932
Motor Skill	executes	executes by *backing* a car into a driveway
Attitude	chooses	chooses by *playing golf* as a leisure activity

Source: From *Principles of Instructional Design,* Fourth Edition, by R. M. Gagné, L. J. Briggs, and W. W. Wager. Copyright © 1992 Harcourt Brace Jovanovich. Reprinted by permission.

The second step is to specify the conditions under which the behavior will be performed or demonstrated during training. Conditions specify (1) what the trainee will be provided when demonstrating a trained behavior; (2) restrictions or limitations imposed on the learner; (3) tools, equipment, and clothing used; (4) references or other job aids that can be used; and (5) physical and environmental conditions surrounding the task (see Mager, 1975; Gagné et al., 1992). An example is *"with a digital oral thermometer,* take the temperature of a patient."

The third step is to state the criterion of acceptable performance. The criterion specifies how well the trainee must be able to perform a particular task. The criterion can consist of minimum standards, time to perform, and the quality or quantity of work or service produced. For example, "with a digital oral thermometer, take the temperature of two patients *to within 0.1 degree of accuracy."*

Once identified, training objectives must be sequenced in such a way as to enhance learning activities in the training program (Gagné, Briggs, & Wager,

1992). The key to sequencing is to ensure that the prerequisite knowledge and skills have been acquired prior to the introduction of advanced content or skills. Consequently, the instructional sequence chosen may or may not mirror the order in which knowledge and skills are used on the job. Sequencing can be done on the basis of (1) logical order—present the least difficult material first and build to the most difficult; (2) problem-centered order—focus on a general problem and develop various ways to solve the problem prior to moving to another problem area; (3) job performance order—order based on the sequence in which a job or task is actually performed; or (4) psychological order—determine whether it makes more sense to move from abstract concepts or concrete examples and hands-on experience, or visa versa. For example, Annett (1991) states that training of skills should begin with instruction on rules, procedures, and factual knowledge relevant to the skills to be learned and, once mastered, move on to practicing the skill.

Once objectives are placed in a sequence, lesson plans can be developed. For each training objective, training experts can identify the specific facts, concepts, principles, and skills needed to build competency in an area. The plans include the instructional activities and the training time needed to accomplish each objective. Table 4.3 presents part of a POI for training aerospace ground equipment specialists in the U.S. Air Force. The POI provides the objectives, instructional approaches, and the time for training each component. As can be seen in the table, the instructional activities are divided into lecture/discussion, performance and feedback, and self-study. Thus, some activities are delivered by an instructor in a classroom setting and part of the training is delivered in a simulated work setting.

Any POI must be examined for the adequacy of course objectives, testing consistency, and presentation consistency. A group of researchers at the Navy Personnel Research and Development Center have constructed indicators of instructional quality around these areas (Wulfeck, Ellis, Richards, Wood, & Merrill, 1978). Their pioneering work is based on the idea that there is a task dimension and a content dimension to training. The task dimension refers to tasks a trainee is expected to perform. The trainee can either be expected to remember information or use information to accomplish the task. In addition, the trainee who uses the information can either do it unaided or aided—where some form of performance support is provided. The content dimension is divided into five areas of facts, concepts, procedures, rules, and principles. These researchers create a task by content matrix to analyze the objectives, the presentation, and the tests used in a training program to establish instructional quality. An example of this system for analyzing training presentation is shown in Table 4.4. Across the top of the table are content dimensions (facts, concepts, procedures, rules, and principles) and along the side are various types of presentation components (statements, practice in remembering, examples, and practice using). The body of the table gives the appropriate presentation

TABLE 4.3	PLAN OF INSTRUCTION FOR AIR FORCE AEROSPACE GROUND EQUIPMENT SPECIALISTS

Hydraulic Test Stands

Troubleshooting and Correcting Malfunctions

a. Using a hydraulic test stand, technical order, workbook, electrical diagrams, test equipment, and AFTO Form 349, troubleshoot a malfunction.

b. Using a hydraulic test stand, technical order, electrical diagrams, and test equipment, correct one malfunction.

Training Equipment

Hydraulic Test Stand (3)
Multimeter (1)
Ear Protectors (1)

Training Methods

Lecture/Discussion (0.5 hour)
Performance and Feedback (9.5 hours)
Self-Study (4 hours)

Instructional Guidance

The instructor will issue applicable programmed text, workbooks, multimeters, and technical orders and conduct a briefing on safety hazards and precautions. Ensure students wear proper ear protection during operational checks to verify malfunctions. The first problem will be a demonstration problem that the students will follow in the workbook. After completion of demonstration problem, students will practice troubleshooting additional problems, stating the proper corrective action to be taken to the instructor. The instructor will give individual assistance as required. Upon completion of practice troubleshooting, each student will be administered a progress check. Each student will troubleshoot three problems and complete an AFTO Form 349 in the workbook for each problem to document work performed. For safety, only one unit will be operated to identify problems. After identifying a problem, the students will isolate the problem on another nonoperating unit. After satisfactory completion of progress check, instructor will annotate the criterion checklist. After troubleshooting, the students will correct one malfunction on the test stand as designated by the instructor. Two instructors are required for ten hours of student demonstration/performance on the Hydraulic Test Stand when class size exceeds six students.

Source: From the Apprentice Aerospace Ground Equipment Mechanic, Plan of Instruction, Chanute Technical Training Center (POI C3A BR42335 000), 1987.

method—for example, when presenting statements in a training program for a concept, all critical characteristics and their combinations must be given. Similar typologies that link training content and training process for developing lesson plans have been developed and are used to ensure that the training program is being developed in a systematic way (e.g., Gagné et. al., 1992; Yelon, in press).

TABLE 4.4 **PRESENTATION CONSISTENCY**

Presentation Component	Content Type of the Objective				
	Fact	Concept	Procedure	Rule	Principle
Statement	Complete fact presented	All critical characteristics and their combinations are given.	All steps are given in the correct order.	All steps and branching decisions are given in the correct order.	All causes, effects, and relationships are given.
Practice Remembering	Recall or recognition required	Recall of concept definition required	Recall of all steps in correct order required	Recall of all steps and branch decisions in correct order required	Recall of all causes, effects, relationships required
For all content types:	Practice Remembering items must be the same as the test item. They must be the same format as the test item. All practice items must include feedback.				
Examples	Not applicable	Examples show all critical characteristics required for classification; non-examples show absence of critical characteristics.	Application of the procedure must be shown in the correct order.	Application of each step or branching decision must be shown in the correct order.	Interpretation or prediction based on causes, effects, and relationships must be shown.
Practice Using	Not applicable	Classification of both examples and non-examples is required.	All steps must be performed in the correct order.	All steps and branching decisions must be performed in the correct order.	Explanation or prediction based on the principle is required.
For all content types:	Practice Using items must reflect what is to be done on the job or in later training. The task/content level, conditions, and standards must match the test item and objective. The practice item format must be the same as the test item format. All practice items must include feedback.				
For CONCEPTS, RULES, and PRINCIPLES:	Some practice items should be different than either the test items or the examples. (Common error items might be the same.)				

Source: From "The Instructional Quality Inventory: IV. Job Performance Aid," by J. A. Ellis and W. H. Wulfeck II. In (*NPRDC SR 79-5*). Navy Personnel Research and Development Center, 1978.

INCORPORATING LEARNING PRINCIPLES

The amount of learning that occurs in the instructional setting is an important determinant of the amount of transfer that is possible to the job situation. Instructional theorists have developed information about a large number of concepts that can be used to enhance the degree of learning in a training setting. In this section, we present a number of features of the learning environment that have been found to be most useful to incorporate into a plan of instruction to contribute to learning. However, it is important to remember that the usefulness of any particular condition or principle of learning is very dependent upon the type of task and the learning outcomes expected. Thus, feedback or knowledge of results is an important principle of learning but is not a guarantee of learning. How these principles are incorporated into a program is critical.

Feedback

The use of feedback is one of the earliest known variables to support learning found in the literature. The classical study that started the research was provided by E. L. Thorndike (1927), who had two groups of subjects (both blindfolded) draw hundreds of lines measuring three, four, five, or six inches over a period of several days. The members of one group were given feedback that indicated whether their response was right or wrong within the established criterion of a quarter-inch of the target area. The members of the second group were not given any feedback. These data indicate that the group that received the knowledge of results improved considerably in its performance, whereas the other group continued making errors. A later study repeated this experiment but included a group that received feedback stating the degree of error (Trowbridge & Cason, 1932). The subjects in this group gained even greater accuracy than the group that was just told that the answers were right or wrong. These are two examples of the numerous studies that have demonstrated the importance of feedback. Researchers suggest that the reason knowledge of results improves performance can be attributed to motivational and informational functions.

A study examining training practices in a safety program addressed the issue of feedback (Komaki, Heinzmann, & Lawson, 1980). Komaki and her colleagues specifically asked whether training alone was sufficient or if it was necessary to provide feedback to maintain performance on the job. This study was conducted in the vehicle-maintenance division of a large city's public works department. The researchers selected a department that had high accident rates. The researchers conducted a needs assessment, including examination of safety logs, to determine safety incidents that had occurred. With the help of supervisors and workers, they designed procedures to eliminate accident problems. Thus, if it was found that an accident occurred because a worker had fallen off a jack stand, an item was included in the training program related to the proper use of jacks and jack stands. These training items also formed the basis for a system for observing the effects of performance. The training program involved a number of procedures, including slides depicting posed scenes of unsafe behavior followed by discussions of safety procedures. For example, one slide depicted an employee working under a vehicle without appropriate eye-protection devices. Komaki found that preceding training, employees were performing safely one- to two-thirds of the time. After training, performance improved about 9%. Komaki then added another condition, including feedback on a daily basis in the form of a graph showing the safety level of the group and the safety goals that the group was trying to achieve. This extra condition resulted in an improvement of 26% over the pretraining phase and 16% over the training-only phase. Komaki makes the point that training alone is not sufficient to improve and maintain performance. Rather, training plus feedback provides the most effective strategy.

Most training analysts have placed considerable emphasis on the importance of knowledge of results in the learning process. Unfortunately, many of those who emphasize its importance simply assume that any form of feedback with any sort of timing will accomplish the purpose. Yet, Schmidt and Wulf (1997) found that continuous feedback during the acquisition of a motor skill actually interfered with rather than supported the rate of learning. Ilgen, Fisher, and Taylor (1979) have developed a model describing some important aspects of the processes involved in perceptions of feedback and have summarized some of the conclusions that can be gleaned from the literature:

1. There is evidence that feedback must be accurately perceived by the recipient to have an effect, and yet it appears that it is often misperceived. This seems to be particularly true of negative feedback.
2. Results indicate that the accuracy of feedback may be affected by the credibility of the source of the feedback. This implies that individuals who wish to use feedback need to work to develop credibility based on their expertise or on the basis of a trust relationship.
3. High-frequency levels of feedback are not always better as it may connote a loss of personal control. It may also lead recipients to excessively rely on feedback and not develop their own capabilities at judging their performance.
4. The individual needs of the person should be taken into account when choosing feedback. Thus, individuals who are high performers with growth-oriented needs require feedback that emphasizes competency and does not take away from personal initiative. However, poor performers need to be monitored carefully and given very specific feedback.

Automaticity and Overlearning

Automaticity refers to the idea that the performance of tasks can become automated in the sense that they require limited attentional capacity to be performed. As described in classic studies by Shiffrin and Schneider (1977), processing that once demanded active control can become automatic, thus freeing the learner's limited attentional capacity for other tasks. As described by these investigators, one condition under which this occurs is where there is extensive practice on a task so that responses can become consistently mapped to particular stimuli.

The automatic processes demand little attentional resources, thus becoming easily accomplished while the individual still performs other tasks. They also make the performance of these automatic tasks very quick and efficient. Perhaps the most dramatic example of the use of automated processing as a training procedure involves the vigilance decrement. The *vigilance decrement* refers to the problem of decline in performance over time during a watch-keeping period when the number of signals to be detected are infrequent. Finding a solution for this decrement problem has puzzled many investigators. Literally thousands of studies have been devoted to this problem because of its implications for areas of work such as radar signal detection, monitoring machine malfunction warning signals (including those in nuclear power plants), and detection involving product quality control on the assembly line. In a dramatic study, Fisk and Schneider (1981) were able to eliminate this decrement by automatizing the activity through a training program that presented the stimulus and then required a response. These pairings went on for over 4000 training trials. In other words, the trainees' responses through this large number of pairings became automated. This meant that much less attentional capacity was needed to perform the task. Later, the trainees performed the real task with only eighteen targets presented over 6000 presentations. Instead of the usual performance decrement occurring, there was virtually no decrement over time because the responses had become automated and thus required very little attentional capacity from the trainee. A recent review of the research on training design and the principle of automaticity highlights other examples of how to capitalize on cognitive theory of automaticity to maximize training effectiveness (Rogers, Mauer, Salas, & Fisk, 1997).

Historically, it is also interesting to note that the concept of automaticity has a relationship to the classical concept of overlearning. *Overlearning* is a situation where the learners are presented with a number of extra learning opportunities even after they have demonstrated learning mastery on the task. Overlearning has been judged to be particularly important when the task is not likely to be practiced often on the job or when it is necessary to maintain performance during periods when there will be few practice opportunities. An investigation by Schendel and Hagman (1982) examining psychomotor skills studied the disassembly and assembly of weapons and demonstrated the positive benefits of overlearning. They trained soldiers to a criterion of one errorless trial and then gave 100% overtraining. Thus, if a particular performer took ten trials to perform one errorless disassembly and assembly of the weapon, then he or she received ten additional trials as part of initial training. Another group of soldiers received overtraining, but in this case each person received the particular extra trials midway through the eight-week retention period. This training was referred to as refresher training. At the end of the eight-week interval, both the overtrained and the refresher group performed significantly better than a control group that was given just initial training. The overtrained group was superior to both the refresher group and the control group in terms of the amount retained. Driskell, Willis & Cooper (1992) found in a review of over 50 studies that overlearning is an even more effective strategy for cognitive tasks. Overtraining and automaticity are powerful methods, especially in those situations where performance must be maintained over long periods without much practice.

Production of the Response

Classical learning theory states that it is important for trainees to be active during the learning period. Thus, classical learning theorists would advise students reading materials for an examination to outline, underline, write in the margins, rehearse the materials in some way, and so on. This concept has been further developed by cognitive theorists to emphasize the importance of having the learner actively produce whatever capability is to be mastered during training. As Campbell (1988) notes, this is just as critical for knowledge capabilities as it is for a physical or cognitive skill. Too often, the training program does not require the demonstration of the required skill but rather some alternative form that is not necessarily the desired end product. For example, learning the principles of management in working with a complaining employee is not the same as demonstrating the skills necessary to conduct a discussion with the person to resolve the difficulties. Behavioral role modeling, a training technique that will be discussed in Chapter 8, is a procedure for teaching such skills. Also, the interaction of the process of producing the behavior along with many of the active cognitive organizing strategies such as mnemonics should produce strong dividends. Again, however, a lecture on mnemonics would not be helpful by itself as compared to learners demonstrating they have learned the material while using a mnemonic scheme.

Bjork (1995) delights in giving the following example. He notes that many of us have taken numerous airline flights and heard the flight attendant lecture on the use of life-saving vests many times. Yet, he bets that most of us would not know exactly what to do if we would be so unfortunate as to be required to use the life-saving vest. On the other hand, Bjork is willing to bet that if we were required to actually produce the response, that is, put on the life vest and go through the operations a few times, we would know how to perform the activity. In other words, produce the response or, as it is often said colloquially, walk the talk.

Advanced Organizers

An organizer can be any type of cue—including verbal, quantitative, or graphic cues—that is used to present new knowledge by taking advantage of the existing knowledge of the learner. It is called an *advanced organizer* if the material is presented before training and a *comparative organizer* if it is used later in training to clarify later distinctions. Advanced organizers can include outlines, text, diagrams, and graphs that provide the trainee with a structure for information that will be provided later in the training (e.g., see Cannon-Bowers, Rhodenizer, Salas, & Bowers, 1998).

In an important series of initial studies, Mayer and his colleagues (Mayer, 1975; Mayer & Bromage, 1980) used a simplified diagram of the functional structure of a computer to greatly enhance learning of the technical terms and rules in a college course on computer programming. The organizer employed familiar language such as shopping lists and ticket windows in the diagrams. According to Mayer (1989), these organizers (or mental models) help improve learning for several reasons. First, they focus attention on the important components and relationships. Second, they help the trainee organize incoming information. Finally, they help show the relationships between incoming information and existing relevant knowledge.

Massed versus Spaced Practice

Another set of principles comes from the more classical learning literature, but it fits in very nicely with the idea that different principles might apply to different types of learning. Generally, it is considered important to determine whether learners benefit more from as little rest as possible until they have learned their task or from rest intervals within practice sessions. The data suggest that spaced practice for one of the learning categories, motor skills, is typically more effective in acquisition and leads to better retention. In a classical study, DeCecco (1968) presents data that examined massed versus spaced practice on a motor skill task. The subjects were required to draw a figure from a mirror image. One group, performing the task under massed-practice conditions, was given twenty trials without any rest periods. The other two groups performed the task under spaced conditions. One group was given one-minute rest periods between trials and the other group one-day rest periods between trials. As Figure 4.4 indicates, there were consistent differences between the spaced-practice groups and the massed-practice group, with the

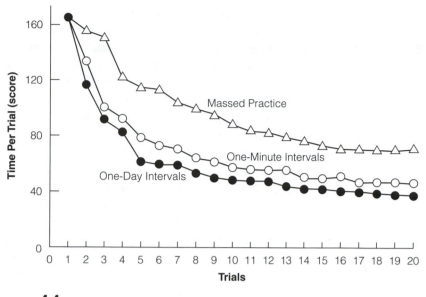

FIGURE 4.4

The effect of distribution of practice on mirror drawing.

Source: Adapted from *Influence of Regularly Interpolated Time Intervals Upon Subsequent Learning*, by I. Lorge. Copyright © 1930 by Teachers College, Columbia University.

spaced-practice groups demonstrating better performance. Interestingly, a recent review of the training literature by Baldwin and Ford (1988) concludes that these types of results for motor skills are still the norm.

Whole versus Part Learning

This is another classical learning variable that is related to the size of the units practiced during stages of the training session. When whole procedures are employed, the learner practices the task as a single unit. The utilization of part procedures breaks the task into components that are practiced separately. The complexity of the task and the relationship among the components determine the usefulness of whole and part methods (Baldwin & Ford, 1988). Naylor (Naylor, 1962; Blum & Naylor, 1968) originally suggested that the difficulty of any particular subtask (complexity) and the extent to which the subtasks are interrelated (organization) determine total difficulty. He uses the example of a person driving a car to illustrate both the complexity and the organization functions. Driving in rush-hour traffic usually places the greatest strain on forward-velocity control (assuming the driver stays in the same lane), because the operator must continually use the accelerator and brake pedals to maintain varying degrees of speed. When the driver operates the vehicle on a curved section of highway, the steering component becomes the most complex part of the task. Task organization can be illustrated by the interrelationship of forward-velocity control and steering. When the operator desires to make a turn, the two components must be interrelated to properly carry out the turning sequence. The examination of the part–whole literature supports the following basic training principles concerning part and whole methods: When a task has relatively high organization, an increase in task complexity leads to whole methods being more efficient than part methods; when a task has low organization, an increase in task complexity leads to part methods being more efficient. Recent research also suggests that part–task training is appropriate if the task components draw on different parts of working memory (Detweiler & Lundy, 1995).

The use of part methods does raise some concerns related to the eventual performance of the entire task. The job must be analyzed to discover the important components and to determine the correct sequence for learning the components. During this process, it is necessary to ensure that the trainee has developed the capabilities necessary to proceed to the next part of the task. If the job is properly analyzed and ordered, a progression method can be used. Here, the learner practices one part at the first session. Then, at the next session, a second part is added, and both parts are practiced together. The addition of parts continues until the whole skill is learned. Strategies for improving training effectiveness using a part–task approach are provided by Goetil and Shute (1996) and Kramer, Larish, and Strayer (1995).

TRAINEE ISSUES

Before trainees can benefit from any form of training, they must be ready to learn, that is, they must have the particular background experiences necessary for being successful in the training program, and they must be motivated to learn. There is reason to believe that individuals often perform poorly in training because they were ill-prepared to enter the program, did not think the program would be useful, or did not want to learn. The importance of understanding the trainee has led to a virtual explosion of studies (for reviews see Tannenbaum and Yukl, 1992; Thayer and Teachout, 1995; Quiñones, 1997) examining trainee characteristics. In addition, there is a developing literature on expectations about whether training will be useful. In the sections that follow, we present first material related to trainee readiness, then material on motivation to learn. This is followed by a discussion of motivational theories that help us to understand why and under what conditions learners see training as useful and become motivated to learn.

Trainee Readiness

Because trainee readiness is critical in the learning process, the instructor must be concerned with the trainee's ability to perform certain tasks. This point has particular significance for instructors responsible for designing instructional programs involving adult learners. Programs will fail if the prerequisite skills necessary to perform successfully are not considered.

These ideas have led researchers to consider various measures to predict who will gain more from training situations. Investigators interested in predicting training performance suggest that a person who can demonstrate proficiency in learning to perform on a job sample will learn in training and eventually perform more effectively on the job (Siegel, 1983; Robertson & Downs, 1989). They suggest the need to develop a trainability test that can predict later training performance. Note that the trainability test is not the entire training program but a sample of the tasks that reflect some of the required knowledge, skills, and abilities (KSAs) needed for job performance. Clearly, this sample must be based on a careful needs assessment and does not serve in lieu of a training program. Rather, the purpose is to use a learning measure based on performance on a relevant sample of tasks, to predict later performance in the training program or on the job.

Many trainability tests have been developed for predicting psychomotor performance. A good example of the variety of such tests that have been developed is provided by Robertson and Downs (1989), who report on over twenty years of research using trainability tests to predict later training performance. They found it possible to predict training success in a large number of jobs, including carpentry, welding, sewing, forklift operating, dentistry, and bricklaying. In some studies, they even found that people who performed poorly on the training tests were less likely to turn up for training and more likely to leave in the first month. This suggests that the trainability test might have provided potential trainees with more realistic expectations about what the training and job would be like. Robertson and Downs selected relevant sample activities based on what was taught in training. Thus, the carpentry test involved making a certain kind of T-joint, and the welding test consisted of several straight runs along chalk lines on steel. The procedure consisted of the following:

1. Using a standardized procedure, the instructor provides training and demonstrations with the applicant free to ask questions.
2. The applicant is asked to perform the task unaided.
3. The applicant's performance is recorded according to a standardized checklist.

While most of Robertson and Downs's trainability tests have a strong psychomotor component, Reilly and Israelski (1988) demonstrate that the same principles work on more knowledge-based tests. They used mini-courses that had material representative of training content in order to assess a trainee's ability to acquire knowledge relevant to a full-scale training program.

There is an important distinction between predicting training performance and actual job performance. Studies that have employed this type of design do not necessarily offer data about the relevance of the training and its relationship to on-the-job performance. Some of these investigators (for example, Siegel, 1983) found, however, they could also use training performance to predict later on-the-job performance. The emphasis here is on trainability. Clearly, the point is that the use of appropriate selection devices to determine who could benefit from training could substantially reduce instruction costs. This view is supported by Reilly and Manese (1979), who employed a short, self-paced training course as a sample to predict trainee performance for programs in electronic switching systems for Bell Systems employees. The average cost for this six-month course was $25,000 per trainee. Duke and Ree (1996) found similar data for pilot training and demonstrated that pilots with higher cognitive ability scores flew fewer hours to complete training and achieved a higher class rank. In another study, researchers (Ree, Carretta, & Teachout, 1995) demonstrated that persons with higher cognitive ability influenced the amount of job knowledge gained in training. In turn, the amount of job knowledge gained in training affected performance on work samples with people who had more job knowledge performing better on the work samples.

A related point is that understanding the capabilities of incoming trainees has important implications for the design of training programs. In the last chapter, we stressed the point that the needs assessment provides the information necessary to design an instructional program. Measuring trainees on what they know before they begin training provides information indicating which trainees may already know this material, which trainees may require remedial work, and which trainees are ready for training. Also, of course, a training pretest is useful to compare the results to a posttest to evaluate the instructional program. But, pretests also provide information about trainee readiness.

Whereas trainability tests focus on selection of people into a training program, cognitive psychologists have been intrigued by the idea that one training program (or treatment) may not work equally well for all trainees. As described originally by Cronbach (1957, 1967), this approach strives to match alternative modes of instruction to the different characteristics of the individual so that each person uses the most appropriate learning procedure. This approach is often called *aptitude–treatment interaction,* or ATI. Figures 4.5 and 4.6 illustrate two types of ATI relationships.

Figure 4.5 shows that all people, regardless of aptitude level, improve with treatment A. In that case, there is no reason to use treatment B; thus, all individuals should be presented with treatment A. Figure 4.6 illustrates an

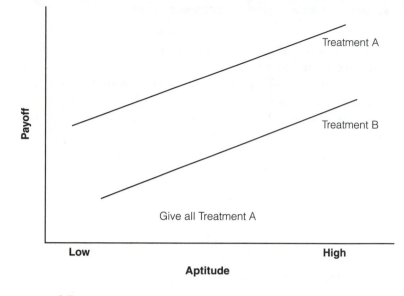

FIGURE **4.5**

Illustration of no aptitude–treatment interaction.

Source: From "The Two Disciplines of Scientific Psychology," by L. J. Cronbach. In *American Psychologist*, 1957, *12*, pp. 671–684. Copyright © 1957 by the American Psychological Association.

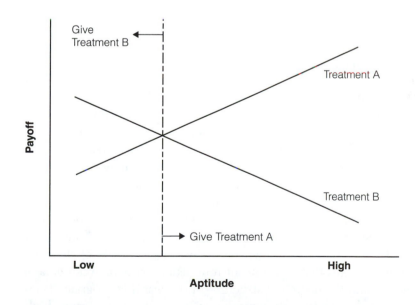

FIGURE **4.6**

Illustration of a disordinal aptitude–treatment interaction.

Source: From "The Two Disciplines of Scientific Psychology," by L. J. Cronbach. In *American Psychologist*, 1957, *12*, pp. 671–684. Copyright © 1957 by the American Psychological Association.

interaction called the *disordinal ATI*. In this case, individuals to the right of the cutoff line (those with higher-aptitude levels) perform best with treatment A. Persons to the left of the cutoff line (those with lower-aptitude levels, who might be labeled as less ready to learn) perform best with treatment B. Thus, the aptitude level of the individual determines the form of treatment that will lead to superior performance. In these cases, aptitude refers to any personal characteristics that relate to readiness to learn and thus can include a broad range of variables, such as styles of thought, personality, and various scholastic aptitudes.

It turns out that very few consistent ATI interactions have been found. But one interaction between general academic ability and the degree of structure in the training program has been found fairly consistently and is important for the design of training programs. The original study showing this interaction came from a study of navy technical training made by Edgerton (1958) and reanalyzed by Cronbach and Snow (1969) for ATI effects. Two methods of instruction were used in a course for aviation mechanics. In one method, which was essentially rote learning, the trainees were told to memorize the material and reproduce it on examinations. In the second method, the instructor presented explanations and stimulated students to ask questions. This procedure was dubbed the "why" method. The test predictors taken by the 150 trainees in each group were the Tests of Primary Mental Abilities. The interaction analyses showed that those individuals who scored highly on the verbal abilities tests were more likely to perform well under the rote treatment. However, a similar relationship was not found for the "why" group. Cronbach and Snow suggest that the explanations in the "why" condition overcame some of the potential learning difficulties for those trainees who scored poorly on the test. On the other hand, the high-ability students did not need that extra information to learn the material. Another interesting interaction was established between scores on an interest test and performance in the course. Those individuals who performed best in the rote treatment had previously expressed interest in the kind of content being taught. There was no relationship between interests and performance in the "why" treatment. In this instance, the more meaningful treatment in the "why" condition may have compensated for whatever handicaps were established by the lack of interest.

A paper by Snow and Lohman (1984) captures some of the promise of ATI effects. This review of their own research as well as that of their colleagues clearly indicates that a significant interaction exists between general academic ability and the degree of structure in the learning program. These data show that low-ability students benefit much more from high-structure/low-complexity programs. The opposite is true for high-ability students. They benefit much more from low-structure/high-complexity programs. For example, one study (Gray, 1983) examined the effect of reorganizing, elaboration, and grouping systems for studying science-related topics. The intervention strategy increased the ability of lower-aptitude students to work with the materials. However, higher-aptitude students complained that the intervention interfered with the strategies they would ordinarily use. Snow and Lohman's review of their own and other studies found consistently similar relationships from instructional method studies, learning strategy studies, and ability-training studies.

Whereas most of this research explored only student performance from grade school through college, other important efforts are concerned with individual differences and actual training performance, which continue to demonstrate the need to consider these issues. Thus, Fleishman and Mumford (1989) found that shorter training programs can be used for trainees who are experienced and have high levels of task-related abilities, whereas less experienced or lower-ability trainees benefit from longer training programs. Again, this can be related to explanations provided by the cognitive theorists. It appears that the less experienced, lower-ability trainees are in an earlier stage of learning such as the declarative stage, which involves a high concentration on gaining knowledge. Thus, it has high attentional demands where it is not possible to do much else. The work described by Snow and Lohman (1984) and by Fleishman and Mumford (1989) provides the type of information that can benefit training programs. It essentially says that analysts should measure the existing ability level or readiness of their trainees before beginning training and should tailor the content of the instructional program accordingly.

Trainee Motivation to Learn

Motivation involves psychological processes that cause arousal, direction, and persistence of behavior (Mitchell, 1982). *Arousal* and *persistence* focus on the time and effort that an individual invests, and *direction* refers directly to the behaviors in which the investment of time and effort are made (Naylor, Pritchard, & Ilgen, 1980). Training analysts need to recognize a variety of factors that influence motivational levels in human beings and that the factors might not be the same for each individual. Using as many motivational variables as possible in the instructional setting, in order to enhance learning, is important. On the other hand, individuals who are already motivated upon entry into the training program clearly have an advantage from the very beginning.

One of the early studies concerning motivation of trainees upon entry was collected in a study of the Navy School for Divers (Ryman & Biersner, 1975). The investigators had trainees fill out a training confidence scale before training. Some of the motivational items on the scale were

- If I have trouble during training, I will try harder.
- I will get more from this training than most people.
- I volunteered for this training as soon as I could.
- Even if I fail, this training will be a valuable experience.

The trainees rated these items on a five-point scale from "disagree strongly" to "agree strongly." The investigators discovered that scores on these items predicted eventual graduation from the program. Thus, the more the pretrainees agreed with these statements, the more likely they were to graduate. Sanders and Yanouzas (1983) have further developed these ideas in terms of the trainers' ability to socialize trainees to the learning environment. They note that trainees come to the learning environment with certain attitudes and expectations, and these may or may not be helpful in the learning process. Trainees who have expectations that are positive and supportive of these types of activities are more likely to be ready for training. If attitudes are generally negative, then it becomes necessary to determine the source of the difficulties and to correct the problems before training begins. Without such intervention, learning is not as likely to occur.

Noe (1986) presented a model specifying some of the motivational factors and their relationships to learning and transfer. Since then, a number of researchers have provided evidence suggesting a positive relationship exists between a trainee's motivation to learn and scores on learning measures (Noe & Schmitt, 1986; Mathieu & Martineau, 1997; Mathieu, Tannenbaum, & Salas, 1992). Such research has also examined the influence of individual differences (demographic variables such as age, education, and work experience; personality factors such as locus of control and goal orientation; and work-related attitudes such as job involvement, career planning, and organizational commitment) on motivation to learn, learning, and transfer. Some of these factors are presented next along with the research evidence that has been collected since the model was developed. This section concludes with a discussion of a recent integrative review of the literature on motivational factors and training effectiveness as well as some needed future research directions.

Self-efficacy.   Motivation to learn and achieve will be higher to the degree that trainees feel that they can actually learn the training content. This concept is usually labeled *self-efficacy,* or the belief in one's capability to perform a specific task. In exploring some of the mechanisms involving self-efficacy, Gist (1989) notes that it is possible to actually learn required knowledge and skills, yet self-efficacy perceptions might be so debilitating that trainees are prevented from using the learning. There have been a number of research studies that show the importance of the relationship between self-efficacy and a number of indicators of training effectiveness. Thus, in a study of managers being trained in the use of computer software, researchers studied the self-efficacy of trainees entering the program (Gist, 1989; Gist, Schwoerer, & Rosen, 1989). They found that trainees who had higher self-efficacy before and at the midpoint of the program performed better on assessments at the completion of training.

Self-efficacy has also been found to be related to the degree of activity or the seeking out of other opportunities. Thus, Hill, Smith, and Mann (1987) found that individuals high in self-efficacy were more likely to seek opportunities to develop their computer skills. Ford and his colleagues (Ford, Quiñones, Sego, & Sorra, 1992; Quiñones, Ford, Sego, & Smith, 1996) found that individuals high in self-efficacy were more likely to be active in trying out trained tasks and attempting more difficult tasks on the job. In summary, self-efficacy appears to be a very potent factor. There is strong evidence that self-efficacy relates to learning performance. Also, there is evidence that learning enhances self-efficacy, and this enhanced self-efficacy relates to later performance on the job.

Locus of control. Noe predicted that an individual's locus of control is likely to affect an individual's motivation and ability to learn. *Locus of control* refers to the degree to which an individual is likely to make internal or external attributions about outcomes. As described in the original theory by Rotter (1966), internals believe that events occurring at work are based on their own behavior and are therefore under their own control. Externals believe that work outcomes are beyond their personal control. Thus, externals attribute work outcomes to factors like luck or the actions of others, whereas internals are more likely to exhibit high levels of motivation to learn in a training program because they are more likely to accept feedback and take action to correct performance problems. Williams, Thayer, and Pond (1991) found such a relationship with locus of control. That is, individuals who have an internal locus of control also have higher expectancies in terms of effort regarding training performance, which is also linked to higher motivation to learn.

Commitment to career. Noe and Schmitt (1986) found trends suggesting that trainees who are more involved in career planning, have a career strategy, and are more job involved are more likely to benefit from training. In a study of entry-level managers in the pharmaceutical industry, Williams, Thayer, and Pond (1991) found that the degree of trainee engagement was related to the individual's motivation to learn in training. The complexity of these issues is demonstrated in a training study designed to enhance proofreading skills (Mathieu, Tannenbaum, & Salas, 1992). In this instance, career planning and job involvement were not found to be related to training performance. However, these investigators carefully note that proofreading is only related to the trainees' current job. Thus, individuals with higher career goals are not likely to value training because it was only designed to enhance skills for the present job.

Integrative review. There are many trainee characteristics that have been examined for their impact on learning and transfer. Colquitt, LePine, and Noe (2000) have completed a meta-analysis (a technique that allows individual study results to be aggregated to examine patterns of results across studies) of the various studies that have examined the link of trainee characteristics, motivation to learn, and learning outcomes. They examined the results of over 100 studies and found a number of important relationships. In particular, they found that there was a strong relationship between locus of control and motivation to learn, with internals showing higher motivation levels. In addition, trainee anxiety was related to motivation, with highly anxious trainees being less motivated to learn and less self-efficacious. Motivation to learn was also related to an individual's level of organizational commitment, job involvement, and career orientation. In addition, age was negatively related to motivation to learn and self-efficacy across the studies. The level of motivation to learn was positively related to knowledge and skill acquisition, reactions of the trainees to the training program, and training transfer indices.

The results of the meta-analysis support the original model of motivation to learn by Noe (1986). In addition, the results highlighted the identification of particular trainee characteristics that are most predictive of motivation to learn as well as various learning outcomes. For example, trainees with high self-efficacy have been found to perform better in training. One logical conclusion is that we should select people with higher self-efficacy (readiness to learn) for our training programs. However, another more developmental question is whether it is possible to design an intervention that raises the level of self-efficacy, thereby raising the general performance level of all trainees. Also, can an intervention be designed to raise the level of expectations of the trainees, the trainers, or both, and does that have benefits? Or, is it possible to develop materials showing how training programs fit career plans, and will this result in trainees understanding the value of the training program and being more highly motivated?

A good example of this linkage of our advanced knowledge of trainee characteristics and their impact on motivation to learn is provided by Cannon-Bowers and her colleagues (Cannon-Bowers, Rhodenizer et al., 1998). They provide a number of examples of how one can prepare trainees for a training experience to enhance the likelihood that training would be successful. For example, they suggest the need to provide trainees with mastery goals early in the training process to enhance self-efficacy and to focus trainee attention to learning the material rather than trying to look good to other trainees and the trainer. Similarly, Quiñones and Ehrenstein (1997) contend that motivation to learn is affected by a number of issues such as

1. Are the decisions about the opportunity to participate made *fairly*?
2. Do trainees get the opportunity to help decide whether to *participate* in training?
3. Is the information about training *framed* in a way that it is viewed positively by the trainee?

A number of studies point to these issues as being important. Thus, Baldwin and his colleagues (Baldwin, Magjuka, & Loher (1991) were interested in whether they should give trainees a choice as to whether to attend training with the possibility that particular options might fill up and they would not be able to honor the choice. They found that the highest motivation to learn was among trainees who received their first choice. In contrast, those trainees who were allowed to choose but did not get their first choice had the lowest motivation to learn and, as predicted from the motivation to learn literature, they also had the lowest scores on the learning measure. In another study with important training implications, Hicks and Klimoski (1987) varied pre-training information given to trainees. One group received a memo from their supervisor requiring attendance. Another group received a memo from the training department describing the program and its benefits and presenting information about the dates and times for training. Trainees who were given a choice reported higher levels of motivation, were more positive about the training program, and received higher test scores.

Similar types of results have been found for how the training work is *framed* for the individual. Tannenbaum, Mathieu, Salas, and Cannon-Bowers (1991) investigated the degree to which recruit training in an eight-week socialization program for a U.S. Naval Recruit Training Command was successful. The socialization program focused on learning the required behaviors and supportive attitudes necessary to participate as a part of the organization. They found that the degree to which the training program met trainees' expectations and desires was positively related to the post-training commitment to the organization.

Quiñones (1997) sums up much of this literature by noting that organizations create the context for training by the kind of information they provide and the way they approach the trainee's participation. Organizations can frame training as punishment for past sins or can present it as a way of advancing trainees' careers and opportunities. Martocchio (1992) found in presenting microcomputer training that a career opportunity approach led to higher self-efficacy and better learning.

It is possible to take these issues and formulate some questions the training designer might consider. In that regard, we offer the following questions:

1. How can the designer increase the trainee's beliefs that training outcomes can be achieved?
2. How can the trainer demonstrate to the trainee the instrumentality of training success for improvements in job performance?
3. How can the trainer positively influence the trainee's beliefs about the value of better job performance?
4. How can the trainer positively influence the level of self-efficacy?

Obviously, answers to these questions require consideration of all issues involved in training systems design. For example, if the needs assessment is not conducted properly, the trainee will learn that the program has not been designed properly and thus has no instrumentality for eventual improvements in job performance. Throughout this text, these types of issues are considered.

The emphasis in this next section will be on motivational approaches that have direct implications for answering the previous questions.

MOTIVATIONAL THEORIES

Motivation involves psychological processes that cause arousal, direction, and persistence of behavior. Arousal and persistence focus on the time and effort that an individual invests, and direction refers to the behaviors in which the investment of time and effort are made (Naylor, Pritchard, & Ilgen, 1980). In that sense, motivation is reflected both in the choice of behaviors that individuals decide to engage and the amount of effort devoted to those behaviors. For the interested reader, a review of motivational theories and empirical research can be found in Ilgen and Klein (1989) and Kanfer (1991). Most of this research is related to performance on the job rather than to learning in a training environment. However, the role of motivation to job performance can provide important insights into performance in training environments. Also, if the motivational level in the transfer or on-the-job setting is extremely poor, learning in the instructional setting becomes an academic exercise. Some of the motivational theories that appear particularly relevant to training systems follow. Thus, these theories seem particularly relevant to the design of pretraining, training, and post-training environments.

Social Learning Theory

Early learning theorists argued that a person makes a response to a stimulus and, when that response is reinforced, a connection is formed between the stimulus and response. Eventually, reinforcements of the response strengthen the neural connections so that the behavior will occur in the presence of the stimulus. (Reinforcement theory is discussed in more detail later.) However, many contemporary psychologists think that this explanation for behavior ignores the mental activity going on inside the person and cannot, by itself, provide explanations for more complex human behavior, such as the cognitive processes involved in actions like thinking and decision making.

As described by Ilgen and Klein (1989), cognitive theories attribute the causes of actions to an individual's processing of information. Thus, the resulting behavior stems from decisions based on the processing of information. Psychologists who espouse the cognitive viewpoint argue that the learner forms structures, or schema, in memory that preserve and organize information about what has been learned. Social learning theory argues that it is "the cognitive representations of future outcomes that generate the motivation for future behavior" (Ilgen & Klein, 1989, p. 151). According to Bandura (1977, 1986), who has been instrumental in the development of social learning theory, people process and weigh information concerning their capabilities in the situation. This clearly relates to training in the sense that achievement will be greater to the extent that trainees believe they are capable of mastering the material, the degree to which they have self-efficacy. Wood and Bandura (1989) describe three particularly relevant aspects of social learning or cognitive theory:

1. The development of the individual's cognitive, social, and behavioral competencies through mastery modeling;
2. The development of an individual's beliefs in his or her capabilities, thus enabling high self-efficacy and use of abilities; and
3. The enhancement of the individual's motivation by the use of goals.

Wood and Bandura (1989) note that if an individual could only learn through direct experiences, then human development would be severely limited. Instead, they propose that individuals can learn by watching another person make a particular response. Bandura states that this observational learning occurs when an observer watches a model exhibit a set of responses. This set of learned behaviors becomes part of the individual's repertoire of potential behavior even though it may not be overtly performed for some time.

Bandura believes that these responses, known as modeling, are acquired through symbolic mental processes that function as the observer watches the behavior of a model. Also, there are several other processes, including retention of the information, which is an active process aided when people symbolically transform the modeled information into memory codes and mentally rehearse the information. If the strategies result in desired outcomes rather than unrewarding or punishing events, people will produce the desired behavior. These ideas fit in well with the expectancy theory, which states that motivational level is based on a combination of individuals' beliefs that they can achieve certain outcomes from their acts and the value of those outcomes to them. (Expectancy theory is discussed further later.) In addition, social learning theory has provided an important foundation for a training technique appropriately known as behavioral role modeling, which is discussed in Chapter 8.

Wood and Bandura's (1989) second point relates to people's beliefs about efficacy and how it can be strengthened. One way is through mastery experiences. Here, the authors indicate that it is important for the individuals to achieve success and not be discouraged by failure. On the other hand, the experiences must be designed so that people learn to overcome failure. Also, they need to observe proficient models that demonstrate effective strategies. Finally, they must receive realistic encouragement to help them exert greater effort even if they have self-doubts. This last factor is labeled social persuasion. Again, many of these points relate to other motivational theories described later. For example, reinforcement theory refers to the importance of the use of positive reinforcement. Also, the implications of social learning theory have resulted in research that is examining various procedures for modifying self-efficacy. Thus, Gist and her colleagues (Gist, 1989; Gist, Schwoerer, & Rosen, 1989) have found that by using a modeling approach they can generate higher self-efficacy scores. In addition, it appears that modeling enhances the participants' beliefs about their own capabilities to perform. Thus, modeling might work because it enhances self-efficacy, which in turn influences performance. It will take some time to determine whether the results are completely supportive of such an idea. Eden and Aviram (1993) add further support for the potential power of using training for self-efficacy. They used a number of behavioral role modeling workshop sessions over several weeks to boost general self-efficacy in a group of unemployed persons. They found that the treatment boosted job search activity among persons who were initially low in self-efficacy but had no extra effect for persons who already had higher general self-efficacy.

In a real sense, social learning theory is an overarching model that contains many important aspects of other theories. That becomes even more obvious in the discussion of Wood and Bandura's (1989) third point, which emphasizes goals and their enhancement of an individual's motivation. They describe some of the many relationships between self-efficacy and goals by noting that when there is stronger perceived self-efficacy, individuals set higher goals and have firmer commitments to the goals. The goal systems relate to the belief that individuals have capacities for self-direction and self-motivation. They seek self-satisfaction by fulfilling goals. Thus, goals provide a sense of purpose and direction. Also, by setting these goals, individuals try to sustain the level of effort needed to achieve them. In this way, they also help to build self-confidence. Individuals use goals as standards to measure their progress and their ability. From Wood and Bandura's point of view, motivation is best achieved by setting long-range goals that determine the course an individual will take and by having a series of attainable subgoals that lead the way. Many of the conditions involving the use of goals are specified in goal theory, which is discussed next.

Goal Setting

Locke and Latham (1990) have conducted and reviewed an extensive set of studies describing the effects of setting goals on behavior. In their various reviews, they found that in 90% of the laboratory and field studies, specific and challenging goals led to higher performance than easy goals, do-your-best goals, or no goals. These authors postulate that goals affect task performance by "directing energy and attention, mobilizing energy expenditure or effort, prolonging effort over time (persistence) and motivating the individual to develop relevant strategies for goal attainment" (Locke, Shaw, Saari, &

Latham, 1981, p. 145). These authors have also detailed a number of specific conditions that affect performance:

1. Individuals who are given specific, hard, or challenging goals perform better than those given specific easy goals, do-best goals, or no goals at all.
2. Goals appear to have more predictable effects when they are given in specific terms rather than as a vague set of intentions.
3. The goals must be matched to the ability of the individual such that the person is likely to achieve the goal. Being able to achieve the goal is important for the individual's self-efficacy, for that is how the individual will judge his or her ability to perform well on the tasks. This means that it is likely that the analyst will need to design intermediate goals to reflect progress in the learning process.
4. Feedback concerning the degree to which the goal is being achieved is necessary for goal setting to have an effect.
5. For goal setting to be effective, the individual has to accept the goal that is assigned or set. Often the acceptance of the goal is related to the degree of support or commitment of the organization to the goal-setting program.

An example of an application of goal-setting techniques is offered by Kim (1984), who had salespeople participatively set goals in terms of specific selling activities and specific sales in dollar terms. Supervisors were given training on how to implement the approach, and feedback on performance was given every two weeks. For departments in which goal setting was introduced, there was significantly higher selling performance than in a control group. The goal-setting points previously described are based on extensive research studies. They suggest a number of ways that training programs can be more effective. The setting of specific challenging goals that are matched to the ability of the individual, followed by feedback on degree of goal achievement, provides a solid foundation for the design of an instructional program. Also, as noted earlier, the use of goals allows a person to measure his or her capabilities against standards, thereby increasing the sense of self-efficacy and achievement.

Expectancy Theory

Vroom (1964) has developed a process theory of motivation related to the question of how behavior is energized and sustained. The theory is based on cognitive expectancies concerning outcomes that are likely to occur as a result of the participant's behavior and on individual preferences among those outcomes. The expectancy can vary, as can the valence, or strength, of an individual's preference for an outcome. Vroom states that outcomes have a particular valence value because they are instrumental in achieving other outcomes. For instance, money and promotion have potential valence value because they are instrumental in allowing an individual to achieve other outcomes, like an expensive home or a college education for his or her children. The motivational level is based on a combination of an individual's belief that certain outcomes can be achieved from his or her acts and of the value of those outcomes to the individual. Training programs have a valence value for individuals if they believe the programs will permit them to achieve other outcomes. Thus, training becomes a low-level outcome that permits the achievement of higher-level outcomes (such as a job, a promotion, or a raise), which in turn might lead to other outcomes. The theory implies that it is necessary to show the individual the value of the instructional program in order to properly motivate the person. Programs that appear unrelated to future outcomes will probably not meet the desired objectives. Note that this is a central point in Noe's (1986) motivation to learn model discussed earlier. Also, it is an important aspect in Wood and Bandura's (1989) discussion of social learning theory. If these strategies result in desired outcomes rather than in unrewarding or punishing events, a person will produce the desired behavior. Some other conditions concerning rewards are presented next.

Reinforcement Theory

When the consequence of a response leads to the response being repeated, the consequence is called a *positive reinforcer*. B. F. Skinner is most often associated with the development of reinforcement theory. In this form of learning, the person's response is instrumental in gaining a consequence that reinforces, or rewards. The responses being reinforced can vary in complexity but certainly include a person producing a product at work, and the rewarding stimuli can vary from praise for the person to monetary incentives. The list of stimuli that have served as reinforcers in various environments is endless but could include praise, gifts, money, and attention. An example of the use of reinforcement principles is illustrated by the early work of Pedalino and Gamboa (1974), who were concerned with the reduction of absenteeism and lateness in a manufacturing/distribution plant. These researchers used a poker game incentive plan as a reinforcement device. In this incentive plan, each day an employee comes to work and is on time, he is allowed to choose a card from a deck of playing cards. At the end of the five-day week, the person might have five cards, a normal poker hand. The highest hand would win $20. In Pedalino and Gamboa's study, there were eight winners, one for approximately each department. Over a four-month period, the experimental group achieved an 18.27% reduction in absenteeism. Other researchers, such as Luthans, Paul, and Baker (1981) found that rewards also increased relevant behaviors for salespeople.

Equity Theory

Equity theory is based on the belief that people want to be treated fairly. Thus, individuals compare themselves with other people to see if their treatment is equitable. As stated by Adams (1965), "Inequity exists for a person when he perceives that the ratio of his outcomes to inputs and the ratio of others' outcomes to inputs are unequal" (p. 280). This definition includes all factors viewed as having value—for example, pay, status, education, and seniority—and perceived as being important for obtaining some benefit (Pritchard, 1969). Inequity is said to create tension that has motivating qualities, requiring the person to reduce or eliminate the discrepancy. This tension is created whether the person compared is perceived as underrewarded or overrewarded.

Although equity theory appears to be especially relevant to the subject of wage factors, it may also have important implications for training. Training may be viewed as an input or as an output. In the input case, individuals who have acquired the necessary training experiences may view as inequitable promotions and pay raises earned by individuals without equal educational experiences. In the output case, individuals may perceive that they are not given the same opportunity to attend advanced training courses. For example, in the employment discrimination area, female managers may view their opportunities from an equity theory framework. That is, they may feel that, given the same training background as males, they do not have equal opportunities for job advancement or for participation in advanced training. This theory is also consistent with the research discussed at the beginning of this section, which noted that individuals who felt they were not treated fairly in obtaining training opportunities developed lower motivation to learn tendencies, which resulted in poorer learning performance. These perceptions might even result in people leaving the organization. For example, Iverson and Roy (1994) in a study conducted in Australia found that employee perceptions of inequity were correlated with intentions to quit the job and with increases in job search behavior.

Need Theory

A number of content theories emphasize learned needs as motivators of human behavior. These theories concentrate on the needs that are to be satisfied and do not attempt to specify the exact processes by which these needs motivate behavior. The theories suggest to the training researcher that his or her programs must meet particular needs in order to have a motivated learner. One need theory given considerable attention involves the need for achievement motivation (nAch), which is described as a behavioral tendency to strive for success (Spencer & Spencer, 1993). It is assumed to operate when the environment signals that certain acts on the part of the individual will lead to need achievement. An illustration of this approach can be found in the studies of Miron and McClelland (1979), which were designed to instill achievement motivation through training programs. They found that participants in their training program were successful in terms of increased sales and profits. Another series of studies, combining the approaches of the need and expectancy theories, indicates that people capable of high achievement do not necessarily perform well unless their behavior is viewed as being instrumental for later success (Raynor & Rubin, 1971). Thus, students with high achievement motivation earned superior grades when they regarded the grades as important for career success.

THE CONDITIONS OF TRANSFER

The previous sections have emphasized instructional design principles and learning processes. Of course, unless the individual learns during training, the question of transfer to the actual job setting is meaningless. Thus, all discussion ranging from the motivation of the learner to the use of advanced organizers is extremely relevant to understanding transfer issues (see Figure 4.1). Issues concerning transfer are paramount, especially for those concerned with instructional programs. For example, Robinson and Robinson (1995) contend that less than 30% of what people learn in training actually gets used on the job. The concern over the "transfer problem" has become even stronger given today's changing job requirements, the view of people as the key to competitive advantage, and the movement toward learning as a key mechanism for fully utilizing human resources in organizations.

Prior to taking constructive steps to solve the transfer problem, there must first be consensus as to the meaning of training transfer. The commonsense notion of transfer is that we want learners to use the knowledge and skills gained through training in the appropriate settings. While this provides a general definition of transfer, it belies a deeper understanding and appreciation for the complexities underlying transfer. In fact, this general definition fails to capture two important questions that one must ask to clearly define transfer.

1. *What behaviors and in what settings do you expect the learner to apply the newly acquired knowledge, skills, or attitudes?*

One key component of a definition of transfer must include an answer to what behaviors are expected to change after completion of training. This calls for clearly linking the changes in knowledge, skills, or attitudes as a function of training to observable changes in behaviors in the job to show that the expected changes have indeed occurred.

In addition to defining the behaviors expected to change, one must also identify how often and in what context transfer is expected. Two types of transfer involve whether the newly acquired KSAs are expected to be applied directly or indirectly through generalization. The direct application of learning outcomes refers to the transfer of the knowledge, skills, attitudes, and behaviors to the exact situations or settings depicted in the educational activity. For example, a program may focus on improving supervisory skills such as problem analysis, listening skills, and action planning or goal setting. The direct application of transfer focuses on whether the learner demonstrates effective supervisory skills in situations and settings that are identical or very similar to those used in the skills training program (e.g., how to handle an employee who is constantly late for work). Beyond direct application, one could be more interested in the extent to which a learner is able to take new knowledge and skills and apply them to a variety of new situations and settings. This issue of generalization requires trainers (perhaps in partnership with the participants or learners) to clearly identify prior to transfer how often and in what situations and settings one could reasonably expect the learner to demonstrate effective application of knowledge, skills, or attitudes to behaviors. If generalization is an important goal, then direct application without attempts to use the KSAs acquired in other appropriate situations would be considered a transfer problem. Yelon, Reznich, and Sleight (1997) used a case study approach to examine the process of generalization relevant to how medical fellows applied training to their work context. They found wide variation in what content the fellows applied as well as how they applied the skills that they had learned. They suggest that trainers should recognize that trainees will customize the training themselves to fit their own needs and thus incorporate time during training to help trainees identify and plan for such customization.

Finally, trainers must also decide to what extent the trainee should be able to demonstrate behavioral adaptability in the face of changing conditions in the transfer setting (Smith, Ford, & Kozlowski, 1997). This issue concerns whether one is interested in the learner's ability to accurately reproduce or mimic the same behaviors that were part of the learning process or to adapt skills to fit the situation. For example, in behavioral modeling training for improving sales, a salesperson could be asked to transfer training to a variety of sales situations by closely following the learning points from the training program. In another type of behavioral modeling program, one might be more interested in whether the salesperson can adapt the trained behaviors to deal effectively with a unique situation encountered on the job.

2. How long do you expect the acquired KSAs to be maintained over time, and what factors can enhance knowledge and skill development on the job?

The second question addresses the length of time that the newly acquired knowledge, skills, attitudes, and behaviors should continue to be in use. This is an issue of maintenance and concerns the continued use of new behaviors in the transfer setting. A review of the literature (e.g., see Baldwin & Ford, 1988; Ford & Weissbein, 1997) reveals that there has been a great deal of work on the acquisition of skills but relatively little on the maintenance of skills once they have been acquired. Similarly, issues of forgetting and memory loss after educational programs are rarely discussed in the transfer literature. Not much attention has been given to strategies for enhancing rather than maintaining the knowledge and skills learned in training once back on the job.

The maintenance of behaviors requires trainers to specify the changes that are expected to occur in the level of KSAs acquired through training as a function of time elapsed from the completion of the program. The specification of expected maintenance is important, as learners who exhibit similar levels of skill proficiency soon after a program can differ substantially on long-term skill retention. Ford and his colleagues (Ford, Quiñones, Sego, & Sorra, 1992; Quiñones, Ford, Sego, & Smith, 1996) contend that a key factor is that some learners obtain many more opportunities to use their new skills and thus retain skills longer than those who obtain fewer opportunities. They found empirical support for this wide variation in opportunities in a study of aerospace ground equipment personnel. They also found that supervisors were the key gatekeeper as to what and how often trainees obtained opportunities to perform trained tasks on the job. In addition, trainees who were more motivated and had learned more during training had an impact on supervisory attitudes toward the trainee, which translated into greater opportunities to perform.

Even when knowledge and skills are used on the job, another key issue is how frequently continuing educational experience is needed to ensure continued use and enhancement of the KSAs obtained through the initial training experience. Such refresher training has been shown to aid the long-term retention of knowledge and skills by not only reinforcing the knowledge and skills previously learned but by also producing new learning. In addition, particular skills acquired might not be activated for use for considerable time periods—this disuse may lead to skill deterioration, which might mean that a skill is no longer functional when needed. Interestingly, how long it takes a learner to rebound or to relearn to the expected level of proficiency can be used as a good index of the successful transfer of the original educational experience in the face of no opportunities to use the skills in the transfer setting.

Research has examined factors that affect the application of training and the long-term maintenance and improvement of skills. We first focus on the more traditional approaches to considering transfer, which centered on the similarity of the training and the transfer contexts. We then focus on research on work context factors that can influence the extent to which what is learned in training is actually transferred to the job.

Classical Approach to Transfer

To determine transfer effects, researchers have traditionally compared an experimental group that learns one task and then transfers to a second task with a control group that performs only the second task. If the experimental group performs significantly better than the control group on the second task, *positive transfer* has occurred. It can be assumed that the learning that occurred in the first task has transferred and aided performance in the second task. If the experimental group performs worse than the control group on the second task, *negative transfer* has occurred. The learning of the first task has resulted in poorer performance on the second task. When there are no differences in performance between the experimental and control groups on the second task, there is *zero transfer.*

Although the basic paradigm of transfer of training have been examined for some time, the exact conditions leading to positive or negative transfer are not easily specified because settings outside the experimental laboratory rarely lend themselves to the type of analysis necessary to accurately specify the degree of transfer. However, it is important to understand the theories that predict varying degrees of transfer because they provide information about the type of environment necessary to achieve positive transfer. The two classic viewpoints that describe the conditions necessary for transfer are the identical-elements and the transfer through principles theories.

The *identical-elements theory* stems from classical learning theory that predicted that transfer would occur as long as there were the same elements in the two situations. These identical elements included aims, methods, and approaches and were later defined in terms of stimuli and responses. Table 4.5 adapts some of the classical work on transfer by detailing the type of transfer expected based on the similarity of the stimuli and responses. In the first case, the stimuli and responses are identical. If the tasks are identical in training and transfer, trainees are simply practicing the final task during the training program, and there should be high positive transfer.

The second case assumes that the task elements, both stimuli and responses, are so different that practice on one task has no relationship to performance on the transfer task. It would be farfetched to design a training

TABLE 4.5 TYPE OF TRANSFER—BASED ON STIMULUS AND RESPONSE SIMILARITY

Task Stimuli	Response Required	Transfer
Same	Same	High positive
Different	Different	None
Different	Same	Positive
Same	Different	Negative

Source: Adapted from *Principles of Training,* by D. H. Holding. Copyright 1965 by Pergamon Press, Ltd. Adapted by permission.

program that is totally unrelated to the transfer situation. The third case is common to many training programs. The stimuli are somewhat different in training and transfer settings, but the responses are the same. The learner can generalize training from one environment to another. The person who has learned to drive one type of car usually has little difficulty switching to another (assuming the required responses remain the same), even though minor features may be different (for example, dashboard arrangement). The fourth case presents the basic paradigm for negative transfer. A certain response to training stimuli is practiced so that the same response is given each time those stimuli appear. If the response becomes inappropriate, negative transfer results. As technology develops, producing continual modifications in control and display equipment without considering the role of human beings, there are frequent instances of negative transfer.

Some trainers have a tendency to ignore stimulus and response elements as being too mechanistic and detailed. They make the assumption that analyses of stimulus and response elements are too difficult and that much of the research stems from the laboratory and therefore is not relevant. Although these are difficulties, that is an unfortunate judgment. A large number of jobs require responses to large, complex displays where such analyses would be extremely useful. An example of this situation is the nuclear power industry, where there is extreme concern about transfer issues resulting from nuclear control room modifications. The life cycle of a nuclear power plant is approximately forty years, and in that time period there will be many changes in the control room. The concern is that the changes introduced must be carefully analyzed to avoid negative transfer effects. An analysis of this problem notes that the most serious negative transfer problem was the situation where "new, conflicting responses on the transfer task are required while stimuli identical or similar to those used in the original task are retained" (Sawyer, Pain, Van Cott, & Banks, 1982, p. 6). Sawyer and colleagues performed an analysis of the potential changes in control room design and designated preferred versus less preferred solutions. An example of one of those situations is shown in Figure 4.7.

Over the years, many of the original ideas concerning identical-elements theory have been broadened to include general principles and attitudes, as well as the more specific components. The *transfer through principle theory* suggests that training should focus on the general principles necessary to learn a task so that the learner may apply them to solve problems in the transfer task. Here the focus in the transfer situation is very similar except that the focus is broadened away from elements such as stimuli and responses to relevance of general principles in the original learning and transfer situations.

It seems particularly appropriate to close this section on the classical views of transfer of training by adding a discussion on how the cognitive analyses

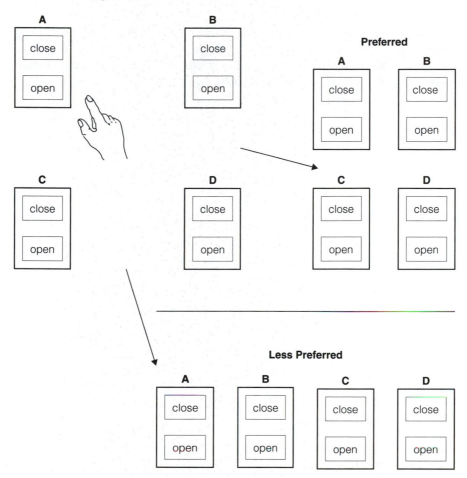

Original Position

A

close
open

B

close
open

C

close
open

D

close
open

Preferred

A

close
open

B

close
open

C

close
open

D

close
open

Less Preferred

A

close
open

B

close
open

C

close
open

D

close
open

PROBLEM: The top legend-controls are difficult to reach and thus should be lowered.

EXPLANATION: The top alternative is preferable because it retains the basic perceptual relationship among the controls while at the same time moving the top controls within easy reach. Although the bottom alternative is not necessarily a bad one, because of prior experience (conditioning) operators may have some problem identifying the array rapidly.

FIGURE 4.7

Example of possible control board modification.

Source: From "Nuclear Control Room Modifications and the Role of Transfer of Training Principles: A Review of Issues and Research," by C. R. Sawyer, R. F. Pain, H. Van Cott, and W. W. Banks, 1982. In (NUREG/CR-2828, EGG-2211). Idaho National Engineering Laboratory.

discussed earlier can affect the consideration of positive transfer of training. As discussed previously, studies by Shiffrin and Schneider (1977) demonstrate that processing can become automatic, thus freeing the learner's limited attentional capacity for other tasks. The condition under which this occurs is where there is extensive practice on a task so that responses can become consistently mapped to particular stimuli. This results in performance of these automatic tasks in a very quick and efficient way. A particularly vexing problem has been the vigilance decrement that occurs during watch-keeping periods when the number of signals to be detected are infrequent, such as monitoring of warning signals indicating machine malfunctions, or watch-keeping tasks such as early-warning signals of nuclear attack.

As noted earlier, Fisk and Schneider (1981) were able to eliminate this decrement by automatizing the activity through a training program that presented the stimulus and then required a response. These pairings went on for over 4000 training trials, and it is called *consistent mapping*. When the trainees performed the real task with only eighteen targets presented over 6000 presentations (in a fifty-minute period), there was virtually no decrement over time. Another condition of the study involved the same training on 4000 trials, but here the group only received the same small number of targets that would occur in the transfer session. This condition was known as *variable mapping* because there was not a consistent mapping of each stimulus and response. When this group transferred to the 6000 trial session, they had the typical 65% vigilance decrement over time.

Howell and Cooke's (1989) analysis of this study notes that the ineffective variable-mapping strategy was identical to what occurred in the transfer condition and thus should have produced the best results according to the traditional identical-elements theory. Consistent mapping, which seemed like unrealistic preparation for the transfer tasks, produced the best results. The theoretical explanation for this result is that consistent mapping resulted in automatizing the subjects' detection responses. Again, the point that Howell and Cooke make is that intensive training on certain procedural elements of a task can make them more cognitively automatic and free capacity for other, more unpredictable or creative demands.

The Work Context and Transfer

In the preceding sections, we discussed issues involved in the specification of stimuli and responses and their relationship to the transfer issue. However, it is critical to remember that transfer of training occurs from an instructional setting (such as a company training program) to a work context that may or may not be supportive of the training. In particular, people who participate in training are faced with a problem; they are required to learn something in one environment (training situation) and use the learning in another environment (on the job). Druckman and Bjork (1994) conducted a review of learning and its implications for the National Research Council. One of their conclusions is that learning is a social activity and the performance environments tend to be social in nature. Thus, it is not possible to understand performance without understanding the social situations in which it occurs.

This requires an examination of the systemwide components of the organization that may affect a trainee arriving with newly learned skills. Thus, training programs are often judged to be a failure because of organizational constraints that were not originally intended to be addressed by the instructional program. An example of the issues comes from the Independent Commission on the Los Angeles Police Department that published a report on the police department after the 1991 riots. The common statement made to new police officers on the beat was "Forget everything you learned at the Academy" (Druckman & Bjork, 1994, p. 36). If this is a common perception, this implies that these officers believed the training program does not prepare the officer for the environment in which they will work. Clearly, workplace analyses would need to be done and the training program would need to consider what issues have to be explored.

As discussed in "Organizational Analysis" in Chapter 3, there is not much research on this issue. However, Rouillier and Goldstein's (1993) work found two major components of transfer climate, situational cues and consequences, that predicted the extent to which transfer occurred. Some of the types of items included in each of those categories were presented in Table 3.1. This research provides evidence that the degree of positive-transfer climate affects the degree to which learned behavior is transferred onto the job, independent of the degree to which the trainees had learned in the training program. A followup study by Tracey, Tannenbaum, and Kavanagh (1995) examined managers in a supermarket chain. Using a similar measure, they found that trainees coming from a more supportive environment showed the largest increase in performance after attending the training program.

There is also one study that actually intervened to change a work environment factor—in this case managerial support—and examined its impact on training transfer (Brinkerhoff & Montesino, 1995). The researchers designed a study where supervisors had discussions with trainees prior to training regarding course content, the importance of the training to the job, and expectations as to how training could be applied to the job. In addition, supervisors discussed post-training issues with the trainees, including the extent to which the trainee learned the material, what barriers the trainee might envision while applying the training to the job, and an emphasis on supervisory expectations regarding the use of trainee skills to improve job performance. Results supported the use of the intervention strategies to improve training transfer.

Unfortunately, the only measure of transfer obtained was through self-reported degree of transfer six weeks after the course. A followup study that also examined more objective performance data as well as supervisory perceptions of change would increase confidence that the intervention was useful and had impacts on bottom line results. Nevertheless, these studies illustrate the powerful role that climate perceptions can have on training transfer.

Another important area of research is the identification of high-risk situations that the trainee would face and the need for coping skills in those situations. The importance of maintaining behavior and overcoming obstacles is clearly detailed in a model developed by Marx (1982, in press). His model is based on a model that was originally designed to examine relapse problems in addictive behavior such as smoking and alcoholism. The model, as shown in Figure 4.8, outlines the importance of having coping responses in the repertoire of managers, to prevent relapses in their learned behavior. Thus, as part of his training program, Marx makes managers aware of the relapse process. He also has them diagnose situations that are likely to sabotage their efforts at maintaining their new learning. For example, he notes in the model that if one problem is increased stress resulting from time pressure, then a coping skill such as time-management techniques would be taught. As described in the model, these coping responses are seen as resulting in increased self-efficacy and a decreased probability of relapse. The model also describes the situation that occurs when no coping response is available. In this situation, the results can lead to giving up on attempts to incorporate new learning. Opportunities for positive transfer then disappear regardless of what has been learned in training.

Although many of the ideas in the model remain to be tested, researchers are beginning to investigate the important issues concerning transfer. In a series of studies, Gist and her colleagues (e.g., Gist, Stevens, & Bavetta, 1991; Stevens & Gist, 1997) examined the impact of post-training goal setting and relapse prevention (or self-management training) on training transfer in a complex negotiation skills context. They found that self-management training can lead to more efforts to enhance skills after training and that post-training goal setting can lead to higher levels of transfer performance—especially for those who came into the program with high levels of self-efficacy. In addition, Burke and Baldwin (1999) found that the organization's transfer climate can impact what types of relapse strategies have the most impact on long-term retention. In particular, they found that a full dose of relapse prevention strategies can be effective in improving transfer when the organizational climate was not very supportive, whereas a reduced set of relapse prevention activities was effective when the transfer climate was more supportive.

In conclusion, transfer of training is a critical issue for effective training practice. There are a number of factors that can be introduced to facilitate the

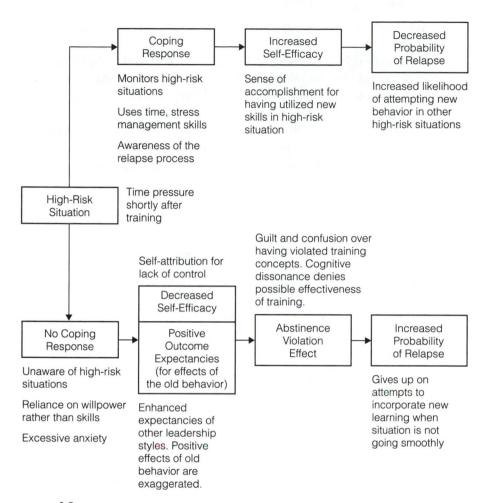

FIGURE 4.8

Cognitive behavioral model of the relapse process.

Source: From "Relapse Prevention for Managerial Training: A Model for Maintenance of Behavioral Change," by R. D. Marx. In *Academy of Management Review*, 1982, *7*, pp. 433–441. Copyright 1982 by the Academy of Management. Reprinted by permission.

transfer of knowledge and skills from training to the job. Some overall comments for enhancing transfer are as follows:

1. We must have a system that unites trainer, trainee, and manager in the transfer process.
2. Before training, the expectations for the trainee and the manager must be clear.

3. We must identify obstacles to transfer and provide strategies to overcome these problems.
4. We must work with managers to provide opportunities for the maintenance of trainees' learned behavior in work organizations.
5. Many people believe that we will need to develop a continuous learning climate so that an atmosphere emerges where employees feel it is important to continually learn and develop. This probably includes support for situations where formal training does not even exist. This point regarding continuous learning approaches is discussed further in Chapter 9.

CONCLUSIONS

In a recent review of the training literature, Salas and Cannon-Bowers (in press) noted that there has been an explosion in the number of new and expanded theoretical frameworks as well as concepts and constructs of learning. These advances have improved our understanding of the learning environment and the conditions and interventions that can enhance training effectiveness. In particular, the assessment of the learning and cognitive literature has led to a number of guidelines for improving training practice (e.g., Tannenbaum & Yukl, 1992; Salas, Cannon-Bowers, & Kozlowski, 1997):

1. The instructional events that comprise the training method should be consistent with the cognitive, physical, or psychomotor processes that lead to mastery.
2. The learner should be induced to actively produce the capability (e.g., practice behaviors, recall information from memory, apply principles in doing a task). The more active the production, the greater the retention and transfer.
3. All available sources of relevant feedback should be used, and feedback should be accurate, credible, timely, and constructive.
4. The instructional process should enhance trainee self-efficacy and trainee expectations that the training will be successful and lead to valued outcomes. For example, training should begin with simple behaviors that can be mastered easily, then progress to more complex behaviors as trainees become more confident.
5. Training methods should be adapted to differences in trainee aptitudes and prior knowledge.

Finally, as a review of the concepts this chapter has addressed, return to Figure 4.1. The diagram postulates various relationships among the trainee inputs, outputs, and conditions of transfer. Good training outcomes can result when there is an effective instructional design, high trainee ability and motivation, and when there is a feeling that it makes sense to learn because there is support in the work environment or that training leads to positive outcomes. Then, if the trainee has learned or retained, there will be an opportunity to perform in transfer onto the job. Finally, if the work environment has a positive climate, the transfer is likely to occur and be maintained. The next two chapters describe approaches for evaluating the extent to which training is or is not effective, including issues of measuring learning and training transfer.

InfoTrac College Edition

For additional readings, go to http: www.infotrac-college.com/wadsworth and enter a search term related to your interest. The following key terms will pull up several related articles.

Cognitive Learning   Mental Models
Employee Motivation   Self-Efficacy
Experts and Novices   Training Feedback
Instructional Design   Training Objectives
Learning Environment   Transfer of Training

THE CRITERION CHOICES: INTRODUCTION TO THE EVALUATION PROCESS

Evaluation is the systematic collection of descriptive and judgmental information necessary to make effective training decisions related to the selection, adoption, value, and modification of various training activities. The objectives of training programs reflect numerous goals ranging from trainee progress to organizational goals. From this perspective, evaluation is an information-gathering technique that cannot possibly result in decisions that categorize programs as good or bad. Rather, evaluation should capture the dynamic flavor of the training program. Then the necessary information will be available to revise instructional programs to achieve multiple instructional objectives.

The history of evaluation of training programs indicates that much more effort is necessary to acquire the information needed for the decision-making process. Thus, one survey of 611 companies indicates that 42% of companies did not evaluate the effectiveness of MBA programs and 32% did not evaluate short-course programs (Saari, Johnson, McLaughlin, & Zimmerle, 1988). However, the positive side of those figures indicates a substantial number of organizations did evaluate programs; it turns out that 92% of the companies surveyed did conduct some evaluation of company-specific programs. On the other hand, most of those evaluations focused on trainee reactions to the program rather than determining whether learning had taken place and job performance had been positively impacted.

BARRIERS AND CONTRIBUTIONS IN THE EVALUATION PROCESS

Grove and Ostroff (1991) describe some of the barriers to training evaluation in work organizations. They include the following points:

1. Top management does not emphasize training evaluation. Although top management is usually interested in evaluating all aspects of business practice, they do not tend to apply the same pressure on training management to evaluate their products. Some people feel that is because top management's fervor in emphasizing the importance of training and career development results in their accepting training on the basis of faith in its value.

2. Training directors often do not have the skills to conduct evaluations. Many directors were direct-line managers or are human resource generalists and are rarely trained in the complex enterprise of evaluations. Further, Grove and Ostroff think that there are few well-written books on how training evaluation should be conducted. Given that there are two chapters on this topic in our book, we will not offer any comments about this point except to hope that some of this material is helpful!

3. It often is not clear to training human resource people what should be evaluated and what questions should be answered by an evaluation. This is the criterion issue, which is discussed next in this chapter. Basically, it is difficult to conduct evaluation without a clear idea of the program's objectives. Grove and Ostroff note that one manager of a corporate learning center told them he could not match up the objectives with the various course descriptions in his company's own catalog. Also, managers are not sure whether they are supposed to evaluate trainee reactions, learning, job performance, utility, or all of the above.

4. There is a view that training evaluation can be a risky and expensive enterprise. Some fear that an evaluation will indicate that a publicly endorsed program is not meeting its objectives. As noted previously, this view is an unfortunate misunderstanding of the purpose of evaluation, which should be to provide the information to help improve programs. The purpose is not to declare programs as good or bad but to gain as much knowledge as possible from the effort.

One of the authors of this book experienced the fourth point recently with a new web-based training course. We were asked to provide a detailed evaluation of the pilot version of the program before it was to become available to all employees. We did our job "too well" in the sense that we identified a number of corrections and modifications that could be made to improve the course and the accessibility for trainees of the various options within the web course. A high-level human resource generalist saw the evaluation report and at one point wanted to pull the plug on the whole course due to "all its errors" found in the evaluation and expressed disappointment in the consulting group and internal company people who had developed the program. Each modification, though, was relatively minor, and was intended to improve the course when delivered to all employees. Much effort had to be expended by the consultants, internal personnel, and by us as evaluators to convince the manager that the evaluation did not show that the course was "bad" but that it only needed some modifications to make it an even better course. In fact, the course finally did go on-line after some modifications were made and eventually won a Brandon Hall award for best web-based computer training program for 1998.

This latter view that evaluation can help improve training in a variety of ways is also discussed by Grove and Ostroff (1991). They note the following ways in which training evaluation can make a contribution:

1. Training evaluation can serve as a diagnostic technique to permit the revision of programs to meet the large number of goals and objectives. Thus, the information can be used to select or revise programs. It can also be used to determine whether people liked the program, whether they learned, and whether it positively affected their job performance.
2. Good evaluation information can demonstrate the usefulness of the training enterprise. This type of information can actually show the benefits and the costs of training. These data can be very useful when economic realities force difficult decisions on how organizational budgets should be allocated.
3. As discussed in our Chapters 1 and 9, legal issues have become important considerations in human resources. Fair employment discrimination lawsuits often question the criteria for entrance into training and the value of training, especially when it is used as a requirement for promotion or job entry. In those cases, evaluation data are required to show the job-relatedness of the training program.
4. There have been important advances in the development of evaluation models during the past ten years. Many of these advances have been spurred by demands for accountability in the areas of criminal and civil justice, social welfare, mental health, and medical treatment. Many of the evaluation issues facing these evaluators, including the establishment of relevant criteria and innovative experimental designs, are exactly the same concerns facing the training evaluator.

In discussing the value that evaluation brings to understanding the utility of training programs, Campbell (1988) states the issue very well. He notes that it is nonsensical to ask whether training affects productivity. We all know that it does, and no one would seriously suggest that a pure trial-and-error strategy would be a good way to learn the job. On the other hand, it is very difficult to know when the marginal costs of training equal the marginal benefit. There are just too many other variables such as the effectiveness of the selections systems, new technology, and new incentives. Thus, it is very difficult to specify how resources should be allocated across all these different approaches, especially when they interact with each other.

However, as Campbell notes, a whole host of questions can be answered between those two extremes. They include whether a particular training program leads to better job performance and how much utility results from the program. It is even possible to ask whether the program produced the specific objectives for which it was designed and whether there are particular approaches to training or teaching of skills that are more effective than others.

An evaluation will not solve all training problems, but it is an important step forward. In many instances, the utilization of a simple procedure—for example, giving participants a pretest that can be used in later comparisons will dramatically improve the validity of the obtained information. The complexities of evaluation should not be underestimated; however, the most serious problem has been the failure to always consider evaluation an ordinary part of the instructional design process.

Rational decisions related to the selection, adoption, support, and worth of various training activities require some basis for determining that the instructional program is responsible for whatever changes occurred. Instructional analysts should be able to respond to the following questions:

1. Does an examination of the various criteria indicate that a change has occurred?
2. Can the changes be attributed to the instructional program?
3. Is it likely that similar changes will occur for new participants in the same program?
4. Is it likely that similar changes will occur for new participants in the same program in a different organization?

Although the answers to these questions provide information about the accomplishments of training programs and the revisions that may be required, investigators may be interested in asking other types of questions. In some cases, they are interested in the relative accomplishments of two different training approaches. It is also possible to ask which training approach works best with what type of training participant or in what type of organization. Researchers may also be interested in testing various theoretical hypotheses that provide the foundation for the design of a new training approach. In this latter instance, researchers still want to know if a change has occurred and whether it can be attributed to the training program. However, they may also ask questions concerning the effects of the training program on trainees with varying characteristics (for example, high and low verbal ability).

Before discussing criterion development (in this chapter) and particular methodologies for training evaluation (in Chapter 6) that help answer these types of questions, it is important to recognize that there are many different viewpoints about the desirability of evaluation, the approach to evaluation, and

the effects of evaluation. In the following sections, we discuss the most promi-
nent of these viewpoints.

VALUES AND THE EVALUATION PROCESS

Before beginning a discussion of evaluation models and strategies, it is important to consider the context in which evaluation occurs. There are a whole set
of values and attitudes that belong to the evaluator, the trainees, the decision
makers in the organization, the trainers, and so on. It is important to suggest
that these values and attitudes do affect many of the decisions involving both
the evaluation and the resulting data interpretations. Some of the more obvious factors can be controlled by some of the evaluation designs. Thus, medical
researchers use designs so that the investigator does not know which patients
were given the experimental drug and which subjects were given a placebo.

There is a growing recognition that all our decisions in conducting
research have an effect on the study itself. This point of view is often described
as the philosophy of intervention. It recognizes that even the decision to evaluate affects the data collected. Cochran makes this point with the following
tale about Grandma Moses:

> It is reported that Grandma Moses told an art dealer who purchased one of her
> early paintings from a gallery exhibit that there were 15 more like it at home. He
> bought them sight unseen and paid the same price for each as he paid for the one
> on display. Arriving at her home the next day to pick them up, the dealer found
> Grandma Moses with a saw, cutting one of her paintings in half. It seems that
> when she got home she found she had only 14 paintings and, not wanting to fall
> back on her agreement, she was correcting the discrepancy. (1978, p. 366)

In an example that is more relevant to work organizations, Cochran also
points out that changes in the use of criterion data occur when organizations
discover that these data are being used in an evaluation study. For example,
when there are programs to lower crime, the criterion data often consist of the
number of larcenies of $50 or more, which are counted in the Uniform Crime
Act. Sometimes, statistics give the appearance of a decrease in crime when
none actually exists. In some cases, the pressures being felt result in the out-
right falsification of data. In other cases, it is more subtle. Larceny figures are
based on stolen goods, which are used items. Thus, there is some value judgment in setting the actual dollar value of a stolen item. Many psychological
studies indicate that the criteria used in making these judgments are often
altered by the context and purposes of the study.

These types of intervention effects can have a dramatic influence on the
outcome of evaluation studies. In one instance, an entire city police force was
criticized in the press publicly and ordered back to training. Most officers took

the training seriously, "others were furious at being sent for more schooling, arriving for class late or not at all and reading newspapers during the instruction" (*Washington Post,* 1996, p. A12). In another study (Pfister, 1975), the researchers' procedure of assigning twenty-four of seventy-eight police officer volunteers to a control condition resulted in officers who wanted to attend becoming angry and withdrawn and making unpublishable comments regarding the research investigators.

The most important aspect of these types of issues is the understanding that trainees are cognitive and emotional human beings with concerns about their relationship to the organization for which they work. The development or the evaluation of a training program is an intervention in their lives. In some instances, having training opportunities actually determines whether a person is eligible for promotion. Training takes place in a particular context, the work organization. Therefore, it is part of a large system and interventions like training programs have consequences for the trainees and the organization. Many evaluation models discussed in this chapter reflect these types of issues.

The following material focuses on various components of evaluation. The criteria are discussed in this chapter, and then the methods and designs of evaluation approaches are presented next in Chapter 6.

INTRODUCTION TO CRITERION DEVELOPMENT

Choosing the Criterion Measures

Industrial psychologists concerned with the selection of personnel have developed programs based on tests that predict a standard of success or criterion of the job. The users and developers of training programs are faced with determining the choice of measures against which they can determine the viability of their program. In some cases, the training program is the instrument used to predict job success. In this situation, the evaluator attempts to establish the relationship between performance in the training program and performance on the job. In a different model, the training evaluator attempts to determine if people undergoing one form of training perform better on the job than those who have either been trained in another program or simply have been placed on the job. In all these situations, the measures of success are standards by which the value of the program can be judged. The most carefully designed study, employing all the sophisticated methodology that can be mustered, will stand or fall on the basis of the adequacy of the criteria chosen.

In Chapter 3, we traced the development of objectives through the techniques of organizational, task, and person analyses. These objectives state the terminal behavior, the conditions under which the terminal behavior is expected, and the standard below which the performance is unacceptable. Thus, as discussed in Chapter 4, good instructional objectives clearly state the criteria by which the trainee is judged. At this point, declaring the problem solved and proceeding to the next chapter would be tempting. Unfortunately, that is not possible. First, the choice of criteria is complex. Finding adequate measures of the success of a training program begins with the specification of objectives, and then it is necessary to determine that the measure is reliable and free from bias. Also, in addition to measuring success in the training program, it is necessary to measure success on the job, where the environment often makes the collection of valid criteria more complex.

There is also the question of the relationship between the measures chosen in training and subsequent performance on the job. Campion and Campion (1987) describe a carefully designed training program to help people entering the job market learn effective interviewing skills. The class members responded very positively to the program and demonstrated on an essay test that they had learned the principles being taught. However, interviewer evaluations of behavior produced no differences between trained and untrained groups, and there were also no differences in job offers received by the two groups. The careful evaluation by these researchers produced some reasons why this may have occurred, including the fact that the program may have been too short to produce actual behavior change, even though the candidates could express the principles on a written examination. One of the most important points is that the evaluation gave the researchers information on the impact of the program and what changes should be considered. In addition, these investigators carefully designed their criterion measures to provide the relevant required information. In many instances, problems begin with the choice of criteria as the complex goals represented by organizational objectives that are often difficult to measure. Guion (1961) describes with pointed humor the whole sequence of criterion selection. The following is an abbreviated version:

1. The psychologists have a hunch (or insight) that a problem exists and that they can help solve it.
2. They read a vague, ambiguous description of the job.
3. From these faint stimuli, they formulate a fuzzy concept of an ultimate criterion.
4. They formulate a combination of measures that will give them a satisfactory composite for the criterion they desire.
5. They judge the relevance of this measure—that is, the extent to which it is neither deficient nor contaminated.
6. They then find that the data required for their carefully built composite are not available in the company files, and there is no immediate prospect of having such records reliably kept.

7. Therefore, they select the best available criterion.

Wherry (1957) further warns us that this choice is often dictated by measurement considerations that are no more valid than an arbitrary choice. He notes that selecting a criterion just because it can be measured says, "We don't know what we are doing, but we are doing it very carefully, and hope you are pleased with our unintelligent diligence" (pp. 1–2). Little understanding can be gained by carefully measuring the wrong thing. Thus, these researchers suggest that criteria must also be carefully evaluated so that a good indicant of the impact of our instructional program may be obtained. In the following section we consider these issues of criterion evaluation.

More recently, Austin and Villanova (1992) stress the importance of clearly articulating the values involved in decisions as to what criterion measures to examine. They note that values in criterion research can be viewed from multiple stakeholder perspectives such as the employer, employee, and the researcher. Each stakeholder holds a different perspective as to what needs to be evaluated and how to evaluate success. For example, a poorly performing employee might favor less sensitive criterion measures that cannot distinguish between individuals very well. As they conclude, "decisions to include some measures of performance as criteria while excluding others makes the criterion problem that much more oblique" (p. 836).

THE EVALUATION OF CRITERIA

Criterion Relevancy

One purpose of needs assessment is the determination of the KSAs required for successful job performance. As shown in the instructional model developed in Chapter 2, that information must provide direct input into the training program to determine the actual content of the instructional material. The same information concerning the KSAs necessary for successful job performance should also provide the input for the establishment of measures of training success. Logically, we should want our training program to consist of the materials necessary to develop the KSAs to perform successfully on the job. Just as logically, we should determine the success of our training program by developing measures (or criteria) that tell the training evaluator how well the training program does in teaching the trainees the same KSAs necessary for job success. These criteria should be used at the end of the training program to determine how well it is doing. Then, they should be used again later on, when the trainee is on the job, to determine how much of the KSAs learned in training transferred to the actual job.

The chosen criteria are judged relevant to the degree that the components (KSAs) required to succeed in the training program reflect what is needed to succeed on the job. The fundamental requirement that transcends all other considerations related to criterion development is its relevance. Accurate job analysis and the ensuing behavioral objectives suggest more clearly the actual criteria to be employed in achieving the behavioral objectives. This relationship between objectives and criteria is an exercise in determining relevance. Figure 5.1 presents the relationship that can exist between items established by needs assessment and the items represented in the criteria chosen to assess the training program. The degree of overlap between these two sets establishes the relevance of the criteria. The term *criteria* refers to the many measures of success that must be used to evaluate instructional programs and the numerous objectives of training programs. The set on the left side shown in Figure 5.1 refers to KSAs. Most perspectives concerning training relate in some way to the trainee performance in learning and using the KSAs stemming from the needs assessment.

Marx and Hamilton (1991) argue for a much broader multiple perspective of the value of training programs. For example, they note that training often results in other positive benefits such as new networks and coalitions that can be built between trainees. We might argue that if such a benefit is a goal of the organization, it should be established as a result of a needs assessment so

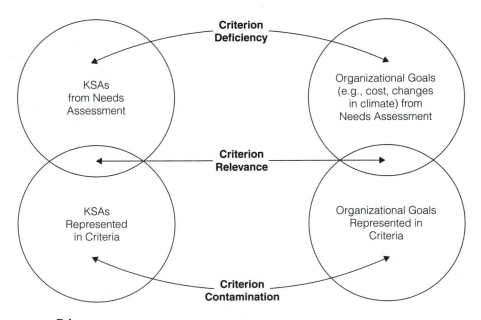

FIGURE 5.1

The constructs of criterion deficiency, relevance, and contamination.

that the programs can be designed to enhance such outcomes. Then, it would be useful to design relevant criteria to determine whether such outcomes occurred and, if necessary, how the program could be modified based on feedback concerning these results. However, it is just as possible to describe organizational goals established from a needs assessment and the degree to which these organizational goals are characterized in the criteria.

For example, Skarlicki and Latham (1997) describe a training program to train union leaders in the administration of organizational justice principles on union members. The criterion measures for this organizational-level change included measures of the perceptions of union members about their leaders' fairness and members' subsequent citizenship behavior toward their unions. These criteria were chosen to reflect organizational goals that the union wished to achieve. Again, the degree to which the criteria overlap with the organizational goals established through a needs assessment determines the relevance of the criterion set. These relationships are represented on the right side of Figure 5.1.

Another way of conceptualizing these relationships is presented in Figure 5.2. In this case, to simplify the diagram, the relationships are just presented for KSAs. However, the diagram could be redrawn to show the same relationships for organizational goals such as cost or citizenship behavior. In this diagram, the horizontal axis across the top of the figure represents KSAs determined by

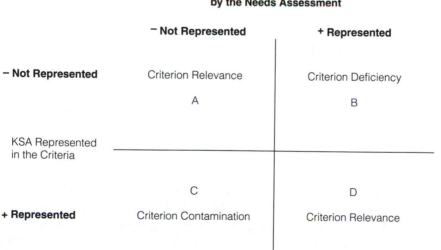

FIGURE 5.2

The relationship between criteria and needs assessment.

a needs assessment. As indicated below that title, there are two possibilities: The KSAs either are or are not represented. Similarly, along the vertical axis, the KSAs are shown as either represented or not represented in the criteria. This results in the four boxes labeled A, B, C, and D in Figure 5.2. Using this method of conceptualizing, boxes A and D are labeled criterion relevance. Box D identifies a situation where the KSAs are represented in both the needs assessment and the criteria. Box A represents a situation where the KSAs are not identified by the needs assessment as being part of the situation being studied, and thus the criteria appropriately are not designed to represent these KSAs. Essentially, this point of view says that relevance is determined by making sure the criteria contain components that have been determined as relevant for job success. Of course, it is only fair to point out that although we have drawn this diagram as a four-part table, it is actually a continuum. Thus, particular KSAs may be identified by a needs assessment as very important, a little important, not at all important, and so on. However, the idea that the criteria should measure those KSAs determined as relevant and not focus on those KSAs determined not to be relevant is still the essential point. Of course, the same point can be made about the contents of the training program. It also is supposed to contain materials related to the relevant component and not contain materials that are judged, as a result of a needs assessment, not to be relevant. This same model is presented for training programs later in Figure 6.6. The kinds of errors that can be made in this process are discussed next.

Criterion Deficiency

Criterion deficiency is the degree to which components are identified in a needs assessment that are not present in the actual criteria. This situation is represented in Figure 5.2 as box B. It is also represented in the upper circles in Figure 5.1. In many cases, it is necessary to make careful judgments about the relationship that is expected between the KSA components established in the needs assessment and the criteria used in the training program. Actually, there are several kinds of deficiency. The most obvious kind is the type represented in Figure 5.2. That is, an important KSA is identified but omitted from the criterion constructs. It may also be omitted from the training program itself. For example, an organization may expect all middle-level managers to be able to appraise the performance of their employees and provide feedback to the individual so each can improve his or her level of performance. However, the training courses may give managers general information about human relations but not provide any instructional material on the complex process of appraising the performance of employees. The material may not only be omitted from the training programs but also the criterion-development package. If this unfortunate event occurs, the manager is left not knowing how to perform the task, and the organization does not know that the manager cannot perform it. Sometimes the material is included in the training program, but criteria are still not developed to measure the manager's performance either in training or on the job. This also represents a deficiency. Again, the organization does not have information about the capabilities of the manager. The solution is to determine, throughout the methodology of needs assessment, the most appropriate multiple criteria to measure success. The complexity of these criteria should be represented in those criteria chosen to judge the initial success of individuals in the training program and on the job. Of course, depending on the level of expertise expected by the organization, there will be many instances in which the trainee does not perform with the same skill as an experienced worker. The criteria must reflect these differences.

A system's perspective that regards training as one part of an organizational system suggests that there are probably other forms of deficiency. It is quite possible that a needs assessment indicates that particular KSAs are required for the job but that there is no intention for the material to be learned through training. For example, a salesperson could be hired with the understanding that the individual already has all the necessary knowledge concerning the advantages and disadvantages of various advertising media. In this case, even though this knowledge component is identified as a critical item for job success, it is not to be learned in the training program. Thus, criteria developed for evaluation of the training program for the salesperson would not be deficient if criteria to measure this knowledge component were excluded. However, it should be represented in the selection system.

The issues related to deficient criteria are just as important in measuring organizational objectives. This adds a degree of complexity. It is one matter to specify all components that determine the success of an individual on required tasks, but it is another matter to determine appropriate criteria to measure organizational goals. Often this requires tracing out the entire process at multiple levels, including what criteria would be used to reflect changes at the organizational level as well as the individual employee level. Ford and Fisher (1994) developed such an analysis for issues regarding safety. A diagram (Figure 9.1) and discussion of such issues is presented in Chapter 9.

Criterion Contamination

Box C in Figure 5.2 and the lower circles in Figure 5.1 present a third concept—*criterion contamination*. This construct pertains to extraneous elements present in the criteria that result in the measure inaccurately representing the construct identified in the needs assessment. The existence of criterion contamination can lead to incorrect conclusions regarding the validity of training programs. For example, a supervisor may give better work assignments to those individuals who have participated in the new training program as compared with persons who have not been trained because they are "better equipped" to handle the assignment than those persons who have simply been placed on the job. When the data are collected, the persons who have been in training perform better but you don't know whether that was because of the training program or the increased opportunities to learn due to better work assignments. This type of contamination is known as *opportunity bias*.

Similar to this type of bias is the situation where trainees are rated higher by supervisors because they know that they have just finished the training program. Thus, when the training program is evaluated, it comes off well, but this may be because the supervisor is aware of who has been trained and gives them the benefit of the doubt when rating their performance as compared with people who have not been trained yet. This type of problem makes it difficult to evaluate what has been accomplished by the introduction of the training program.

Another type of contamination is known as *group-characteristic bias*. This type of bias stems from characteristics in the transfer setting that do not permit a person to perform at the level to which he or she has been trained. In some instances, trainees are not permitted to demonstrate the skills they have gained from the training program because informal or formal regulations do not permit them to work at capacity levels. For instance, experienced personnel may socially ostracize workers who produce at too rapid a rate, or regulations may restrict the use of particular equipment that might raise the level of production.

It is important to be continually aware of the potential danger of criterion contamination because, in many instances, control is possible. For example, training designers should keep trainee scores confidential and should control for factors like trainee work assignments.

Criterion Reliability

Criterion reliability refers to the consistency of the criteria measures. If the criteria are ratings of performance and little agreement exists between two raters, then there is low reliability. Correspondingly, consistently different performance scores by the same individual at different times also reflect low consistency and thus low reliability. Reliability is a necessary condition for stable criteria measures, but it is important to recognize that it will not replace the need for relevant criteria. Because reliability can be measured statistically, some evaluators emphasize it rather than relevance, but, as mentioned earlier, there is no utility in carefully measuring the wrong indicant of success.

There are many factors that can determine the reliability of a criterion measure. For example, if a rating scale is used to measure performance, low reliability sometimes results when the dimensions are not carefully specified. For example, the ability to provide leadership is not something that can be rated easily without further specification of what is meant by leadership. Some raters might try to determine whether the person provides information about what needs to be done and who should perform the task. Others might look to see if the individual has strong interpersonal skills such as providing positive feedback on performance. Unless the dimensions are carefully specified in ways that suggest what is to be observed and rated, low reliability results. Another reason for low reliability is when the rater does not have much opportunity to observe the performance of the individual.

Other Considerations

Besides relevancy and reliability, there are several other considerations in the evaluation of criteria. These include acceptability to the organization, cost, and realistic measures. These factors cannot replace relevancy and reliability, but they are of consequence to the organization. If these various factors have been accepted by the organization, the training analysts know that they are convincing the decision makers to accept criteria that are the most valid measures to judge the adequacy of the training program.

THE MANY DIMENSIONS OF CRITERIA

There are few, if any, single measures that can adequately reflect the complexity of most training programs and transfer performance. A study by O'Leary (1972) illustrates the importance of considering the many different dimensions of the criteria. She used a program of role playing and group problem-solving sessions with hard-core unemployed women. At the conclusion of the program, the trainees had developed positive changes in attitude toward themselves. However, it also turned out that these changes did not reflect the lack of positive attitudes toward their tedious, structured jobs. Rather, these trainees apparently raised their levels of aspiration and subsequently sought employment in a work setting consistent with their newly found expectations. In this instance, it was obvious that the trainees were leaving the job as well as experiencing positive changes in attitude. However, there are many other cases in which the collection of a variety of criteria related to the objectives is the only way to effectively evaluate the training program.

Considering that training programs must be examined with a multitude of measures, including participant reactions, learning, performance, and organizational objectives, it is necessary for training evaluators to view the criteria as multidimensional. Training can best be evaluated by examining many independent performance dimensions. However, the relationship between measures of success should be closely scrutinized because the inconsistencies that occur often provide important insights into training procedures. Decisions and feedback processes depend on the availability of all sources of information.

For instance, a particular training program might lead to increased achievement but dissatisfied participants. It is important to find out why the program is not viewed favorably so changes that might improve the reactions of the trainees may be considered.

There are many different dimensions by which criteria can vary, including the time the criteria are collected and the type of criterion data collected. These dimensions are not independent. For example, learning criteria and behavior on the job are not only different types of criteria but also vary according to the time of collection. Some of the more important dimensions that should be considered are discussed in the following sections.

Levels of Criteria

It is difficult to discuss any set of training criteria without beginning with Kirkpatrick's four levels of criteria—reaction, learning, behavior, and results. He first suggested that model in 1959 and 1960 in articles that are now considered classics. He has updated his observations concerning these criteria in 1994. Kirkpatrick's system is certainly by far the most influential and most used approach by training practitioners as well as being used by many researchers and thus is presented next. We do note that there have been debates about the usefulness of this system, and we will discuss those issues after presenting the approach.

Reaction.   Kirkpatrick defines *reaction* as what the trainees thought of the particular program. It does not include a measure of the learning that takes place. The following are suggested guidelines for determining participant reaction:

1. Design a questionnaire based on information obtained during the needs assessment phase. The questionnaire should be validated by carefully standardized procedures to ensure that the responses reflect the opinions of the participants.
2. Design the instrument so that the responses can be tabulated and quantified.
3. To obtain more honest opinions, provide for the anonymity of the participants. One of the best methods is a coding procedure that protects the individual participant but permits the data to be related to other criteria, like learning measures and performance on the job.
4. Provide space for opinions about items that are not covered in the questionnaire. This procedure often leads to the collection of important information that is useful in the redesign of the questionnaire.

5. Pretest the questionnaire on a sample of participants to determine its completeness, the time necessary for completion, and participant reactions.

Participant reaction is often a critical factor in the continuance of training programs. Responses on these types of questionnaires help ensure against decisions based on the comments of a few very satisfied or disgruntled participants. Most trainers believe that initial receptivity provides a good atmosphere for learning the material in the instructional program but does not necessarily cause high levels of learning. It is important to realize that reaction measures may not be related to learning and eventual performance on the job. It is entirely possible for participants to enjoy the training but not to produce the behavior that is the objective of the instruction. The study by Campion and Campion (1987) on interviewer training is such an example. In that instance, trainees not only had favorable reactions to the program but also demonstrated book knowledge of the principles on an essay exam. However, they could not demonstrate the required behaviors any better than a control group that had not been trained. The issue of the interrelationships of criterion measures is further discussed later. However, even if there is not a consistent relationship between trainee reactions and performance, few people would argue that it makes sense to run a training program that results in participants having unfavorable reactions.

One issue related to reaction measures might be that there are multiple facets to what is being examined. Morgan and Casper (2000) examined the multidimensionality of reaction measures taken from over 9000 government employees collected over three years across a variety of training programs including 800 classes for 400 different courses. Using factor analysis statistical techniques, they were able to find that the reaction measure seems to fall into six different groupings. As noted in Table 5.1, these groupings include various categories such as satisfaction with the instructor, satisfaction with the training management process, testing process, materials used, course structure, and utility of the program for the trainee. A few sample items for each of these categories is included to give you a feel for what types of participant reaction items make up each grouping. Their research suggests that more work needs to be done to actually understand what makes up participant reactions to training programs. An example (Grove & Ostroff, 1991) of an actual trainee reaction measure is shown in Table 5.2.

Learning.   The training analyst is concerned with measuring the learning of principles, facts, techniques, and attitudes that were specified as training objectives. The measures must be objective and quantifiable indicants of the learning that has taken place in the training program. They are not measures of performance on the job. There are many different measures of learning

TABLE 5.1   CATEGORIES REFLECTING THE MULTIDIMENSIONAL NATURE OF PARTICIPANT REACTIONS TO TRAINING

Category 1. Satisfaction with the Instructor

How satisfied are you with the instructor's ability to keep the class's interest?
How satisfied are you with the instructor's overall effectiveness?

Category 2. Satisfaction with the Training Management/Administration Process

How satisfied are you with the communication of training information to employees in your facility?
How satisfied are you with the registration process and information you received prior to arrival at training?

Category 3. Satisfaction with the Course Testing Process

How satisfied are you with exam coverage and importance of material tested?
How satisfied are you with feedback you received as a result of course testing?

Category 4. Utility of Training Program

How satisfied are you with the relevance of the course content to your job?
How satisfied are you with the extent to which the course prepared you to perform new job tasks?

Category 5. Satisfaction with the Course Materials

How satisfied are you with the audio and visual aids used by the instructor?
How satisfied are you with the classrooms, furniture, learning environment, and so on?

Category 6. Satisfaction with the Course Structure

How satisfied are you with the pace of the course material presented?

Source: Adapted from "Examining the Factor Structure of Participant Reactions to Training: A Multi-dimensional Approach," by R. B. Morgan and W. Casper, 2000, *Human Resources Development Quarterly, 11*, pp. 301–317. Copyright © 2000 Jossey-Bass, Inc. Reprinted by permission of Jossey-Bass, Inc., a subsidiary of John Wiley & Sons, Inc.

performance, including paper-and-pencil tests, learning curves, and job components. Again, the objectives determined from a needs assessment must be the most important determinants of the measure to be employed.

The importance of developing good proficiency measures for training is illustrated in a study training older adults to use an automatic teller machine ATM (Rogers, Fisk, Mead, Walker, Cabrera, 1996). In this study, participants who had never used an ATM were trained on a computer-simulated ATM that had all the standard features. Participants used a computer mouse (on which they were pre-trained) so that the finger on the mouse could point to the desired button, graphic, object, or keypad numbers. Data were collected on the percent correct responses for obtaining account information, fast cash, deposits, withdrawal, and transfer. There were several different training pro-

TABLE 5.2	PART OF A FORM USED TO OBTAIN TRAINEE REACTIONS

Instructions: For each statement below, circle the number that best describes the extent to which you agree or disagree with that statement using the following scale: (1) "Strongly Disagree;" (2) "Disagree;" (3) "Neither Agree nor Disagree;" (4) "Agree;" and (5) "Strongly Agree." If you do not agree with a statement, please clarify this issue further in the "Other Comments" section at the end.

	Strongly Disagree	Disagree	Neither Agree nor Agree	Agree	Strongly Agree
1. The objectives of this program were clear.	1	2	3	4	5
2. The instructor(s)/trainer(s) was/were helpful and contributed to the learning experience.	1	2	3	4	5
3. There was an appropriate balance between lecture, participant involvement, and exercises in the program.	1	2	3	4	5
4. The topics covered in this program were relevant to the things I do on my job.	1	2	3	4	5
5. I can see myself performing more effectively after attending this program.	1	2	3	4	5
6. The logistics for this program (e.g., arrangements, food/beverage, room equipment) were satisfactory.	1	2	3	4	5

7. The length of the program was (circle one):
   (1) Too long   (2) Too short   (3) Just right

8. Overall, how would you rate this program (circle one)?
   (1) Poor   (2) Fair   (3) Good   (4) Very good   (5) Excellent

9. What from this program was *most* valuable for you?

Source: Reprinted by permission from Chapter 5.6 "Program Evaluation," by David A. Grove and Cheri Ostroff, Figure 2, pp. 5–211, from *Developing Human Resources*, edited by Kenneth N. Wexley and John Hinrichs. Copyright © 1991 by The Bureau of National Affairs, Inc., Washington, D.C. 20037. For copies of BNA Books publications call toll free 1-800-960-1220.

cedures ranging from reading a description of the ATM, a pictorial guide, a text guide, and an on-line learning tutorial. The tutorial proved to be the most effective technique. Learning data was collected across a series of 20 trials and then later on after a twenty-four-hour retention period had passed. The information in Figure 5.3 shows the data for these conditions. Each of the initial practice blocks averages 5 of the 20 learning trials. The twenty-four-hour retention period is also shown.

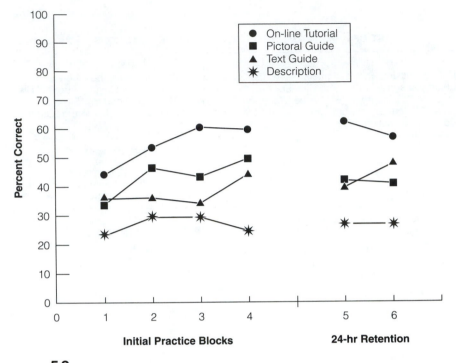

Initial Practice Blocks   **24-hr Retention**

FIGURE **5.3**

Percentage of correct transactions across the initial practice and 24-hour retention blocks for each instructional group.

Source: From "Training Older Adults to Use Automatic Teller Machines," by W. A. Rogers, A. D. Fisk, S. E. Mead, N. Walker, and W. Cabrera. In *Human Factors, 38,* 3, 1996, pp. 425–431. Copyright © 1996 by the Human Factors and Ergonomics Society, Inc. Reprinted by permission. All rights reserved.

Another illustration, involving peer evaluations of police trainees at the end of their eleven-week training program, is offered by Goldstein and Bartlett (1977). Trainees were to rate each other based on the following instructions for a recruit backup questionnaire:

> Again, assume that your recruit class has graduated, and that all of you are police officers in X city. If you were to find yourself in a crisis situation (such as an armed robbery, a high-speed chase, a domestic dispute, a drug raid, a multiple-car accident), which five members of your recruit class would you *most like to have as your backup.* On the following page is an alphabetical list of the members of your recruit class. *First,* find you own name and draw a line through it. *Second,* go through the remaining names and circle the five names you would most like to have as your backup in a crisis situation. Make sure you consider all names before choosing. *Then circle five and only five names.*

The paper nominations did not correlate with grades and other learning measures at the end of the eleven-week police academy training measures. However, the peer nominations did predict a later training performance measure. That is, the police trainees, after graduating from the academy, went into field training, with each trainee assigned to an individual field-training officer. The length of time that the trainee stayed in field training was determined by each trainee's performance as judged by the training officer. The peer nominations at the end of academy training correlated $r = -.43$ with the number of days that a trainee spent in field training. That is, the more positive the peer nominations, the *fewer* days were spent in field training. Evidently, the trainees' peers saw something in the performance of their fellow trainees that was not reflected in their grades in the police training academy.

Behavior.   Kirkpatrick uses the term *behavior* in reference to the measurement of job performance. Just as favorable reaction does not necessarily mean that learning occurs in the training program, superior training performance does not always result in similar behavior in the transfer setting. Data related to these types of relationships is presented in another section of this chapter. A large number of measures can be employed to assess on-the-job performance. It is important to ensure that on-the-job measures are related to the objectives of the training program. Because training is not usually intended to relate to all job functions, using a job-performance measure that is unrelated to the objectives of the training program can be misleading.

Latham and Wexley (1981) offer a large number of behavioral rating item examples for a number of different jobs, based on careful needs assessment. For example, managers who had been trained in these areas could be rated from "almost never" to "almost always" on the following types of items based on job performance:

- Establishes mechanisms for spotting trends/patterns in key departmental/functional areas.
- Clearly defines the role responsibilities of key managers.

A mechanic in a bowling alley might be rated on the following items:

- Asks the mechanic leaving the shift what machines need watching.
- Checks the tension of chains weekly and keeps them oiled.

In another example, a training program might be developed to teach police officers to state factual information objectively when describing a crime incident. In that instance, some on-the-job behaviors that might be examined could include those presented in Table 5.3. As you might imagine, being able to perform such behaviors is just as important as being able to accurately fire a weapon.

Results.   Kirkpatrick uses this category to relate the results of the training program to organizational objectives. Some results that could be examined include costs, turnover, absenteeism, grievances, and morale. In Chapter 3, we described the various components of organizational analysis, including goals

TABLE 5.3   **EXAMPLE OF ONE PERFORMANCE DIMENSION FOR EVALUATION OF POLICE OFFICERS**

1. Ability to state factual information objectively without interjecting personal biases
   Please rate the behaviors listed below from

Almost Never				*Almost Always*
1	2	3	4	5

   A. Clearly separates fact from personal opinion.

   B. Uses neutral words and professional terminology in presenting situation.

   C. Develops conclusions that flow logically from incident facts.

   D. Does not attempt to hide or minimize rule violation even when directly questioned.

   E. Does not attempt to omit discrepant information from presentation of facts.

   F. Does not attempt to embellish or exaggerate facts.

and objectives, which in turn should suggest relevant organizational criteria. Again, it is important to emphasize the tracing-out process so that relevant criteria stemming from the needs assessment are developed. A criterion that has received increasing attention over the last several years is cost. Many organizations have designed instructional programs in the hope that it will reduce other costs. Thus, an entry-level sales-training course is used in the hope that the trainee, upon beginning the job, can produce at a higher rate than might otherwise be expected. Obviously, these kinds of analyses require very careful detailing of all the costs and gains associated with training.

Mirabal (1978) outlines the costs associated with the actual instructional program. Table 5.4 shows some of these costs as related to the trainee, the instructor, and the facilities. Other charts developed by Mirabal address items such as training development costs. An important addition to the concept of cost in evaluating training programs is the idea of utility. Most of the work involving utility has been applied to the usefulness of selection programs, but Cascio (1989) has applied the concepts to training programs. The basic idea is that the utility of a training program is the translation of validity information into cost figures that permit comparisons between different types of programs. The use of such concepts considerably increases the number of ways one would measure the success of a training program. For example, it is possible to ask what the training program will add to other interventions, such as a selection system, which itself has varying degrees of success. It is also possible to ask what the utility of a formal training program is, as compared to expecting employees to learn on the job from other, more experienced people. Here, it becomes necessary to ask what differences in productivity for the new employee result from the two approaches, what is the loss in productivity from people on the job who have to teach the employee (compared to the cost of

TABLE 5.4 CHART FOR SPECIFYING TRAINING COSTS

DATE:

Chart I: Trainee Costs

Course Title	Trainees and Hours				Salary		Travel and Per Diem	Materials and Supplies	Total Trainee Costs	
	No. of Trainees	Level and Step	Curriculum Hours	Trainees Hours	Hourly Salary Plus Benefits	Total Salary	Annual Travel and Per Diem	Annual Cost	Total Trainee Cost	Trainee Cost per Trainee Hour
	1	2	3	4	5	6	7	8	9	10

Chart II: Instructor Costs

Course Title	Agency Instructors							Non-Organization Instructors			Travel and Per Diem		Total Instructor Costs	
	No. Instructors and Level	Salary per Hour	Over-head per Hour	Salary Plus Over-head	Hours per Year	Annual Salary Plus Over-head Cost	Annual Salary Plus Over-head Cost per Trainee Hour	No. Instruc-tors	Annual Salary or Fee	Annual Salary per Trainee Hour	Annual Travel and Per Diem	Annual Travel and Per Diem per Trainee Hour	Total Annual Instruc-tor Costs	Annual Instruc-tor Costs per Trainee Hour
	1	2	3	4	5	6	7	8	9	10	11	12	13	14

(Continued)

159

TABLE 5.4 CONTINUED

DATE:

Chart III: Facilities Costs

Course Title	Non-Organization Owned Space				Improvement to Space		Equipment and Furnishings			Total Facilities Costs	
	Annual Cost of Required Space	% of Time Used for Course	Annual Cost of Space for Course	Cost per Trainee Hour	Cost per Year	Annual Cost per Trainee Hour	Total Cost of Items	Annual Cost of Items for Course	Annual Cost of Items per Trainee Hour	Total Annual Facilities Cost	Annual Facilities Cost per Trainee Hour
	1	2	3	4	5	6	7	8	9	10	11

Source: Adapted from "Forecasting Future Training Costs," by T. E. Mirabal. In *Training and Development Journal,* 1978, *32,* pp. 78–87. Copyright 1978 by the American Society for Training and Development, Inc. Adapted by permission.

the formal training program), and what is the dollar payoff to the organization? If the cost of formal training is very great and the production return is very little and if the employee moves on to other jobs in a short time, a formal training program may not be worth it. A study (Gattiker, 1995) conducted on semiskilled employees, such as telephone operators and mail clerks, in Canada demonstrated such effects. The study involved approximately 170 firms and examined government-subsidized computer training for these semiskilled workers. The results analyzed wages earned for the individual as well as training costs for the organization. These data indicated that government sponsorship resulted in positive returns for the firms and individuals when the training was general and not firm-specific. High turnover made firm-specific training unattractive.

The Interrelationship of Reaction, Learning, Behavior, and Results

Although all these categories of criteria are important, and comparisons across the four types would be interesting, few studies have collected data across all types of criteria. Also, as noted in a survey of over 600 firms, the most commonly collected criterion measure is the reaction of participants (Saari, Johnson, McLaughlin, & Zimmerle, 1988).

In 1982 Clement reported being unable to find any literature that might clarify the relationships between these types of measures. In 1989, Alliger and Janek reported they found twelve articles on training programs reporting twenty-six correlations between various criteria. More recently, Alliger and his colleagues (Alliger, Tannenbaum, Bennett, Traver, Shotland, 1997) reexamined the literature. Consistent with the growth of the training literature, they found 34 studies with 115 correlations to examine. Based on their analyses, they suggested an augmented framework for Kirkpatrick's taxonomy of reaction, learning, behavior, and results. That framework is presented in Table 5.5.

In their conception, Alliger et al. divide the reaction category into two types: affective, which typically means whether the participant found the program enjoyable; and utility, in other words, whether the training was viewed by the participant as being relevant and having practical value in the sense that it improved the trainee's ability to perform his or her job. Of course, it is also possible for a measure to contain both affective and utility aspects. Interestingly, another set of investigators (Warr & Bruce, 1995) also suggested enjoyment of training and usefulness of training as components of reaction measure. Furthermore, they suggested a third concept, training difficulty, but there do not seem to be many reaction measures that incorporate this component so data on this later concept is very limited.

<table>
<tr><td>TABLE
5.5</td><td colspan="2">TRAINING CRITERIA TAXONOMIES</td></tr>
</table>

Kirkpatrick's Taxonomy	Augmented Framework
Reaction	Reaction Affective Reactions Utility Judgments
Learning	Learning Immediate Knowledge Knowledge Retention Behavior/Skill Demonstration
Behavior	Transfer
Results	Results

Source: From "A Meta-Analysis of the Relations Among Training Criteria," by G. M. Alliger, S. I. Tannenbaum, W. Bennett, H. Traver, and A. Shotland. In *Personnel Psychology,* 1997, *50,* pp. 341–358. Copyright 1997 by Personnel Psychology, Inc. Reprinted by permission.

The study by Morgan and Casper (see Table 5.1) suggests six possible reaction components. These authors note that their utility category is very similar in makeup to the utility factor identified by Alliger and Janek and that was the category that actually seemed to relate to learning and transfer measures. However, Morgan and Casper also note that their category of satisfaction with the instructor carried great weight in the trainees' overall judgment of the training effort and also was highly linked to trainee perceptions of the utility of the training program. They note that perhaps understanding what leads to satisfaction with the instructor will help us understand further how this relates to perception of the utility of the training program. Clearly, this is a topic that will be explored further in research studies over the next several years.

As presented in Table 5.5, Alliger and his colleagues also divide the learning measure into a number of categories. The first is immediate post-training knowledge, which is a fairly common assessment in training programs. This is an assessment of what the trainee knows about the topic presented, and the most common measure of this category is a traditional paper-and-pencil test. The second category, knowledge retention, is where evaluators assess what has been learned at a later period of time. The third category is behavior/skill retention. These authors have developed as part of the learning a category referring to a measure of behavior during training. This could refer to behavioral role plays, performance on a simulator, and so on. The reader probably will note that the first two knowledge measures are traditional: one right after training and one at a retention period some time later. It could actually be possible to have two such levels for behavior/skill demonstration, one immediately after training and one later on as a retention test. In that case, the learning category would look as follows:

	Knowledge Measurement	Behavior/Skill Demonstration
Immediate		
Retention		

The 24-hour retention period in the study of the ATM shown in Figure 5.3 is an example of behavior/skill demonstration as a retention measure.

Alliger and his colleagues make it clear for Kirkpatrick's Level 3, known as behavior, that they mean behavior that is part of transfer performance or on-the-job performance. In our judgment, this is a useful clarification. Using the 34 studies and the 115 correlations, the researchers then examined the inter-relationships and the patterns of results between the criteria in the augmented framework. In general, they found the following:

1. *Correlations involving reaction measures.* Previous analyses (Alliger & Janek, 1989) found that the relationships among reaction measures and the other three criteria in the Kirkpatrick system were very limited, and the only conclusion that could be reached at that time is that there is no established relationship. Using the augmented system, they again found that when reaction measures focused on affective reactions, there was virtually no relationship to learning. On the other hand, when reaction measures focused on utility reactions, there were some relationships with the learning measures. Thus, the reaction measure known as utility correlated $r = .26$ with immediate learning measures and $r = .18$ with transfer measures but did not relate well to behavior measure. As the authors note in quoting a reviewer who had read their paper, perhaps "what we think is useful may correlate with what we use" (p. 352). One could certainly make the argument that positive perceptions of the future utility of a training program should logically lead to stronger learning performance than perceptions of whether the experience was enjoyable. On the other hand, it is interesting to note that there is also a relationship between the two types of reaction measures, that is, the affective perception and utility perception of $r = .34$. All of this seems to say that people enjoy the program more when they think it is related to their job.

2. *Correlations involving learning measures.* These authors found that immediate knowledge and knowledge retention measures (see Table 5.5) were related (correlation of $r = .35$). The immediate knowledge and behavior measures had a less robust relationship (correlation of

$r = .18$) as did the measures of knowledge retention and behavior (correlation of $r = .14$). Of course, the issue here is that typically the immediate and retained measures as knowledge measures are more similar in nature, and thus the relationship could be partially based on method similarities. On the other hand, the relationship of either immediate knowledge or retained knowledge with behavior/skill demonstrations really matches up very different methods and is probably a better test of whether relationships actually exist. Still, they did find some limited relationships. In addition, while there were many more studies to draw these analyses as compared to when these relationships were first examined in 1989, it is still the case that the number of studies is quite small. Thus, it will probably take several sets of other studies to be sure of these relationships.

3. *Correlations between learning and transfer onto the job.* The relationships between immediate, retained, and behavior within training with transfer were also quite modest with correlations of .11, .08, and .18. This indicates that the current learning measures obtained in these studies are not very predictive of how well a person actually transfers the learning to the job.

Two studies correlated immediate learning with results, and the finding was a robust $r = .52$, but with only two studies those data sets are not yet large enough to be quite sure of the relationships. On the other hand, almost all of these relationships are going in the right direction and more data are being collected. The signs are encouraging. Also, when these authors examined the reliability of each of these training measures, the results were very good. This is an important sign that data are being collected carefully and systematically. While one can lament the fact that there is not yet more data, it is also fair to say that the positive change in the number of carefully crafted studies over the last ten years is very encouraging.

A Conceptually Based Classification Scheme of Learning

Kraiger, Ford, and Salas (1993) criticize most of the criterion classification schemes such as Kirkpatrick's model as simplistic and unidimensional. They argue that classification schemes need to be developed that probe the richness of the learning variables being explored and described in models such as those presented in Gagné's systems. Gagné's model is described in Chapter 4, and Table 4.2 describes some of its components. Figure 5.4 describes parts of the model derived by Kraiger, Ford, and Salas. In their model, these authors divide learning outcomes into three central types. They are the *cognitive outcomes*, which reflect concepts like knowledge and cognitive strategies. Then, there are the more *skill-based outcomes*, such as the automaticity constructs presented in Chapter 4. And finally, there are *affective outcomes*, such as atti-

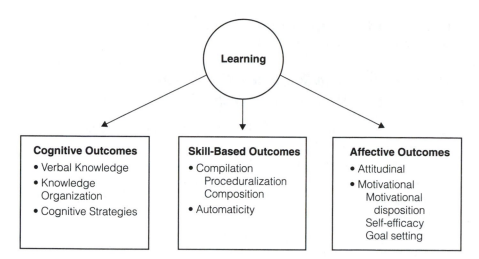

FIGURE 5.4

A preliminary classification scheme of learning outcomes.

Source: From "Applications of Cognitive, Skill-based, and Affective Theories of Learning Outcomes to New Methods of Training Evaluation," by K. Kraiger, J. K. Ford, and J. E. Salas. In *Journal of Applied Psychology*, 1993, *78*, pp. 311–328. Copyright 1993 by American Psychological Association. Reprinted by permission.

tudinal or motivational constructs like self-efficacy and goal setting. The reader will probably note that the presentation by Kraiger, Ford, and Salas parallels Chapter 4 in this text, which describes exactly these kinds of learning variables. The authors essentially argue that when you think of Kirkpatrick's scheme, it is misleadingly simple because it does not fully describe many of the relevant learning outcomes. Also, these authors argue that when you are designing training to influence one of these types of outcomes, such as affective outcomes, you have to design the criteria to match those types of outcomes. They further argue that you will have a better measure of whether anything is being achieved in training if you match the outcomes most carefully to what is being learned. The use of a simple measure such as a multiple-choice knowledge test at the end of training does not examine the richness of what is going on during the learning process in training. Thus, in examining cognitive outcomes, they would recommend that we carefully specify for each of the components what is to be measured. For example, in testing for knowledge organization, the authors would test for how knowledge is organized by examining the mental models of the learner. They might test a pilot by determining what mental models he or she has for preflight briefings, takeoffs, landings, and so on. The reader should note that in Chapter 4 we describe how novices and experts differ in the complexity of their mental models. These authors extend that work by suggesting the development of criteria that are specific to the types of learning described in Chapter 4. This kind of work has serious implications for how you develop and measure changes that are specific to what the trainer is trying to achieve.

Outcome Criteria and Summative Evaluation: Process Criteria and Formative Evaluation

Outcome measures refer to criteria, like learning and performance, that represent various levels of achievement. Some investigators use the term *summative evaluation* when referring to evaluations that focus on outcome measures such as those in the Kirkpatrick model. Thus, summative evaluation describes assessments using outcome measures that focus on the effectiveness of completed interventions. Campbell (1988) discriminates between two types of summative evaluations. The first type, simply labeled summative evaluation, refers to the question of whether a particular training program produces the expected outcomes. The comparison is between a trained and untrained group. Campbell notes that a more powerful question is the comparative summative evaluation where the question is which of two or more training methods produces the greatest benefits. There have been much fewer of these types of efforts. One instance of such comparisons is in work on investigating programmed instruction versus a conventional method, usually a straight classroom lecture procedure. In those comparisons, the usual outcome has been that programmed instruction produces quicker learning to mastery of the subject, but the eventual level of learning retention is the same with either technique.

Although outcome measures and summative evaluations are critical in determining the viability of instructional programs, reliance only on outcome measures often makes it difficult to understand why certain kinds of results were achieved. Another approach to evaluation is known as *formative evaluation*, which focuses on process criteria to provide further information to help understand the training system so that the originally intended objectives are achieved. Brown and his colleagues (Brown, Werner, Johnson, & Dunne, 1999) note several potential benefits that can occur from formative evaluation. These include collecting information to change training programs to reach their original objectives. In addition, their approach focuses on collecting information from participants and stakeholders to ensure that the program meets their needs. It also inquires as to how the program can be improved and provides information about why a particular program might work.

In past editions of this text, Goldstein stressed the importance of process measures that examine what happens during instruction. This emphasis is illustrated in the training instructional model in Figure 2.1 by the arrow between "Training" and "Use of Evaluation Models." It is not unusual for a training program to bear little relationship to the originally conceived format. One of Goldstein's favorite examples occurred in a basic-learning laboratory, where the experimenter's ability to control the setting supposedly prevents these events. In this study, a pigeon was trained to peck at a key for food. Later in the experiment, the researcher noted that the response rate of the animal was surprisingly low. The researcher decided to observe the pigeon and discovered that it was not pecking the key to earn reinforcement. Instead, it was running across the cage and smashing into the wall that held the key, thereby setting off the mechanism and earning food! This example was used in the very first edition of this book, and it often prompted readers to ask if the incident was true or made up for the sake of the book. It was enjoyable to inform people that it was true! Even in basic research laboratories, complete reliance on outcome measures often misleads the investigator.

Even the use of rigorous experimental designs does not necessarily provide the investigator with the degree of understanding that is anticipated. Evaluation designs and specification of outcome criteria have often been based on a product, or outcome, view of training validity. Thus, researchers sometimes collected pre-criterion and post-criterion measures, compared them with control groups, and sometimes discovered that they did not understand the results they had obtained. This problem becomes especially apparent when these data collectors were outside consultants who collected pre-data and post-data but had no conception of the processes that had occurred in training between the pre-measurement and post-measurement. An experience of one of the authors of this text illustrates this issue.

> In a study of computer-assisted instruction (CAI) in a school setting, two teachers agreed to instruct a geometry class by traditional methodology and by computer-assisted instruction. Each teacher taught one traditional and one CAI class. Further, the teachers agreed to work together to design an exam that would cover material presented in each of the classes. At the end of the first testing period, the traditional classes taught by each teacher significantly outperformed the CAI groups taught by the same teachers. However, at a later testing, one of the CAI groups improved to the extent that it was equivalent to the two traditional groups. The other CAI group performed significantly worse than the other three instructional groups. One reasonable conclusion for this series of events might be that one of the teachers learned how to instruct the CAI group so that it was now equivalent to the two traditional groups, but the other teacher had not been able to perform that task with the other CAI group. Indeed, if the investigators had only collected the outcome measures, this or other similar erroneous conclusions would probably have been offered as explanations for the data. In this case, the investigators also observed and maintained diaries describing the instructional process to provide further information about the program. In this way, the evaluators learned that the instructor for the CAI group that eventually improved had become disturbed over the performance of his students. As a result, the teacher offered remedial tutoring and essentially turned the CAI class into a traditional group.

From an organizational psychology perspective, process measures might provide important insights for the analysis of instructional programs in organizations. As indicated, process measures can help determine the source of the effect. If it is found that the trainers' attitudes or the trainees' expectations account for a substantial portion of the variance in the outcomes, those variables must be considered in the design of instructional programs. The utilization of process measures may provide all sorts of unanticipated dividends. For example, in one case we experienced, high-level executives were astonished to discover that the reason entry-level grocery clerks could not operate the cash register was that the instructional sequence was no longer part of their carefully designed instructional program. It turned out that over a period of time, various trainers had modified the contents of the program.

Another perspective on these events is that there are both intended and unintended outcomes that result from our programs. This view stresses the concern for side effects, which is familiar to medical researchers but has not been emphasized by many training researchers. For example, it is possible to consider the side effects of a training program for hard-core unemployed workers. Because such a program would place more minority group workers on the job, it might have the unintended and unwanted effect of increasing racial tensions by introducing workers with different sets of personal and social values. Or, the program might have a positive side effect by making management more aware of the need to enhance efforts to improve the climate in the organization toward diversity. By carefully considering these possibilities, criteria could be established to measure these unintended outcomes so that information is available to determine side effects. In many cases, these criterion data become important elements in shaping policy and determining future objectives.

Again, this view reinforces the belief that criterion development should be approached with thoughtful emphasis on broadly relevant criteria. Research involving formative evaluation and the collection of process criteria has been fairly limited. However, some of the kinds of process measures that could contribute to formative evaluations could be the collection of information through daily diaries and the use of expert review.

Time Dimension

Criteria also vary according to time of collection. Thus, learning criterion measures are taken early in training, and behavior criterion measures are taken after the individual has completed the training program and transferred to the new activity. Figure 5.5 depicts the time dimensions of criteria. In this diagram, *immediate criteria* refer to those measures that are available during the training program. *Proximal criteria* are measures that are available shortly after the initial training program. They might include performance in an advanced section of the training program or initial success on the job. *Distal criteria* are available after considerable time in the transfer setting. There are no exact rules that tell when to measure or when a proximal criterion becomes a distal criterion. Several previously mentioned examples in this chapter illus-

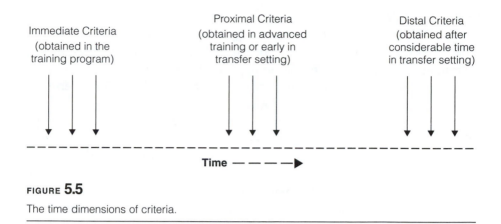

FIGURE **5.5**

The time dimensions of criteria.

trate the time dimensions of criteria. Goldstein and Bartlett (1977) discuss the use of peer nominations collected at the end of a police academy training program and a later field-training measure consisting of the number of days required to complete field training.

TYPES OF CRITERIA

This section provides a few general criterion categories that are meaningful for training research but have not been emphasized in previous sections. These categories include criterion- and norm-referenced measures and objective and subjective measures.

Criterion- and Norm-Referenced Measures

Criterion-referenced measures depend on an absolute standard of quality, whereas norm-referenced measures depend on a relative standard. *Criterion-referenced measures* provide a standard of achievement for the individual as compared with specific behavioral objectives and therefore provide an indicant of the degree of competence attained by the trainee. *Norm-referenced measures* compare the capabilities of an individual with those of other trainees. Thus, schools administer nationally standardized exams that determine the individual's standing in comparison with a national sample. The norm-referenced measures tell us that one student is more proficient than another, but they do not provide much information about the degree of proficiency in relationship to the tasks involved. Unfortunately, many training evaluations have employed norm-referenced measures to the exclusion of other forms of measurement. To properly evaluate training programs, it is necessary to obtain criterion-referenced measures that provide information about the skill level of the trainee in relationship to the expected program achievement levels. Data informing us that the student is equal to or above 60% of the population provide little information about his or her specific capabilities; thus, it is difficult to design modifications to improve the program.

Although there are not many examples of the use of criterion-referenced measures in training settings, it is obvious that many of the rules for the development of test items follow the philosophy of the critical importance of criterion relevancy espoused in this chapter. Readers interested in the procedures necessary to develop criterion-referenced measures should consult an excellent book by Swezey (1981).

One example of the development of such measures in a training situation is offered in a study by Panell and Laabs (1979). These investigators were interested in using criterion-referenced measures for a training program for navy boiler technicians. They designed a set of 186 items by setting up hypothetical job situations that required the knowledge and skills contained in each of the training modules. They then had job experts check the items to determine the correspondence between the job situations and the knowledge and skills and to ensure adequate question representation for each module. The hypothetical job situations were also checked to determine that each situation was based on known job requirements and that each situation used job materials such as maintenance requirement cards, charts describing maintenance actions, and illustrations of tools and equipment.

Panell and Laabs (1979) followed these procedures with empirical methods to establish the reliability of the items and cutoff scores for passing and failing. This resulted in 127 usable items. The investigators then administered the test to seventy-five trainees who were about to enter the training course and another seventy-five trainees who had just completed the course. They then compared the results of the performance of the two groups on the test items. Those results are presented in Table 5.6. Using the cutoff scores established by these investigators, it is possible to see that in a large number of cases, the test items did differentiate between the two groups. For example, in module 1, 88% of the individuals who were in either the group entering training or who had completed training were identified correctly by their test-score performance. That is, people who had completed training knew the test items stemming from the needs assessment, whereas people entering training did not know the test items. For that same module, 4% of the pre-instruction group did well enough on the test that they were identified as not needing training, and 8% of the group that had completed training was still identified as needing training. Of course, there could be many reasons why some people were misidentified. It is possible that some trainees knew the materials before they entered and that others did not know the materials after they completed the course. If that happened with large numbers of people, it could also be

TABLE
5.6

TABLE 5.6   HITS AND MISSES IN CLASSIFICATION OF TRAINEES

Module	% False Positives[a]	% False Negatives[b]	% Hits
1	8	4	88
2	22	0	78
3	16	16	68
4	8	6	86
5	12	14	74
6	2	6	92
7	8	6	86
8	18	10	72
9	12	10	78
10	16	4	80
11	10	2	88
12	8	4	88
13	12	2	86
14	8	2	90

[a] A false positive is diagnosing a preinstruction group member as not needing training.
[b] A false negative is diagnosing a postinstructional group member as needing training.
Source: From "Construction of a Criterion-Reference Diagnostic Test for an Individualized Instruction Program," by R. C. Panell and G. J. Laabs. In *Journal of Applied Psychology,* 1979, *64,* pp. 255–261. Copyright 1979 by the American Psychological Association. Reprinted by permission.

possible that the test items were not very well constructed or that the training course was not doing its job.

As Swezey (1981) points out, it is critical that the criteria be developed with an emphasis on criterion relevance. Otherwise, it is not possible to make any judgments about the training program or the level of knowledge of the trainees. In conducting these types of studies, it is important to consider the quote by Swezey:

> First, it must be determined that objectives have been properly derived from adequate task analyses that prescribe clearly what an examinee must do or must know in order to perform the task under examination. Second, each item must be carefully evaluated against its associated objective to ensure that the performances, conditions, and standards specified in the item are the same as those required by the objective. (p. 151)

Objective and Subjective Measures

Measures that require the statement of opinions, beliefs, or judgments are considered subjective. For example, rating scales are subjective measures, whereas measures of absenteeism are more objective. (However, supervisors' ratings of the absenteeism level of employees could turn that measure into a subjective criterion.) Objective measures—for example, rate of production—are especially vulnerable to criterion contamination based on opportunity bias, whereas subjective measures are affected by the difficulties that one individual has in rating another without bias. For various reasons, rating scales have been the most commonly employed measures in applied settings. This appears to be the case partially because there are not many objective measures of the performance of individuals in complex jobs, such as that of manager. Professionals who have developed relevant-criterion measures know that the steps in the process are very similar for objective and subjective measures and that shortcuts do not work in either case. For any criterion, the issues discussed in this chapter, such as relevance, deficiency, and contamination, are critical. The tracing-out process from the needs assessment in order to develop relevant criteria is the same for both objective and subjective measures.

Goldstein and Bartlett have developed an approach for linking behavioral rating scale items directly to a needs assessment. They run workshops where job-knowledge experts are trained to write rating scale items. As input, they are given task items and asked to write behavior items that reflect effective, ineffective, and average performance on the task. Thus, they tie the rating items directly to the needs assessment by using input tasks identified in the needs assessment as critical tasks. The instructions they use for this procedure are presented in Table 5.7. After the development of these behavioral items, they still have to be edited, judged to be certain they are important behaviors (as described in Chapter 3), and checked for reliability. However, the starting point is that these behaviors are tied to important tasks for that job.

Some interesting research by Ostroff (1991) raises the possibility of using ratings more effectively in evaluating training research. Her analysis suggests that ratings, which are the most commonly used measures of behavior change, often do not show positive effects of training. On the other hand, the use of other measures such as work samples seems to produce more positive results. She suggests that might occur because the traditional rating scales are not designed in a way that allows raters who are judging the performance of trainees to easily and accurately recall and report observations of others. Ostroff notes that cognitive psychologists contend that scripts specifying a sequence of events or behaviors leading up to an outcome can enhance performance. In a rating situation, it is possible to have a script that might enhance the performance of raters by making it easier for them to recall and remember specific behaviors. In this case, the script would contain sequences of interconnected behaviors, rather than the individual items usually found on a rating scale. An example of a script is found in Table 5.8.

TABLE
5.7

INSTRUCTIONS FOR PERFORMANCE-MEASUREMENT WORKSHOP

Industrial/Organizational Psychology Program
Department of Psychology
University of Maryland
College Park, Maryland 20742

The industrial/organizational psychology program at the University of Maryland has agreed to help develop rating scales for the use of the Police Department. This rating scale will be used as part of the appraisal system for police officers. During the past several weeks, the personnel department has conducted a job analysis in order to obtain a list of job tasks performed by officers in X city. For example, a few of the many tasks include:

Check bars for liquor law violation.

Engage in high-speed pursuit driving to apprehend suspects.

Administer first aid to injured persons.

Conduct bank security checks to determine level of protection.

The next step in obtaining relevant items for a rating scale is obtaining performance examples for each of these tasks. For example, consider the task of "conduct conflict resolution between members of the community." Performance examples for this task might be:

Effectively calms the emotions of others at the scene of an incident.

Demonstrates good self-control when harassed by the public.

Note that you would probably consider these performance examples to be illustrations of effective behavior. We would also like to have performance examples which might illustrate ineffective behavior. For example:

Makes insulting remarks to law violators.

Becomes belligerent when interacting with citizens.

Questions the sincerity of rape victims.

Finally, we would like to obtain some behavior statements which you would judge to be of average effectiveness. For example:

Discuss police actions with private citizens affected.

Explain court procedures to complainants.

Thus, we would like you to write out examples of behaviors according to the instructions that are given to you.

Instructions to job knowledge experts:
Please write out examples of effective behavior* for items _____ through _____ on the enclosed sheet. An example of effective behavior should be a sign of good performance in the sense that it contributes to the goals of good police functioning. The behavior should also have the following characteristics:

(a) The behavior should be realistic in the sense that this type of behavior has occurred in the police department.

(b) The behavior should be relevant to the jobs of police officers.

(c) The behavior should consist of specific behavioral examples that tell us what happened.

For example, saying the officer "showed good judgment" does not tell us what the person did (or did not do) that made you feel it was effective. An effective example here might be "did not fire at an escaping criminal when it would endanger innocent bystanders."

---

* Similar instructions are used to obtain examples of ineffective and average performance.
Source: Adapted from instructions developed by I. L. Goldstein and C. J. Bartlett. Copyright 1982 by I. L. Goldstein and C. J. Bartlett.

TABLE 5.8   EXAMPLE OF SITUATIONAL ITEM

The administrator receives a letter from a parent objecting to the content of the science section. The section topic is reproduction. The parent objects to his daughter having exposure to such materials and demands that something be done. The administrator would most likely (check one):

_____ Ask the teacher to provide handouts, materials, and curriculum content for review.

_____ Check the science curriculum for the board-approved approach to reproduction and compare board guidelines with course content.

_____ Ask the head of science department for his or her own opinion about the teacher's lesson plan.

_____ Check to see if the parent has made similar complaints in the past.

Source: From "Training Effectiveness Measures and Scoring Schemes: A Comparison," by C. Ostroff. In *Personnel Psychology*, 1991, *44*, pp. 353–374. Copyright © 1991 by Personnel Psychology, Inc. Reprinted by permission.

In examining a two-day training program to improve the administrative and interpersonal skills of educators, Ostroff (1991) used both a traditional rating scale format and the script format. The traditional rating scale required rating a person on items such as "skill in recognizing when a decision is required to act quickly" on a five-point scale ranging from little to a great deal. It turned out that the script method was much more sensitive in showing differences between trained and untrained individuals and that, in many cases, the traditional rating format did not distinguish between people who had been trained and others in a control group. Clearly, further research on the script method might produce a more sensitive measure of training performance.

CONCLUSIONS

In summary, the following suggestions about the determination of criteria appear relevant.

1. Place the greatest degree of effort on the selection of relevant criteria. Relevance should be conceptualized as a relationship between the operational measures (criteria) and KSAs determined from the needs assessment. Thus, several suggestions can aid in the selection of relevant criteria. First, carefully examine the behavioral objectives established from the needs assessment procedures. Because the objectives

are statements about terminal performance, they suggest potential criteria. Next, carefully examine all components suggested by the needs assessment so that the criteria are not deficient. For example, criteria that measure the performance of grocery cashiers include not only measures of register skills but also ratings of various aspects of customer service. Finally, carefully reduce the extraneous elements that often cause criterion contamination. As described earlier, two contaminating factors that can be effectively eliminated are opportunity bias and preknowledge of training performance.

2. After establishing relevant criteria, statistically determine the reliability or the consistency of the measure. If the criteria are not measured reliably, they are useless as indicants of success. Because ratings are often used as measures of success, consider the difficulties in rating a bus driver on a trait like "being careful." Compare that to the following rating statements used by a bus company:

    SLOWING AND STOPPING

    1. Stops and restarts without rolling back.
    2. Tests brakes at tops of hills.
    3. Uses mirrors to check traffic in rear.
    4. Signals following traffic.
    5. Stops before crossing sidewalk when coming out of driveway or alley.
    6. Stops clear of pedestrian crosswalks.

    Note that the behaviors are overt, easy to observe, and well defined. Certainly, more reliable measures could be expected by using these statements than by simply rating "being careful" or even "slowing and stopping" without further defining the behaviors.

3. Because of the complexity of most training programs and the corresponding evaluation efforts, criterion selection must reflect the breadth of the objectives. One useful paradigm is suggested by Kirkpatrick's (1994) measures of reaction, learning, behavior, and results. This particular analysis provides for measures of training performance, transfer performance, and organizational objectives. It is critical that the criteria chosen not only be relevant but also reflect the breadth of the program. Thus, it makes little sense to have measures that reflect training performance but not job performance. Similarly, it is not as useful to have measures of various types of performance without also considering cost or utility factors. The criteria must be chosen so that they reflect the breadth of the approach. Thus, it is not only important to have measures that reflect the outcomes but also equally important to collect data that provide information about why those

outcomes occurred. Also, criteria must reflect the organizational objectives as determined by the organizational analysis. Otherwise, no matter how successful individual performance is, the organization might judge the training intervention as not meeting the strategic goals of the company.

INFOTRAC COLLEGE EDITION

For additional readings, go to http: www.infotrac-college.com/wadsworth and enter a search term related to your interest. The following key terms will pull up several related articles.

Criterion Measures   Training Measures
Formative Evaluation   Training Values
Training Evaluation

CHAPTER 6

EVALUATION PROCEDURES

As previously stated, evaluation is the systematic collection of descriptive and judgmental information necessary to make effective training decisions related to the selection, adoption, value, and modification of various training activities. The objectives of instructional programs reflect numerous goals ranging from trainee progress to organizational goals. From this perspective, evaluation is an information-gathering technique. The necessary information will then be available to revise training programs to achieve multiple instructional objectives. In Chapter 5, we presented several types of questions that could be asked about the outcome of training programs:

1. Does an examination of the various criteria indicate that a change has occurred?
2. Can the changes be attributed to the instructional program?
3. Is it likely that similar changes will occur for new participants in the same program?
4. Is it likely that similar changes will occur for new participants in the same program in a different organization?

These questions could be asked about measures at each criterion level (reaction, learning, behavior, results). Thus, evaluations of training programs are not likely to produce dichotomous answers. Although the answers to these questions provide information about the accomplishments of training programs and the revisions that may be required, investigators may be interested in asking other types of questions. In some cases, they are interested in the relative accomplishments of two different training approaches. It is also possible to ask which training approach works best with what type of training participant or in what type of organization. Researchers may also be interested in testing various theoretical hypotheses that provide the foundation for the design of a new training approach. In this latter instance, researchers will still

177

want to know if a change has occurred and whether it can be attributed to the training program.

VIEWS OF THE EVALUATION PROCESS

Phases of the Evaluation Process

In the opening section of Chapter 5, we described some of the reasons why evaluation is avoided and what advantages can be gained from a thoughtful evaluation. In a real sense, evaluation has evolved through a series of phases (Goldstein, 1980). In the very early phases, appropriate methodology was ignored, and decisions were at best based on anecdotal trainee-trainer relations. In this text, we argue that many developing methodologies now permit the investigator to gain valuable information about training programs—even those that are used in complex work organizations. We believe that training programs should be considered dynamic entities that evolve to accomplish their purpose in meeting predesigned objectives, and through the use of systematic evaluation, we are able to provide the information necessary to improve programs or generate quality information to make decisions.

Another early view about evaluation was the belief that only the most rigorous scientific evaluation of training was worthwhile. Advocates of this approach would have had the researcher avoid studying a situation where the sample size was too small for traditional designs or where control groups could not be used. Fortunately, few researchers feel constrained by this view today. Instead, evaluation research is evolving into another much more sophisticated phase. People recognize that training programs must be evaluated and are concerned with designing appropriate methodologies to perform the evaluation. From this perspective, programs should be evaluated, either formally or informally. Yet, the concern is with the quality of the evaluation rather than with the question of whether to evaluate. It is important to use the most systematic procedures available that fit the particular setting being investigated, to control as many of the extraneous variables as possible, and to recognize the limitations of the design being used. The better experimental procedures control more variables, permitting a greater degree of confidence in specifying program effects. Although the constraints of the environment may make a perfect evaluation impossible, an awareness of the important factors in experimental design makes it possible to avoid a useless evaluation. The job of the training analyst is to choose the most rigorous design possible and to be aware of its limitations. These limitations should be taken into account in data interpretation and in reports to the program sponsors.

METHODOLOGICAL CONSIDERATIONS IN THE USE OF EXPERIMENTAL DESIGNS

Each research design has different assets and liabilities in controlling extraneous factors that might threaten the evaluator's ability to determine (1) if a real change has occurred, (2) whether the change is attributable to the instructional program, and (3) whether the change is likely to occur again with a new sample of subjects. Specific research designs are discussed in a later section, but several general design concepts, including control groups and pre- and posttesting, are mentioned here as background for the presentation of the sources of error that can affect the validity of the experimental design.

Pretesting and Posttesting

The first question is whether the participants, after exposure to the instructional program, change their performance in a significant way. A design to answer this question includes a pretest administered before the instructional program begins and a posttest given after exposure to the instructional program. The timing of the posttest for the evaluation is not easily specified. A posttest at the conclusion of the training program provides a measure of the learning that has occurred during instruction, but it does not give any indication of later transfer performance. Thus, other measures should be employed after the participant has been in the transfer situation for a reasonable time period. Comparisons can then be made between (1) the pretest and the first posttest, (2) the pretest and the second posttest, and (3) the first and second posttests. For convenience, only pretests and posttests are referred to in this section, but it is important to remember that one posttest immediately after training ordinarily will not suffice.

The variables measured in the pretests and posttests must be associated with the objectives of the training program. The expected changes associated with the instructional program should be specified so that statistically reliable differences between the pretests and posttests can confirm the degree to which the objectives have been achieved. An additional factor in the analysis of pretest and posttest scores is how scores on the pretest affect the degree of success on the posttest. One possibility is that the participant who initially scored highest on the pretest will perform best on the posttest. To examine this effect, it is necessary that the pretest scores be partialed out of the posttest.

Control Groups

The specification of changes indicated by premeasurement and postmeasurement is only one consideration. Posttests might indicate improvement in scores over pretest scores, and one might be tempted to declare that the training program was successful. Yet, it still must be determined that these changes occurred because of the instructional treatment. A control group is used (treated like the experimental group on all variables that might contribute to predifferences and postdifferences, except for the actual instructional program) to eliminate the possibility of other explanations for the changes between pretest and posttest. With control procedures, it is possible to specify whether the changes in the experimental group were due to instructional treatments or to other factors, like the passage of time, or events in the outside world. The kinds of errors that can occur in interpreting evaluation data are specified in the next section, but, as an example of the necessity for control groups, we can consider the placebo effect. As mentioned earlier, the placebo is an inert substance administered to the control group by medical research so that patients cannot distinguish whether they are members of the experimental group or the control group. This allows the researcher to separate the effects of the actual drug from the reactions induced by the patients' expectations and suggestibility. In instructional research, similar cautions can be taken to separate the background effects sometimes employed in the experimental setting and the actual treatment.

It is also becoming increasingly clear that the use of experimental design, including the assignment of persons to control groups, sometimes can produce profound changes in the behavior of participants, with consequences that can include the sabotaging of program outcomes. Obviously, if these effects are not detected by investigators, misinterpretations of the results of the study are very likely. Before discussing specific research designs, it is necessary to consider those factors that contribute sources of error. D. T. Campbell and Stanley (1963) originally organized and specified these threats to experimental design. Cook and D. T. Campbell (1976, 1979) and most recently Cook, Campbell, and Peracchio (1990) have updated these findings and include discussions of many of the intervention threats stemming from a growing appreciation of the values of trainees, trainers, evaluators, and organizational sponsors. For the most part, these researchers' labels and framework are used in this text.

INTERNAL AND EXTERNAL VALIDITY

Internal validity asks the basic question, did the treatment make a difference in this particular situation? Unless internal validity has been established, interpreting the effects of any experiment, training or otherwise, is not possible. *External validity* refers to the generalizability, or representativeness, of the data. The evaluator is concerned with generalizability of results to other populations, settings, and treatment variables. External validity is always a matter of inference and thus can never be specified with complete confidence. However, the designs that control the most threats to internal and external validity are, of course, the most useful. In this presentation, we focus on the internal threats that are most relevant in the analysis of training programs. There are threats to the interpretation of experimental results such as maturation, which are changes that in human beings over long periods of time regardless of what is being done in the training program. However, because training programs typically don't usually occur over a long period of time, maturation is not typically a threat and is not discussed here. For a complete listing of internal and external threats to validity, consult Cook, Campbell, and Peracchio (1990).

Threats to Internal Validity

These threats are variables, other than the instructional program itself, that can affect its results. The solution to this difficulty is to control these variables so that they may be cast aside as competing explanations for the experimental effect. Threats to internal validity include the following.

History.   History refers to specific events, other than the training treatment, occurring between the pretest and the posttest that could provide alternative explanations for results. When tests are given on different days, as is almost always the case in instructional programs, events occurring between testing periods can contaminate the effects. For instance, an instructional program designed to produce positive attitudes toward safe practices in coal mines may produce significant differences that have no relationship to the material presented in the instructional program. Instead, a coal mine disaster occurring between the pretest and posttest may lead individual miners and the organization to take additional steps to improve safety. History is often a threat to validity, and one way to determine whether it is a possibility is to use process criteria to describe work conditions and key events in the organization that occur during training.

Testing.   Testing refers to the influence of the pretest on the scores of the posttest. This is an especially serious problem for instructional programs in which the pretest can sensitize the participant to search for material or to ask colleagues for information that provides correct answers on the posttest. Thus, improved performance can occur simply by taking the pretests and posttests, without an intervening instructional program. When this occurs, one can question whether the tests are appropriate and, if so, whether a training intervention is therefore even needed to accomplish the objectives.

Instrumentation.   Instrumentation results from changes in the measurement instruments that might result in differences between pretest and posttest scores. For example, changes in grading standards (e.g., grading more leniently on the posttest) can lead to "improvement" between pre- and post-tests, regardless of the instructional program. Because rating scales are a commonly employed criterion in training research, it is important to be sensitive to differences related to changes in the rater (for example, additional expertise in the second rating, bias, or carelessness) that can cause error effects.

Statistical regression.   Participants for instructional research are sometimes chosen on the basis of extreme scores. Thus, trainees with extremely low and extremely high intelligence-test scores may be chosen for participation in a course using programmed instruction. In these cases, a phenomenon known as statistical regression often occurs. On the second testing, the scores for both groups regress toward the middle of the distribution. Thus, trainees with extremely high scores would tend toward lower scores, and those with extremely low scores would tend toward higher scores. This regression occurs because tests are not perfect measures; there will always be some change in scores from the first to the second testing simply because of measurement error. Because the first scores are at the extreme ends, the variability must move toward the center (the mean of the entire group). Trainees with extremely high pretest scores might have had unusually good luck the day of the first testing, whereas trainees with extremely low scores may have been upset or careless that day. On the second administration, however, each group is likely to regress toward the mean.

Differential selection of participants.   This effect stems from the way people are chosen to be part of comparison groups. If volunteers are used in the instruction group and randomly chosen participants are used in the control group, differences could occur between the two groups simply because each group was different before the program began. This variable is best controlled by random selection of all participants, with appropriate numbers of participants (as determined by statistical considerations) for each group. Random selection is a particular problem in educational settings where one class is chosen as the control group and another class as the experimental group. Establishing experimental and control groups by placing individuals with matched characteristics (for example, intelligence, age, gender) in each group may still not be the best alternative. Often, the critical parameters that should be used to match the participants are not known, and thus selection biases can again affect the design and interpretation of results. One alternative is a combination of matching and randomization in which participants are matched on important parameters; then, one member of each pair is assigned randomly to the treatment or control group.

Experimental mortality.   This variable refers to the differential loss of participants from the treatment or control group. In an experimental group of volunteers, those people who scored poorly on the pretest may drop out because they are discouraged. Thus, the group in the experimental program may appear to score higher than the control group because the low-scoring performers left.

Internal Validity and Intervention Threats

The following threats to internal validity can be labeled intervention threats because they stem mainly from the decision to evaluate a program. Interestingly, many of the internal threats to validity discussed previously can be constrained by the use of experimental design procedures. For example, the internal threat of history effects can often be investigated by having an experimental and a control group so that whatever the historical occurrence, it affects both groups. However, most of the next set of threats cannot be constrained by experimental methodology. Rather, as discussed in the section on values and evaluation, it will take other approaches—for example, working with the participants as part of the evaluation model so that they do not feel threatened by events such as being assigned to a control group. It is no surprise that a mysterious announcement from a training analyst that assigns only certain individuals to a training program might be viewed by the control subjects as a message that they are not in favor with the organization. We all know that human beings are involved in training, and many individuals are highly motivated and deeply care about their future. It is useful to consider that perspective when considering these threats to validity. Some of these types of threats include the following.

Compensatory equalization of treatments. When the training treatment is perceived to produce positive benefits, there is often a reluctance to permit perceived inequalities to exist. Thus, administrators or trainers might provide control subjects with similar or other benefits that wipe out any measured differences between the control and training groups in the evaluation. Cook, D. T. Campbell, and Peracchio (1990) note that in several national educational experiments, what were meant to be "control schools" tended to be given other federal funds by well-meaning administrators. This resulted in the control schools actually being another form of experimental condition. Unfortunately, as later analyses often indicate, it also wipes out the differences between the experimental and control treatments, leaving many confused individuals wondering why their training treatments had no effect. The powerful effect of this category is supported by lawsuits being brought by minorities, women, and other protected classes because they believe they are not being permitted on an equal basis to enter training programs that are required as stepping stones for promotional opportunities. In this instance, the question is not how the evaluation data should be evaluated but rather the impact of the perceived positive benefits of training programs. Again, this is a clear indication of the importance of understanding value issues and how they effect interventions. This is an instance where the training designer has to work with the organization so that the benefits of training can first be determined and any necessary changes to enhance its utility can be made. Often, the designer will need to work with all individuals over many sessions to explain the process and also explain how everyone will eventually receive the same opportunities.

Compensatory rivalry between respondents receiving less desirable treatments.   In some situations, competition between the training group and the control group may be generated. This is more likely to occur when individuals in the control condition are not brought into the process and are not told when they will have the same opportunities. The problem is that this special effort may wipe out the differences between the two groups but not be a reflection of how control subjects would ordinarily perform. This kind of effect is also possible where the control condition is the old training procedure. Here again, the controls might work extra hard so that their performance would be equivalent to the persons assigned to the new treatment condition. Saretsky (1972) labels this type of effort the "John Henry effect." As memorialized in the folk song, John Henry competed against a steam drill. He worked so hard that he outperformed the drill and died of overexertion. In several firefighter jurisdictions, women have worked together outside the organization to set up special training programs to help them build the upper-body strength necessary to qualify for the job. If these women had been assigned to the control group in large numbers, data comparing the "control" to a more traditional program would not be meaningful.

Resentful demoralization of respondents receiving less desirable treatments.   In some instances, people selected for a control condition can become resentful or demoralized. This is especially possible when control subjects believe that the assignment might be a message that they are not as highly valued by management. This can result in the person not performing as capably as possible. In this instance, the control subjects' drop in performance could make the training group look that much better, leading to the incorrect conclusion that the training program has been successful.

Threats to External Validity

External validity refers to the generalizability of the study to other groups and situations. Internal validity is a prerequisite for external validity because the training program must be judged effective before there can be concern over whether the program will be effective for other groups. As noted by Cook, D. T. Campbell, and Peracchio (1990), the concern in external validity is generalizing to or generalizing across times, settings, and people. In general terms, the representativeness of all aspects of the investigation to the categories the investigator wishes to extrapolate determines the degree of generalizability. For example, when the data are initially collected in a high-socioeconomic setting, claiming that the instructional program will work equally well in a low-socioeconomic area may be problematic. In that sense, threats to external validity are those threats that limit the generalizations. The following are examples of threats that are potentially relevant to external validity generalizations.

Reactive effects of pretesting.   The effects of pretests often lead to an increased sensitivity to the instructional procedure. Thus, the participants' responses to the training program might be different from the responses of individuals who are exposed to an established program without the pretest. The pretested participants might pay attention to certain material in the training program only because they know it is covered in test items. Usually, it is speculated that pretest exposure will improve performance. However, Bunker and Cohen (1977) discovered that the posttest scores of individuals low in numerical ability were hindered by exposure to the pretest. They offer two possible reasons for this development: (1) Trainees may mistakenly have attended to only the limited sample of material appearing on the pretest; (2) trainees who were low in numerical ability may have become quite anxious because of the pretest and that might have interfered with later learning. Further research is needed to explore that possibility. However, generalizations to subsequent training populations that would not be exposed to a pretest would be in error. Interestingly, however, the problem occurred only for low-ability students. Thus, the external validity threat of pretesting interacted with the selection of the participating group. That type of threat is discussed next.

Reactive effects from the group receiving the treatment.   In this case, the characteristics of the group selected for experimental treatment determine the generalizability of the findings. The characteristics of employees from one division of the firm may result in the treatment's being more or less effective for them, as compared with employees from another division with different characteristics. For example, individuals on a busy production line might not see the value in computer training, whereas those individuals in engineering may see such training as critical to reducing job obsolescence. Similarly, characteristics such as the low numerical ability example may make trainees more or less receptive to particular instructional programs.

Reactive effects of the experimental settings.   The procedures employed in the experimental setting may limit the generalizability of the study. Observers and experimental equipment often make the participants aware of their participation in an experiment. This can lead to changes in behavior that cannot be generalized to those individuals who will participate in the instructional treatment when it is not the focus of a research study. The Hawthorne studies have become the standard illustration for the "I'm a guinea pig" effect. This research showed that a group of employees tended to increase production regardless of the changes in working conditions designed to produce both increases and decreases in production. Interpreters believe that the experimental conditions resulted in the workers' behaving differently. Explanations for the Hawthorne effect include novelty, awareness of being a participant in an experiment, changes in the environment due to observers, enthusiasm of the instructor, recording conditions, social interaction, and daily feedback on production figures. The important point is that, because the factors that affect the treatment group may not be present in future training sessions, the performance obtained is not necessarily representative of that of future participants.

The potency of these types of variables was demonstrated by Eden and Shani (1982) in their "Pygmalion effect" study of military combat training for the Israeli Defense Forces. Instructors had been led to expect that some of these trainees were better students than others, although actually there were no greater ability differences for the people chosen. The individuals for whom trainers had high expectancies scored significantly higher on objective achievement tests, exhibited more positive attitudes toward the course, and had more positive perceptions of instructor leadership. These types of variables become an external validity threat because there is often more enthusiasm when courses are first being offered (and evaluated). However, that enthusiasm sometimes disappears when the course becomes more routine. To the extent that the training effect was due to factors such as enthusiasm, it will disappear with the more routine course. On the other hand, if organizations can learn to use and maintain the conditions that lead to factors such as enthusiasm, there are indications that training performance will improve. It would be terrific if the positive attitudes and performance generated in the Eden and Shani study would continue on the job. However, further studies are needed to make that determination.

EXPERIMENTAL DESIGN

In the sections on internal and external validity, we discussed some of the factors that make it difficult to determine whether the treatment produced the hypothesized results. As will become apparent, these threats are differentially controlled by the various experimental designs. Some of the many designs that examine the effects of experimental treatments are presented in this section. Given any particular setting, the researcher should employ the design that has the greatest degree of control over threats to validity.

For convenience in presenting the experimental designs, T_1 will represent the pretest, T_2 the posttest, X the treatment or training program, and R the random selection of subjects. Cook and his colleagues (1990) have organized a detailed examination of the variables that should be considered when choosing a research design. The designs in this text, organized into several different categories, provide examples of the numerous approaches available. The first category includes preexperimental designs that do not have control procedures and thus make it more difficult to specify cause-and-effect relationships. Experimental designs, the second category, have varying degrees of power that control some threats to validity. The third category includes quasi-experimental designs that are useful in many social science settings where investigators lack the opportunity to exert full control over the environment.

Preexperimental Designs

1. The one-group posttest-only design:

$X \qquad T_2$

In this method, the one-group posttest-only design, the trainees are exposed to the instructional treatment (without a pretest) and then are tested once at the completion of training. Without the pretest, ascertaining any change as a result of the training treatment from before to after training is not possible. Just because trainees might do well on the posttest does not mean that training led to those high scores—the participants might have done just as well on the posttest without any training intervention. Also, without the control group, it is difficult to infer if the cause of the change is the training treatment rather than an internal threat to validity, such as history. Thus, the limitations include the lack of hypothesis testing and problems in generalizability. However, some valuable information and very rich descriptions can stem from this type of design. For example, case-study approaches used in the social sciences often employ a posttest-only design that provides considerable information based on the collection of a large number of measures at the posttest time. This information can provide very important hunches and hypotheses, which can be used as input for another study.

Sackett and Mullen (1993) argue that in some instances, depending on the question being asked, this type of design is appropriate. The example they offer is a situation where investigators are interested in determining whether a person has achieved a certain level of competence. The illustration they present is of assessors being trained to provide accurate ratings of individuals who are taking part in management work simulations. These simulations are usually referred to as assessment centers, and individuals take part in these assessment centers as a way of being tested for promotion into a managerial position. These type of assessment centers will be discussed in Chapter 8, but essentially they are simulations of critical aspects of a manager's job, such as responding to a complaining customer or providing training for an incumbent employee. In order to score performance on these exercises, individuals (called assessors) are trained on the performance dimensions to be rated. Then, at the end of training, the assessors give ratings on a few simulated examples to ensure that they are rating performance accurately. After training, these assessors are then themselves evaluated to determine if they have reached the right performance level. Sackett and Mullen argue that in this situation all you need is an assessment at the end of training to evaluate whether the individual has reached the desired performance level. They also argue that you do not even need a pretest because you are not interested in the degree of change from pre- to posttest but rather only that the person has achieved the desired performance level (meeting training objectives). However, one could argue here that if you had a pretest, you might identify some persons who can already perform the task without this level of training. In general, interpretations of causality and generalizability in a single posttest-only design remain questionable.

2. The one-group pretest/posttest design:

$$T_1 \quad X \quad T_2$$

When this design is employed, the participants are given a pretest, presented with the instructional program, and then given a posttest. This design is widely used in the examination of training settings because it provides a measure of comparison between the same group of trainees before and after treatment. Unfortunately, without a control group, it is difficult to establish whether the experimental treatment is the prime factor determining any differences that occur between the testing periods. Thus, the many threats to internal validity, including changes in history, testing effects, changes in instrumentation, and statistical regression, are not controlled.

Research Example of Preexperimental Designs

Golembiewski and Carrigan (1970) carried out a training program that used a pre- and postdesign without a control group in one of a series of investigations designed to change the style of a sales unit in a business organization. They had a series of goals including the integration of a new management team, an increase in congruence between the behaviors required by the organization and those preferred by the salespeople, and a greater congruence of individual needs and organizational demands. The training program consisted of a laboratory approach using sensitivity training to encourage the exploration of the participant's feelings and reactions to the organization. The program also included confrontations in which management of various levels was given an opportunity to discuss its ideas and feelings. The instrument used to measure preexperimental and postexperimental changes was Likert's profile of organizational characteristics, which includes items related to leadership, character of motivational forces, communication, interaction influence, decision making, goal setting, and control.

After statistical analyses, the researchers concluded that the learning design had the intended effect in terms of the measured attitudes. The authors indicate that they had included all managers in the treatment and so did not have a control group. Thus, their design did not permit them to be certain that the effects were a result of the training program rather than of random factors or the passage of time. This design uncertainty is expressed by Becker in an article entitled "The Parable of the Pill," which presents complex design issues with a simplicity that most writers, including us, would love to achieve (see Table 6.1). The point in the parable is that Skeptic One, Skeptic Two, or the inventor of the pill may be right. There is no way of being certain, given the present design, what was responsible for the effect.

The next group of designs shows how easily many of the preexperimental designs can be improved. Design 1 can be strengthened by adding a pretest, and both design 1 and design 2 can be improved by adding a control group. Even where the environment makes a control group impractical, these designs can be improved by using the approaches described in the section on quasi-experimental designs, which will be discussed later. One of the points of quasi-experimental design is the use of innovative and thoughtful ways of collecting information that help control the threats to validity even when a true experiment with trainees assigned randomly to a control and experimental groups cannot be accomplished. Of course, it is also possible to strengthen training designs even when it is just a pre- and postdesign without a control group.

An example of this can be found in a training study designed by Haccoun and Hamtriaux (1994). These investigators examined a management training program administered to intermediate-level managers in a university. The program focused on a number of human resources management issues such as communication, power relationships, leadership, performance appraisal, and motivation. The 45-hour course given over a period of eight weeks was evaluated in terms of knowledge gained on a multiple-choice paper-and-pencil test given both before and after training. The test items were written by the developers of the course and reflected mainly applications of knowledge that were the theme of the course. These investigators came up with the idea of examining patterns of change by including in their criterion measure some test items that were relevant to the course in the sense that they were included in the training program and some items that were irrelevant to the course. The irrelevant items in this study reflected themes that fit into the course but simply were not covered. The investigators named this strategy the Internal

| TABLE 6.1 | THE PARABLE OF THE PILL |

There once was a land in which wisdom was revered. Thus, there was great excitement in the land when one of its inhabitants announced that he had invented a pill which made people wiser. His claim was based on an experiment he conducted. The report of the experiment explained (1) that the experimenter secured a volunteer; (2) the volunteer was first given an IQ test; (3) then he swallowed a pill which he was told would make him more intelligent; (4) finally he was given another IQ test. The score on the second IQ test was higher than on the first, so the report concluded that the pill increased wisdom. Alas, there were two skeptics in the land. One secured a volunteer; gave him an IQ test; waited an appropriate length of time; then gave him another IQ test. The volunteer's score on the second test exceeded that of the first. Skeptic One reported his experiment and concluded that taking the first test was an experience for the subject and that the time between the tests allowed the subject to assimilate and adjust to that experience so that when he encountered the situation again he responded more efficiently. Time alone, the skeptic argued, was sufficient to produce the increase in test score. The skeptic also pointed out that time alone could have produced the change in test score reported in the experiment on the Wisdom Pill.

Skeptic Two conducted a different experiment. He held the opinion that most people were to some extent suggestible or gullible and that they readily would accept a suggestion that they possessed a desired attribute. He further believed that people who accept such a suggestion might even behave in a way such as to make it appear, for a time at least, that they indeed did possess the suggested ability. Therefore, the skeptic secured a volunteer; gave him an IQ test; had him ingest a pill composed of inert ingredients; told him the pill would increase his intelligence; then gave him another IQ test. Skeptic Two dutifully reported his subject achieved a higher score on the second test and, based on his hypothesis, explained how the disparity arose. He also pointed out that the increase in test score in the Wisdom Pill experiment could have been due to the taking of the pill and expectations associated with taking the pill rather than to the ingredients in the pill.

The inventor of the wisdom pill drafted a reply to the two skeptics. He wrote that, although he did not employ a control group or a placebo group, he is confident that the pill's ingredients caused the observed change because that change is consistent with the theory from which he deduced the formula for his pill.

Source: From "Parable of the Pill," by S. W. Becker. In *Administrative Sciences Quarterly,* 1970, *15,* pp. 94–96. Copyright 1970 by Administrative Sciences Quarterly. Reprinted by permission.

Referencing Strategy (IRS) and said that effectiveness of the training program could be inferred when pre- and postchanges on relevant items were greater than changes on irrelevant items.

The investigators were very careful in the design of both the relevant and irrelevant items. They pretested the items for clarity and made sure that the items for the relevant and irrelevant aspects of the course were matched on various aspects including difficulty level. They also made sure that the items were difficult enough that they did not get a ceiling effect where everyone managed to get all the items correct. The outcome of their study is shown in Figure 6.1. Note that the increase in performance for the trained relevant items in terms of pre-post differences is much higher than the increase in the performance for the trained irrelevant items. The authors note that the likelihood of there being certain types of threats to internal validity such as history would be low, the reason being that if there was an external threat, such as

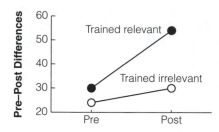

FIGURE **6.1**

Internal referencing strategy—relevant versus irrelevant.

Source: Adapted from "Optimizing Knowledge Tests for Inferring Learning Acquisition Levels in Single Group Training Evaluation Designs: The Internal Referencing Strategy," by R. R. Haccoun and T. Hamtriaux. In *Personnel Psychology*, 1994, *47*, pp. 593–604. Copyright 1994 by Personnel Psychology, Inc. Reprinted by permission.

some event that occurred between the pre- and posttests, it would be unlikely to just affect performance on the relevant items and not on the irrelevant items.

Actually, this study was much more complex than just having the pre- and postdesign without a control group. They also had other conditions where they did have a control group, but their point was introducing the IRS strategy as a way of obtaining additional information even when just using a pre- and post-measurement without a control group. Notice in Figure 6.1 that there was an increase in performance between the pre and post for the irrelevant items also but it was not nearly as high as that for the relevant items. The authors postulate here that the increase for the irrelevant items may have been due to pretest sensitization. It is thought that because the irrelevant items were part of the same domain of management of human resources, performance might improve because the trainees were sensitized to apply the knowledge they were gaining to topics other than those directly taught in the training program. This kind of analysis again permits the investigators to provide thoughtful information about the effectiveness of the training intervention. Further examples are covered next in the section on experimental designs.

Experimental Designs

3. Pretest/posttest control-group design:

Experimental Group	(R)	T_1	X	T_2
Control Group	(R)	T_1	X	T_2

No training for control group [handwritten annotation]

In this design, the subjects are chosen at random from the population and assigned randomly to the experimental group or control group. Each group is given a pretest and posttest, but only the experimental group is exposed to the instructional treatment. If there is more than one instructional treatment, it is possible to add additional experimental groups. This design represents a considerable improvement over designs 1 and 2 because many of the threats to internal validity are controlled. The differential selection of subjects is controlled by the random selection. Variables like history and pretesting should affect the experimental group and the control group equally. Statistical regression based on extreme scores (if trainees are chosen that way) is not eliminated but should be equal for the two groups because of the random-selection procedures. However, any effects not part of the instructional procedure that are due to differential treatment of subjects in the control and experimental groups must still be controlled by the experimenter. This includes the problems of intervention threats such as compensatory rivalry or resentful demoralization of control groups.

This design is affected by external threats to validity that are not as easily specified as the threats to internal validity. The design does not control the effects of pretesting; thus, T_1 could have sensitized the participants to the experimental treatment. Generalizations would also be hampered because trainees in the experiment might be different from those who will participate at later times and because the guinea pig effect could lead to differences between the experimental and control groups. This latter concern depends on the ingenuity of the experimenter in reducing the differences between groups by treating the control group in the same manner as the experimental group (except for the specific instructional treatment).

The difficulties associated with external validity should not freeze the researcher into inactivity. Although most threats to internal validity are reasonably well handled by experimental designs, generalizations, which are the core of external validity, are always a matter of judgment calls. As D. T. Campbell and Stanley (1963) originally pointed out, experimenters try to generalize by scientifically guessing at laws and by trying out generalizations in other specific cases. Slowly, and somewhat painfully, they gain knowledge about factors that affect generalizations (e.g., there is now ample evidence that pretesting does sensitize and affect participants). As shown in the following design, a control for pretest sensitization is relatively easy to achieve by adding a group to design 3 that is exposed to the treatment without first being presented with the pretest.

4. Solomon four-group design:

Group

1 (R)	T_1	X	T_2
2 (R)	T_1		T_2
3 (R)		X	T_2
4 (R)			T_2

The Solomon four-group design represents the first specific procedure designed to consider external validity factors. This design adds two groups that are not pretested. If the participants are randomly assigned to the four groups, this design makes it possible to compare the effects of pretesting. (Group 4 provides a control for pretesting without the instructional treatment.) It also permits the evaluator to determine the effects of some internal validity factors. For example, a comparison of the posttest performance for group 4, which was not exposed to pretesting or instructional treatments, to the pretest scores for groups 1 and 2, permits the analysis of the combined effects of maturation and history.

Research Example of Experimental Designs

A number of carefully carried out empirical research efforts have been reported. A study by Latham and Saari (1979) sets an excellent standard for the conduct of training research. In their study, they randomly selected 40 supervisors from a total group of 100, and then randomly assigned 20 of them to a training condition and the other 20 to a control group. The control group was informed that they would be trained at a later date. They were trained at a later time, but in the interim they served as a control condition for the study. In Chapter 8 in the section on behavioral role modeling, we describe the procedures used in the training sessions in some detail. Basically, the program consisted of presenting key behaviors of effective performers, viewing a film where an individual modeled the key behaviors, group discussion of the behaviors, practice of the key behaviors through role playing, and feedback from the class. At the end of each session, the trainees were sent back to their jobs with instructions to use the supervisory skills they had gained. The purpose here was to facilitate transfer of the learned skills back to the job. At the next session, the trainees reported their experiences, and for situations where they had experienced difficulties, they repracticed the desired behavior.

Besides carefully designing a training program, the researchers also evaluated the results using reaction measures, learning measures, behavioral measures, and job performance measures and found strong evidence supporting the training program. For example, they used job performance indicators consisting of ratings made by supervisors of the trainees; the rating scales were based on a job analysis that produced critical incidents depicting effective and ineffective supervisory behavior. The investigators found no difference between pretest measures of the training and control group. Posttest measures indicated that the training group performed significantly better than the control group.

As a final step, Latham and Saari (1979) trained the control group. After their training was complete, all differences on all four measures between the control group, which was now trained, and the original training group disappeared. This kind of careful implementation and evaluation in a real work environment should serve as a model for what can be accomplished with some thoughtful effort. For the interested reader, Frayne and Latham (1987) employed a similarly powerful design in examining self-management training programs as a tool in reducing absenteeism. That research will be also discussed further in Chapter 8, which emphasizes training techniques for managers and interpersonal skills.

Quasi-Experimenal Designs

5. The time-series design:

$$T_1 \qquad T_2 \qquad T_3 \qquad T_4 \qquad X \qquad T_5 \qquad T_6 \qquad T_7 \qquad T_8$$

This design is similar to design 1, except that a series of measurements are taken before and after the instructional treatment. This particular approach illustrates the possibilities of using quasi-experimental designs in situations in which it is not possible to gain the full control required by experimental designs. An examination of internal validity threats shows that this design provides more control than design 1. If there are no appreciable changes from pretests 1 to 4, it is unlikely that any effects found after the training can be attributed to testing effects or regression to the mean. The major internal validity difficulty with this design is if the investigator was unfortunate enough to have a history effect that occurs between T_4 and T_5.

The use of such time-series design does not control external validity threats. Thus, it is necessary to be sensitive to any relationships between the treatment and particular subject groups (like volunteers) that might make results difficult to generalize to other groups. It is also necessary to be aware that trainees might be sensitized to particular aspects of the instructional program through the use of pretests.

6. The nonequivalent control-group design:

Experimental Group T_1 $\qquad$ X $\qquad$ T_2
Control Group $\qquad$ T_1 $\qquad$ $\qquad$ T_2

The nonequivalent control-group design is the same as design 3, except that the participants are not assigned to the groups at random (the choice of the group to receive the instructional treatment is made randomly). This design is often used in training settings where there are naturally assembled groups such as several factories producing the same product. If there is no alternative, this design is well worth using and is certainly preferable to designs that do not include control groups (such as design 2). The more similar the two groups and their scores on the pretest, the more effective the control becomes in accounting for extraneous influences—for instance, internal validity factors like history, pretesting, and instrumentation.

However, the investigator must be especially careful because this design is vulnerable to interactions between selection factors and history and testing. Because the participants were not chosen randomly, there is always the possibility that critical differences exist that were not revealed by the pretests. For example, some studies use volunteers who might react differently to the treatment because of motivational factors. Thus, the investigator must be sensitive to potential sources of differences between the groups. The dangers of instrumentation changes and of differential treatment of each group (unrelated to the treatment) remain a concern for this design as well as for design 3. Although the external validity issues are similar to those for design 3, the non-equivalent control-group design does have some advantages in the control of the reactive effects of experimental settings. The utilization of intact groups makes it easier to design the experiment as part of the normal routine, thus reducing some of the problems associated with the guinea pig effect. Because this design is not as disruptive, it is also possible in some settings (for example, educational systems), to have a larger subject population, thus increasing generalizability.

Research Example of Quasi-Experimental Designs—Time Series

An ingenious example of the use of a quasi-experimental design is offered by the research of Komaki, Heinzmann, and Lawson (1980). This study was described briefly in Chapter 4 in the section on feedback of results. Because it is a good illustration of quasi-experimental designs, we will describe it here in more detail. These investigators were studying safety problems in the vehicle-maintenance division of a city's department of public works. The department being studied had one of the highest accident rates in the city. Komaki and her colleagues performed a needs assessment including an analysis of the factors that led to unsafe practices and hindered safe acts. They examined safety logs for the previous five years to determine what type of accidents occurred and then wrote safety behavioral items that would have prevented that accident. Throughout this procedure, they interacted with supervisors and workers on the specification and development of safety procedures. Some examples of safety items generated for the vehicle-maintenance department are

1. *Proper use of equipment and tools.* When reaching upward for an item more than 30 cm (1 ft.) away from extended arms, use steps, stepladder, or solid part of vehicle. Do not stand on jacks or jack stands.
2. *Use of safety equipment.* When using brake machine, wear full face shield or goggles. When arcing brake shoes, respirator should also be worn.
3. *Housekeeping.* Any oil/grease spill larger than 8 × 8 cm (3 × 3 in.) in an interior walking area (defined as any area at least 30 cm [1 ft.] from a wall or a solid standing object) or an exterior walking area (designated by outer white lines parallel to the wall and at least 30 cm [1 ft.]

from the wall) should be soaked up with rice hull or grease compound.

4. *General safety procedures.* When any type of jack other than an air-jack is in use (i.e., vehicle is supported by jack or off the ground), at least one jack stand should also be used. (pp. 262–263)

Komaki and her colleagues designed a training program that used slides to depict the unsafe practices employed in the department, examined the trainees on their knowledge of appropriate safe behaviors, discussed correct safety behaviors, and then showed the same slides but this time demonstrated safe practices. Also, employees were given copies of the appropriate safety rules to take with them. This procedure was designated the Training Program. Another procedure used later in the program was called Training and Feedback. In this procedure, besides the training given earlier, employees were informed about realistic safety goals that were set on the basis of their previous performance. Then, randomly timed, daily safety observations were made, and the results were posted on a graph so that the employees could see how they were progressing toward their goals. The design of this study was a time-series with at least four or five observations for each of the first three phases of the study and an average of three observations per phase for the last two phases (see Figure 6.2).

The first phase, referred to as baseline, consisted of the collection of data before any training or feedback. It essentially consisted of multiple pretests. The second phase was the training program, and the third phase added feedback to the already trained employees. The fourth phase went back to training only with no feedback being given, and the final phase reinstituted feedback to the already trained employees. Note that all trainees proceeded through the entire sequence of five phases and that there are multiple data-collection points in each phase. The data collected consisted of the number of incidents performed safely.

Data were collected by trained observers, and there was high-level agreement between the observers. In the data shown in the graph for two departments (preventive maintenance and light-equipment repair), performance improved from baseline to after training and then improved more when feedback was added. When feedback was taken away, performance went down, but performance improved again when feedback was put back in the last phase of the study. Komaki's point is that, besides training, feedback on employee performance is a critical component of the program. In two other departments, Komaki obtained similar data for the first four phases, but improvement did not occur again as a result of the fifth phase. The investigators in this study considered the various threats to validity and how their quasi-experimental design accounted for these factors. Plausible alternative hypotheses (history, maturation, statistical regression) were ruled out because the two phases were

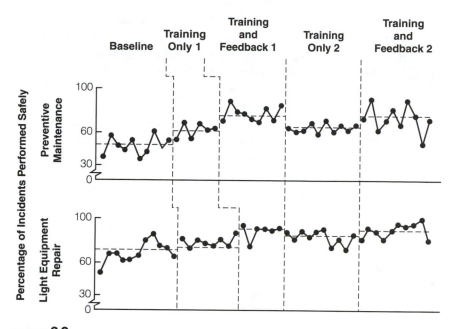

FIGURE 6.2

Percentage of incidents performed safely by employees in vehicle-maintenance departments under five experimental conditions.

Source: From "Effect of Training and Feedback: Component Analysis of a Behavioral Safety Program," by J. Komaki, A. T. Heinzmann, and L. Lawson. In *Journal of Applied Psychology*, 1980, *65*, pp. 261–270. Copyright 1980 by the American Psychology Association. Reprinted by permission.

introduced to the sections at different points in time and improvements occurred after, and not prior to, the introduction of these phases. History was ruled out as a source of internal invalidity because it is not likely that an extraneous event would have the same impact in separate sections at different times. If maturation was responsible, performance would be expected to improve as a function of the passage of time; however, improvements occurred, with few exceptions, after the introduction of phase 3. The effects of statistical regression were ruled out because regression effects would be seen in any series of repeated measurements and not just after the introduction of the two phases.

Reactivity of measurement was also not likely to be a plausible explanation for the improvements obtained because the observers were present during all phases. Therefore, improvements in performance during any one phase could not be due to the reactivity of the measure per se. Questions concerning reactivity and external validity, however, were not so straightforward. Although the issue of the generality of improvements was not addressed directly in the present study, support was provided by accident records, which showed that injuries were reduced by a factor of seven from the preceding year. Because the observers were present during a relatively small percentage of working hours, it is unlikely that improvements were confined to these times. This wonderfully detailed explanation of the threats to validity and how they can be controlled by quasi-experimental designs serves as a teaching tool and reminds us that these type of designs can be extremely effective in field settings.

Another excellent example of a time-series design is offered by Murray and Raffaele (1997). They explored quality awareness training as a way of reducing scrap in a vitreous china production plant that manufactures items such as vanities. The organization had six different product lines. There were two major production processes. One process was called the greenware process, which involved mixing and molding wet clay. The other was the firing process, which dealt with baking the clay. Here timing and temperature were critical variables. Another aspect of the quality process involved the handling of the materials. The organization was motivated by the high cost of scrapped items, estimating the value of lost items to be millions of dollars. Their approach was modeled after a quality-training program proposed by Crosby (1988). The program was based on the following principles: quality relates to the prevention of defects, and it is a skill that can be trained; the quality improvement process needs to be an ongoing process, not a single event; meeting production requirements in terms of quality needs to occur at every point in time; and it is possible to measure quality in terms of the cost of deviations from the production requirements.

The investigators' study, carried out over twelve years from 1981 to 1992, is described in Figure 6.3. The data gathered in the pretreatment measurement period from 1981 through 1986 came from archival data. These data permitted an analysis of quality that was defined as the percent of good pieces following a production process. The total training program took approximately one year to complete. It consisted of a series of steps ranging from discussions of organizational commitment, the development of quality improvement teams, measurement of potential problems and costs, establishment of goals, and zero defects days. First, all managers were trained offsite by the consulting organization on all elements of the plan. Then, managers trained salaried employees. Afterwards, all hourly employees were trained. After training, all employees were tested on the principles and techniques that had been learned. After completion of the training, employees were able to identify needed improvements, make recommendations, and identify costs. Following initial training, the program continued for five more years (see Figure 6.3 for the postmeasurement period) and all new members of the organization were also trained.

The organization went from a scrap rate of 30% to a scrap rate of 22% to 26%, depending on which part of the production process is being analyzed. Using a utility analysis similar to that described in the next section, the inves-

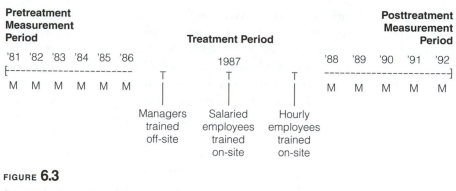

FIGURE **6.3**

Summary of experimental design.

Source: From "Single-site, Results-level Evaluation of Quarterly Awareness Training," by B. Murray and G. C. Raffaele. In *Human Resource Development Quarterly, 8,* 1997, pp. 229–245. Copyright © 1997 by Jossey-Bass, Inc. Reprinted by permission of Jossey-Bass, Inc., a subsidiary of John Wiley & Sons, Inc.

tigators estimated the savings in terms of lower defects minus the increased costs, such as the cost of training. They estimated that the manufacturer saved more than $400,000 just in terms of one production.

All the threats to validity, such as not having a control group, are similar to those described earlier in the Komaki safety study. An additional component here is that it is unusual to have a study continue across this many years, and there is the question of controlling for major changes in the individuals who joined and left the organization during these time periods. One aspect of this company that permitted the control of many extraneous variables is that the employees at the facility were long-term, with an average tenure of eleven years and a very low turnover rate of 1.5%. In addition, the organization did not make any changes in the technology of its production process. Of course, it is also unusual to have a study carried out over twelve years. But in this case, it resulted from the investigators' thoughtful approach to the problem. It turned out that there was archival data that provided information for many years prior to the introduction of the training procedures. Also as it happened, once the training procedure was implemented, the production process remained the same for many years. So again, it was possible to collect long-term data after the training program was completed. This type of study shows how the use of imaginative quasi-experimental designs can provide powerful information even if it is not possible to use a true experimental design.

Research Example of Quasi-Experimental Designs— Nonequivalent Control-Group Design

Skarlicki and Latham (1997) provide an excellent example of the nonequivalent control-group design. The participants in this study were members of the

Canadian Auto Workers Union (CAW). This is Canada's largest private-sector union, and they are employees of an international airline. All union members and shop stewards participate in an employee investment plan. As such, they are the largest stockholders of the airline with a 25% share. The focus of the program was to train shop stewards in principles of the administration of organizational justice. The shop stewards were the most immediate contact for union members, and their role consisted of keeping members aware of union meetings and activities, handling complaints and grievances, and supporting labor community activities. The goal was to increase the perceptions of fairness by union members and to increase their citizenship behavior.

The training condition involved twelve shop stewards located in Vancouver, and the control condition consisted of thirteen shop stewards located in Toronto. For the treatment condition, questionnaires were sent to 305 members of their local union located in Vancouver; and for the control condition, questionnaires were sent to the 240 members located in Toronto. The questionnaire consisted of a rating scale asking for the union members' perceptions of the procedural justice demonstrated by union stewards. They also collected from several peers of the various union members an assessment of the union members' citizenship behavior. This included assessment of behaviors such as "co-workers help new members learn the ropes at work and in the union," and "co-workers volunteer for union-related activities." All of these measures were collected prior to the training of the shop stewards and then again at a post-measurement time three months after training.

The training consisted of lectures, case studies, and role playing to practice principles of procedural justice including consistency, bias suppression, representativeness, and ethicality. An example of the kinds of training provided was the focus not only on being fair but the importance of being perceived as being fair. The trainees set goals such as interacting with each member in his respective area at least once a month, sitting with different members during lunch and coffee breaks, and hosting monthly meetings to provide information to the members. Also, the trainees were asked to contact a union member who felt he or she was treated unfairly and to practice using the skills they had learned in the training program. The trainees would be asked during later training sessions to report back on their experiences, and the trainees would provide help and support for one another.

The results indicated that the reaction of the trainees to the program as far as its benefits were concerned was very high. Data indicated that union members whose leaders had been trained as compared with the control group showed significantly greater levels of positive citizenship behavior both directed at fellow union members and at the union itself. Similar results were obtained concerning the union members' perceptions of the shop steward's fairness. Skarlicki and Latham also report on some qualitative evidence supporting their program. Thus, there was greater participation in union activities such as an increase in the number of candidates running for office over past elections.

Of course, the threats to validity here involve the fact that these are intact groups where one group (Vancouver) was trained and the other group (Toronto) was not trained. In other words, the individuals in training were not randomly assigned to training or control conditions. As the authors note, they used this design because it was not possible to randomly assign members, and ethical considerations did not allow union leaders to behave differently toward members of the union local within the same group. Thus, as previously discussed, the concerns here are that there might be other differences that could explain these results. The authors do as much as possible to examine many issues that might make for differences between groups. Thus, they discovered that there were no differences between the shop steward training group and the control group in terms of sex, employment status, age, education, and years as a union member. The authors even investigated whether there were differences in the union members themselves. Again, there were no differences in terms of age, education, employee status, and number of years as a member. About the only difference found was that union members in the treatment group were younger and had a lower level of education. Thus, if we were to search for an alternative explanation of the results, there does not seem to be much evidence to challenge the interpretation of the finding that training was effective. It's always possible that there might be some other variable that was not investigated that might explain the results. Such a variable might focus on some structural or organization differences between the Vancouver and Toronto site that would explain the results in such a way that it provided evidence that the training intervention was not the reason for the effect. Given the lack of differences between the participants at the two sites and the number of different kinds of measures that showed consistent differences between the training and control group, that does not seem likely, but the training analyst always needs to be aware of such possibilities. This study provides an excellent example of research where the authors analyzed the conditions and employed the best design possible. And most important, they recognized the potential limitations and worked at providing process data that tended to mitigate concern about threats to validity.

UTILITY CONSIDERATIONS

An important consideration in the evaluation of training programs is the concept of utility. Meaningful terms for management usually involve monetary considerations. For example, when a production manager requests a new piece of machinery, it is usually supported by projected increases in productivity and resultant decreases in unit cost of production. Maintenance managers support hiring requests with figures showing decreases in downtime due to equipment problems and the resulting savings. This means translating our validity evidence into dollar values even if the translations are somewhat crude. These kinds of translations are called *utility analysis*. The analysis not only enables researchers to have information about the costs of their programs but also permits comparisons between the costs of different programs—for example, a formal training program versus on-the-job training or a training program versus a selection program.

Again, this is an area where there have been important developments. Cascio (1989) has developed a methodology for the application of utility analysis to the assessment of training outcomes. His considerations involve several steps. First, Cascio introduces the use of capital budget methodology to analyze the minimum annual benefits in dollars required from any program. This phase of the analysis requires specifying the cost of the program, the increased benefits expected for any given period, the duration of the benefits, and a determination of the discount rate to specify the firm's minimum expected return on investment. The acceptance ratio that Cascio specifies for a training program based on these figures is that the net present value of the program must be greater than zero.

Second, Cascio details the use of a break-even analysis originally introduced by Boudreau (1984) to estimate the minimum effect size for a program to produce the required benefits. Basically, this operates on the premise that if the training program has any effect, the mean of the job performance of the trained group should exceed the untrained group. The degree to which there is a difference between the trained and untrained group, expressed in standard deviation units, represents the effect size. Once the effect size is corrected for unreliability of the criterion, it is an estimate of the true differences between the trained and untrained group.

As a third step, Cascio (1989) uses data across multiple studies to estimate the expected actual payoff from the program. Further, he also provides information on the effects of the outcome when other factors are considered, such as an enhancement or decay of the size of the training effect. As a result of this work, it is now possible to express the gains resulting from effective training in terms of a number of outcomes such as dollar, percentage increases in output, or reductions in the size of the workforce while accomplishing the same level of work.

An important point raised by Cascio (1989) is that these analyses depend on a careful tracing out of the costs of training. An examination of such costs and issues in the examination of structured training versus unstructured training for a production worker is presented in Cullen, Sawzin, Sisson, and Swanson's (1978) work, illustrated in Figure 6.4. Training costs would include training development, training materials, training time, and production losses. The

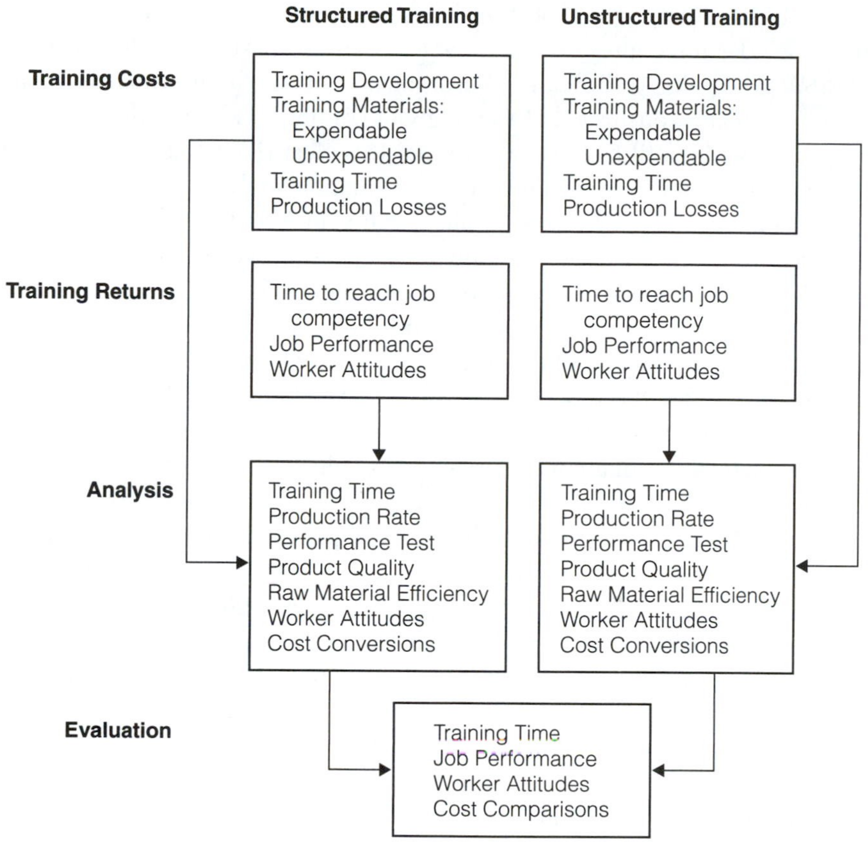

	Structured Training	**Unstructured Training**

Training Costs	Training Development
	Training Materials:
	    Expendable
	    Unexpendable
	Training Time
	Production Losses
		Training Development
		Training Materials:
		    Expendable
		    Unexpendable
		Training Time
		Production Losses

Training Returns	Time to reach job
	    competency
	Job Performance
	Worker Attitudes
		Time to reach job
		    competency
		Job Performance
		Worker Attitudes

Analysis	Training Time Production Rate Performance Test Product Quality Raw Material Efficiency Worker Attitudes Cost Conversions	Training Time Production Rate Performance Test Product Quality Raw Material Efficiency Worker Attitudes Cost Conversions
Evaluation	Training Time Job Performance Worker Attitudes Cost Comparisons	

FIGURE 6.4

Industrial training cost-effectiveness model.

Source: From "Cost Effectiveness: A Model for Assessing the Training Investment," by J. G. Cullen, S. A. Sawzin, G. R. Sisson, and R. A. Swanson. In *Training and Development Journal,* 1978, *32,* pp. 24–29. Copyright 1978 by the American Society for Training and Development, Inc. Reprinted by permission.

analysis requires that measures be developed for each of the categories (training costs, training returns, and analysis). This involves the criterion issues (relevancy, reliability, and so on) previously discussed. The final stage of assessing the cost effectiveness (as shown in the figure) is evaluation. Here, the structured and unstructured training methods are compared on all variables in the diagram. Each variable is translated into monetary terms. Thus, each factor in the analysis would be specified and translated. For example, raw material usage would be specified as the "weight of the raw material supplied to the machine versus weight of scrap and amount of quality product produced"

(Cullen et al., 1978, p. 27). The translation of these measures into monetary figures includes the conversion of variables such as worker attitudes. As Cascio (1989) notes, this is difficult to accomplish, but the failure to analyze our programs in dollars ensures that training will continue to be viewed as a cost rather than as a benefit to the organization. It is clear that utility analyses will become an increasingly important part of evaluation analyses.

Mathieu and Leonard (1987) applied utility analysis to examine a behavioral role modeling training program to teach supervisory skills for bank tellers, branch managers, and operations managers. Their analyses indicated that the training program was effective, and the future utility to the organization for training a group of fifteen supervisors in each of the three job classes was over $13,000 for the first year and over $100,000 by year 3. The increase over a period of years resulted from the increased effectiveness of supervisors already trained who remain in the organization plus training other new supervisors. In addition, these researchers provide utility estimates showing that there is more to be gained financially from emphasizing training for branch managers as compared with operations managers or as compared with tellers. Thus, the organization can receive information from utility analysis that not only permits decisions on the effectiveness of the program but also permits important comparisons related to a large number of factors, such as the effects of training people in different jobs, the effects of different rates of turnover of trained individuals, or even estimates of what would occur if the training program decreased in efficiency over several years.

More recently, Morrow, Jarrett, and Rupinski (1997) investigated the economic utility of corporate-wide managerial and sales/technical training programs. They used quasi-experimental designs to investigate the effects of the training programs on job performance and utility analysis to estimate the economic impact of the training programs. The results showed that the training did have an impact with sales/technical training programs having more of an effect on job performance (as indicated by supervisory, peer, or subordinate ratings) and a greater return on investment than the managerial training programs. This shows that return on investment approaches to evaluating training might be more useful for training programs that focus on specific skills rather than managerial training, which often focuses on broader and more general skills and competencies.

Finally, Tesoro (1998) examined the return on investment for sales negotiation training provided to Dell Computer Corporation. The specific measures examined included profit margin, unit sold, and total revenue. Results from 57 participants showed that there was an overall improvement over a control group of employees of almost 61% for profit margin and 42% for revenue sales as a function of the training. A cost-benefit analysis calculated the return on investment of over 500% for a three-month period after the training with a net profit to the company of $763,000.

OTHER METHODS OF EVALUATION

The experimental models of evaluation that center on pretests and posttests, control groups, threats to validity, and so on represent the traditional models used to assess the effects of training programs. However, there are a number of other evaluation models. For example, there is the adversarial model, which stems from a criticism of the classical experimental model (Levine, 1974). This point of view maintains that the traditional approach to experimental design is not well suited to decision making and does not focus well on questions of the value or worth of the program being evaluated. The adversarial model is developed around a system similar to a court of law. The model takes the point of view that all researchers are biased and the best way to counteract this problem and determine the value of the program is to have two sets of researchers. Each group gathers its own data to support its position and advocates a point of view to a judge or jury, who then renders a decision about the value of the program. Many of the rules of data gathering, analysis, and so on are similar to the experimental model. However, the final decision is based on a judge's or jury's determination of worth based on the evidence presented by the advocates.

Unfortunately, it is not possible to discuss all evaluation models in this book; however, a few other models are particularly relevant to the evaluation of training programs. They are individual-differences models and content-validity models.

Individual-Differences Models of Predictive Validity

Many industrial and organizational psychologists have emphasized the use of training scores as a way to predict the future success of potential employees. The use of trainability scores (discussed in Chapter 4 in the section on trainee readiness) is an example of the use of a pretraining measure to predict training performance. It is also possible to use performance in training to predict either later training performance or actual job performance. Figure 6.5 presents a hypothetical set of scores on a sales training test and a criteria consisting of sales volume at the end of one year on the job. One way of characterizing the relationships between these two variables is by the statistical determination of the correlation coefficient. The value of the correlational coefficient ranges from +1.00 for a perfect positive relationship to −1.00 for a perfect negative correlation. A .00 correlation indicates that there is no evidence that the two variables are associated. In this example, a positive correlation means that people with higher scores on the training test also tended to perform better on the job in terms of sales volume. Thus, the better performers in training were better performers on the job, and the poorer performers in training were poorer performers on the job.

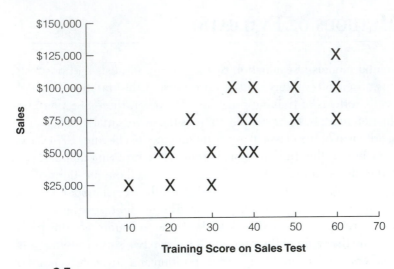

FIGURE **6.5**

Hypothetical scores on a sales test at the end of training and sales volume after one year on the job.

A number of these types of predictive studies show meaningful relationships between training performance and on-the-job performance. For example, Kraut (1975) found that peer ratings obtained from managers attending a month-long training course predicted several criteria including future promotion and performance appraisal ratings of job performance.

Other investigators have used early training performance to predict performance in more advanced training. An example of this approach is offered by Gordon and Cohen (1973), whose study involved a welding program that was part of a larger manpower development project aimed at training unemployed and underemployed individuals from the eastern Tennessee area. The program consisted of fourteen different tasks that fell into four categories and ranged in difficulty from simple to complex. Advancement from one task to the next depended on successful completion of all previous tasks. Thus, trainees progressed at a rate commensurate with their ability to master the material to be learned. For each trainee, data were collected on the amount of time spent on each task. The correlations between the completion times for the four categories of tasks and total time to complete the plate-welding course are given in Table 6.2.

Gordon and Cohen indicate that the results show that early performance in the lab generally is an excellent predictor of final performance. Furthermore, the greater the number of tasks included in our predictor, the better our prediction will become. It is possible, therefore, to identify those trainees who will take longer than average to complete the plate-welding course by simply examining their performance on the first few tasks.

| TABLE 6.2 | CORRELATIONS BETWEEN THE TIME TO COMPLETION FOR VARIOUS SEGMENTS OF THE COURSE AND TOTAL TIME REQUIRED TO COMPLETE THE PLATE-WELDING COURSE |

	Correlation of Task			
	1 with Finish	1 and 2 with Finish	1–3 with Finish	1–4 with Finish
I (N = 21)	0.55	0.76	0.81	0.84
II (N = 19)	0.70	0.83	0.94	0.96
III (N = 18)[a]	0.09	0.18	0.77	0.78
Total (N = 58)	0.69	0.79	0.87	0.87

Note: Groups I, II, and III differed in their starting dates.
[a] A word of explanation is due regarding the poor predictability of tasks 1 and 2 in Group III. Discussion with the training supervisor of the welding program indicated that illness had caused two of his three instructors to be absent for most of the period during which Group III was learning tasks 1 and 2. Consequently, the amount of supervision and guidance provided was necessarily below normal. It is probable that this temporary understaffed situation changed the usual conditions of learning and caused the correlations observed in Group III to be unlike those recorded for Groups I and II.
Source: From "Training Behavior as a Predictor of Trainability," by M. E. Gordon and S. L. Cohen. In *Personnel Psychology*, 1973, *26*, pp. 261–271. Copyright 1973 by Personnel Psychology, Inc. Reprinted by permission.

These investigators understood that they were predicting the performance of individuals on a later task—for example, on the job or later in training—based on performance in the training program. As a matter of fact, once these relationships have been established in an appropriately designed study, it is possible to select individuals for a job or for later training based on these training scores. In other words, the training score serves as a validated predictor of future performance.

However, caution should be used when this technique is considered as an evaluation of the training program. The relationship between training performance and on-the-job performance means that individuals who perform best on the training test also perform well on the job. This does not necessarily mean that the training program is as properly designed as possible or that individuals learned enough in training to perform well on the job. It is entirely possible that the training program did not accomplish as much as possible and that trainees did not learn as much as possible. In those cases, the training test is predictive of future performance. That is, some people would perform poorly in training and some would perform well. Even if the training program did not teach as much as it should, a strong relationship would still be indicated if the people who performed well on the test also performed well on the job and the people who performed poorly on the test performed poorly on the job. That is, the training program might not have achieved as much as desired but it still might maintain the individual differences between trainees that existed before they entered training.

At least several suggestions could be helpful in this instance. First, the use of appropriate pretests and control groups will establish whether learning has occurred and whether it is likely to be a result of the training program. In other words, even when the purpose is to use the training scores as a predictive device, it is useful to use experimental methodology evaluation to ensure that the training program has actually accomplished its learning objectives. For example, if you find correlations between training performance and job performance, and you can also demonstrate that performance improved in training from pre- to posttest, you would feel much more comfortable in knowing that the training program had achieved its desired effects.

Another procedure that lends some support to individual-differences and predictive validity methodology is to demonstrate that the training program and the criteria used to evaluate training are based on a thorough needs assessment so that the training program really does reflect the required knowledge, skills, and abilities (KSAs). In this instance, you would feel more comfortable with the outcomes because you have better assurances that the training program itself did properly map what is needed on the job. This latter procedure introduces another evaluation methodology—training content validity.

Content-Validity Models

If the needs assessment is appropriately carried out and the training program is designed to reflect KSAs, then the program will be judged as having content validity. That is, the training program should reflect the domain of KSAs represented on the job that the analyst has determined should be learned in the training program. Yet, in many instances, a training program originally formed on the basis of a needs assessment might be modified over the time it is offered. Or, the program might not change over the course of years that it is taught. Thus, an interesting question is whether a training course has maintained its level of content validity or job-relatedness over time. This question is operationalized by examining whether a training program designed several years ago is content-valid in the sense that it reflects the content established by a newly completed needs assessment. The research examples provided next present ways of exploring these issues.

One way of conceptualizing the content validity of a training program is presented in Figure 6.6. In this figure, the horizontal axis across the top of the figure represents the dimension of importance, or criticality, of the KSAs as determined by a training needs assessment. Although the diagram only presents KSAs as being important or not important, it is vital to realize that this is an oversimplification of a dimension with many points. The vertical axis represents the degree of emphasis for the KSAs in training. Again, to simplify the presentation, the dimension indicates that the KSA is or is not emphasized in the training program.

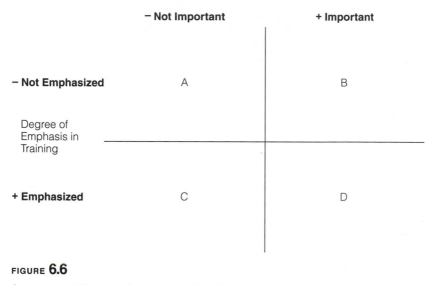

FIGURE 6.6

A conceptual diagram of content validity of training programs.

This results in the fourfold table presented in Figure 6.6. Using this approach, both boxes A and D provide support for the content validity of the training program. KSAs that fall into box D are judged as being important for the job and are emphasized in training. Items in box A are judged as not important for the job and are not emphasized in training. Conceptually, to the degree to which KSAs fall into categories A and D, it is possible to think about the training program as being content-valid. Of course, this is an oversimplification. There will be KSAs that are judged as moderately important for the job or KSAs that are moderately emphasized in training. However, it is possible to conceive of this type of relationship and to actually measure the degree to which those KSAs judged as important are emphasized (and hopefully learned) in training. Very few people would be unhappy with a training program that tends to emphasize the objectives associated with KSAs that are judged critical or important for job performance.

Box B represents a potential error and could affect the degree to which a program is judged content-valid. KSAs falling into the B category are judged as important for the job but are not emphasized in training. From a systems perspective, these items must be analyzed to determine whether the organization intends for these KSAs to be gained as a result of training. If that is the case, then there is a problem. However, it is also possible that individuals are expected to be selected with that particular KSA or that individuals are expected to learn the material related to that KSA on the job. To that extent, the training program should not be expected to emphasize the item, and its content validity would not be questioned. However, training designers should still determine whether KSAs judged as important or critical are covered in another system, such as the selection of employees. If the item is not represented, then the organization must decide whether revision of the training program is necessary or if some other system must be designed to cover that material.

Box C represents KSAs that are emphasized in training but are judged as not being important for the job. This is sometimes a criticism of training programs. That is, they tend to spend time emphasizing material that is not job-related. Most analysts agree that the use of needs assessment procedures and examination of training content results in a decrease in the amount of training time necessary to complete the training program. This usually occurs because of a reduction in the program based on an elimination of the types of items present in Box C. Interestingly, a systems view of this process would even suggest a reduction of items that would appear in Box D. Selection experts would note that sometimes KSAs included in Box D are unnecessary because they have already been used as a basis for selection. Thus, if such materials are included in the training program, trainees are again subjected to materials on KSAs that are already in their repertoire. Of course, in other instances, it is the complexity of the KSA that makes the difference. For example, you might test for one level of ability on a KSA during the selection process. Then, you might be trying to raise the ability level on the particular KSAs in the training program.

You should also note that Figure 6.6 and Figure 5.2 are identical except that one refers to criteria and one refers to training programs. The point is that in each case the model is designed to assess the content validity of either criteria or training programs. And in each case the content validity is determined by matching the criteria or the training program against data established in a needs assessment.

There are a number of analyses in the research literature based on these types of content-validity strategies. Ford and Wroten (1984) explored some of these strategies in an examination of police officer training programs. The objectives of the research were (1) to determine the extent to which the training content of the existing course was job-related and content-valid and (2) to identify needed changes in training content to improve the job-relatedness of the program. On the basis of training needs assessment procedures, these investigators identified 383 KSAs as incorporated into a police training program for entry-level officers and an additional 57 KSAs identified as important for job performance. They then had 114 experts independently rate the importance of each of the 440 items (383 included in the training program and the additional 57 deemed important on the job) for job performance. For the first objective of the research, these investigators chose KSAs that were identified as emphasized in training and determined whether the item fell into category

C (not important for job performance) or category D (important for job performance). They discovered that 237, or 62%, of the KSAs met the criteria they specified as being important for job performance. Thus, the training program was deemed to have a high degree of content validity.

To meet the second objective of the project, training designers then examined the KSAs that were not seen as important for job performance but were included in the training program to determine whether they should remain in the program. Based on this analysis, some KSAs were eliminated from the program or deemphasized in the program. In addition, in a separate analysis of the job performance domain, these investigators also examined the 57 items that were rated as important for job performance but not included in the training program. A few of those items were judged to be KSAs that were trainable and important, and they were thus added to the program. This study shows a systematic approach to examining content-validity issues as well as the use of evaluation data to modify an existing training program.

As part of a research program involving Goldstein's attempts to develop content-validity models to understand training, Newman (1985) conducted research examining the implications of the diagram presented in Figure 6.6. His study was conducted on the job of cook supervisor for the Federal Bureau of Prisons. First, a needs assessment was conducted to determine the KSAs needed for the job as well as the KSAs taught in the training program. The training program was a two-week course covering the basics of institutional cooking and baking for cook supervisors who oversee inmates in the preparation of meals in the federal prisons. A KSA analysis was done for the training program, as well as the job, to include the possibility that KSAs not important on the job (box C in Figure 6.6) might be emphasized in training. Both sets of KSAs were combined in an inventory. Newman then had eighty-seven job subject-matter experts (SMEs) rate the KSAs in terms of importance on the job, difficulty of learning, and where best acquired. The same KSAs were also rated by two training SMEs (the training director and the course instructor) on importance on the job, difficulty to learn, and time spent in the program teaching the KSAs. As an indicator of content validity, Newman correlated the KSA job-importance ratings and the training-emphasis ratings (as reflected by time spent). For the cooking and baking KSAs, the correlation was $r = .52$. For another set of KSAs related to supervision and administration, the correlation was $r = .55$. These data provide positive evidence that KSAs judged higher in job importance were KSAs most emphasized in training. Also, the trainer SMEs and the job SMEs agreed on what was important for cooking and baking KSAs and for supervision and administration KSAs. As a result of this study, it was also possible to do an analysis of where KSAs should be learned and which KSAs fell into the four boxes diagrammed in Figure 6.6. Newman (1985) collected other quantitative and qualitative data about the program. For example, he found improvement from pretraining to posttraining based on test scores and found that trainees as compared with a control group received higher performance ratings on training-relevant dimensions.

Another example of the kind of thoughtful information that can be collected using content type analysis is offered by Teachout, Sego, and Ford (1997/1998). They examined a technical training course offered in the U.S. Air Force. These authors used the type of analysis described previously in the work of Ford and Wroten and Newman and Goldstein. However, they added some further indicators. One indicator was referred to as training efficiency—the degree to which training time was actually used on the tasks that had been rated in a training needs assessment as most difficult to learn. They also examined transfer opportunity—the degree to which trainees were given the opportunities to actually perform the trained tasks on the job. They also examined whether on-the-job supervisors thought that trainees were effectively performing these tasks.

Their content validity matchup procedure produced very interesting results. They found that twelve of thirty-three tasks were considered potentially overtrained in that more time was being spent on them in training than appeared warranted given the difficulty rating of the tasks. Perhaps even more important, six of the tasks were considered undertrained in the sense that less time was being spent on them than might be expected given their difficulty ratings. Then, the researchers examined the opportunities for the trainees to perform these tasks on the job. For the twelve overtrained tasks, the trainees averaged performing them approximately eighteen times over an eight-month period. For the six undertrained tasks, trainees were given an opportunity to perform them only about two times on average over the course of eight months on the job. Thus, not only was less training time devoted to these tasks but the trainees had less opportunity to perform them when on the job. Most interestingly, when supervisors rated the trainee's effectiveness in performing these tasks, they gave the highest effectiveness ratings to those where training time and training opportunities were the highest. The lowest performance ratings were given to tasks that were undertrained in terms of time devoted in training and where trainees had fewest opportunities to perform on the job. This type of analysis certainly provides the kind of information necessary to suggest revisions in both the training program itself and in the design of training opportunities on the job to produce more positive transfer from training to the job.

A word of caution should be added to any conclusion about the use of content-validity models for training programs. Obviously, content validity is very important, and all training programs should be content-valid. It makes no sense to have training programs that do not cover the KSAs necessary for the job. The whole purpose of performing a needs assessment and then tracing out the training program objectives based on the needs assessment is to have a content-valid program. As noted earlier, the concept of criterion relevance is based on exactly the same idea. Also, if both the criterion and the training program are based on a properly conducted needs assessment, then the criterion should form a good basis for the evaluation of the training program. However, the point is that the reason for concern about the development of criteria is the importance of having a measure of trainee performance both in the training program and on the job. That is why using only the concept of content validity in the evaluation of a training program is a problem. The program may very well be content-valid, but that does not provide information about whether trainees learned the material in the training program and whether trainees were able to transfer that knowledge to the job. Nevertheless, some of the additional data that Newman (1985) collected about predifferences and postdifferences allow stronger inferences about training program effects than content-validity information by itself could permit. Information concerning that issue requires the use of principles of experimental design and quasi-experimental design to ensure that learning occurs and that it transfers to the job. As noted earlier, the same point might be made about the use of individual-differences methodology to examine predictive validity. As described previously, a correlation between scores in training and on the job does not guarantee that the program is effective. It does mean that individuals who perform well on the training test also perform well on the job, and those individuals who perform poorly on the training test perform poorly on the job. These same relationships may exist regardless of whether the training program accomplished anything. If the training program was also shown to be content-valid, then there is reason to be more optimistic. It is also possible to consider training evaluation as a succession of steps that provides information of better and better quality. Thus, as a next step, adding a pretest and posttest on relevant criteria is possible. More certainty is then possible because there will be information on changes in trainee performance from before to after training. If, in addition, it is possible to add a control group, there will be more information about ruling out other reasons for the changes from pretest to posttest.

In summary, establishing the validity of training programs involves building a network that gives more and more information with better and better controls so that the evaluator has more faith in the information. In some cases, it may be possible only to start with an individual-differences methodology for examining predictive validity. On that basis, the investigator will know whether people who perform well on training test measures also perform well on the job. Then, it might be possible to obtain a pretest, then content validity, and so on. As Goldstein stated previously,

> In order to gain an appreciation for the degree to which training programs achieve their objectives, it is necessary to consider the creative development of evaluation models. The models should permit the extraction of the greatest amount of information within the constraints of the environment. . . . Researchers cannot afford to be frozen into inactivity by the spectra of threats to validity. (Goldstein, 1980, p. 262)

Practical, Statistical, and Scientific Significance

Analysts often emphasize the importance of statistically significant changes. The achievement of *practically significant* changes assumes that the differences are indeed meaningful and will recur when the next instructional group is exposed to the treatment. Interacting with both ideas is the concept of *scientific significance*—that is, the establishment of meaningful results that permit generalizations about training procedures beyond the immediate setting being investigated. As Campbell, Dunnette, Lawler, and Weick suggest for managerial training, "once the effects of such a program are mapped out for different kinds of trainees and for different types of criterion problems under various organizational situations, the general body of knowledge concerning management training has been enriched" (1970, p. 284). If the instructional program is well designed, it should contribute to the solution of organizational goals and add to the body of instructional knowledge.

In one way, statistics serve as the gatekeeper for social scientists. Cook, Campbell, and Peracchio put it this way: "Though statistics function as gate-keepers, they are fallible even when properly used, sometimes failing to detect true patterns of covariation and sometimes indicating there is covariation when it does not exist" (1990, pp. 493–494). Thus, if statistical power is low because the sample size is small or the reliability of the criterion measure is low or because a statistical test is not powerful, then relationships that actually exist might not be found using the data that could be gathered. On the other hand, when large numbers of comparisons are made, some will be statistically significant by chance. In addition, with very large sample sizes, statistical differences might be found that are not especially meaningful in the sense that they are too small to have practical value.

Some of these measurement considerations are beyond the scope of this chapter. Statistical considerations and the choice of design interact. This has been made more obvious by an important article by Arvey and Cole (1989). One factor these authors explore is the likelihood of detecting a difference when it is really there (otherwise known as statistical power). They note that when they compared different designs, they were not all comparable in detecting differences that really existed. The designs compared were a posttest-only design that ignored pretest information completely, a gain-score design that analyzed the differences between pretest and posttest, and an analysis of covariance (ANCOVA) design that statistically treated the pretest as a covariate in a between-group design. In general, they found that the ANCOVA was more powerful. However, the extent of these power differences between designs was dramatically affected by a host of other factors including the sample sizes and the degree of correlation between the pretests and posttests. For example, in the gain-score and ANCOVA design, power always increased as the correlation between pretest and posttest increased.

Alternatively, when the correlation was very small, the advantage of ANCOVA over the gain-score approach was substantial, and any advantages for the posttest-only design became nonexistent. Also, the effect of greater score reliability increases the power of all three designs but the benefits are more substantial in the gain-score and ANCOVA design than in the posttest only design. Most important, in all the work described in this article, the assumption is made that the pretest scores are equivalent. The effect of non-equivalent groups at the pretest phase is crushing on the power of all of these designs. Further data (Yang, Sackett, & Arvey, 1996) has shown that the power to detect statistical differences between experimental and control groups is maximized by having an equal number of persons in each group. These authors also provide information on how it is possible to use a larger sample size even with unequal numbers of participants in each group to overcome some of these challenges. It is clear that evaluators should pay careful attention to these types of considerations before choosing experimental designs and procedures.

FROM NEEDS ASSESSMENT TO TRAINING VALIDITY: SOME CONCLUDING WORDS

Researchers, training designers, and managers need to ask ourselves what we want our training program to be able to do. At one level, we usually want our program to result in trainees who perform better at the end of the training program. Then, we usually also ask that our programs result in trainees who perform better at both the end of the training program and on the job. If the training program is not a one-shot affair, we would also be interested in knowing how another group of trainees (after the program has been developed and evaluated) are going to perform. Then again, if you are a consulting company developing training programs, you would also be interested in how the program might work in another organization with other trainees. The answers to these questions require the analyst to consider what systems-training issues must be addressed. It is possible to characterize the evaluation methodology in this chapter as an attempt to achieve one of the following types of validity (Goldstein, 1978):

1. *Training validity.* This particular stage refers only to the validity of the training program. Validity is determined by the performance of trainees on criteria established for the training program.
2. *Transfer validity.* This stage of analysis refers to the validity of the training program as measured by performance in the transfer or on-the-job setting. Ordinarily, training and transfer validity are both considered indicators of internal validity. That is, they indicate whether

the treatment made a difference in a very specific situation. Here, transfer validity is considered an external validity concept because training programs are typically developed in a particular environment that is different from the organizational settings in which the trainee will eventually be expected to perform.

3. *Intra-organizational validity.* This concept refers to the performance of a new group of trainees within the organization that developed the original training program. In this instance, the analyst is attempting to predict the performance of new trainees based on the evaluated performance of a previous group.

4. *Inter-organizational validity.* In this instance, the analyst is attempting to determine whether a training program validated in one organization can be used in another organization.

The first two stages, training validity and transfer validity, have been the topics of the first five chapters of this book. Thus, training validity begins with the needs assessment process and continues with criterion development, evaluation, and the feedback necessary to revise the program. Transfer validity requires attention to all aspects of training validity but includes the idea that the trainee must perform on the job. Considering the needs assessment procedures and evaluation procedures necessary to establish training validity, it would seem that there is little to add to a section on transfer validity. This is not the case as the focus is on external validity operations, which involve the transfer of performance in one environment (training) to another environment (on the job). As noted earlier in this chapter, the tracing-out process from needs assessment to criterion development must now be concerned with relevant on-the-job criteria while avoiding deficiency and contamination. Also, transfer validity is affected by the fact that the trainee enters a new environment and is affected by all the interacting components that make up organizations today. Certainly, some aspects of the environment contribute to the success or failure of training programs beyond the attributes the trainee must gain as a result of attending the instructional program. For example, as described in Chapter 3 in "Organizational Analysis," the training program and the organization often specify different performance objectives, and trainees are caught in a conflict that sometimes results in difficulties. The trainee and the training program may be declared inadequate because the training analyst never considered the relevant variables that determine success or failure at each of the four stages of validity. We have become convinced that many training programs are judged failures because of organizational systems' constraints. Transfer validity thus requires the use of organizational analysis as a critical component of program development. Most of these concepts have been discussed in the preceding chapters in this book. However, the concepts of intra-organizational and inter-organizational validity prompt several new considerations. These are discussed next.

Intra-organizational Validity

Intra-organizational validity presupposes that the trainer has established training and transfer validity and is concerned now with the performance of a new group of trainees. Just as transfer validity presupposes the consideration of the points established for training validity, intra-organizational validity presupposes that the points discussed for training and transfer validity have been established. We have already described evaluation as an information-gathering process that provides feedback about the multiple objectives of most training programs. Thus, it becomes apparent that evaluation should be a continual process that provides data as a basis for revisions of the program. New data should be collected based on the performance of a new group of trainees. The new data provide further understanding about the achievement of objectives or about the variables that affect the achievement of objectives. That does not mean that each effort must start from the very beginning. However, collecting further new information about the effects of revisions should be possible. Also, it should be possible to collect data that can be checked against previously collected information to ensure that the instructional program is having the same effect.

Given this philosophy, it is still possible to ask how likely it is that one can generalize results from the previous training program to a new group of trainees in the same organization. The answer to that question stems from a consideration of many of the factors already discussed. First, it is necessary to consider the components of the needs assessment process, including task, person, and organizational aspects. If the job tasks and resulting KSAs have been revised or if their frequency, importance, or degree of difficulty have changed, then the training program requires revisions. In these cases, generalizations based on the old program are speculative at best. These kinds of task changes can occur for a variety of reasons, including technological developments or revisions in jobs being performed at various levels in the organization. Similarly, if the kinds of people entering the organization are different, then it is difficult to generalize from the old program. These kinds of changes also occur for a variety of reasons, including moving the organization from an urban to suburban environment or market and career shifts that result in differences in the KSAs of individuals desiring particular types of employment. Also, of course, modifications in the organization or constraints in the organization can affect the degree to which generalizations are safe. Although time itself is not ordinarily considered a variable, these types of changes eventually occur in all organizations, rendering long-term generalizations of training results to new populations increasingly suspect. A good procedure might be to recheck the needs assessment for applicability before attempting to generalize to new trainee populations. If needs assessment procedures have not been carried out, the original program is questionable, and generalizations are difficult to make.

A second factor to consider before generalizing is how well the evaluation was performed in the first place. If the data on which the generalizations are based are only the reactions of the trainees to the instructional program, then the original evaluation and any future generalizations are limited. In the same sense, properly evaluated instructional programs provide a variety of information about the achievement of multiple goals. It is necessary to consider what has been achieved and what remains questionable before deciding whether to generalize to new trainees.

A third consideration is whether the training program will be the same. This factor is misleadingly simplistic. Almost everyone would agree that it is dangerous to generalize to new trainee populations when they are not being instructed in the same training program. However, training analysts are sometimes surprised to discover how different established training programs tend to be from the original training program from which evaluation data were collected. Some of these difficulties generally can be labeled problems of reactivity. Observations, experimental equipment, and questions being asked often result in changes in behavior that are not a result of the actual training program. To the extent that these variables are a source of training results and to the extent that these variables are not present the next time training is offered, it is difficult to generalize. There is a certain aura of excitement surrounding new instructional treatments or training programs that simply disappears over time.

To the extent that these factors change over time, the training program has changed, and it is difficult to generalize. Also, programs tend to change over time as trainers and managers add to and delete from the originally designed program. Sometimes changes in carefully designed programs radically alter the training system. One of the most compelling reasons for the use of process criteria is to attempt to specify these variables and their effects. When the process criteria indicate that the training programs have not changed, then it is obviously safer to generalize. From a consideration of the needs assessment component, the quality of the evaluation, and the similarity of the training program, the decision of whether to generalize becomes easier. It should also be clear that the greater the confidence in training and transfer validity, the easier it is to generalize. Even so, our personal choice will always be to collect some evaluative information to ensure that the program continues to work.

Inter-organizational Validity

In *inter-organizational validity,* the analyst attempts to determine whether a training program validated in one organization can be used in another organization. All factors discussed in training validity, transfer validity, and intra-organizational validity affect this decision. As indicated in the previous section, when the needs assessment shows differences (that is, the task, person, or organizational components), or the evaluation is questionable, or the training program will differ, then generalization is difficult. In this instance, the needs assessment and evaluation may not have been performed for the organization that desires to use the training program. Clearly, the more similar the organizations, as shown by a needs assessment, the more likely similar results will occur. Still, considering the incredible number of ways organizations differ, attempting to generalize the training results in one organization to trainees in another organization is hard to do. On the other hand, borrowing needs assessment methodologies, evaluation strategies, and training techniques to try out in different organizations is entirely appropriate. Through these procedures, organizations can establish techniques that work, and perhaps it will be possible to begin to understand what variables affect the success of programs across organizations. However, given the present state of knowledge, simply borrowing results from another organization as a shortcut in the training process probably does not serve the organization well.

INFOTRAC COLLEGE EDITION

For additional readings, go to http: www.infotrac-college.com/wadsworth and enter a search term related to your interest. The following key terms will pull up several related articles.

Evaluation Design   Quasi-Experimental Design
External Validity   Training Evaluation

TRAINING DELIVERY:

Traditional Instructional Approaches and Emerging Learning Technologies

The previous chapters have examined the instructional-systems design (ISD) model for the assessment, design, and evaluation of training programs. Needs assessment tells us what, where, when, and who needs to be trained. Based on that information, training objectives can be specified. Program design is the process of developing a plan of instruction for each training program to be offered to meet training objectives. Training design includes the sequencing of training events, deciding the evaluation strategy, and incorporating learning principles to maximize learning and transfer.

To maximize learning potential, training designers must examine the methods and techniques available and choose the training approach most appropriate for the behaviors being trained. This procedure should be appropriate for all different types of objectives from motor skill specifications in pilot training to styles of managerial behavior in various organizations. For example, machine simulators are useful for the development of motor skills, whereas role playing is designed to acquaint managerial trainees with a variety of interpersonal situations.

A key dilemma for training designers is how to determine the behaviors that are likely to be modified or enhanced by the various instructional approaches. Campbell (1971) originally expressed this dilemma by noting that it is impossible to organize empirical research around dependent variables. Campbell and his colleagues (Campbell, McCloy, Oppler, & Sager, 1993) further lament the lack of conceptual understanding about the dependent variable or performance. These authors note that

> People can get goose-bumps over a new treatment (e.g., empowered work groups), or a new ability variable (e.g., tacit knowledge), but spending a lot of time or resources to understand performance itself seems not to be very exciting or fundable.

Although these authors are referring to any type of treatment, the remarks apply to training interventions. Campbell and his colleagues argue for examining which kinds of experiences produce particular outcomes and which variables affect the relationship between treatments and outcomes. However, for a variety of reasons, the training field has not arrived at that state of knowledge. First, the empirical research necessary to establish these relationships has been insufficient. Second, as noted in Chapter 6 on evaluation, most research efforts have emphasized reactions and learning in the training setting rather than performance in the transfer setting. Third, empirical studies have tended to cluster around demonstrations of the value of an instructional approach rather than the nature of the learning activities for which the method is useful. Nevertheless, there is a large body of research and practice that can be used to organize the literature on instructional approaches.

Part 3, titled "Instructional Approaches," involves the next steps in the design of training—the selection of instructional techniques and training methods. Instructional techniques emphasize the variety of ways in which training content can be delivered. It is the physical means by which training content is communicated. For example, training material on how to properly fill out accounting forms for automobile leasing agreements could be conveyed by an experienced trainer through the traditional lecture and discussion format. On the other hand, training administrators might decide that the best way to convey this information is through a web-based course in which trainees can access the information whenever they have the time and need for this training on how to fill out forms. The need to develop troubleshooting skills could lead to the delivery of training via a heavy emphasis on skill practice on the actual equipment with feedback from an instructor. Or, money might be invested in developing capabilities to train via virtual reality that do not require a physical machine to troubleshoot but immerse trainees into a virtual world in which they can manipulate and work on equipment to solve the problem. Chapter 7 describes the variety of training delivery techniques from the traditional classroom and work simulation approaches to the emerging learning technologies.

Chapter 8 describes the variety of training methods and learning experiences for developing employees, teams, and leaders. For example, to train leadership skills such as resource management, training designers might develop a business simulation game. The simulation puts the leader in the position to make a variety of important decisions that can be analyzed once the game is completed. Or, the desire to develop the technical proficiency of newcomers could lead to assigning the newcomer to complete an on-the-job training program with an experienced worker. We have selected techniques that have aroused the interest of the training community and that appear likely to be used in the twenty-first century. We have also favored approaches that elucidate the topics presented in the first six chapters. For example, behavioral role modeling represents a technique that is a direct development of cognitive and social learning approaches.

The tremendous variety of delivery mechanisms and training methods requires a flexible presentation format in these chapters. In those cases where the technique consists of well-defined approaches, we include descriptive background material and specific research examples. For those approaches that do not have well-defined characteristics, we can provide only general descriptions. Where enough empirical information is available, we engage in a general discussion of the evaluation data, with particular emphasis on the advantages of the instructional approaches as well as the problem areas that the researcher and practitioner must face.

In particular, Chapter 7 presents two major discussions. We begin by discussing traditional approaches to training delivery—instructor-led with trainees present in a classroom setting, self-directed learning programs, and simulated work settings. With face-to-face training delivery mechanisms, the trainer typically chooses how much time to devote in training to lecture, discussion, self-study, evaluation, and feedback. With self-directed learning programs the trainee is in more control of the pace of instruction. With simulated work settings, trainees can watch instructors demonstrate skills, obtain practice, and receive immediate feedback. The second major topic focuses on the emerging training delivery platforms that are based on rapid advances in technologies. These new platforms include distance learning, computer-based instruction via CD-ROM, web-based instruction, intelligent tutoring systems, and virtual reality training. Distance learning expands the view of traditional classroom instruction by including trainees from different geographical locations at the same time. CD-ROM, web-based, and intelligent tutoring systems expand the options for self-directed learning opportunities. Virtual reality training provides trainees with a work simulation setting via computer instead of the traditional simulations that require the physical equipment to be present.

TRADITIONAL INSTRUCTIONAL APPROACHES

Traditional instruction involves learning in classroom settings, self-directed learning programs, and learning in simulated work settings. For training technical skills, both classroom and simulated work settings are often utilized. For enhancing knowledge, self-directed instructional programs can be used. This section on traditional instruction focuses on four issues. First, we describe training methods used in classroom settings. Second, we explain self-instructional programs as an adjunct to the more traditional classroom settings. Third, we discuss use of simulated training environments that go beyond what can be accomplished through classroom instruction. Finally, because the effectiveness of traditional instructional methods relies heavily on the quality of the instructors, we address issues of instructor effectiveness.

Classroom Instruction

Classroom instruction continues to be the way the majority of training content is delivered in work settings. Classroom instruction can include the use of lecture and discussion, case studies, and role playing. Each aspect of classroom instruction is described. Much of this research was conducted in the 1960s and 1970s as the focus then was on how to improve training delivery through classroom instruction.

Lecture and discussion.   The lecture and discussion method continues to be a major delivery process for training programs. Originally, many authors (e.g., McGehee & Thayer, 1961) questioned the usefulness of the lecture method as an instructional technique. Their criticisms focused on its one-way communication aspects. Too often, the lecture method results in passive learners who do not have the opportunity to clarify material. In addition, the lecturer may have difficulty presenting material that is equally cogent to individuals who have wide differences in ability, attitude, and interest. By the time a criterion test is employed, some individuals may be hopelessly behind. Many of these difficulties can be overcome by competent lecturers who make the material meaningful and remain aware of their students' reactions by effectively promoting discussion and clarification of material.

Studies have compared programmed instruction or televised instruction to the lecture technique. The results indicate that these techniques do not necessarily lead to superior student achievement, although there is some evidence that the student completes the material faster. Thus, there appears to be little empirical reason for the bias against the lecture procedure. Interestingly, research does not fully support the poor opinions of the lecture technique as an instrument in the acquisition of knowledge. Certainly, the lecture method has shortcomings. It is insensitive to individual differences, and it is limited in providing immediate feedback to the learner. However, considering the low cost of the lecture method, it is important to determine empirically when and how it can be used. Evidence indicates that the technique is not appropriate when complex responses (for example, motor skills) are required but may be quite applicable when acquisition of knowledge is the goal. There is general uncertainty about the benefits of the lecture method for other behaviors, such as attitude change. Most authors and training directors think that the lecture method is not useful in promoting attitude change, but, again, little empirical evidence supports their view. Actually, several studies conducted by Miner (1963) suggested that the lecture was appropriate as an attitude-change technique. One study examined seventy-two supervisors in the research and development department of a large corporation. These employees had been neglecting their supervisory activities in favor of scientific interests. Miner developed a course that placed considerable emphasis on scientific theory and research findings relevant to supervisory practices. He found that the experimental group developed more favorable attitudes toward supervisory training as compared with a control group that did not participate in the lecture program. Interestingly, the control group developed negative feelings during the training period because of the threat of department reorganization.

Unfortunately, few studies have examined lecture courses that are specifically designed as part of a training program. Usually, when the lecture method is employed as a control procedure, most of the effort is devoted to the development of the experimental technique. Almost all other techniques have many proponents who excitedly proclaim the validity of their procedure with little, if any, empirical evidence. Conversely, the lecture technique is viewed with disdain without much empirical evidence.

Lectures are unlikely to disappear. Rather, as training has become more sophisticated, many different instructional techniques have begun to merge together. For example, audiovisual techniques can complement instruction by extending the range of stimuli that can be brought into a training program. Television and film productions can present dynamic events that unfold over time. Thus, it is possible to present events that cannot be recreated in the traditional classroom such as simulated accidents that vividly demonstrate what happens to individuals who are not wearing a seat belt. Audiovisual techniques can also be used to demonstrate the terminal performance expected in a complex motor sequence. Instructors can discuss the expected performance and the knowledge needed to perform the task and then show a film to demonstrate the appropriate sequence of steps. The medium can be sped up when trainees have the requisite knowledge and skills or slowed down for particularly important aspects of behavior.

An additional example of this blending of instructional delivery mechanisms beyond simple lecture is the use of on-the-job training to supplement and reinforce lecture material. For example, on-the-job training can include job or performance aids. These are instructional devices that facilitate learning by serving as reminders in recalling training information. One interesting application of job aids is employed by Domino's Pizza (Feur, 1987). They place large, glossy illustrations of exactly what a pizza is supposed to look like at each stage of preparation. Domino's does this even though it expects employees to produce pizzas at high speed and to memorize thoroughly the production procedures. One display shows a different type of cutting error for each slice presented in the picture, and the other shows a perfect pizza. These types of learning aids have been a common feature of military training programs and are now making their appearance in a large variety of civilian on-the-job situations. This blurs the distinction between formal training and informal training and learning opportunities. Chapter 8 provides a detailed examination of various methods used to build employee capabilities through structured learning experiences on the job.

Both the lecture method and one-on-one instruction are used often and are relatively inexpensive compared with other methods like computer-based instruction. Burke and Day (1986) employed a technique called meta-analysis, which is a statistical procedure that permits comparisons across studies, to examine various managerial training techniques. They found that the lecture method fared well as a training method. They note that these results were encouraging especially because criticisms of its use often arise.

Case study.   Once training content has been communicated to trainees through lecture and discussion, trainers often use case studies to build skills in analysis and problem solving. With case studies, trainees receive a written report that describes an organizational dilemma or problem. The report may be of an actual or fictitious organization. Trainees are expected to analyze the problem and offer solutions based on a number of factors including people, environment, rules, and physical parameters. The trainee usually studies the case individually and prepares solutions. He or she then meets with a group that discusses the various solutions, comes to consensus as to which actions to take, and tries to identify the basic principles underlying the case. The group procedure is designed to promote feedback and allow the individual to learn by observing others developing their respective solutions. Oftentimes there is no correct solution; the trainees are thus encouraged to be flexible. An assumption of this training approach is that trainees can retain and use what is learned though this guided discovery process of understanding key principles from the case.

For example, one case used in a leadership training program focused on decision making under uncertainty and time pressure (Brittain & Sitkin, 1989). The case involved a race car team that must decide whether to race. The problem in the case was that the racing team had experienced blown engines in seven of their twenty-four races. One of the mechanics on the team contends that the blown engines are more likely in colder weather, and the temperature for this morning's race is in the 40s. While a gut reaction suggests not racing, this particular race is very important to the racing team because a major sponsorship is riding on the outcome. Another blown gasket would lead the sponsor to seek other racing teams as well as leave the team in debt for the racing season. Racing and finishing in the top five would lead to a key sponsorship and the ability to compete the following year in the top racing venues. The pit crew is excited about the opportunity and considers the race car sound. Another member of the racing team presents data that seems to indicate no relationship between air temperature and the frequency of blown gaskets and encourages the leader to race. Table 7.1 presents a part of this case.

TABLE 7.1 CARTER RACING

"What should we do?"

John Carter was not sure, but his brother and partner, Fred Carter, was on the phone and needed a decision. Should they run in the race or not? It had been a successful season so far, but the Pocono race was important because of the prize money and TV exposure it promised. This first year had been hard because the team was trying to make a name for itself. They had run a lot of small races to get this shot at the bigtime. A successful outing could mean more sponsors, a chance to start making some profits for a change, and the luxury of racing only the major events. But if they suffered another engine failure on national television . . .

Just thinking about the team's engine problems made John wince. They had blown an engine 7 times in 24 outings this season with various degrees of damage to the engine and car. No one could figure out why. It took a lot of sponsor money to replace a $20,000 racing engine, and the wasted entry fees were no small matter either. John and Fred had everything they owned riding on Carter Racing. This season had to be a success.

Paul Edwards, the engine mechanic, was guessing the engine problem was related to ambient air temperature. He argued that when it was cold the different expansion rates for the head and block were damaging the head gasket and causing the engine failures. It was below freezing last night, which meant a cold morning for starting the race.

Tom Burns, the chief mechanic, did not agree with Paul's "gut feeling" and had data to support his position (see Exhibit 1). He pointed out that gasket failures had occurred at all temperatures, which meant temperature was not the issue. Tom had raced for 20 years and believed that luck was an important element in success. He had argued this view when he and John discussed the problem last week: "In racing, you are pushing the limits of what is known. You cannot expect to have everything under control. If you want to win, you have to take risks. Everybody in racing knows it. The drivers have their lives on the line, I have a career that hangs on every race, and you guys have got every dime tied up in the business. That's the thrill, beating the odds and winning." Last night over dinner he had added to this argument forcefully with what he called Burns' First Law of Racing: "Nobody ever won a race sitting in the pits."

John, Fred, and Tom had discussed Carter Racing's situation the previous evening. This first season was a success from a racing standpoint, with the team's car finishing in the top five in 12 of the 15 races it completed. As a result, the sponsorship offers critical to the team's business success were starting to come in. A big break had come 2 weeks ago after the Dunham race, where the team scored its fourth first-place finish. Goodstone Tire had finally decided Carter Racing deserved its sponsorship at Pocono—worth a much needed $40,000—and was considering a full season contract for next year if the team's car finished in the top five in this race. The Goodstone sponsorship was for a million a year, plus incentives. John and Fred had gotten a favorable response from Goodstone's racing program director last week when they presented their plans for next season, but it was clear that the director's support depended on the visibility they generated in this race.

"John, we only have another hour to decide," Fred said over the phone. "If we withdraw now, we can get back half the $15,000 entry and try to recoup some of our losses next season. We will lose Goodstone, they'll want $25,000 of their money back, and we end up the season $50,000 in the hole. If we run and finish in the top five, we have Goodstone in our pocket and can add another car next season. You know as well as I do, however, that if we run and lose another engine, we are back at square one next season. We will lose the tire sponsorship and a blown engine is going to lose us the oil contract. No oil company wants a national TV audience to see a smoker being dragged off the track with their name plastered all over it. The oil sponsorship is $500,000 that we cannot live without. Think about it—call Paul and Tom if you want—but I need a decision in an hour."

John hung up the phone and looked out the window at the crisp fall sky. The temperature sign across the street flashed "40 DEGREES AT 9:23 A.M."

(Continued)

Exhibit 1: Note from Tom Burns

John,

I got the data on the gasket failures from Paul. We have run 24 races this season with temperatures at race time ranging from 53 to 82 degrees. Paul had a good idea in suggesting we look into this, but as you can see, this is not our problem. I tested the data for a correlation between temperature and gasket failures and found no relationship.

Relationship between Temperatures and Gasket Failures

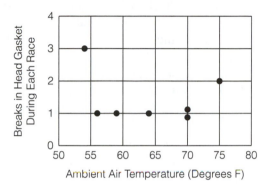

In comparison with some of the other teams, we have done extremely well this season. We have finished 62.5% of the races, and when we finished we were in the top five 80% of the time. I am not happy with the engine problems, but I will take the four first-place finishes and 50% rate of finishing in the money over seven engines any day. If we continue to run like this, we will have our pick of sponsors.

Source: From "Facts, Figures, and Organizational Decisions: Carter Racing and Quantitative Analysis in the Organizational Behavior Classroom," by J. Brittain and S. Sitkin. In *The Organizational Behavior Teaching Review,* 1989, *14,* pp. 62–81. Copyright 1989 by Sage Publications. Reprinted by permission.

Leaders read the case and have to decide whether to race using a rational decision-making approach of (1) defining the problem, (2) determining the overall objective, (3) weighing the criteria, (4) generating alternative courses of action, and (5) weighing alternatives and coming to a decision. The reasons for or against racing are captured by the instructor. The instructor then probes for more in-depth analysis of the case and the reasons for or against racing.

In presenting this case to experienced managers, almost all the teams opt to race—a common sentiment is "nothing ventured, nothing gained." Once the decisions have been made and the rationale obtained, the instructor reveals that the car racing example has many of the same contextual and motivational factors that led to the decision to launch the ill-fated space shuttle *Challenger.* For example, there were tremendous pressures to launch in spite of the fact that some engineers feared a relationship between ambient temperature and O-ring leakage. This leads to a discussion about the underlying principles of decision making that this case (and the *Challenger* explosion)

highlights. These principles include issues such as the reality of making decisions with limited or partial information, the importance of asking the right
questions to obtain the best data before making a decision, the need to listen
to negative information rather than downplaying the source of the information, and the need to avoid escalating commitment due to a focus on meeting
planned deadlines.

Proponents of the case-study method contend that the self-discovery
occurring during these sessions is likely to lead to longer retention of the principles. The case study provides an atmosphere that might be more conducive
to the examination of general principles and issues. Cases like the race car
example can help unfreeze current beliefs and open trainees to learning more
about themselves and the decision-making process they use (Alden & Kirkhorn, 1996). This can lead learners to be more willing to attend to and to more
deeply process the principles from the case than would be likely to occur if the
instructor just lectured on those principles. After the case, trainees can
develop their own stories from past experiences and highlight how the principles were or were not incorporated in the decision-making process. In addition, trainees can be asked to think of a decision that will have to be made in
the near future and address how the general principles learned from the case
study can be directly applied to this everyday job situation to result in higher
quality decisions.

Critics of this approach think that the method is not useful for learning
general principles and that the lack of guided instruction generally characterizing the group process can even be detrimental. For example, participants in
the case-study technique can become entangled in the large amount of information presented and never find the basic issue. Or, trainees can become so
engrossed in the case study that they never see the relevance of the principles
to everyday life.

Argyris (1999) provides a detailed criticism of the case-study method. He
believes that there are two types of learning. First, there is the form that
involves the detection and correction of error. An example of this type of
learning, known as *single-loop*, is a thermostat, which detects when a room is
too hot or cold and corrects that situation. Argyris describes the second form
of learning as *double-loop;* this involves changes and corrections in underlying
policies, assumptions, and goals. In this case, the thermostat would be a
double-loop learner if it questioned why it was set at 65 degrees or even why
it was measuring heat. Argyris's concern is that the case method may uninten-
tionally undermine double-loop learning and instead focus trainees on single-
loop learning.

Specifically, this view about case studies stems from his observations and
tape recordings of management-development programs that use the case-
study method as a major form of instruction. He observed that trainers domi-
nated classroom activities, designed procedures to save face for trainers and

participants, and generally designed the atmosphere to avoid confrontation and open discussion of new ideas. Trainers espoused views such as "people should expose their ideas, maps, strategies for solving the problem; yet instructors do not expose many of their ideas and strategies about the case" (Argyris, 1980, p. 295). He also thinks that there was little time or effort spent on ensuring that learning is transferred back to the organizational environment, a criticism that is common to most training programs. Argyris argues that trainers should be taught to be less dominating, that open discussion should be encouraged, and that cases from their own organization should be used to enhance transfer. This concern for transfer is a continual issue and is one of the reasons that evaluation is so important.

Argyris's views concerning single- and double-loop learning remain controversial. He strongly believes in experiential learning and group confrontation as a way of unfreezing old values rather than simply through case analyses. However, there may be instances where single-loop learning is the goal of the training program. Even if it is not, however, the training environment must still be designed to achieve the appropriate goals and must be analyzed to determine if the goals are realized. Actual studies demonstrating both the need for and the achievement of double-loop learning remain an important agenda item.

Role playing.   In this technique, trainees act out characters assigned to them for a particular type of scenario or setting. Role playing is used primarily for analyses of interpersonal problems and attitude change and development of human relations skills (Baldwin, 1997). This technique gives trainees an opportunity to experience a variety of on-the-job problems. Trainees learn by trying out different approaches or solutions to the problems and considering which approaches are more successful and why.

The method's success depends on the participants' willingness to actually adopt the roles and to react as if they really are in the work environment. The use of role playing in training exercises has a long history developed out of research on team building. There are many different role-playing techniques. In one variation, trainees who disagree are asked to *reverse roles*. This procedure is intended to make a person more aware of the other's feelings and attitudes. In another variation, called *multiple role playing*, a large number of participants are actively involved in the role-playing process (Maier & Zerfoss, 1952). The entire group is divided into teams that role-play the situation. At the end of a specified period of time, participants reunite and discuss the results achieved by each group.

One of the more unique uses of role playing is called *self-confrontation*. In this procedure, the trainee is shown a videotape replay of his or her entire performance. While viewing the tape, the trainee is given a verbal critique of the performance by the trainer. In an early study of this technique on cross-cultural skills, King (1966) gave trainees information about a culture and the desired general behavior. Then, the learner plays the role of an adviser in a foreign country. Typically, the trainee interacts with a person from the foreign country who is a confederate of the trainer. After role playing, the trainee views the tape and is given a verbal critique of the performance by the trainer. The results of this study indicated that trainees who participated in self-confrontationperformed consistently better than another group of subjects who had spent an equivalent amount of time studying the behavioral requirements outlined in the training manual. Retention tests given two weeks later indicated that the self-confrontation group maintained its skills. Although self-confrontation techniques can be applied as a feedback supplement for a variety of training techniques, it is especially useful with interaction procedures like role playing. As already mentioned, the key to these techniques is the feedback and critique session. The self-confrontation method provides accurate and detailed feedback, and, when it is combined with sensitive analyses of performance, it appears to be a very useful procedure. Several other studies have indicated that the role-playing, videotape, and feedback sessions do result in changes in behavior (see Triandis, 1994 and our discussion in Chapter 8 on cross-cultural issues and training).

In an important illustration of the unintended consequences of interventions, Teahan (1976) reports on a study that investigated role-playing effects on the attitudes of police officers. As part of their academy training, both white and black police officers role-played sensitive racial situations. Attitude-change scores indicated that black officers became more positive in their views of whites. However, white officers, while becoming more sensitized to the presence of black-white problems, became more prejudiced toward blacks. The author's interpretation of these results indicates that white officers perceived that the program was intended for the benefit of blacks rather than whites. Independent of the interpretation, the results underscore the importance of examining the outcomes of our interventions rather than simply assuming that all is well.

Besides the studies mentioned here, relatively few research efforts directly focus on role playing. Interestingly, one reason is that role playing by itself does not seem to be used very frequently. Rather, it has become part of other techniques such as behavioral role modeling, which will be discussed in Chapter 8. Early concerns about the technique were that participants might find the role playing childish and that they might have a tendency to put more emphasis on acting than on problem solving (Bass & Vaughan, 1966). If the emphasis is on the acting of roles, participants might behave in a manner that is socially acceptable to other members of the group but not reflective of their actual feelings. In this case, role playing may not lead to any behavioral changes outside the role-playing environment. In the traditional format, the feedback is controlled by the participants in the role-playing setting. If the feedback focuses more on the acting ability of the participant than on the solution to problems, the entire learning process can be circumvented. Again, the leader becomes the key element to a successful training session. Later techniques such as behavioral role modeling have focused on specific problem situations in the work environment in order to avoid such difficulties.

Self-Directed Learning Programs

Organizations utilize a range of self-directed learning programs to address the training needs of their workforce, including the assignment of outside readings, workbooks, correspondence courses, and programmed instruction methods. The advantages of self-directed programs include flexibility in terms of time and location for completing training assignments, reduced instructor and facility costs, and time and resource efficiency. Self-directed learning activities are also consistent with the move in organizations to place more responsibility on employees for their own development (see Chapter 8 for further discussion of this trend).

Readings, Workbooks, and Correspondence Courses

Self-directed learning can be as simple as preparatory reading to be done prior to attending a training program or targeted readings to be completed once classroom instruction has been completed. The preparatory readings can serve two functions. First, the readings can bring all trainees up to speed on an issue so that they are at a similar knowledge level going into the training. This allows the instructor to focus on meeting training objectives without the tension of talking over the heads of some participants while boring the more knowledgeable participants. Thus, bringing everyone up to speed lessens the tendency of instructors to teach to the lowest common denominator. Second, preparatory readings allow trainers to devote less time on lecturing to enhance basic knowledge about a subject and thereby allow more time for training more complex (e.g., procedural) knowledge or skill development. This can lead to a more efficient and effective training program. Posttraining readings can be used to reinforce training material and to facilitate transfer to the job.

Organizations often use assigned readings and workbooks to target individuals who need additional learning opportunities. For example, managers might be evaluated by subordinates, peers, and supervisors on key job competencies. This person analysis information can be useful in identifying specific training needs for each manager. If a manager is found to be rated low on coaching and guiding skills, the manager might be assigned to classroom instruction, targeted readings on leadership, or required to complete a workbook on how to be a better coach and guide. One of the authors worked with a hospital that developed workbooks for managers relevant to an identified skill need. The workbook included self-assessment instruments on leadership styles, a discussion of key behaviors of effective coaches, and exercises that focused on the participant creating action plans for becoming a more effective coach. The workbook also had a reference list of books and chapters for the participant to read to obtain more information about coaching skills. While the workbooks were created to be voluntary self-directed learning experiences, a contact person in the organizational development group was available for assistance in completing the workbook and for mentoring opportunities.

Readings and workbooks are typically targeted to a specific knowledge or skill need. For a more comprehensive developmental approach, organizations and individuals have opted to complete correspondence courses. The correspondence method includes an exchange of learning material and tests through the mail (or computer) with little verbal communication between the trainee and the instructor (Ford & Wasson, 1997). Progress is monitored through assignments and exams returned to the instructor at the trainee's pace. Course completion depends on the learner's speed in mastering the assigned materials. Correspondence courses are often seen as an efficient way for specialists to remain technically up to date. However, long feedback lag times, low learning motivation, little or no opportunities for interaction or learning from experts, limited subject matter, and often high rates of incompleteness of course material can occur. The concern is that correspondence courses can turn into a check-off system in which participants gain the credentials for completing the course, yet the organization does not see much in the way of transfer and improved performance on the job.

In general, there is limited evidence as to the effectiveness of readings, workbooks, and correspondence courses. Clearly, active participation in these knowledge and skill upgrade and development activities is a function of both individual characteristics and work environment factors. For example, upgrading knowledge and skills is more likely when individuals have a realistic assessment of their strengths and weakness (career insight); are fully involved in the job, career, and profession (career identity); and are the type of people who deal with work disruptions by taking control of their own work environment (career resilience); Noe, Wilk, Mullen, & Wanek, 1997). In addition, supervisory support (e.g., career counseling) and management policies (e.g., rewarding innovation) have been found to be related to organizational commitment and updating activities such as continuing education (Kozlowski & Hults, 1987).

Programmed Instruction

Programmed instruction (PI) involves taking a systematic approach to presenting information to the learner (workbooks, computer) using principles of reinforcement. In the early 1900s, Thorndike introduced the *law of effect*. This law states that stimulus-response associations that are followed by satisfying states of affairs are learned, whereas those that are followed by unsatisfying states of affairs are weakened and eliminated. Skinner (1954) applied this idea and his models of operant conditioning to the educational process. Skinner argued that a program could successively shape the learner by reinforcing the achievement of small steps. He believed that positive reinforcement of correct responses is the most efficient way to produce learning. Therefore, he designed self-instructional programs to condition the learner through a series of small steps so that few errors occurred. The only variability that is permitted among learners is the speed with which they complete the program. Because a student proceeded through each successive step, the technique became known as *linear programming*. To develop a more customized PI approach, intrinsic or *branching programming* has also been developed.

Linear programming.   Linear programming has been defined as having five key steps:

1. All material is presented in small units called frames. Each frame varies in size from one sentence to several paragraphs, depending on the amount of material necessary to guide the learner.
2. Each frame requires an overt response from the learner. The trainee reads the frame and then constructs a response by filling in the blank. Thus, the learner is actively involved in the learning process.
3. The learner immediately receives feedback indicating the correctness of the response. Because the program is constructed for a minimum number of errors, the learner usually receives immediate positive reinforcement.
4. The program is predesigned to provide proper learning sequences. Because the units must be presented in small steps to achieve low error rates, the programmer must carefully analyze both the material and the learner's characteristics in order to obtain the most appropriate step size and sequence. This process requires pretesting of the program and revisions based on trainee responses. If a criterion of approximately 90% correct by all trainees is not met, the material must be rewritten.
5. Each trainee proceeds independently through the program at a pace commensurate with his or her own abilities.

For example, Wexley and Latham (1981) reported on a gift shop that used programmed instruction to train their Christmas rush sales force. The material consisted of self-paced texts and diagnostic pretests that permitted trainees to skip material that they already knew. The material covered many work-related topics ranging from customer relations to operating the cash register, handling refunds, and cashing checks. With linear programming, the training content across all participants is the same (although a pretest can help participants skip sections they already know). More recent approaches have focused on developing branching programs, which allow for more individualized instruction in this self-paced environment.

Branching programs.   In branching programs, correct responses by the learner lead directly to the next step of the program, whereas incorrect answers lead to a branch designed to correct the mistake. The branches can vary in complexity from a few short frames to an elaborate subprogram. Typically, the learner is presented with text to read and a series of multiple-choice questions. After reading a frame and answering the question, the learner is given immediate feedback. If the chosen answer is correct, the response is confirmed and the learner is directed to the next frame. If the answer is incorrect, learners proceed to a remedial set of frames designed to correct the previous response. Table 7.2 presents a unique branching program developed by Mager (1975) to train novice training designers on how to write good training objectives. In the example given in the table, Mager presents information about how to include accuracy criteria into the writing of a training objective. The reader then is asked to apply the knowledge gained from this reading and determine which part of a written training objective is concerned with stating the accuracy of performance. Depending on the answer chosen, the learner is sent to different pages in the text to determine if the response chosen was correct. A correct response leads to a reinforcing statement (in the example the correct response leads to page 83), "You said 'bisections must be accurate to one degree' are the words describing the criterion of success. That's exactly right. These are the words by which we will be able to tell when to certify the student as having accomplished the objective." Depending on which incorrect response is given, the learner moves on to page 80 or page 81 in the text. The page tells the learner that the response was incorrect and why. The learner is then asked to reexamine the issue on a subsequent page.

Branching programs cannot eliminate all errors; however, trainees do not proceed until they can demonstrate by their performance on the branching step that they understand the concept previously missed. Often the branching frames include smaller, more incremental steps in the learning process. In this way, superior trainees can progress through the program without becoming bored while the slower student receives more special attention. Typically, branching programs have had limited flexibility. Only a certain number of branches can be designed for the individual trainee without the whole project becoming cumbersome. Computer-assisted programs have helped in increasing flexibility for branching.

Two major reviews have examined the relative effectiveness of PI in both academic and industrial settings (Hall & Freda, 1982; Nash, Muczyk, & Vet-

TABLE 7.2   EXAMPLE BRANCHING PROGRAM

Accuracy

Speed is only one way to determine a criterion of success. Sometimes the accuracy of a performance is more important than its speed, and sometimes both speed and accuracy are important.

Here's an example of accuracy:

Be able to state the time shown on the face of any clock to within one minute of accuracy.

Since the rapidity of the performance is unimportant, no speed criterion is shown.

Or, your objective might include criteria like these:

. . . And solutions must be accurate to the nearest whole number.

. . . With materials weighed accurately to the nearest gram.

. . . Correct to at least three significant figures.

. . . With no more than two incorrect entries for every ten pages of log.

. . . With the listening accurate enough so that no more than one request for repeated information is made for each customer contact.

Use whatever words or means will communicate how well your students must perform before you will be willing to certify them as competent.

Try this example:

Given a compass, ruler, and paper,

page 80

be able to construct and bisect any given angle larger than five

page 81

degrees. Bisections must be accurate to one degree,

page 83

Turn to the page indicated beneath the words that describe the criterion of acceptable performance.

Source: From *Preparing Instructional Objectives*, by R. F. Mager. Copyright 1985 by Fearon Publishers. Reprinted by permission.

---

tori, 1971). Table 7.3 presents the data for three different criteria including training time, immediate learning, and retention. The results comparing conventional lecture and discussion methods with PI support the conclusion that there are no significant differences in achievement scores (immediate learning and retention) but that the same level of learning was met in less time through PI. The average reduction in learning time was about 30%. Although the data concerning learning time has been consistent, they must be interpreted cautiously. The PI group is self-paced, and the learners may leave the program whenever they have completed the material. However, the more traditional

| TABLE 7.3 | COMPARISONS OF PROGRAMMED INSTRUCTION VERSUS CONVENTIONAL METHODS FOR EACH CRITERION IN STUDIES THAT INCLUDE TWO OR MORE CRITERIA |

	Conventional Method Superior	No Significant Difference Between Methods	Programmed Instruction Superior
Training time	1	2	29
Immediate learning	3	20	9
Retention[a]	5	16	5

[a]Of the 32 studies that included measures of both training time and immediate learning, only 26 also had a measure of retention. *Source:* From "The Relative Practical Effectiveness of Programmed Instruction," by A. N. Nash, J. P. Muczyk, and F. L. Vettori, In *Personnel Psychology*, 1971, *24*, pp. 397–418. Copyright 1971 by Personnel Psychology, Inc. Reprinted by permission.

programs have a fixed time limit, and superior learners cannot leave even if they have learned enough material to achieve the objectives. Of course, that is one of the advantages of programmed learning, but it might be interesting to see what would happen if learners in the control condition could take their achievement tests when they have completed the program to their own satisfaction.

SIMULATED WORK SETTINGS

Training simulators are designed to replicate the essential characteristics of the real world that are necessary to produce learning and transfer. These efforts can vary from very sophisticated flight simulators to PC-based simulations (Salas, Bowers, & Rhodenizer, 1998). A variety of simulators have been designed for specific training purposes, including skills development, decision making, and problem solving. In this section, simulators designed for skill training are discussed. These types of devices are more likely to be found in flight training, maintenance training, and the like. Simulations that are designed for training interpersonal skills or management skills, such as business games, will be discussed in Chapter 8 in the section that focuses on management and leadership training. Instead, we focus here on three key issues in training simulation: (1) reasons for using training simulators, (2) fidelity issues and simulator training, and (3) transfer of training issues.

Reasons for Using Training Simulators

A good early example of a relatively simple but effective simulation was provided in a study by Salvendy and Pilitsis (1980). They investigated its use in teaching medical students suturing techniques needed in surgical procedures. The traditional method consisted of a lecture-slide presentation and videotape describing the technique. Included in the instructions were materials related to the general geometry of the suture path, descriptions of the instruments and their functions, and general guidelines. The student then used these instructions while practicing on pigs' feet until the instructor determined that the student was performing the task appropriately. The simulator created as an alternative to this procedure was called the Inwound procedure simulator:

> The "Inwound" procedure simulator . . . assists the student in acquiring the manipulative motor skills during the inwound procedure phase by puncturing a simulated tissue with an electrically activated needle holder. . . . The simulated tissue contains related wound path geometry such as "entry" and "exit" points. The overall unit is mounted on a revolving fixture located in a mannequin-type arm. The student is able to monitor his/her progress by gaining information as to correctness of motions through the student feedback console. This console consists of 11 clearly marked amber and red lights that correspond to correct and incorrect motions. Both audio and visual channels are activated by the suture needle as the needle is guided by the student through the "wound." If the various phases (entry, depth, exit) are performed correctly, the amber lights are activated. . . . An incorrect needle motion while the needle is in the wound causes a corresponding red light and tone generator to be activated momentarily. When the needle is corrected in its path, the related visual and auditory feedback is discontinued. Number of errors, time in the wound, and number of cycles performed for each of the procedure phases are recorded individually on the monitoring console. (pp. 155–156)

In their research study, the investigators found that simulation training improved the performance of the medical students beyond the traditional training methods. In addition, the investigators collected psychophysiological measures of stress such as heart-rate variance and muscle tension. The data confirmed that students trained by simulation method showed less stress when they were required to perform new suturing tasks.

From these early attempts, the use of simulators for training technical skills has risen markedly over the last twenty years. For example, military and commercial aviation use complex simulations to train for a variety of tasks such as stick and rudder skills, combat maneuvering skills, and instrument reading (Salas et al., 1998). Four reasons for this increase include the potential for controlled reproducibility of the work environment, safety considerations, learning considerations, and cost effectiveness.

1. *Controlled reproducibility.* Simulations permit the environment to be reproduced under the control of the training analyst. They represent a training laboratory outside the real-world setting, where uncontrolled parameters make it difficult to produce the desired learning environment. By careful design and planning, environments can be created

that supply variation in the essential characteristics of the real situation. In addition, a simulation permits the trainer to expand, compress, or repeat time, depending on the needs of the trainees. For example, a flight simulator can provide months of aircraft-landing experience in several hours.

2. *Safety considerations.* In many cases, the required terminal behavior is too complex to be safely handled by a trainee. The simulator permits learners to be slowly introduced to the essential task characteristics, without any danger to themselves, their fellow workers, or the expensive equipment. Many observers recognize the validity of carefully planned introductions to complex tasks like flying an airplane, but they fail to realize that many jobs, like assembly-line operations, also require considerable pretraining. Some industrial firms solve this problem by a vestibule-training program, which consists of a simulation, off the production line, of the equipment and materials used on the job. Simulations also permit the trainee to practice emergency techniques before being exposed to hazardous situations in real settings. One of the most striking examples of a simulator designed to produce a dangerous safety event is the wind shear simulator. Wind shears are a sudden shift of wind that has killed thousands of air travel passengers. United Airlines training center produces all the effects of wind shear, including hydraulic stilts that mimic every bump and roll, aircraft sounds, rain pelting the windshield, and thunder. Table 7.4 presents the conversations and happenings from a training session. After reading the material, we think that most observers would prefer to have pilots learn how to fly under those conditions in a simulator rather than be on board if there was a real practice try.

3. *Utilization of learning considerations.* Most simulations permit the effective utilization of learning principles. Because the environment is carefully controlled by the trainers, they can easily (1) introduce feedback, (2) arrange for practice, (3) use part or whole and massed or spaced methods, and (4) design the environment according to the best-known principles of transfer. Thus, careful design of simulations can produce an environment conducive to positive transfer.

4. *Cost.* The acquisition of skills requires practice, and if practice is not feasible in the real world, simulation provides a viable alternative. Although most simulation efforts are expensive, they are often an economical alternative to using high-priced, on-the-job equipment. For example, managers being trained to assume vital roles in overseas environments are being exposed to simulated training settings because trial-and-error performance in foreign countries is too expensive. And, quite probably, the behavior of a beginning trainee handling a multi-million-dollar jet might quickly convince passengers to make dona-

TABLE 7.4	TERROR AT ZERO FEET: A CREW'S SIMULATED BRUSH WITH DISASTER

In this accident, one can hear rain pelting the windshield. And there is thunder. "We would never take off in conditions like this," Carter said.

But true to the real event, Hill took the plane's controls while Carter spooled up the engines. They began racing down the runway. "Eighty knots," Carter said. About 92 mph.

As the plane passed 127 knots—the speed that pilots call VI, essentially the point of no return—the air speed indicator abruptly stopped moving.

"Wind shear!" shouted Carter as he slammed the throttles into the full "firewall" position—as much power as he could muster.

"Keep it on the runway," he told Hill, who eased the nose wheel back down onto the runway to gain as much speed as possible on the ground—a maneuver that amounts to "banking energy" for the ordeal ahead. Even with the increased ground speed, the air speed dropped 20 knots—about 23 mph.

As did the real aircraft in the real incident, the simulator began climbing steeply as it neared the end of the runway, pushing everyone back in his seat. Then came the bad news.

"Decreasing air speed," Carter said. "Sinking," he said: "200 feet . . . 160 feet . . . 140 feet . . . 80 feet."

"Bring your stick higher," he said. Hill, already fighting his control yoke as if it were a bull in a rodeo, pulled the nose higher into the air as the engines roared.

With that, pandemonium broke out in the cockpit. Lights began flashing and the control yoke began vibrating loudly like a giant rattlesnake—the "stick shaker" that warns of a stall.

An artificial voice boomed out in a deliberate but loud monotone, "Don't sink! Don't sink! Don't sink!" It was the ground proximity warning having its say.

As all appeared lost, the plane began emerging from the shear. "Air speed recovery," said someone out of the din. A later reading of the simulator tapes showed that the plane dropped within 20 feet of the ground before it recovered and took off.

A lot of people died on the real plane, in the days before pilots were trained to survive wind shear. This was just a simulator. But the cold sweat, fast heartbeat, and weak knees were not simulated.

Source: From "Terror at Zero Feet: A Crew's Simulated Brush with Disaster," by D. Phillips. In *Washington Post,* January 1, 1991, p. A3. Copyright © 1991 The Washington Post. Reprinted by permission.

tions to simulation-training programs. Or, simulations are often developed after a critical event where additional training might have been helpful. For example, after the nuclear power plant accident at Three Mile Island, there was no hesitation to design a $1 million control-room simulator to attempt to avoid future problems.

All the previously mentioned reasons for simulation have prompted the development of skill simulators. These simulators are used when the required skills are explicit and the behavior can be measured objectively. Frequently, these simulations have extensive physical fidelity and can represent a large number of potential environmental situations. Because flight simulators are becoming so complex, many airlines expect that all flight training soon will be done on a simulator. For example, the navy's primary jet trainer is simulated for research purposes at the Naval Training Equipment Center in Orlando, Florida. This simulation includes all normal operations, including carrier arrest landing and carrier simulation, which provides for ship pitch, roll, and heave, as well as variations in sea conditions, wind conditions, and turbulence. (One of the authors of this book has flown the simulator and can attest to the complexities of landing a plane on an aircraft carrier. In weaker moments, the author might even mention that in numerous tries he never even hit the carrier but rather managed to land in the ocean.) The description of the wind shear incident in Table 7.4 indicates just how complex a flight simulator can be.

Fidelity Issues

The cost versus benefit of work simulators is a function of the physical and psychological fidelity that designers attempt to incorporate into the simulation. The design of training simulators can be quite expensive when designers attempt to be completely accurate in terms of physical fidelity—the representation of the real world of operational equipment. For example, airlines often use simulators that not only replicate the cockpit but also include motion that simulates what one would feel in a real aircraft. In addition, costs are high for comprehensive, full-mission simulations that deal with large-scale operations such as those designed to coordinate actions across multiple crews on an aircraft carrier. Other simulation efforts are part simulations, which are often less expensive to design and deliver. Part simulations replicate a critical or difficult portion of the task without attempting to provide the complete context or comprehensive scope of performance on the job. Still other simulation efforts focus on using relatively inexpensive PC equipment with software programs that provide practice on critical skills and important processes that are required for task performance. These low physical fidelity simulators are more limited in scope but often strive to be realistic in terms of the types of issues or problems that need to be addressed back on the job.

Regardless of the level of physical fidelity and cost, most researchers maintain that simulation efforts must have psychological fidelity as their chief objective in order maximize the benefits of simulator training. Designing for *psychological fidelity* requires that the training task provide the trainee the opportunity to reproduce the behavioral processes that are necessary to perform the job. This means that instructional features must be incorporated into the training simulation that help trainees successfully meet the learning objectives for the course. For example, a pilot can use a joy stick with a computer game to practice landings rather than be in a full scale simulator with motion—the issue is whether the skills being learned in each type of setting provide the psychological fidelity that will lead to learning and transfer. As noted by Salas et al. (1998), the quest for more physically realistic simulation may come at a cost of losing sight of the true goal of using a training device that has the psychological realism to impact learning and transfer.

Despite the critical nature of psychological fidelity, the question that remains is how much physical representation is necessary to achieve psychological fidelity. For example, is the simulation of motion a necessary aspect of pilot training? Research has begun to provide some answers to the balancing of physical and psychological fidelity issues. Part simulators have been found to be quite effective when a critical behavior is the focus of the training effort. A clever study of a part simulator is provided by Rubinsky and Smith (1973) as they examined simulated accident occurrence in the use of a grinding wheel. The researchers devised a task that exposed operators to a simulated accident that led to a jet of water being squirted on the operator. The "accident" was designed to occur when the operator stood in front of the grinding wheel during startup operations—the time when there is the greatest danger of the wheel exploding. The investigators found that those trainees who experienced a simulated accident as part of their training program were less likely to repeat the potentially hazardous behavior of standing in front of the grinding wheel at startup then those who were given written instructions or demonstrations of safe procedures. The results were maintained over a series of retention tests. The researchers suggest that simulated accidents might be effective in reducing power-tool accidents—certainly, this procedure provides a creative form of immediate feedback for incorrect responses.

Much research effort has focused on low physical fidelity simulators on PCs and their impact on training effectiveness. Jentsch and Bowers (1998) provide a summary of studies done on lower fidelity flight simulators. The review was conducted to examine the argument that these types of low fidelity flight simulators have more in common with video games than actual work tasks. They examined ten years of research that address issues of content and construct validity of low fidelity flight simulators. The review found that participants often rate the content validity of these simulators as quite high and agree that behaviors elicited by the scenarios in the simulations are important for effective on-the-job performance. They also found evidence that the situations embedded in the low fidelity simulations typically elicited the full range of behaviors that were important for training transfer, such as coordination behaviors among aircrew. Nevertheless, they note that the findings are limited; data is still lacking as to the generalizability of the results. Studies have shown that pilots appreciate the realism embedded in even low fidelity simulators and that learning does occur during training. We have much less data on the extent to which the learning that occurs in low fidelity simulators leads to similar levels of performance on the job than larger scale, high physical fidelity simulators. Such research would need both high and low physical fidelity simulators that elicit similar behavioral responses along with on-the-job performance data. As noted by Dennis and Harris (1998), it is clear that low fidelity simulators may be quite beneficial early in the learning process. What still is unknown is the trade-offs of physical fidelity, cost, and psychological fidelity later in the learning process.

Simulator Design to Facilitate Training Transfer

It is important to remember that simulation efforts are directly related to transfer of training. Individuals are trained on a simulator so that they will perform better in the work situation. Many of the parameters involving transfer were considered in "The Conditions of Transfer" in Chapter 4. However, despite accomplishments in the literature and laboratories, the degree of understanding that might be expected has not been achieved. Unfortunately, very few transfer studies relevant to simulator training have been conducted. Thus, we do not have the empirical base to know what works or why. Consequently, while we wait for more definitive studies, practitioners are moving forward on developing guidelines and standardized procedures for the effective design of training simulators. The assumption of this approach is that effective design that takes into account learning principles and psychological fidelity issues will lead to more effective training and ultimately effective training transfer.

An early example of this approach was completed by Swezey (1983). He applied a transfer process model of two different training simulators to predict which one would lead to more transfer. Some of the parameters of the model include:

1. *Task commonality:* whether the device permits the trainee to practice skills required for actual performance on the real task.
2. *Equipment similarity:* the extent to which the equipment involves physically identical equipment and has identical information requirements.
3. *Learning deficit analysis:* an examination of the task to determine its relationship to the input repertoire of trainees and the difficulty level of training the necessary skills and knowledge.
4. *Training technique analysis:* an estimate of the instructional effectiveness of the device based on the degree to which relevant principles of learning are used.

Building on this foundation, an event-based approach to training (EBAT) has been developed to guide the design of simulation-based training (Fowlkes, Dwyer, Oser, & Salas, 1998). The EBAT approach identifies and introduces events with the training scenarios of the simulation to provide opportunities to perform and then observe the behaviors that are the objectives of the program (e.g., improving the use of assertiveness behaviors among a flight crew). The EBAT system includes four components: (1) training requirements or objectives, (2) event-based triggers, (3) scenario control, and (4) observation and feedback. For EBAT to be effective, there must be explicit linkages among these four components to needs assessment, design, delivery, and the evaluation of the training simulation.

First, training requirements necessitate the identification of competencies that should be the target of simulation training. The competencies can be identified through training needs assessment techniques such as critical incident techniques (see Chapter 3). Critical incidents are those events that distinguish between highly effective and ineffective performance in an area. For example, critical incidents regarding mistakes made by flight crew members have been examined. The results of this analysis indicated that lack of assertiveness and appropriate communication of concerns by junior officers to more established pilots were key areas for improvement. Second, based on these critical incidents, event-based triggers can be embedded into the training simulation to elicit the behaviors related to the competencies being trained such as assertiveness. Thus, events can be scripted where a flight leader (role-played by an instructor) asks crew members to perform an unsafe navigation procedure. Crew member communication patterns and the extent to which crews display assertive behaviors can be observed. Third, the need to standardize training across individual trainees and teams requires scenario control. To maintain scenario control, the design requires the specification of exactly when trigger events are to be introduced into the scenario so there is consistency across individuals and teams going through the simulation. This allows observers to see the variations in the effectiveness of different performance strategies across various trainees and teams. Finally, the use of closely scripted event triggers allows for the anticipation of specific trainee behaviors that can be translated onto observer evaluation forms. These forms are used to detail exactly what occurs in the simulation around these key trigger events so that specific and detailed feedback can be given to trainees about effective and less effective behaviors during the simulation. Lessons learned from these experiences can be drawn across groups of trainees who have experienced the same simulation training. In addition, trainees can undergo additional training with different scenarios and different event triggers that focus on building the same competencies as in earlier scenarios.

Research involving models like this one are an encouraging sign that it may soon be possible to understand what variables contribute to transfer of learning. Simulator training for complex skills, motor or otherwise, offers a real opportunity for research that will contribute to an understanding of the learning process and training transfer.

EFFECTIVE INSTRUCTION

Regardless of whether training is done in the classroom or in simulated training environments, designers and trainers must attend to many instructional considerations to make sure that the instruction given is effective. Even with self-directed learning programs, an instructor is often available for support and feedback. This section focuses on the role of the trainer and the characteristics of good trainers.

Role of the Trainer

The role of the trainer can make the difference between a successful or unsuccessful learning experience. The potency of the trainer's role has been demonstrated in some very important research conducted by Eden and his colleagues (e.g., Eden & Ravid, 1982). In these studies, trainers were informed that they had trainees with very high-success potential attending their course. Learning performance as measured by both weekly performance measures and instructor ratings was significantly higher for the classes with high-success potential as compared with control groups. Interestingly, the control groups in these cases consisted of trainees with the same ability levels as the people in the high-success groups. The only difference was that the trainers were informed that one group had high-success potential. Eden's analyses, which included reports from trainees, indicate that inducing high expectations in trainers similarly enhanced trainee performance. He feels that the high expectations communicated by trainers or immediate superiors lead trainees to expect more of themselves and to perform better. An interesting facet of his data is that several instructors were replaced in the middle of the training program. However, the performance differentials continued unabated. Eden believes that by this time the induction of high-expectancy effects had occurred and the trainees continued to perform at a high level. The researchers have dubbed this the "Pygmalion effect" in honor of George Bernard Shaw's work, which demonstrated the powerful effect our expectations can have on us. Certainly, this research attests to the powerful role that the instructor can have on learning performance. Eden (1990) correctly points out that expectancy effects are part of every training program. He strongly recommends that trainers be made aware of expectancy effects and that they use it in a positive manner by helping trainees raise their self-expectations.

The role of the trainer was also explored by Watkins (1990) in interviews with fifty-seven human resource developers at a government agency, a high technology corporation, and a research hospital. She explored the trainers' beliefs and discovered three themes. One theme is that being able to train is something with which you are born. These people see skillful training as amazing, magical, and something out of reach. People who view training from the second theme believe that training is political. This view states that training cannot be done well because trainers are political pawns. These ideas are reflected by statements such as "the training staff is where you put misfits who cannot do anything else." Given these attitudes, it is not surprising that the magical and political groups do not have the type of expectations that would produce Pygmalion effects. Finally, Watkins identified a group that offers a third theme, "training as learning." These individuals focus on learning as a way of being responsive to organizational needs, and they are characterized by people who continually reflect on their practice and engage in self-learning themselves. All three theme types are presented in Table 7.5. The themes clearly indicate that the organization must take responsibility for what type of training department they are going to have and how the trainers themselves will be trained. You should also reread the material presented in Chapter 1 on the discussion of ethical issues involving trainers.

Characteristics of Good Trainers

Many opinions are offered about the characteristics that an instructor in a training course should have. Unfortunately, there is not much research related to questions about the role of these characteristics in fostering learning. Most of the research on this topic has evaluated teacher characteristics and the reaction of students in academic classrooms. Although it is not possible to state that all these characteristics would be equally important in training settings, it is probably a good guess that instructors who have these characteristics would positively benefit the learning environment. One such list adapted from Bartlett (1982) includes the following items:

Is well-organized.
Presents an outline of the course.
Designs the sequence of materials for maximum learning.
Emphasizes conceptual understanding.
Gives lectures so well-organized they are easy to outline.
Relates lectures to other aspects of course.
Answers questions clearly and thoroughly.
Uses examples.
Sets difficult but attainable goals.
Encourages students to use their talents to achieve.
Points out how materials they are learning can be useful.
Encourages class discussions.
Makes good use of class time.
Gives exams that reveal strengths and weaknesses.
Explains how topics in the course are related to each other.

TABLE 7.5 THREE BELIEFS OF TRAINERS ABOUT TRAINING

Framing Orientation and Beliefs of Trainers	Action Strategies	Consequences for the Training Function	Possible Consequences for Learning
Training is magical.	Support the idea that trainers who have "it" don't need training and those who don't couldn't learn anyway.	Almost no one can do it "artfully," so few achieve a high level of professionalism.	Learning will not be predictable.
	Hold excellent trainers in awe and discount personal capacity to emulate them.	Trainers will not do professional work.	
	Discount technology of training by emphasizing technical expertise over training expertise when choosing own learning activities.	Managers have little solid information about how to use training.	
	Minimize clarifying of outcomes, purposes, time needed for different outcomes and purposes, and cost justification of training.	Training will become expendable.	
	Avoid seeking valid information about performance.		
Training is political.	Assume training is a negotiable benefit for self; blame others for holding the same assumption.	Training is part of the reward and punishment system rather than the task/goal system.	Learning is a political tool.
	Delegate determining training needs and methods to supervisors who enact personal or cultural norms about how best to learn.	Trainers are vulnerable and personally responsible for both means and ends they did not design.	Learning is expendable.
	Remain unaware of implicit priority setting when bending rules, setting budgets for training, or compromising educational goals or time frames.	Trainers are expendable.	
An alternative conception: Training is learning.	Trainers actively engage in learning about learning.	Learners and trainers will experience less defensiveness, more trust.	Training is more likely to lead to learning and to more organizationally productive results.
	Trainers encourage different views of training and design ways to test them.	Learners and trainers will feel mutually responsible for results.	
	Trainers publicly share and test their understandings of human resource development problems.	Learners and trainers will feel freer to experiment, to take risks.	
	Trainers jointly design and implement solutions with learners.		
	Trainers and learners publicly reflect on results.		

Source: From "Tacit Beliefs of Human Resource Developers: Producing Unintended Consequences," by K. E. Watkins. In *Human Resource Development Quarterly,* 1990, 1, pp. 263–275. Copyright © 1990 by Jossey-Bass, Inc. Reprinted by permission.

Is well-prepared.
Encourages students to learn the material.
Designs course so students demonstrate what they have learned.
Introduces many ideas during each class session.
Allows students to express problems related to the course.
Encourages students to share their relevant knowledge or experiences.
Effectively uses blackboard and/or audiovisual aids.
Accomplishes the goals and objectives of the course.
Shows enthusiasm for the subject.
Stimulates interest in the subject.
Is accessible outside of class.

In a comprehensive review of instructional research on effectiveness, Borich (1989) identified five key instructor behaviors: (1) clarity, (2) variety, (3) task orientation, (4) engagement in the learning process, and (5) moderate to high rates of success. For these five behaviors, instructors have been found to vary considerably in their enactment, and this variation has been found to produce significant differences in trainee performance.

Clarity refers to how interpretable or understandable the instructor's presentation is to the trainees. Some instructors are able to communicate without wandering or speaking over the heads of the trainees. Instructors with high degrees of clarity have been found to spend less time going over material.

Variety refers to how flexible the instructor is when presenting training material. For example, effective instructors plan for a mix of different instructional methods like lecture, discussion, case studies, and role plays. Table 7.6 presents a summary of effective and ineffective indicators of using variety in instruction. For example, effective instructors create variety by asking different types of questions like fact questions, process questions, convergent questions, and divergent questions.

Task orientation behaviors refer to the extent to which the instructor is achievement-oriented. Instructors with high task orientation are concerned that all relevant material is covered and is learned, as opposed to following procedures and focusing on the trainee's enjoyment in the course. Effective instructors have high expectations for trainee learning and make efficient use of instructional time. For example, the instructor knows what outcomes are to be achieved in a given period of time, organizes instruction around these outcomes, and adheres to these learning goals in the face of distractions.

Effective instructors also engage learners in the learning process. For example, the instructor can engage learners by having individualized instructional materials available such as extra exercise sets for those who may need them. Or, the instructor can provide opportunities for feedback in a nonevaluative atmosphere.

One other characteristic of effective instructors is their emphasis on moderate to high rates of success from learners. The instructional content is

TABLE

7.6

EFFECTIVE AND INEFFECTIVE INDICATORS FOR VARIETY

	Using Variety (an effective instructor)	Poor Variety (an ineffective instructor)	Recommended Behavior
1.	Uses attention-gaining devices; e.g., begins with a challenging question, visual, or example.	Begins lesson without full attention of most learners.	Begin lesson with an activity in a modality that is different from last lesson or activity; e.g., change from listening to seeing.
2.	Shows enthusiasm and animation through variation in eye contact, voice and gestures; e.g., changes pitch and volume, moves about during transitions to new activity.	Speaks in monotone, devoid of external signs of emotion. Stays fixed in place the entire period or rarely moves body.	Change position at regular intervals (e.g., every 10 minutes). Change speed or volume to indicate that a change in content or activity has occurred.
3.	Varies mode of presentation; e.g., lectures, asks questions, then provides for independent practice (daily).	Lectures or assigns unmonitored seatwork for the entire period. Rarely alters modality through which instructional stimuli are received (e.g., seeing, listening, doing).	Preestablish an order of daily activities that rotates cycles of seeing, listening, and doing.
4.	Uses a mix of rewards and reinforcers; e.g., extra credit, verbal praise, independent study (weekly, monthly).	Rarely praises or tends to use same clichés to convey praise every time.	Establish lists of rewards and expressions of verbal praise and choose among them randomly. Provide reasons for praise along with the expression of praise.
5.	Incorporates student ideas or participation in some aspects of the instruction; e.g., uses indirect instruction or convergent questioning (weekly, monthly).	Assumes the role of sole authority and provider of information. Ignores student input.	Occasionally plan instruction in which student opinions are used to begin the lesson; e.g., "What would you do if . . ."
6.	Varies types of questions (e.g., divergent, convergent) weekly and probes (e.g., to clarify, to solicit, to redirect) daily.	Always asks divergent, opinion questions (e.g., What do you think about . . .?) without followup. Or overuses convergent, fact questions.	Match questions to the behavior and complexity of the lesson objective. Vary complexity of lesson objectives in accord with the unit plan.

Source: From *Air Force Instructor Evaluation Enhancement: Effective Teaching Behaviors and Assessment Procedures,* by G. D. Borich. Copyright 1989 by U.S. Air Force Human Resources Laboratory, Wright-Patterson Air Force Base. Reprinted by permission.

sequenced in a way that reflects prior learning and is lumped into lessons that can be digested easily by learners. Transitions to new materials are presented in easy-to-grasp steps so as to maintain and build learner self-efficacy.

EMERGING TRAINING TECHNOLOGIES

Classroom training, various self-directed learning approaches, and simulation instruction will continue to be major delivery mechanisms in the foreseeable future. Nevertheless, there is a trend toward a decrease in instructor-led classroom instruction and an increase in the use of emerging learning technologies such as distance learning, CD-ROM/multimedia instruction, web-based training, intelligent tutoring systems, and virtual reality training. Figure 7.1 presents the results of a recent survey conducted by the American Society of Training and Development that show these trends. According to the survey, instructor-led classroom instruction is projected to decline from over 80% of all instruction in 1996 to approximately 60% in 2000 with a concurrent increase in emerging training technologies from around 6% in 1996 to over 22% in 2000 (Bassi & Van Buren, 1998). Training expenditures for these emerging training technologies have also shown a sizable increase. Over two-thirds of organizations responding to a human resource executive survey expected their spending on training technologies to increase (American Society of Training and Development National HRD Executive Survey, 1998).

There are a number of limitations with traditional instructional methods that have led to the examination of alternative ways to deliver instruction. First, traditional classroom and simulation instructional methods are often relatively expensive for many multinational companies. Either employees must be flown to a centralized location for training or a number of trainers must be trained to deliver the content and then flown to different locations to train. In addition, equipment for simulation training can also be very expensive to obtain and maintain.

Second, most traditional training approaches are normative in nature rather than individualized to meet trainee needs—the pace and plan of instruction are set by the instructor and do not vary across individual trainees. Even for correspondence courses, the trainee must proceed through a series of assessments that does not vary across trainees. The training literature has described efforts to develop more individualized instruction such as placing high-ability learners in different types of training environments than lower-ability learners. This rather general strategy has not met with high levels of success.

A third limitation is the fact that most traditional training programs are scheduled and delivered at particular times. Individuals may be forced to

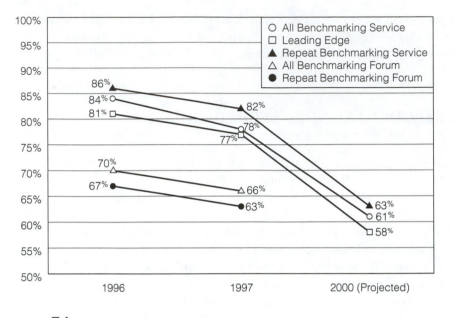

FIGURE 7.1

Percentage of training time for instructor-led classroom.

Source: From *The 1998 ASTD State of the Industry Report,* by L. J. Bassi and M. E. Van Buren. In *Training and Development,* 1998, *52,* pp. 21–43. Copyright 1998 by American Society of Training and Development, Inc. Reprinted by permission.

attend the training before or maybe even after the training is needed. Just-in-time training is very difficult to do with scheduled classroom instruction, correspondence course timelines, and simulated work environments.

A fourth concern is that of skill practice. Most traditional instruction can provide only a minimal amount of time for skilled practice. The practice time must be shared across a number of trainees attending the same course, and for more individualized practice there is a need for multiple trainers. Practice is also often limited to a few types of scenarios or situations.

Emerging learning technologies are leading the way toward trying to address some of the limitations of traditional instructional approaches. The five learning platforms described in this section include distance learning, computer-based instruction through CD-ROM technology, web-based training, intelligent tutoring systems, and virtual reality training. This section describes each new learning technology and presents the limited research that has been conducted to examine their effectiveness. These advances are exciting and changing the very nature of training in the workplace. Nevertheless, keep in mind that the foundation for training continues to be careful needs assessment, the development of training objectives, and the design of the program to maximize the chances that the training objectives will be met. Technology by itself will not and cannot become the Holy Grail of the training field.

Distance Learning

One learning platform that allows for training across multiple sites at one time is distance learning. Through audio and data links, trainees from various sites can access and interact with an instructor from a distant location. The move to distance learning reflects rapidly changing instructional needs as organizations are looking for a more affordable, low time expense, learner-tailored alternative to live instruction (Hannafin & Hannafin, 1995). Distance learning is characterized by a physical separation between learners and the instructor/facilitators where communication between all parties can be done via television, telephone, computer, or radio. The majority of instruction is provided by prepackaged learning resources or courseware (Goodyear, 1995). The success of distance learning is a function of high levels of interactions among peers and instructors. Peer support and instructor help is available to the learner either immediately, through the telephone, or with a slight delay through fax or e-mail systems.

Distance learning is becoming increasingly popular as a way to meet the special training needs of people who are leading busy lives. It is a response to a number of challenges, including rising costs, reduced operating budgets, and overused personnel and physical resources (Ashe & Buell, 1998). Distance learning technology has advanced to a point where almost all aspects of the physical classroom can be recreated in a sort of virtual classroom. Materials can be exchanged, communication can occur in real time, experiential exercises can be included, and so on. The only thing missing is eye contact and nonverbal cues such as body language and posture (Keegan, 1993).

In 1987, the U.S. Distance Learning Association held its first convention. Colleges and universities in all fifty states now offer distance education programs, and many Fortune 500 companies, such as IBM and Kodak, are joining in the delivery of distance courses (Morgan & Hawkridge, 1999), spending more than $40 billion annually (McIsaac, 1999). Federal Express offers more than 4000 courses through interactive video (Martin, 1996). The United Kingdom, Holland, Germany, and Spain all have widely recognized open universities, and the so-called Third World countries have also turned to distance learning to educate large numbers of widely scattered students who might not otherwise have access to educational resources (Hawkridge, 1999). The typical setup in industry is to beam satellite-based programs to several classroom sites that are simultaneously connected by video and sound.

Research on the effectiveness of distance learning programs is sparse. Key problems include the use of small sample sizes that make any conclusions tentative and the reliance on case studies rather than more controlled experimental and quasi-experimental designs. Research generally shows no significant difference in achievement levels between distance and traditional learners, and shows that older students tend to perform better than younger students (Threlkeld & Brzoska, 1994). This is consistent with Knowles's (1990) adult learner profile, which characterizes adult learners as self-directed, problem-oriented, and interested in applying knowledge to life experience.

The call now is for research comparing different instructional designs using the same media, rather than comparing delivery systems. A few researchers are beginning to examine the learning process in interaction with various forms of technology (e.g., Binner, Welsh, Barone, Summers, & Dean, 1997). For example, Linn (1996) uses a knowledge integration framework to provide advice on how designers can enable students to become more independent within a distance learning environment.

Attitudes and satisfaction with distance learning show greater variability than performance outcomes. Zhang and Fulford (1994) report that higher levels of interaction are related to more positive attitudes and greater satisfaction. Feedback remains a key ingredient, and instructor behaviors that promote student involvement are linked with student satisfaction just as in a traditional classroom. Webster and Hackley (1997) found in a review of twenty-nine studies that students in more interactive courses were more satisfied.

Technology reliability has been implicated as an important factor affecting both attitudes and learning outcomes. Problems center on losing class time due to equipment malfunctions and lack of readily available technical support. Some classes reported that they had problems every week (Webster & Hackley, 1997). Technology quality is also important. Slow transmissions cause time-lag difficulties for video and audio, leading to interruptions (often the instructor interrupting students) and uncertainty about what people at other sites are seeing and responding to during the broadcast. In addition, sound can be choppy, overheads lose resolution, and small video images can make it difficult for instructors to see students' raised hands or to watch for facial cues of understanding or confusion. It can also be difficult for students to tell who is speaking. In addition, the level of monitoring the instructor must do to keep track of what is being broadcast by video, watch remote classes, and so forth can detract from the attention focused on teaching local class and can reduce eye contact. Many participants in the courses studied reported a sterile environment, especially at the remote sites, where they felt particularly removed from the instructor. The bright side from the Webster and Hackley (1997) review was that students were positive about being able to take courses and learn from instructors that they wouldn't otherwise have had access to, interacting with students from other places, and getting exposed to technology.

CD-ROM and Interactive Multimedia

A second learning platform is the use of CD-ROM technology to create multimedia training programs. Multimedia is defined as a computer-driven, interactive communication system for various types of text, graphic, video, and auditory information (Reeves, 1992). The integration of these various media formats permits diverse content to be easily accessed by users in multiple ways to enhance learning. Interactive media often include live action video, animation, graphics, text, and audio to deliver training content. As with other emerging technologies, multimedia programs can be expensive to develop with some estimates of 200 to 500 programming hours for every hour of instruction (Stone, 1993). Nevertheless, recent software advances are reducing the number of hours of development per hour of instruction.

An early example of an innovative approach that uses multimedia to improve sales performance is provided in Table 7.7. Training effective interpersonal skills such as selling remains one of the biggest challenges in training. In many top insurance companies, for example, a large number of new sales personnel leave after three years—largely because they are unable to develop sufficient sales skills to make an adequate income from their commissions. This interpersonal skills training program to teach sales skills (or to aid in the early recognition of those not suited to sales) combined the power of multimedia with individual interaction. The results of this program showed much promise as trainees were found to get up to speed much more quickly than those who were trained through traditional methods (Ives, 1990). Of course, not all early attempts at developing multimedia programs were totally successful, as noted by Smith (1990) in evaluating a interactive videodisc program:

> One vignette, showing what probably would not happen, depicts a supervisor terminating an employee who leaps up and profusely thanks the supervisor, claiming enthusiastically that this is just what she wanted. The humor is so overbearing that it defeats its aim. Viewers were laughing so loudly at some of the situations that information was lost. (p. 410)

The scope and complexity of multimedia programs using CD-ROM technology has greatly advanced since the use of videodiscs and early computer-based programs. One of the many well-developed systems of interactive multimedia is PLATO (Programmed Logic for Automated Teaching Operations). PLATO consists of over 5000 individually selectable or assignable learning activities that can be as short as a fifteen-minute lesson to ninety-minute modules that are self-paced (see www.plato.com/ed/solutions/wf.html). This curriculum can be examined to develop a customized plan for workers to upgrade basic skills in math and writing to more complex job skills such as quality fundamentals, workplace communication, and problem solving. For example, with the problem-solving skills module, the learner might enter a simulated workplace and be given a problem by a supervisor that needs to be explored. One problem might be that shipping overhead costs have increased over the last three months, and the trainee needs to find out what is causing the increase and what can be done to reduce costs. To accomplish this task, the learner can click on various "people" within the organization and hear them

TABLE
7.7   **AUTOMATING INTERPERSONAL SKILLS TRAINING**

A combination of automated audio/video feedback and interactive videodisc (IVD) or computer-based training (CBT) is now being used to teach sales skills. One system uses a laserdisc player, touchscreen monitor, and a PC coupled with videotape recorder, camera, and microphone. The IVD presents full-motion/audio demonstrations of skills such as presenting credentials, then provides review exercises with proper and improper examples of those skills. Trainees can interrupt the presentation of a skill when a mistake is made and offer a critique of the action. Feedback is given on the appropriateness of their critique.

The camera or audio recorder is then used to allow the students to demonstrate proper behavior. Trainees face a new customer (provided on the IVD) and practice the skill they just saw modeled.[a] Their performance is recorded on videotape along with the customer's conversation. Students can practice in privacy, then review their performance based on a set of criteria (from the IVD) and evaluate their own behavior. They can erase and repeat, practicing as many times as they wish. When they feel they have successfully transferred the training to their performance, trainees can show the tape to the supervisor, who provides advanced coaching.

In a pilot evaluation program, insurance agents using this training program had a 16 percent increase in calls, a 24 percent increase in kept appointments, and a 43 percent increase in approach interviews with clients. In addition, new hire training time was reduced 30 percent over traditional classroom methods, and the subsequent on-the-job learning curve decreased. For example, one agency that had been using the IVD system for over a year compared 10 agents who used the system with 17 trained by traditional methods. The 10 using the IVD program were at a level 18 months ahead of the control group after the completion of training. While it is difficult to separate the impact of the IVD training from other changes in the company, its revenues also have gone up since introduction of the system, and the agent retention rate has increased.

IBM also experimented with a similar system coupled with a videotape camera for teaching sales skills. In a comparison with their traditional person-to-person role-playing training, they found that trainees using the IVD system did much better in structuring their sales calls and developing sales skills.

A second, similar program uses CD-ROM combined with audio feedback. For some training situations, such as telephone sales, audio feedback is actually closer to the real job situation, and full-motion video is not needed. CD-ROM also costs approximately $2000 less per training station than IVD, has larger storage capacity, and can be used more easily for nontraining applications.

[a] Although the "customer" on the IVD cannot respond in all of the unexpected ways a real person might, this will change with advances in artificial intelligence.

Sources: "Soft Skills in High Tech: Computerizing the Development of Interpersonal Skills," by William Ives, in *Information Delivery Systems,* March/April 1990; and "Goodbye Classrooms (Redux)," by Beverly Geber, in *Training,* 1990, *27* (1). *Source:* From "Worker Training: Competing in the New International Economy," by Office of Technology Assessment, U.S. Congress, 1990, OTA-ITE-457, Washington, DC: U.S. Government Printing Office.

discuss the problem and possible solutions. Figure 7.2 presents a program screen of one employee's response (note that for the actual PLATO program the information is conveyed through audio). The learner gathers the information from the various employees and completes a form that highlights what information has been gathered and what the learner sees as the real problem and the possible solutions to the problem. Once the learner decides what to do about the problem, feedback is given as to the appropriateness of the solution.

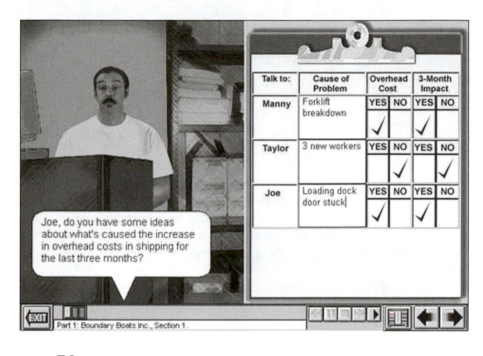

FIGURE 7.2

Problem-solving skills module.

Source: Copyright 2001 by PLATO Learning, Inc. ® PLATO is a registered trademark of PLATO Learning, Inc. Reprinted by permission.

In general, multimedia programs such as those in the PLATO system often embed in the modules intensive drill and practice exercises to build declarative knowledge (what is meant by root cause analysis of a problem?), and to improve procedural knowledge (how does one conduct a root cause analysis?). After drill and practice, feedback is given to the learner to allow for self-monitoring (was the right solution chosen and why or why not?) as well as progress mastery tests that are competency-based (has the trainee demonstrated the declarative and procedural knowledge relevant to problem-solving skills?). This testing process allows for targeting what training module should come next for the learner. In addition, this technology enhances the potential for just-in-time training as individuals can go through the course when the content is most directly relevant to their job.

The effectiveness of computer-based instructional approaches such as CD-ROM multimedia programs is encouraging. Case studies show that multimedia programs can be effective in improving learning. For example, Amoco Fabric and Fibers in North Carolina offers the PLATO system to its employees for continuous learning and improvement. An examination of the math curriculum showed that learners gained an average of 1.6 grade levels after an average of 26 hours spent logged onto the program (see www.plato.com/ed/results/adultjob.html#1). More comprehensive reviews and meta-analytic studies have repeatedly found that computer-based instruction saves time (about 30%) and leads to higher scores on mastery tests compared with traditional classroom instruction (Johnston, 1995; Kulik, 1994)

As noted by Tessmer (1995), formative evaluations of multimedia systems need to be investigated to enhance the effectiveness of such systems. Tessmer contends that the important aspects to evaluate include program clarity, ease of use, feedback quality, content accuracy, and trainee appeal. Table 7.8 presents a number of user interface issues that must be considered and the evaluation questions that can be asked to help in the formative evaluation of a multimedia training program. For example, one issue is transparency, or the intuitiveness of the computer program interface to the user. A question that might be asked is whether users can operate the CD-ROM with minimal training.

Interactive multimedia instruction through CD-ROM technology is better suited for situations where the necessity for updating content is fairly infre-

TABLE 7.8   INTERFACE EVALUATION CRITERIA AND QUESTIONS

Evaluation Criteria	Evaluation Questions
Interface transparency	Where do learners become lost?
	Users operate with minimal training?
	Operate with minimal help system use?
Match between interface metaphor and learning experience	Metaphor understandable to users?
	Match user expectations of program?
	Match system structure and functions?
Interface forgiveness	Where do learners make mistakes?
	Users easily undo their actions?
	Easily reverse directions?
Interface informativeness	Where do users seek information?
	Users tell where they are?
	Tell where they have been?

Source: From "Formative Multimedia Evaluation," by M. Tessmer. In *Training Research Journal, 1,* 1995/1996, pp. 127–149. Copyright 1995 by Educational Testing Publications. Reprinted with permission.

quent. For example, training individuals in math skills such as dividing fractions can probably stay the same for years. In addition, when organizations want individuals to go through the same training experience (except for testing out of some beginner modules), CD-ROM can be quite effective as individuals can be led through the program with the same content. When training content is more volatile or frequently changing as well as when variations of the same general program might be needed, web-based instruction might be a more viable option.

Web-based Instruction

The growth of the World Wide Web has triggered an interest in web-based instruction (WBI) delivered via the Internet or corporate intranet. With this third learning platform, information is sorted and transmitted as requested by trainees at remote sites accessed through widely available web browsers such as Explorer or Netscape. Trainees can access this training at any time— twenty-four hours a day by seven days a week.

There are many potential benefits of placing training on the web. Information on the web is generally stored in one location and transmitted across company intranets or the Internet as requested by remote sites. Thus, web training is easy to update and increases the accessibility of training to a broad audience. WBI can also take place at work. This cuts down on travel expenses. Web-based instruction also allows for just-in-time training delivery as trainees can access the material when needed. The learners have control over how much information to attend to through the use of hyperlinks to additional material, practice exercises, and feedback. This allows learners to determine the depth of information and practice desired from the training to better fit their individual training needs. For example, icons on the screen can be clicked on to move to another site (e.g., a picture of a schoolhouse to represent a link to the trainer), or the icons can be web addresses that are linked to other Internet or intranet sites. In addition, the web programs can be set up to promote sharing of information and ideas during a training program. Trainees can gain access to company bulletin boards or be allowed to carry on a discussion regarding applications of training content with other employees, trainees, or experts in the company. The web also offers sophisticated tracking features that can record individual training performance for training administration (Filipczak, 1996).

The number of companies that have jumped on the web training bandwagon has risen dramatically over the last few years. Eighty-one percent of the companies that are members of the American Society of Training and Development Benchmarking Forum anticipated a major increase in using the web for internal training (Bassi, Cheney, & Van Buren, 1997). As one example,

Steelcase has launched an Internet site that offers on-line training courses and career development information for its employees and for the 450 furniture dealers in its network. The company expects 12,000 Steelcase and dealer employees to use the system, which provides material on product updates, selling skills, and problem solving.

WBI is most appropriate when self-directed learning is a possible and preferable teaching mode. Instruction is self-contained and therefore there can be only a minimal need for outside assistance. In addition, all instructional elements, including practice and feedback, must be easily accomplished without interaction with a live instructor. Nevertheless, WBI can only be as effective as face-to-face learning if proper support and feedback are available (Threlkeld & Brzoska, 1994). Proper support may include time to proceed through the modules and a physically and psychologically supportive environment—maximizing encouragement and minimizing distraction.

A report by Brown, Milner, and Ford (1998) provides a comprehensive review of the literature on the design of effective web-based instruction. From this review, they identified effective strategies for designing content, building a learning environment, planning for continued success beyond the course, and using the web-based technology. For example, one aspect of building a learning environment is providing the learner with guidance during the web-based program. Guidance can include information about what material to focus on and how to learn the material effectively as well as instruction and help on how to use the web medium in these efforts. When learners are left on their own, they are often not good judges of their needs for practice in weak areas or of when they have mastered material sufficiently (Gail & Hannifin, 1994). Thus, in self-directed web-based programs, guidance that helps learners make better decisions can be offered. This support can take the form of default paths, audit trails, and easily accessible help information. Table 7.9 presents a summary checklist for providing guidance in web-based programs. Checklists were also formed for other aspects such as navigation (moving from page to page), interface (completing activities and answering questions), and screen layout (how the information is presented). Brown et al. (1998) stress that the most important principles for navigation, interfacing, and screen layout should be simplicity, consistency, and usefulness. Options for learner movement and response should be carefully planned so that learners do not become frustrated or lost within the system. Disorientation can lead to trainees giving up so these issues need to be considered early in the design process to ensure the course is user friendly. The programming should also provide trainees easy access to features they want and need. Trainees with different instructional needs will use the system differently, and the interface must account for this by ensuring that the vast majority of trainees can efficiently locate the information, activities, or resources for which they are looking.

TABLE 7.9	LEARNER GUIDANCE

Guidance

- The system helps learners maintain a sense of mission/purpose?
- The system provides a model for the inquiry process, and instructions to assist learners with questions or problems?
- Expected learning outcomes are clearly specified at all times?
- Advice is provided on how to approach the learning task (e.g., where to begin, what to focus on)?
- Advice is provided about ways to learn effectively from the system (e.g., instructions about how to study the information)?
- Instruction and feedback emphasizes that learners have control over the level of their success?
- Self-check questions are provided to prompt learners to monitor their comprehension and revise learning strategies?
- Help is available about how to use the system (e.g., navigation, accessing index or help features, printing materials) at all times?

If Any Form of Learner Control Is Determined to Be Appropriate

- Extra guidance is provided for low-ability or low-confidence learners to improve the choices they make during learning?
- Audit trails are available to show learners where they have been and what they have accomplished?
- A default path/choice for "what to do next" is available for those who want or need it?
- Learners have had training (or have demonstrated competence) in how to identify their learning needs, how to set goals, how to select practice exercises, how to evaluate progress, and how to decide when learning is done?

Source: From "Design of Asynchronous Distance Learning Courses" by K. Brown, K. Milner, and J. K. Ford, 1998. In *Instructional Design Handbook for Distance Learning: Designing Effective Satellite Web-based Training.* Copyright © 1998 National Center for Manufacturing Sciences. Ann Arbor, MI. Reprinted by permission.

Although there is much advice on how to develop web-based training programs, few systematic evaluation efforts have been conducted on the effectiveness of such programs. Brown and Ford (1998) evaluated a training course on problem solving that was "repurposed" from a three-day instructor-led course to a web-based course. The repurposing resulted in a complex web-based course that contained approximately 1100 pages of text and computer code! The cost was between $11,000 and $60,000 per instructional hour. There were many interactive elements embedded into the program such as content-related, thought-provoking activities and a practice case to examine at the end of each module. Data on the web course was obtained from eighty engineers from one large manufacturing company who were brought into a learning center to complete the course. The results of the evaluation were that trainees responded positively to the web-based course and felt it was effectively designed. Most trainees also enjoyed the self-pacing and flexibility afforded by the web course. The results also indicated that trainees learned (based on a knowledge test) as well from the web as they did in the instructor-led course (mean posttest scores for the web and the instructor-led groups were nearly identical). Finally, trainees completed the web course in half the time of the instructor-led course—indicating a possible gain in learning efficiency as the same amount of "learning" was achieved in less time.

Although results are encouraging, it must be noted that the web course was voluntary and that with the absence of pretest scores of current knowledge state it is difficult to conclude that training had equal effects. In addition, although the web course was completed in half the time, many trainees felt that completing the course at their own work desks rather than at a learning center would have been problematic due to work pressures and distraction. Thus, the results may not generalize to situations where trainees have to complete the course on their own time and work space.

The field needs many more empirical studies that use rigorous evaluation designs and more sophisticated learning measures to examine the effectiveness of web-based courses—especially in terms of training transfer. Self-directed learning activities may be an efficient use of trainee time, but the trainees may not receive the support needed on the job to directly apply the new knowledge and skills. We also need more research on self-directed learning on the web, including how to help learners to make good choices about what to study, how to learn, and whether to examine additional information or perform additional skill practice exercises. Unfortunately, there has also been little systematic research examining how learners proceed in a web-based training program (what they look at, which hyperlinks they use and why), which individuals benefit most (e.g., mastery goal-oriented learners) from web-based self-directed learning programs, as well as what interventions (e.g., various types of guidance and feedback systems) improve trainee learning and retention in web-based training courses. Brown (2000) provides a first step by showing that trainee choices regarding how many practice activities as well as time taken to complete the web-based course influenced knowledge gain in trainees.

Intelligent Tutoring Systems

A fourth learning platform involves intelligent tutoring systems (ITS), which are computer-based programs that strive to completely individualize instruction. Through various methods, this platform can diagnose the trainees' current level of understanding or performance and select the appropriate intervention that can advance a trainee toward more expert performance.

Intelligent tutoring systems offer the potential to customize the training experience for individuals to better meet individual needs.

Intelligent tutoring systems are the new, high-tech version of traditional programmed instruction. ITS are designed to infer trainee models as a result of watching the trainee solve tasks and comparing them through computerized expert models in a domain. Pioneering work on ITS was conducted by Carbonell (1970) and led to the development of a system called SCHOLAR. The system was originally designed to provide training on South American geography. The SCHOLAR program presented information to the student, asked questions, assessed the answers, corrected mistakes, and answered student questions. The idea was that the system be more like human tutors rather than the rigid models of interaction typical of programmed instructional approaches. The system was further developed to permit the integration of graphic information with verbal information in a program called Map-SCHOLAR (Collins, Adams, & Pew, 1978). Students are asked to name blinking cities on a map of South America. When the student answers correctly, the system prints the name on the map—if an incorrect name is given, the map blinks where the city is actually located, thus giving both verbal (e.g., Lima is in Peru not Brazil) and visual feedback to help the student learn the material. The researchers found that the SCHOLAR program was more effective in promoting student learning than more linear program instruction methods.

Research and development activity on ITS has expanded greatly since the mid to late 1980s (Steele-Johnson & Hyde, 1997). The research activity has focused on meeting the basic goals of intelligent tutoring systems—to diagnose the types of errors trainees make when solving problems and to react to these errors with targeted tutoring—often called Model Based Remediation. Table 7.10 presents the key attributes of an intelligent tutoring system that includes student, expert, and instructional modeling components (Woolf, 1992). As ITS has become more sophisticated, developers have increased their capacity to develop meta-strategies based on a history of the student's learning. These meta-strategies guide selection of more specific teaching strategies (next topic, detail level, teaching action) based on the results of tests given at various points in the lessons. ITS can also compare student learning with domain models of learning, and automatically change styles (Benyon & Murray, 1993). The system itself also can learn over time as it tutors many students, storing information about suggestions that helped students and those that did not. By comparing models of the learner's behaviors and cognition with expert content and instructional models, ITS can select training goals and example types, provide tailored feedback, and make decisions about when to stay at a particular module, when and where to advance, and when and where to remediate. Feedback can also be hierarchically structured so that at first vague hints are given, then direct analogies, and finally explicit instructions for the trainee. In addition, trainees can ask questions of the system. These design

TABLE 7.10	ATTRIBUTES OF INTELLIGENT TUTORING SYSTEMS
Generative:	the capacity to generate appropriate instructional interactions at run time, based on learners' performance
Mixed-initiative:	the capacity to initiate interactions with a learner as well as to interpret and respond usefully to learner-initiated interactions. Natural language dialogue is sometimes a focus of this feature.
Interactive:	the provision of appropriately contextualized, domain relevant, and engaging learning activities
Student modeling:	the capability to assess the current state of a learner's knowledge and the implied capability to do something instructionally useful based on the assessment
Expert modeling:	the capability to model expert performance and the implied capability to do something useful based on the assessment
Instructional modeling:	the capability to make pedagogical inferences and decisions based on the changing state of the student model, based on the prescriptions of an expert model, or both
Self-improving:	the capability to monitor, evaluate, and improve its own teaching performance as a function of experience

Source: From "AI in Education," by B. Woolf. In *Encyclopedia of Artificial Intelligence* (2nd ed., pp. 434–444) edited by S. Shapiro. Copyright 1992 by John Wiley & Sons. Reprinted by permission.

issues can prevent frustration from interventions given too early or from lack of help. The design can also prevent trainees from wandering too far off track (Gold, 1998).

Thus, these high-end systems respond adaptively to both learning level and learning style, making judgments about student knowledge and learning needs. For example, NASA has employed ITS to train flight dynamics officers how to deploy satellites in space—a complex task that requires performing the correct sequence of activities (Steele-Johnson & Hyde, 1997). The ITS presents a deployment problem with information based on the types of errors committed in performing the tasks. The trainees can also engage in dialog with the system by querying the system with help messages. The success of the trainee in navigating these sequences of activities affects the type of feedback and tutoring the trainee receives.

As might be expected, ITS are at the moment costly to design and implement. Estimates range from 100 to 500 hours of development time for every hour of instruction (Orey, 1993). Improvements in technology (e.g., voice recognition, third-generation authoring languages) are making it easier to build ITS. Nevertheless, for now they are mainly used in the military and in some larger businesses. There is also controversy about whether these systems can replace human teachers in the education and learning systems. Over the past fifteen years, the U.S. Air Force has developed several programs to increase levels of technical expertise quickly and effectively while responding to training needs of personnel from diverse educational backgrounds. One such program, the Intelligent Computer-Assisted Training Testbed supports simulation-based training for equipment maintenance tasks, with the goal of minimizing errors in complex maintenance and operations tasks. Another program, the Fundamental Skills Research Program, addresses the critical thinking skills required for basic literacy. Intelligent tutors have also been developed for weather forecasting, satellite console operations, auxiliary power unit maintenance, and cryptographic equipment maintenance. Since 1990, the U.S. Air Force has been working with Texas schools to incorporate these programs into the educational process to help teachers cope with increasingly demanding and diverse student populations. For example, the Word Problem Solving Tutor teaches general problem-solving strategies, as well as how to solve specific word problems. The Writing Process Tutor facilitates the development of basic writing process skills, whereas the Instruction in Scientific Inquiry Skills focuses on the development of students' scientific skills.

Most of the work on ITS has been focused on developing its underlying architecture, such as how to represent knowledge structures in areas like those just described. This work is a function of advances in artificial intelligence research and advances in our understanding of cognitive issues in psychology. While this work is exciting and there are test programs, existing ITS have not reached their potential. For example, critics contend that one shortcoming of ITS is that the systems make decisions for the user rather than teaching users to become more self-directed learners. This can lead to a dependence on the technology rather than learning to learn. In addition, we have limited understanding of how customized training needs to be to maximize effectiveness.

Of course, the key question is how effective ITS is in affecting learning, retention, and transfer. Unfortunately, even after more than twenty-five years of research on ITS, there is limited data on its effectiveness (Bloom, Linton, & Bell, 1997). The limited information available is mainly positive in terms of trainee interest and time to complete. For example, Bloom et al. (1997) reported on a program that teaches U.S. West employees how to converse with customers to problem solve and sell services. They found that trainees liked the system and thought it was interesting and fun to use and were more confident over time in the program.

Despite these positive reactions, definitive answers require more extensive and rigorous evaluation. For example, Gott (1995) reported a study of 54 participants trained in ITS on electronic system problem solving. She found that the tutored participants did better in troubleshooting a new system in a transfer task than nontutored apprentice technicians. The apprentices used a less efficient process of testing the whole system than the tutored participants. Aleven and Ashley (1997) reported on a system designed to help beginning law students learn basic skills of making arguments with cases. The system generated different argumentation examples dynamically as a function of the student's ongoing work. Results in an actual legal writing course for thirty first-year law students found that the ITS instruction led to significant improvement in students' basic argumentation skills that were comparable to that achieved by an experienced legal writing instructor teaching small groups of students. Despite these types of successes, in a review of the research, Gold (1998) notes the inconsistent results from the few controlled studies of ITS versus other types of instructional approaches. The author contends that we need to move away from the race horse mentality of which technique works better to a more complex examination of what specific instructional strategies need to be incorporated into ITS to enhance effectiveness.

Despite this lack of empirical evidence, ITS continues to attract attention for its potential in customizing training. In addition, ITS are beginning to be applied to virtual reality training systems to allow for a more dynamic and visual learning environment to go along with the customization of training made possible by ITS (Loftin & Kenney, 1999).

Virtual Reality Training

A fifth platform is the development of work simulations through virtual reality technology. With virtual reality (VR) training, trainees can view a 3D world of the kinds of situations they might typically face on the job and encounter objects in this simulated world that can be touched, looked at, and repositioned. VR training has been advocated because it is purported to be a highly motivating, interesting, and effective training tool. It capitalizes on visual learning and experiential engagement very similar to the transfer context without the physical space requirements of full-scale training simulators. A single VR training system can simulate many different types of situations and learning events within a short time frame (Wesley, Shebilske, & Monk, 1993). VR training also adds zoom in/out capabilities to study something at various levels of detail as well as the ability to control time (faster, slower, reverse, halt). VR is now being developed in modules that can be updated, integrated, and reused—making it very flexible especially compared with other computer-based training systems. In addition, Rickel and Johnson (1999) reported on the development of an animated person named Steve who is embedded in a three-dimensional simulated mockup of a work environment. Trainees who can move around in this 3D world have Steve as their tutor. Steve can be asked to demonstrate how to perform tasks and even provide assistance to the trainees while they are practicing tasks in this VR work environment. Figure 7.3 shows Steve pulling out a dipstick in the VR work environment.

Experts in the area predict that VR will become available over the Internet, allowing many users to share and manipulate a common virtual environ-

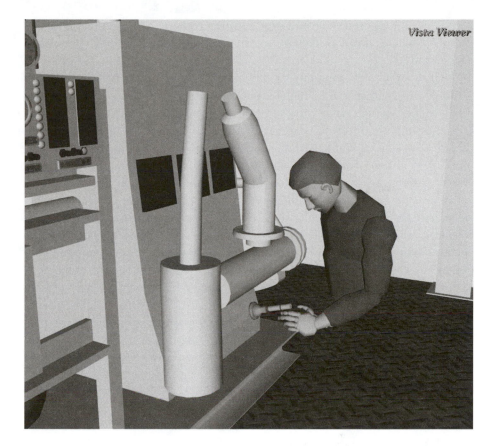

FIGURE **7.3**

Animated Steve pulling out a dipstick.

Source: Copyright 1999 From "Animated Agents for Procedural Training in Virtual Reality: Perception, Cognition, and Motor Control," by J. Rickel and W. L. Johnson. In *Applied Artificial Intelligence, 12,* pp. 343–382. Reproduced by permission of Taylor and Francis, Inc., http://www.routledge-ny.com.

ment. Forecasts also predict that VR will expand from the technical skills domain to interpersonal skills. For example, negotiation skills could be practiced in a room full of virtual people, where opponents are modeled after people's speech patterns, gestures, and experiences (Gunther-Mohr, 1997).

Costs for basic system hardware can easily reach $250,000, with software development costs of over $200,000 for immersion systems where trainees can actually touch and manipulate the environment within the 3D world. Estimates for course development are $30,000 to $60,000 per instructional hour (Harmon & Kenney, 1994). This cost has constrained the use of VR to situations in which the current training is quite costly (like high fidelity training simulators) or where the cost of errors during training can have major consequences, such as injury or damage to expensive equipment (Steele-Johnson & Hyde, 1997).

Applications are emerging in the military; NASA; and in areas such as architecture, medicine, and engineering. For example, the U.S. Air Force uses VR training to teach aircrew how to fly their emergency parachutes. The system can simulate different landing terrain, wind conditions, hostile locations, and time of day or night. NASA has been involved in virtual reality training since 1995 to help prepare international crews for space travel (Loftin, 1996). An interesting application of successful VR training was the preparation of astronauts for fixing the Hubble Telescope. Over 100 flight controllers experienced simulated extravehicular activities designed to familiarize them with the location, appearance, and operability of the telescope's components and the maintenance components of the space shuttle cargo bay, to verify and improve procedures, and to create contingency plans. In particular, the VR technology allowed Bernard Harris, a U.S. astronaut stationed in Houston, Texas, to enter a virtual environment and interact with astronaut Ulf Merbold, who was physically located in Germany. They spent over thirty minutes performing the procedures for replacing the damaged lens and communicating with each other. As noted by Loftin, at the conclusion of the procedure, the two astronauts "shook hands and waved goodbye" to each other.

VR training is also being considered for more traditional skilled trades. For example, the U.S. Army's National Automotive Center in Warren, Michigan, has teamed up with Detroit's Focus: HOPE and Center for Advanced Technologies to demonstrate the effectiveness of virtual environments for machinist training (*HOPE in Focus*, 2000). This project focuses on applying military training simulations to desktop personal computers. They assert that learning production skills in this environment produces benefits that extend from the factory floor through a product's lifetime, including maintenance, repair, and upgrading and thus reducing time-to-market. A reduction in the cost of training can occur as actual production equipment does not have to be used.

Similarly, Motorola offers VR training for machines on the manufacturing line and has trained several hundred employees at several locations. Learners can start, run, and stop machines, as well as troubleshoot problems. When they operate buttons and switches, audio and visual reactions of the machine are mimicked. Each course can be completed in eight to twelve hours, with specific coursework included, activities scored, and feedback given. They do not include the glove technology that allows users to "touch" the virtual machines and learn about how much force it takes to flip a switch or other sensory tasks. Preliminary results suggest that workers are more comfortable with this training than traditional approaches and that the VR training speeds on-the-job training. Pre- and posttests show that transfer of knowledge had increased by 30%.

As a final example, Penn State is developing a system that will train surgeons on microsurgical vascular anastomosis (surgical joining of two blood vessels to allow blood flow from one to the other). The tools used are computerized to create lifelike resistance when the surgeon moves them, and the visual image moves as the surgeon moves. The goal of this system is to allow training in a safe, predictable, reproducible setting and to allow performance measures such as accuracy and tissue/surface damage.

Data on the effectiveness of VR training is just becoming available. Most of this research has focused on participant reactions and the examination of physical symptoms such as headaches and dizziness during and after experiencing a VR world. Testimonials by companies such as the Research Triangle Institute in North Carolina that produce custom-made VR training systems (e.g., detecting hazardous conditions) report that VR technology can reduce training time from ten days of classroom and lab instruction to one and a half days. They also cite cost savings in training delivery time (per learner) and training-related travel.

From a more systematic perspective, the U.S. Air Force (Wesley et al., 1993) conducted some basic tests of two VR environments, comparing them with simpler, two-dimensional learning environments. Thirty-one paid temporary employees participated in a console task in which they had to learn a sequence of seventeen buttons and knobs (a procedural motor sequence in small scale space—limited vision area). All trainees completed the task perfectly; however, trainees in the VR condition performed the task more quickly. The same set of trainees also completed a maze navigation task (configurational knowledge in large-scale space—can't see whole area in one frame of vision). Trainees were taken through three guided explorations of the 3D maze and then allowed an hour of free exploration. They then completed three tests of navigation. Trainees in the VR condition performed better (i.e., took more direct paths from the start point to the end point) than trainees in the 2D condition. Trainees in the 2D condition also complained that the hour of free exploration was too long.

The lack of effectiveness studies is not surprising. In many ways, VR is still very much a prototype technology. Critics of VR training contend that the technology at present does not allow for the level of high physical fidelity obtained from more typical training simulators. Attempts to include high levels of fidelity in VR training may lead to a level of cognitive complexity that ultimately overwhelms trainees. Other drawbacks noted include lack of trainee experience with 3D navigation. This requires fairly intensive practice modules to increase the comfort of trainees in negotiating a 3D world without becoming disoriented so that the trainees can be ready to learn from the actual VR training experience. Although the technology is rapidly improving, there are still issues with the ability to readily display legible text and the delay for a scene to catch up to the learner's movements. Fister (1999) has questioned the promise of VR training. She contends that VR is limited to training for high-end jobs with life-and-death consequences (e.g., pilots, surgeons) and will not become mainstream. She feels that off-the-shelf products and fast lead times are going to dominate the training market as VR training can take at least eight months to produce. Thus, there is some movement toward 3D computer-based training without the manipulability of VR training.

The bottom line is that we need much more research on VR training as compared with other instructional approaches to determine issues of feasibility and effectiveness. In addition, strategies for improving the learning experiences of trainees within a VR training experience are sorely needed.

CONCLUSIONS

The options for delivering training have rapidly expanded over the last ten years. The expanded options are a function of computer technologies that allow for much more sophisticated learning platforms in comparison to early efforts at programmed instruction and simulated training programs. Research consistently shows that emerging technologies like distance learning, multi-media instruction, web-based training, intelligent tutoring systems, and virtual reality training programs, while costly to develop, provide cost savings in terms of time to complete the course. In addition, most research that has compared the effectiveness of these computer-based instruction platforms with more traditional classroom instruction has found better and higher levels of learning for the technology-mediated instruction. It must be noted, though, that these results may say as much about the efforts put into effective needs assessment and training design as it does about the instructional medium. Organizations that invest the money needed to build these new learning platforms (e.g., intelligent tutoring systems) are more likely to make sure that the instructional design (Chapter 2) model is followed carefully in the development of the training programs. For example, in building an expensive web-based problem-solving program, the instructional designers often go to great lengths to include instructional principles such as gaining learner attention at the beginning of training, making sure prerequisites are met by trainees prior to moving to a new training experience, having learning aids embedded into the training, and varying the instructional stimuli to motivate learners. These principles may be given greater weight in developing these programs. This level of attention to design was not as evident in the classroom instruction given for the same problem-solving program.

It is also clear that organizations are moving toward a mix of instructional delivery systems to develop their workforce. For example, the College of Business Administration at the University of Tennessee has responded to an increasing need for physicians to be business-savvy by launching a Physician Executive MBA program in January 1998. This program features three methods of delivery: four Residential Periods, forty computer-based training classes, and weekly Web-Works. Residential Periods are week-long intensive traditional classroom study periods involving the entire class of medical doctors and faculty in one location. The computer-assisted instruction classes are real-time, Internet-based, interactive media (including audio over Internet, synchronized web browsers, shared electronic white board allowing real-time group collaboration, synchronized PowerPoint presentations). They also include anonymous pop quizzes that allow faculty to adjust content and pacing. Participants can talk to each other (audio) before and after class. Web-Works includes twenty-four-hour asynchronous access to discussion groups, documents, video, and e-mail (Dean, 1998). Similarly, self-paced PLATO systems are often combined with live instructional programs and web-based courses to build a targeted curriculum to advance individual knowledge and skills.

In addition, the emerging training technologies are becoming more blended in terms of delivery. CD-ROM multimedia programs are often no longer standalone systems. Instead, the learner can progress through the CD-ROM and hyperlink to web sites to gain additional information. In addition, trainees can take tests from the CD-ROM program and then submit tests for grading or ask questions of experienced tutors through the web. In addition, programs are being developed where trainees can switch from a virtual reality world where they can touch and manipulate objects to more conventional multimedia programs to gain declarative and procedural knowledge.

Finally, although emerging learning technologies offer significant potential for improving teaching and learning, they also complicate training design considerably (Hannifin & Hannifin, 1995). The challenge is to develop training designs that utilize the potential advantages of the training technologies rather than simply providing another means of training delivery. How technological capabilities are used in creative ways to facilitate learning is more critical than the technical capabilities themselves. Managing this creativity to develop effective training is the difficult part. The important aspect here is to use the power of the technology with learning and performance as the key outcomes. For example, designers must be aware of the cognitive demands their training systems place on learners. The training design must thoughtfully apply techniques that support, not interfere with, learner effort. As noted by Krendl et al. (1996), "it is far easier to create something with great cosmetic appeal than an integrated learning system that is consistent with available research and theory." An integrated learning system focuses on meeting important training objectives rather than focusing on delivery of training material through these emerging training technologies. An integrated learning system, regardless of whether we are talking about emerging or traditional instructional delivery mechanisms, must lead trainees to form a deeper understanding of the training material.

INFOTRAC COLLEGE EDITION

For additional readings, go to http: www.infotrac-college.com/wadsworth and enter a search term related to your interest. The following key terms will pull up several related articles.

Distance Learning	Training Simulators
Intelligent Tutoring Systems	Virtual Reality Training
Interactive Multimedia	Web-based Training

A VARIETY OF TRAINING INTERVENTIONS AND LEARNING EXPERIENCES

Training methods have traditionally been developed as a necessary part of bringing new hires up to speed in the organization, ensuring that individuals are technically competent in their individual jobs, training new first-line supervisors on how to manage, and developing individuals identified as having high potential for future leadership positions in the organization. The focus of these training efforts has been to enhance the effectiveness of individuals in particular jobs in an organization.

As noted in Chapter 1, the changing nature of the workplace and work-force has led organizations to recognize a much larger role for training and development. Many companies are realizing that their core productive capacity and long-term viability must be based on the quality of the human resources within the company. Thus, training is viewed as critical not only for improving individual effectiveness but also for enhancing organizational effectiveness through meeting a variety of organizational and individual needs. This move to link training and human resource development efforts to larger organizational effectiveness issues has led to a more holistic approach to training and development.

This more holistic perspective to developing people has led organizations to search for a new approach for identifying those key organizational knowledge and skills that are expected of all employees and leaders in the company. Given the need for a flexible and adaptable workforce, organizations have begun to identify core competencies that they want to establish and nurture in their workplace to enhance organizational effectiveness.

A competency consists of the characteristics, skills, and know-how employees need to successfully operate within an organization (Meister, 1994). Unlike traditional job analysis, the focus on identifying competencies is not on the technical requirements or specific knowledge and skills to perform a particular job (e.g., what knowledge and skills are needed to perform the job of police officer). Instead, this approach emphasizes the characteristics desired across individuals and jobs within an organization (e.g., all police personnel). These more global competencies are expected to not only predict behavior across a wide variety of tasks and settings but also provide the organization with a set of core characteristics that distinguish the company from others in terms of how it operates its business and treats its employees.

One competency modeling approach is to derive competencies that are consistent with the core vision and values of the company. For example, Intel has identified six core values that form the basis for the competencies that every employee at Intel must strive to acquire, demonstrate, and improve upon: (1) taking risks and challenging the status quo; (2) focusing on quality through setting challenging goals and continuously learning; (3) having the discipline to properly plan projects, meet commitments, and conduct business with integrity; (4) serving customers by communicating expectations and delivering innovative and competitive products; (5) being results-oriented by assuming responsibility and focusing on output; and (6) striving to work as a team and having mutual respect for one another (Meister, 1994). A second modeling approach to identifying competencies is to conduct a more traditional analysis of the characteristics held and consistently used by exemplary performers. This method often includes the use of critical incident techniques (Chapter 3) and expert reviews of what characteristics distinguish highly effective from average or less effective performers in the organization, the clustering of this information on critical incidents into categories, and the labeling of the categories as key competencies. For example, Spencer and Spencer (1993) used this approach to identify a generic competency model for salespeople that included competencies of (1) impact and influence, (2) achievement orientation, (3) initiative, (4) interpersonal understanding, (5) customer service orientation, and (6) self-confidence.

Typically, organizations do both types of analyses and combine them into a set of core global competencies for the organization and more specific competencies for particular sets of jobs (e.g., all leadership positions). For example, Prudential HealthCare Group created a competency-based system to integrate human resources (Bina & Newkirk, 1999). They identified core competencies that applied to all jobs in the areas of communication, personal and work management, teamwork, and customer focus. Six additional competency areas were identified for different job families within the organization. The advantage of such an approach is that human resource systems within an organization like selection, training, performance appraisal, and career management can all be linked to achieving and developing these generic, organizational-level competencies.

The increasing importance of training and development for enhancing organizational effectiveness has led to a proliferation of training interventions to develop core competencies as well as job-specific knowledge and skills. We have organized these interventions in terms of their main focus or intended audience. First, interventions can be directed toward employees and improving individual effectiveness. Thus, training interventions have been developed to build individual effectiveness by helping individuals accomplish assigned job duties in an efficient and effective manner, develop interpersonal skills, and revise personal goals as the organization changes. Second, the move to team-based work systems (Chapter 1) and the increasing emphasis on cooperation and coordination of efforts across functions and departments within an organization has led to a number of training interventions to enhance team effectiveness. Interventions have been created to build team-based knowledge and skills such as how to accomplish team goals, how to enhance the internal dynamics of the team, and how the team can go beyond the status quo to improve systems and processes within the organization. Third, there has been a concerted effort in many organizations to increase their emphasis on building the expertise of their leaders to meet the challenges of the changing workplace and workforce and the realities of the increasingly global economy. Interventions to enhance leadership effectiveness focus on building skills such as ensuring that workgroup activities meet organizational goals and objectives, facilitating the growth and development of effective workgroups, and improving organizational processes, products, services, and resource allocations.

In this chapter we discuss interventions to enhance employee, team, and leader effectiveness. These interventions focus on increasing proficiency in the technical aspects of the tasks being performed by organizational members, the development of people skills required to be effective within the organization, and the development of skills for changing the status quo and driving improvements in jobs and systems within the organization. The traditional approach to developing more global competencies and specific knowledge and skills has been to develop a formal training method so that individuals can gain the knowledge and skills needed to meet a perceived need. For example, it might be decided that behavioral modeling training is needed to improve leader effectiveness in how to handle problem employees.

Formal training methods, though, represent only one type of activity within a broader perspective of learning and development. As noted by Baldwin and Magjuka (1997), training is not an isolated event, but an episode that occurs among many other learning opportunities experienced by organizational members. Thus, the development of individuals in organizations must focus on an integrated approach that includes multiple learning events and multiple learning methods that occur over time. In addition to formal training methods, organizations are actively creating structured learning experiences. For example, an organization might set up a structured process in which a new leader is provided with highly challenging work assignments under the direction of a trained mentor. This structured approach to learning is in contrast with the informal learning that occurs on a daily basis in organizations through emerging mentoring relationships and the socialization of newcomers to the organization by established insiders. This unstructured type of learning occurs without the active involvement of the organization in terms of design, direction, or evaluation and has an ill-defined beginning or end (Chao, 1997). In this chapter we focus mainly on formal training methods and well-developed structured learning experiences that have proven to be valuable in improving employee, team, and leadership effectiveness.

BUILDING EMPLOYEE CAPABILITIES

Individuals encounter a variety of training programs and learning experiences during their work career. As noted by Schein (1995), a career can be studied as a series of movements along three different dimensions: (1) moving up in the hierarchy in an occupation or organization, (2) moving laterally across various subfields of an occupation or functional group, and (3) moving toward the centers of influence and leadership in the occupation or organization.

From the individual employee perspective, training and development experiences can have a major impact on what types of career movements are possible and whether the changes involved in each movement are made in a smooth and effective manner. Thus, individuals recognize that their knowledge and skills need to be continually updated to remain current with the present job and to prepare for future career goals. From an organizational perspective, ongoing employee development is a necessary component to improving quality, meeting the challenges of global competition, using new technologies in producing products and services, and capitalizing on the strengths of a diverse workforce (Noe, Wilk, Mullen, & Wanek, 1997).

This section focuses on training methods and structured learning experiences that develop employees from initial entry into the organization (e.g., employee orientation) and throughout the course of an individual's career (e.g., career management/enterprise training). As individuals move from newcomer status to established insider in the organization, employees are often asked to enlarge their knowledge and skill base and more fully utilize their talents for productive employment. Training goals are usually targeted to improving technical proficiency as well as developing more general competencies that lead to a more well rounded individual who can succeed in the workplace over the course of a career.

Employee Orientation

The process of employee development begins when a person enters an organization. Individuals may be exposed to minimal job orientation or to an extensive training experience prior to beginning work. Others may learn on the job after minimal preparation. The quality and quantity of these training experiences can have a major impact on the readiness of the worker (in terms of acquiring needed knowledge and skills) to be a productive member of the workforce.

New employee orientation is typically defined as a planned and systematic attempt by the organization to introduce new employees to job duties, organizational expectations, policies and procedures, and the culture of the organization (Cook, 1992). As noted by Barbazette (1999), the objectives of many orientation programs include attempts to

1. Provide information about the job and the company.
2. Teach essential safety and job skills.
3. Discuss the necessary attitudes that the employee must acquire.
4. Help the new employee get off to a good start by developing an understanding of how things get accomplished in the organization.
5. Make clear what the roles of the supervisor and other employees are in the workgroup.

This list highlights that a key component of any job orientation program is to convey to the newcomer what the organization will be like as well as to provide factual information about benefits or medical plans. An effective orientation program can result in a highly motivated employee ready to be productive in the workplace. An ineffective program can lead to a confused and anxious employee who does not understand what duties to perform or where the job fits into the larger picture of the organization.

Orientation sessions are often packaged as half-day or one-day events in which newcomers fill out forms, are provided with a large amount of information about the company and policies, tour the facility, and are introduced to their workgroup and supervisor. The effectiveness of this type of intensive one-day orientation has been questioned as newcomers are often overwhelmed with information that may not be retained. One option being explored by an increasing number of companies is placing basic information about company structure, policies, procedures, and benefits on the company intranet so that newcomers can access information about the company at orientation time and also review the information at any time once on the job.

Other companies have begun to recognize the importance of orientation programs that are much more extensive and long-lasting. This heightened awareness is due to the recognition of the high cost associated with turnover (up to 50% of new hires leave within the first year on the job) as well as a better appreciation of the need to immediately inculcate values and norms of organizational citizenship among new employees. For example, Intel has executive staff members deliver the message to newcomers as to the company's culture, vision, values, philosophy, and the expected behaviors for success within the company. This orientation also helps differentiate Intel from its competitors. After this initial exposure, new employees take six more orientation seminars over the next fifteen months on the job for a total of thirty classroom hours. Supervisors are also encouraged to provide structured meetings with co-workers to discuss organizational values and customer satisfaction issues and how the work at Intel is consistent with these espoused values (Meister, 1994).

From this emerging perspective, effective employee orientation must be a planned process that ties into the larger organizational vision and strategy rather than a one-day human resource department event. Given broader goals for newcomer orientation, planned learning activities are often embedded during the first week, month, and perhaps a followup three to six months on the job to discover issues that still need to be addressed to help the newcomers fit into the organization. An example of a supervisory checklist for new employee orientation at the University of California—Berkeley is provided in Table 8.1. The orientation covers the steps that should be taken from the first day through six months on the job.

Orientation programs provide the organization with an opportunity to give newcomers a realistic view of what to expect from the organization. If the initial training program provides all the necessary and accurate information required for the newcomer to perform effectively in the new position, then it is possible that some of the "reality shock" of entering the new organization can be minimized (Wanous, 1992). A newcomer with exaggerated beliefs and unrealistic expectations is a likely candidate for poor attitudes and possibly turnover. One approach for integrating training and realistic previews is to develop a miniature job-training program where an applicant is exposed to the actual work conditions and tasks of the job being sought. The results of the miniature job-training program can be used by the organization to make selection decisions or to develop a customized plan for training and development. The program also gives the applicant a realistic preview of what the job will be like. Individuals who do not see a fit between their needs and the job requirements can then self-select themselves out of the applicant pool.

Newcomer Socialization

Once the newcomer is on the job, a key factor influencing how well the individual will fit into the organization is the socialization process. *Organizational socialization* is the formal and often informal process by which a person learns

TABLE

8.1 SUPERVISOR'S CHECKLIST FOR NEW EMPLOYEE ORIENTATION

First Day on the Job

A new employee may be anxious about starting a new job. Try and create a comfortable environment and remember not to overwhelm the employee. On the first day you should:

_____ Give a warm welcome and discuss the plan for the first day.

_____ Tour the employee's assigned work space.

_____ Explain where rest rooms, refreshments, and break areas are located.

_____ Provide required keys.

_____ Arrange to have lunch with the new employee.

_____ Tour the building and immediate area and introduce the new employee to other staff members.

_____ Introduce the new employee to the person you've identified as a buddy (if appropriate).

_____ Review job description card.

_____ Review the department's (or office's) organizational chart and explain its relationship to campus.

_____ Review your office's policies and procedures including:

- Working hours
- Telephone, e-mail, and Internet use
- Office organization (files, supplies, etc.)
- Office resources (directories, dictionaries, style manuals, computer program manuals, staff listing, etc.)

_____ Staff meetings

_____ Accountability

_____ Customer service philosophy

_____ Confidentiality

_____ Ethics

During the First Week

_____ Review employee work area to ensure needed equipment is in place.

_____ Set up a brief meeting with the employee and the assigned buddy to review the first week's activities (if appropriate).

_____ Schedule meeting with Department Personnel Manager to:

- Complete required paperwork
- Review personnel policies and procedures
- Learn about benefits (health & life insurance, select benefits, etc.)
- Schedule Campus New Employee Orientation (if it has not been scheduled)
- Explain time cards
- Review vacation/sick/personal leave policies
- Obtain UC ID
- Obtain Parking Permit (if appropriate)

_____ Have appropriate office personnel review:

- After-hours and weekend office access
- General review of accounting (if appropriate)
- Listing of account numbers (if appropriate)
- Journal vouchers (if appropriate)
- Travel and reimbursement

(Continued)

TABLE 8.1	CONTINUED

- Diners Club credit card
- Campus mail services
- Office supplies
- Copy machine and fax use
- Office safety issues

_____ Review computer competency with CAL PACT self-assessment tools (if appropriate).

_____ Overview of policies and procedures, including confidentiality and software piracy issues.

_____ Assess knowledge of department's hardware and software.

Within the First Month of Employment

_____ Meet with employee to review:

- Job description
- Performance standards
- Work rules

_____ Send employee to New Employee Orientation to review:

- Campus culture
- Campus structure
- Health and safety
- Campus tour
- Benefits overview

_____ Check to be sure employee has signed up for benefits prior to enrollment deadline.

Within Six Months of Starting

_____ Revisit performance standards and work rules.

_____ Schedule performance appraisal meeting.

Source: From *Guide to Managing Human Resources* [On-line]. Available: http://hrweb.berkeley.edu/GUIDE/Gd-new4.htm. Copyright 2000 by Regents of the University of California. Reprinted by permission.

the values, norms, and required behaviors that permit the person to participate as a member of the organization. Socialization takes place over weeks or months after initial entry through both formal methods such as new employee orientation programs and through informal methods such as advice from co-workers, observation, and trial and error (Fisher, 1997).

Wanous (1980, 1992) notes that one of the central themes in the entry process is the idea that people become socialized by the organization. Feldman (1989) suggests that there are "multiple socialization processes," which include interactions between learning and the actual work tasks and all other types of learning that new employees go through in understanding their organization. Wanous indicates that one of the first ways that people become socialized is through the initial training programs. He points out that you can consider a newcomer's effectiveness according to three factors:

1. Having accurate knowledge of what is expected and clarity of the person's role in the organization;
2. Having the knowledge, skills, and abilities (KSAs) necessary to perform the job; and
3. Being motivated to perform the job.

Most of the time, training programs are considered in relationship to point 2—the KSAs necessary to perform the job. Recently, however, the relationship between training and socialization issues has become a topic of interest. Table 8.2 illustrates Wanous's view of the stages in the socialization process. An examination of those stages makes it clear that many of the learning processes involved in stages 1 through 3 begin with a training program as a person enters the organization. These initial training and socialization processes can have a major impact on the inferences the newcomer makes about the organization's philosophy regarding such things as innovation, the value of risk taking, and the importance of continuous learning (Feldman, 1989).

In addition to formal training activities sponsored by the organization, learning occurs for new employees in a variety of ways. Chao, O'Leary-Kelly, Wolf, Klein, and Gardner (1994) have specifically identified six dimensions of socialization where learning is occurring. Performance proficiency focuses on the extent to which individuals learn to perform the required job tasks. People skills focus on establishing successful and satisfying work relationships with established employees. Politics concerns the individual's success in gaining the information about the power structure within the organization—how things get done. Language describes the proficiency of the newcomer in acquiring the technical job-specific language as well as knowledge of organizational acronyms and jargon unique to the organization itself. Organizational goals and values focus on the understanding and appreciation for the rules or principles that underlie how the organization operates and what is expected of its employees. Finally, the issue of history focuses on an appreciation for the organization's traditions, customs, myths, and rituals that drive action and provide explanations for why certain things occur in the organization. In a study of 182 engineers, managers, and professionals, Chao et al. (1994) found that individuals with a stronger understanding of the organizational goals and values and organizational history showed the highest relationships to key outcomes such as personal income, career involvement, and job satisfaction.

A recent study was also conducted to examine the effectiveness of an organizational orientation training program for enhancing the socialization of new hires (Klein & Weaver, 2000). This quasi-experimental field study examined the impact of the training on the six dimensions of socialization developed by

TABLE 8.2	STAGES IN THE SOCIALIZATION PROCESS

Stage 1: Confronting and accepting organizational reality

    a.   Confirmation/disconfirmation of expectations

    b.   Conflicts between personal values and needs, and the organizational climates

    c.   Discovering which aspects of oneself that are reinforced, not reinforced, and which that are punished by the organization

Stage 2: Achieving role clarity

    a.   Being initiated to the tasks in the new job

    b.   Defining one's interpersonal roles

       i. with respect to peers

       ii. with respect to one's boss

    c.   Learning to cope with resistance to change

    d.   Congruence between one's own evaluation of performance and the organization's evaluation of performance

    e.   Learning how to work within the given degree of structure and ambiguity

Stage 3: Locating oneself in the organizational context

    a.   Learning which modes of one's own behavior are congruent with those of the organization

    b.   Resolution of conflicts at work, and between outside interests and work

    c.   Commitment to work and to the organization stimulated by first-year job challenge

    d.   The establishment of an altered self-image, new interpersonal relationships, and the adoption of new values

Stage 4: Detecting signposts of successful socialization

    a.   Achievement of organizational dependability and commitment

    b.   High satisfaction in general

    c.   Feelings of mutual acceptance

    d.   Job involvement and internal work motivation

    e.   The sending of "signals" between newcomers and the organization to indicate mutual acceptance

Source: From *Organizational Entry: Recruitment, Selection, Orientation, and Socialization of Newcomers*, 2nd ed., by J. P. Wanous, © 1992. Reprinted by permission of Prentice-Hall, Inc., Upper Saddle River, NJ.

Chao and her colleagues. With a sample of 116 new employees, results indicated that employees attending the voluntary orientation training were significantly more socialized on three of the six content dimensions—goals, history, and people—than those who did not attend the training. Those individuals who attended were also found to be more committed to the organization.

On-the-Job Training

On-the-job training (OJT) involves assigning trainees to jobs and encouraging them to observe and learn from experienced job incumbents (Baldwin, 1997). Almost all trainees are exposed to some form of on-the-job training after an initial job orientation. This form of instruction might follow a carefully designed off-the-job instructional program. There are very few, if any, formal instructional programs that can provide all the required training in a setting away from the job. At the very least, provisions for transfer to the job setting must be part of the initial learning experience of the actual job environment.

An example of this blending of formal and on-the-job instruction is found in most police organizations. After selection into a police force, new recruits typically attend a formal training academy to learn the basic knowledge and skills to become an effective police officer. Through lectures, discussions, demonstration, and practice, recruits acquire knowledge about basic issues such as the legal system, techniques such as investigation and observation, and skills such as firearms and driving skills. This initial training may take anywhere from three to six months. The recruits are then assigned to a field-training officer for a period of one to two months to learn "on the job." The role of the field-training officer is to model appropriate actions, supply opportunities for the new officer to practice the skills obtained in training, and provide feedback to the new officer on how to improve.

What distinguishes OJT from other instructional methods is that it is carried out at the workplace, delivered while the learner is engaged in performing work tasks, and conducted one on one between a trainer and the learner (Rothwell, 1999). As in the police example, the trainer is typically an experienced employee who has the same job as the learner. In leading-edge companies, these trainers have received much training on how to be an effective coach and mentor.

On-the-job instructional programs are often an informal procedure in which the trainee is expected to learn by watching an experienced worker. A typical example is the new employee in a restaurant who is told to follow an experienced waitstaff person to learn the ropes. This informal approach with an employee who has not received any training on how to coach others reflects the main argument against the use of on-the-job training as the fundamental instructional system. Too often, practicality is the main reason that this unstructured and informal form of training is chosen; it is cheap and easy to implement with no planning at all. The simple instruction to "help the newcomer learn the job" does not make for an effective process. The entire instructional process is placed in the hands of an individual who may consider training an imposition on his or her time. Under these conditions, training and developing the new employee takes second place to the performance of the job. It may not be possible to slow the pace of work, appraise the responses, and supply feedback to the trainee in a job setting where the pressure for performance overwhelms any attempt to create a learning environment for the newcomer.

On the other hand, there is no reason why a carefully designed on-the-job instructional system should not be as successful as any other training approach. The success of the program demands that the objectives and the training environment be carefully prepared for instructional purposes. On-site training must be treated like any other method; the technique should be chosen because it is the most effective way of developing skills. Once the training analyst ascertains that on-site training is the most effective technique to teach the pertinent skills, the on-the-job training environment must be designed as carefully as any other instructional environment. In addition, a selection system can be put into place to find employees motivated to do a good job in training newcomers. The seasoned employee can then be trained to be an effective trainer and mentor and given the organizational support to do the job effectively.

Given these proper conditions, there are certain advantages to on-the-job training. For example, the transfer problem becomes less difficult because the individual is being trained in the exact physical and social environment in which he or she is expected to perform. There is also an opportunity to practice the exact required behaviors and to receive immediate feedback on the effectiveness of various job behaviors. Evidence suggests that companies with effective OJT programs can realize substantial return on their investment. For example, Jacobs, Jones, and Neil (1992) provided data that structured OJT was predicted in a large truck assembly plant to provide approximately twice the financial benefits and five times the efficiency compared with unstructured OJT.

Rothwell (1999) presents an informative case study of a structured on-the-job training program that was carefully planned for employees in a manufacturing plant. There were a series of steps in the program, including the following:

1. Top management fully supported the development of a structured OJT program for improving performance as it was clear that new employees lacked the appropriate training.
2. The goal of the OJT effort was clearly specified to all workers as a means for reducing the unproductive breaking-in period of newcomers, to improve work quality, and to ensure new workers received essential safety training within the job context.
3. The consultant worked with human resources and the plant managers to identify an assembly line where the new OJT program could be implemented and tested for effectiveness.
4. The best performers from each shift along with shift supervisors and internal customers of the assembly line met with the consultant to identify the specific knowledge and skills newcomers needed to acquire relevant to production, quality, and safety.

5. The work flow of the assembly line was identified and the sequence of training events for new hires was determined.
6. A validation meeting was held with other employees, managers, and engineers to review the suggested training events and make modifications.
7. A checklist was developed for each training event to guide the structured OJT process.
8. The exemplary employees on the assembly line were then given training on how to use the checklist and how to instruct newcomers.
9. The success of the OJT was tracked and monitored and the process of developing the structured OJT program diffused to the other assembly lines in the plant.
10. The process of conducting the sessions to develop the OJT program also led to other benefits such as identifying ways to improve transitions from shift to shift and increased consistency across shifts in how the work was completed.

The example makes clear that effective OJT requires a systematic and planned approach to learning. One of the authors of this book worked with a company to develop a train-the-trainer OJT system. Table 8.3 presents a checklist of tasks that were identified relevant to loading/unloading and operating a drilling machine. This checklist was used by experienced (and trained) workers to provide OJT to newcomers in the organization. The OJT process consisted of seven steps. First the trainer showed the newcomer how to do the steps on the checklist. Second, the trainer told the newcomer what the steps were and why they needed to be followed in the proper sequence. Third, the trainer demonstrated the steps again. Fourth, the trainer allowed the newcomer to try out the simple parts of the steps in the task. Fifth, the trainer allowed the trainee to complete the whole set of steps in a task. Sixth, feedback to the trainee was given by comparing the trainee's performance to the checklist and identifying ways in which the trainee could improve. Finally, the trainee would then complete the set of tasks again until all the steps in the task could be completed accurately and efficiently and the newcomer could do the tasks independently.

Apprenticeships

Apprenticeships are formal programs used to teach various skilled trades. Typically, the trainee receives both classroom instruction and supervision from experienced employees on the job. At the end of a specified period of training, the apprentice becomes a journeyman. With more experience on the job, the apprentice becomes a certified skill tradesperson. This system is employed in a wide variety of skilled trades, such as bricklayers, electricians, sheet metal

Source: From *Great Lakes Industry Employee Training Manual.* Courtesy of Great Lakes Industry, Inc., Jackson, MI.

| TABLE 8.3 | BASIC TECHNICAL TRAINING SKILLS CHECKLIST |

Drilling Machine

a. *Load/Unload*

____ Approach the drill with an undrilled part.

____ Remove drilled part from the arbor and set down.

____ Wipe chips from drill arbor and face of flange with your hand.

____ Remove tangled chips from drill below pushing with gloved hand, brush, or hook. (Not your fingers!)

____ Slide part onto arbor (hub side toward flange unless indicated otherwise by the setup man).

____ Use finger locater to orient part if:

    ____ part has two holes, or

    ____ hole has to be located relative to a tooth.

    ____ Setup man will demonstrate use of the locator for each specific part.

b. *Operation*

What trainee should know before operating machine:

____ "ON" button is most always green (used to start machine).

____ "OFF" button is always red (used to stop machine).

To operate machine:

____ Hold part in position on arbor with left hand.

____ Pull down feed handle manually with right hand.

____ When drill has touched the part, pull feed handle down gently to engage automatic feed cycle.

____ Let go of the part when automatic cycle starts (drill feed handle will be rotating slowly).

____ If the part requires two holes

    ____ wait for the first one to drill,

    ____ rotate part to locator stop,

    ____ start second hole.

workers, and pipefitters. It is commonly accepted as a valid mode of instruction for large numbers of trainees.

The original purposes of the apprenticeship-training programs were formulated in 1937 by the National Apprenticeship Act, which created the Federal Bureau of Apprenticeship and Training (BAT) as part of the Department of Labor. These purposes, which have largely remained unchanged, were to formulate labor standards to safeguard the welfare of apprentices and to extend the application of those standards. In addition, another mission was to bring together employers and labor to develop programs and to cooperate with state agencies in developing standards for apprenticeships.

TABLE
8.4

APPRENTICESHIP TRAINING AT NUMMI

New United Motor Manufacturing International (NUMMI), a joint venture between General Motors and Toyota in Fremont, California, cross-trains maintenance mechanics who are responsible for all plant maintenance plus special projects such as building robots. Trainees spend 5 years studying five trades (plumbing, pipefitting, welding, electrical, and machinist). The program includes about 20 percent lecture (theory) and 80 percent lab (troubleshooting small equipment, making projects), supplemented with on-the-job training. It is much less intensive in any one trade than registered apprenticeship programs, however. Graduate trainees receive a United Auto Workers electrical journeyman card and a State of California multi-craft journeyman card, neither of which would be recognized by other unions.

Before entering the program, candidates take placement tests in both basic skills and their individual crafts. Basic skills deficiencies are remediated in class contexts (e.g., math skills in blueprint reading). Classes are 2 hours a day, at the end of each shift; during the most intensive training, classes meet 4 days per week (for this period, a trainee is in the workplace 48 hours per week). The lab component of each course includes 10–15 projects that the trainee has to complete satisfactorily. Each project has three basic steps: describe the process, make a materials list, then return the finished product for review of quality/quantity. The projects range in difficulty from troubleshooting small electrical devices to machining parts to welding. Trainees have to pass each class with a score of at least 80 percent or repeat it. Training continues on the shop floor as those mechanics most skilled in one field assist their co-workers in maintenance tasks.

Training aids in the laboratory include basic electrical units (e.g., volt-ohm-meters, circuits, switches, small motors), machine tools, welding booths and equipment, and other equipment and tools common to the factory (most were scrounged rather than purchased).

The maintenance mechanics feel their productivity has improved as a result of cross-training (e.g., one cross-trained worker often can complete repairs that previously required two or three specialized maintenance workers). However, in some crafts—particularly electrical—the mechanics do not feel they have had sufficient training to tackle complicated repairs without assistance from a union-certified journeyman.

Source: From "Worker Training: Competing in the New International Economy," by Office of Technology Assessment, U.S. Congress, 1990, OTA-ITE-457, Washington, DC: U.S. Government Printing Office.

Federal and state guidelines specify that registered apprenticeship programs must include at least 144 hours of classroom instruction and one year (about 2000 hours) of on-the-job experience. Between 1980 and 1987, the number of apprentices in federal programs declined from 0.3% of the U.S. civilian workplace to 0.16% (Office of Technology Assessment, 1990). In recent years, there has been widespread interest in revitalizing the system because of the concerns about the shrinking supply of young workers and the rising skill requirements in many occupations. Organizations are taking more of a proactive approach to training for increasing the pool of skilled trade workers. Employees are typically certified in one type of skilled trade. Table 8.4 presents an example of a joint venture by General Motors and Toyota to train skilled trades employees in multiple trades through a creative and intensive apprenticeship program.

Two-year or community colleges have also been active in developing and delivering apprenticeship programs. Typically, they involve a partnership among an organization, the relevant trade union, and the community college (Stern, Finkelstein, Stone, Latting, and Dornsife, 1994). For example, General Motors operates over 500 apprenticeship programs involving two-year colleges (Cantor, 1991). Selection into an apprenticeship program can be rigorous as applications can far outnumber available positions. For example, ability tests, high school grades, and selection interviews were used by the Electrical Workers (IBEW) Local #3 to select 700 apprentices from over 2000 applications. Once in a program, apprentices often follow a cycle of working full-time for some months followed by full time schooling. Others work a full-time job and complete training during off-work time.

In addition, there is now interest in using apprenticeship systems for work organizations in occupations other than traditional trades. For example, the Service Employees International Union (SEIU) represents about 875,000 service workers, most of whom work in public or private health care (Office of Technology Assessment, 1990). With the support of BAT, the union has developed joint training programs called Career Ladders. The program specifies exactly what a worker needs to do to be promoted in jobs ranging from housekeepers to pharmacists. One program that has been particularly successful is for phlebotomists, people trained to draw blood from patients. This program has been helpful for a hospital in the Cape Cod, Massachusetts, area where phlebotomists have been in great demand, especially during the summer months. At this point, the hospital does not even have to provide its own training program. All nonmanagement training is done through the Career Ladders program. This effort has been especially important in providing training opportunities for minorities and women.

Embedded Training

As the workplace becomes technically more sophisticated, organizations are trying to take advantage of all possible job-training opportunities. *Embedded training* is an example of this combination, involving the use of new technology and equipment and structured learning experiences on the job. This type of training consists of instruction that is an integral part of the equipment itself. That is, embedded training relies on controlled exercises or vignettes that are called up and need to be worked on by an employee who is operating the equipment on the job. The exercises are developed (1) to provide employees with opportunities to practice skills in a variety of common situations to build automaticity (Chapter 4), or (2) to allow for practice of skills relevant to situations that might not occur very often on the job but are critical to perform. For example, in a nuclear plant, a reactor meltdown is not a likely occurrence, but if it does occur, you want highly trained personnel who have practiced on planned exercises that forced them to deal with possible meltdown situations.

The military has moved quickly to incorporate embedded training opportunities. For example, the U.S. Navy has conducted research since 1990 on tactical decision making under stress on ships. Personnel in a command and information control (CIC) section of a ship must monitor and identify possible airplanes, ships, or submarines that might pose a threat to the battle group of ships and carriers. To maintain readiness, CIC personnel are put through a series of drills that simulate various critical situations. The exercises are embedded in the job such that the crew may not even know if the data presented on the screens in front of them is a practice exercise or the real thing (Cannon-Bowers, Burns, Salas, & Pruitt, 1998).

The U.S. Army also recognizes the need to develop embedded training experiences to improve decision-making capabilities. The embedded experiences can be delivered "just in time" for personnel who may be part of a rapidly deploying force or for geographically dispersed Army Reserve units (Abate, Bahr & Brabbs, 1998). This type of training has several advantages. It is available at the workplace whenever the trainee needs it, and it focuses on the immediate need. The trainees operate under real conditions with opportunities for commanders to watch how each individual and crew responds to a variety of situations. Commanders can then provide immediate and targeted feedback to enhance effectiveness.

The embedded exercises can be repeated or altered to provide new experiences. Training responsibility can revert to individual members and team leaders because there is less need to centralize scheduling and time sharing on training simulators. Also, embedded training permits co-workers to discuss approaches for dealing with a situation and immediately try out new strategies. On the other hand, effectively designing these systems is not easy. The designer must focus on which problems the user is likely to have and anticipate how to answer the questions.

Performance Support Systems

Performance supports have traditionally been viewed as standalone tools that provide information to specific users to help perform specific job tasks. The performance support tool is often in the form of checklists, diagrams, flowcharts, and decision-making aids for the user. For example, word processing and spreadsheet programs have extremely effective instructional systems built into the program. When a user is not sure what to do next, a help button can be pushed to uncover the procedures that must be followed. The advantage of such support tools is that individuals can call up this information from a computer program as they need it to complete a task.

With improvements in technology, more sophisticated embedded performance support systems have been created that provide software application capabilities. The software interface is designed to provide the expert system of information and advice when the user needs guidance (Raybould, 1996). These enhanced support systems can also provide for hypertext, on-line reference, and databases to provide integrated, on-demand access to information, advice, and learning tools (Gery & Jezsik, 1999). For example, Arcand and Trevail (1995) describe a system that allows Avis employees to call up an intelligent help system to aid in making automobile reservations. When a user needs information to complete a task, the expert system takes into consideration known data to supply next steps. The expert system asks questions aimed at reaching a solution to a problem. Rather than concentrating on intensive classroom training experiences, the performance support system enables the users to accomplish tasks on-line.

Oftentimes, more traditional training activities are combined with performance support systems to decrease classroom training time and facilitate the rapid acquisition and transfer of knowledge and skills to effective job performance. As one example, the Canadian Department of National Defence recently combined six existing human resource management systems into one total human resource system for 80,000 employees. Given that these employees are geographically dispersed, the organization took an approach that involved minimal traditional training and added an extensive performance support system. The system, called Enterprise Coach, guides the more than 2300 human resource specialists on how to navigate the new human resource management system. The Enterprise Coach links business and system procedures, providing users with step-by-step instruction to complete tasks. There are 556 business and system procedures embedded in the Enterprise system to aid performance for various functional groups in the military. Employees are given the following expectations about this combination of training and performance support:

> You are not expected to memorize everything we cover during this training session. We want you to come to training with an open mind, and at the end of the session we'd like you to have an understanding of the basic functionality and navigation of the Enterprise system, understanding how to use Enterprise Coach. Enterprise Coach is a tool that you can use at your desktop that provides all of the instructions you will need to perform procedures required with the Enterprise system. Enterprise Coach will contain the most up-to-date procedures that you are expected to perform in Enterprise. Therefore, as long as you are familiar with the functionality of the Enterprise system and are comfortable using Coach, you can depend on the information in Coach to assist you to accomplish all of the Enterprise procedures. . . . Rather than relying on paper-based training manuals that are difficult to maintain, the instructor will use Enterprise Coach to locate the instructional system procedure and will then demonstrate the procedure using the Enterprise System. (Canadian Department of National Defense, quoted from epss.com, "PeopleSoft HRMS User Support and Training"[on-line])

It has been estimated that a traditional training plan would have required from ten to fifteen days of classroom training for each participant supported by a 1500-page manual. By combining training and performance support, the Department of National Defence was able to conduct a two-and-a-half-day classroom training program. An added bonus is the ease of updating and maintaining this type of performance support system on-line rather than sending out new information to be placed into training manuals. A survey found that 91% of the users had a favorable response to the combined training and support approach and that 85% stated that the new system was a valuable tool that assisted them in their daily job duties (see epss.com for more information on this and other case studies).

Enterprise Training

The changing nature of the workplace and workforce has had an impact on career development issues. The career development process has changed from one in which employees assumed they would remain in one company and move up through a progression of mandatory career development training programs and activities. Instead, career management is increasingly seen as a self-directed activity to increase career options within and across companies. *Enterprise training* is a new term being coined for a variety of programs of self-directed career management (Stamps, 1999).

It is estimated that over half of the U.S. firms with 100 or more employees now offer career self-management training (Brockner & Lee, 1995). These companies include such Fortune 500 companies as Hewlett-Packard, IBM, Intel, Motorola, and Sun Microsystems. The main reasons given by these companies for this shift in emphasis is the rapid changes in their industry, compressed product life cycles, and high levels of competition for skilled workers (Griffith, 1998). For example, Sun employees attend a two-day workshop on career self-management (identifying strengths and weaknesses against benchmarks) and also set up four individual counseling sessions. AMD, an integrated circuit manufacturer, has developed a Career Partnership Center that houses a library, multimedia lab, and an MBA program offered on site through a partnership with San José State University.

The goal of such enterprise programs is to build a career-resilient workforce (Waterman, Waterman, & Collard, 1994). This means that employees are willing to continually update their knowledge and skills and manage their careers to enhance their employability within or outside the company. This translates into the employee being more proactive in regularly gathering information and planning for career problem solving and decision making. The focus of training efforts is on the skills and behaviors needed for long-term personal effectiveness.

The variety of techniques used for enterprise training includes self-assessments of the current career state, descriptions of career plans and interests, and the development of career planning goals and action plans. Enterprise training also tries to inculcate the idea that individuals must take on more personal responsibility for career management and direction. This might include suggestions for career networking (inside and outside the company), seeking feedback from others about opportunities, and taking advantage of job opportunities as they arise to make oneself more marketable (again both internally and externally).

Evaluations of enterprise training programs are limited. The Kossek, Roberts, Fisher, and DeMarr (1998) study is one of the few attempts to empirically evaluate the impact of career self-management training. They focused on several hundred salaried professionals of a large transportation company. The three-day training program was specifically designed to "change employees' attitudes to increase their level of initiation of certain behaviors associated with career self-management, informal feedback seeking on current performance and developmental needs, and preparing for internal or external job mobility" (p. 947). The results of the study found little evidence that the training had an impact on self-reported levels (based on telephone interviews) of feedback seeking behaviors or job mobility preparedness. Most surprisingly, the results indicated that trainees were even less likely to engage in career self-management behaviors six to eight months following the training compared with a control group. The researchers suggest that one reason for lack of success was that the training was an isolated event from the traditional HR systems in the organization. Clearly, there must be much effort devoted to understanding when and how enterprise training can be effective in reaching the training objectives.

BUILDING TEAM EFFECTIVENESS

Work organizations have embraced new initiatives such as just-in-time inventory control, total quality management, and advanced computer-based systems. These types of initiatives have led to more integrated approaches to work that require increased coordination of efforts. Many organizations have adopted team-based work systems as a way of meeting these increasing integration needs (Ilgen, 1999). With effective training, teams can tackle complex issues and develop effective solutions.

Teams consist of a small group of people "with complementary skills who are committed to a common purpose, goals, and approach for which they hold themselves mutually accountable" (Katzenbach & Smith, 1993). Team members must have clearly defined, differentiated roles and responsibilities and yet must rely on one another to accomplish goals. To perform effectively, team members must develop an understanding of how their actions affect and are affected by others (Kozlowski, Gully, Nason, & Smith, 1999).

Work teams need the time to become cohesive and training to become an effective and productive unit. Banker, Field, Schroeder, and Sinha (1996) examined a transition from a typical production assembly system to a team-based work system. The transition required months of trust building as employees were given more autonomy and decision-making authority and leaders demonstrated their willingness to implement the decisions made by team members. The trust building was followed by extensive training on teamwork issues. Over a twenty-one month period, the researchers found significant improvements in team effectiveness and manufacturing quality and quantity.

From a training perspective, the transformation of a group of individuals into an effective team requires the development of a variety of team competencies. Team competencies are the knowledge, skills, and attitudes (KSAs) necessary for effective performance of the team's tasks. While similar in nature to the KSA approach typically applied to individual training (see Chapter 3), team competencies are separate and distinct from individual competencies, not merely aggregates of individual-level counterparts. Thus, individual competency is a necessary, but not sufficient condition for effective team performance.

Recent reviews of the team literature indicate a number of team competencies that can be expected to play a large role in team effectiveness (e.g. Cannon-Bowers, Tannenbaum, Salas, & Volpe, 1995). In particular, research has highlighted three key factors that distinguish effective from less effective teams. First, effective teams have members who are highly skilled and who can effectively complete various tasks that the team must perform. Individuals must be competent in their role if they are to become effective team players. This development of the technical competencies of team members have been called taskwork skills (Salas, Dickinson, Converse, & Tannenbaum, 1992). To build taskwork skills, individual team members must be trained to be proficient relevant to their major job duties. Within teams, individuals must also have a larger range of skills than specific technical proficiency to help the team perform to its fullest extent.

Second, effective teams have highly developed teamwork skills in which individual members understand what it takes for a team to work together well as a unit. Teamwork skills are those related to functioning effectively as a team member. The skills focus on the interaction among team members independent of the task to be performed. Salas and his colleagues have identified key teamwork skills that distinguish effective from ineffective teams. Table 8.5 presents these skills of adaptability, shared situational awareness, performance monitoring and feedback, leadership and team management, interpersonal relations, coordination, communication, and decision making along with their definitions and subskills that might be amenable for training. Training teamwork skills can advance the ability of teams to dynamically adapt to the

TABLE 8.5 **TEAMWORK SKILL DIMENSIONS**

Skill Dimension	Definition	Subskills/Alternative Labels

Adaptability	The process by which a team is able to use information gathered from the task environment to adjust strategies through the use of compensatory behavior and reallocation of intrateam resources	Flexibility
		  Capacity for closure
		  Development of innovations
		  Mutual adjustment
		Compensatory behavior
		  Backing-up behavior
		  Provide/ask for assistance
		  Fail stop
		Dynamic reallocation of functions

Shared Situational Awareness	The process by which team members develop compatible models of the team's internal and external environment; includes skill in arriving at a common understanding of the situation and applying appropriate task strategies	Situational awareness
		  Orientation
		  Team awareness
		  Development of integrated model of environment
		  Development of system awareness
		Shared problem-model development

Performance Monitoring and Feedback	The ability of team members to give, seek, and receive task-clarifying feedback; includes the ability to accurately monitor the performance of teammates, provide constructive feedback regarding errors, and offer advice for improving performance	Intramember feedback
		  Performance feedback
		  Planning review
		  Feedback/reinforcement
		  Acceptance of/giving suggestions, criticism
		Mutual performance monitoring
		  Monitoring and cross-checking
		  Systems monitoring
		  Performance monitoring
		  Error identification/correction
		  Intrateam monitoring
		  Strategy development
		  Procedure maintenance

(Continued)

Skill Dimension	Definition	Subskills/Alternative Labels
Leadership/Team Management	The ability to direct and coordinate the activities of other team members, assess team performance, assign tasks, motivate team members, plan and organize, and establish a positive atmosphere	Task structuring Delegation and assignment Task assignment Resource distribution Resource management Performance direction Establishment of priorities Mission analysis Motivation of others Leadership control Goal setting Drive to completion Goal orientation
Interpersonal Relations	The ability to optimize the quality of team members' interactions through resolution of dissent, utilization of cooperative behaviors, or use of motivational reinforcing statements	Conflict resolution Cooperation (interpersonal) Assertiveness Morale building (behavioral reinforcement) Boundary spanning
Coordination	The process by which team resources, activities, and responses are organized to ensure that tasks are integrated , synchronized, and completed within established temporal constraints	Task organization Coordination of task sequence Integration Task interaction Technical coordination Response coordination Timing and activity pacing

(Continued)

TABLE
8.5 CONTINUED

Skill Dimension	Definition	Subskills/Alternative Labels

Communication	The process by which information is clearly and accurately exchanged between two or more team members in the prescribed manner and with proper terminology; the ability to clarify or acknowledge the receipt of information	Information exchange
		  Closed-loop communication
		  Information sharing
		  Procedural talk
		  Volunteering/requesting information
		
		Consulting with others
		  Effective influence
		  Open exchange of relevant interpretations
		  Evaluative interchange

Decision Making	The ability to gather and integrate information, use sound judgment, identify alternatives, select the best solution, and evaluate the consequences (in team context, emphasizes skill in pooling information and resources in support of a response choice)	Problem assessment
		
		Problem solving
		  Emergence of solutions
		  Probabilistic structure
		  Hypothesis formulation
		  Information processing
		  Information evaluation
		
		Planning
		  Plan development
		  Use of information
		
		Metacognitive behavior
		
		Implementation (jurisdiction)

Sources: From "Defining Competencies and Establishing Team Training Requirements," by J. A. Cannon-Bowers, S. I. Tannenbaum, E. Salas, and C. E. Volpe. In *Team Effectiveness and Decision Making in Organizations* (pp. 333–380) edited by R. A. Guzzo and E. Salas. Copyright 1995 by Jossey-Bass. Reprinted by permission of Jossey-Bass, Inc., a subsidiary of John Wiley & Sons, Inc.

demands of the situation under high workload conditions. Due to the great stress and high workload under which many teams must operate (e.g., emergency response teams, air crews), team success is likely to be heavily influenced by the degree to which team members demonstrate effective teamwork skills.

Third, effective teams develop process improvement skills that allow team members to address pressing issues that place constraints on team performance. A core competency for process improvement is problem-solving skills so that team members can identify key problems, analyze root causes, and develop solutions to improve the way the team operates within the organization. Rather than being satisfied with maintaining the status quo, effective teams become drivers for change in an organization.

Training methods developed to enhance taskwork, teamwork, and process improvement skills are described next. While not completely comprehensive in scope, the methods described exemplify the tremendous variety of training and learning activities that have been created to address the changing reality of organizations toward team-based work systems.

Cross Training

One approach for increasing flexibility of individuals within teams is cross training in which individuals learn multiple jobs. The goal of cross training is for all individuals on a team to learn two or more of the jobs that must be performed by the team. With cross training, team members acquire knowledge and skills beyond those previously required so that they can successfully perform the work duties of other members of the workteam. Cross training is typically implemented by organizations to increase flexibility in staffing positions, to prevent employee obsolescence, and to allow teams to become self-managed or autonomous. With skill-based pay systems, team members receive additional pay for acquiring new knowledge and skills.

For example, the work of a manufacturing team might be to transform a piece of steel into gears or sprockets for heavy machinery like farm tractors. To produce a sprocket, the team tasks include sawing the metal into manageable pieces, making a rough cut of the steel rod with a lathe, drilling holes through the metal, creating the teeth of the gear through a hobbing process, and deburring the gear to get rid of excess metal. With cross training, individuals become proficient in many if not all of the tasks to be completed by the team to produce the part. In addition, team members become proficient in more general skills such as checking the quality of the parts produced, enhancing the safety of the manufacturing process, maintaining the machines so they run reliably, and skills in how to set up the machine to allow the team to run different types of parts through the manufacturing process. The more skills an individual learns while on the team, the more flexible the team can be in handling situations that arise. A checklist similar to the one presented in Table 8.3 was developed for each machine. The checklist is used by an experienced trainer to teach the skills needed and to evaluate whether the person has acquired the skills needed to run the machine effectively.

Cross training usually involves the development of train-the-trainer systems in which an experienced team member trains the others to become proficient in a variety of job tasks. For example, one company has formalized the train-the-trainer system and coined it as LUTI—you first *l*earn a new team skill, you next *u*tilize the skills until you become proficient in the skill, you can then *t*each that skill to others, and then you can *i*nspect whether that new person is able to learn and become proficient in that skill.

Cutcher-Gershenfeld and Ford (1993) provide a case analysis of the difficulties in implementing a cross-training program that is sustained and supported within an organization. They report on a company that makes rolled steel that introduced a craft-combination training process. Craft-combination training focused on merging skilled trades. For example, the craft-combination training involved broadening a welder's skills to include pipefitting competencies and expanding a pipefitter's competencies to include welding. Over 900 skilled trades employees had gone through the craft-combination training modules with an average module taking over 1000 hours to complete. Despite these efforts, an evaluation of the system found that many supervisors did not allow those who had successfully completed the training to use the skills learned in training. Instead, the supervisors preferred someone who was originally certified and trained as a welder rather than calling a pipefitter who had been cross trained on welding skills. Thus, the problem was not one of training but of the transfer of training to a work environment where the pressure was to keep production moving and putting out fires as quickly as possible rather than supporting the development of the individuals who had been cross trained by giving them opportunities to perform on the job.

Interpositional Training

One method for enhancing cooperation and coordination of efforts in a team is to facilitate the development of what has been called interpositional knowledge (Volpe, Cannon-Bowers, Salas, & Spector, 1996). The goal of interpositional training is not for members to become cross trained—the method previously described in which members of the team are fully trained on the tasks of other team members. Although one may acquire a great deal of knowledge of their teammates' duties, the goal of *interpositional training* is for individuals to acquire a working knowledge of the tasks performed by one's teammates and the interconnections among them. In this way, the training can lead to the building of a shared mental model among team members as to how the team operates and thus what type of cooperation and coordination is needed to be an effective team. With interpositional knowledge, the goal is to facilitate implicit coordination among team members and foster greater team adaptability.

Interpositional training can take three different forms: positional clarification, positional modeling, and positional rotation (Blickensderfer, Cannon-Bowers, & Salas, 1998). Positional clarification refers to providing members with information-based training, such as verbal or written presentation of information on various facets of their teammates' jobs. Positional modeling refers to a training procedure in which the duties of one's teammates are discussed and observed. Finally, positional rotation is experientially based training, wherein team members actually perform the duties of other team members to get a hands-on perspective of the roles, responsibilities, and coordination requirements.

The form of interpositional training utilized should correspond to the level of interdependence of the team, with positional clarification being sufficient for teams with minimal interdependence and positional rotation appropriate for highly interdependent teams (Blickensderfer et al., 1998). Studies have provided empirical support for the utility of interpositional training for enhancing team effectiveness. For example, Volpe et al. (1996) found that two-member teams operating a PC flight simulator demonstrated greater overall teamwork, more efficient communication strategies, and greater team performance when provided with positional clarification than when trained only on performing their own duties. Extending this initial finding, Cannon-Bowers et al. (1998) found that the benefits of interpositional training were greatest under high-workload situations, in which demands on team effectiveness are the greatest. Such findings are a common characteristic of the situations in which emergency response teams must operate, indicating the utility of interpositional training for such teams.

Team Self-Management

An important outcome of cross training and interpositional training is to allow teams to become more self-sufficient and autonomous. The team can manage its own internal processes such as assigning people to work projects, evaluating team success, taking action to improve team effectiveness, and monitoring its own learning. Tannenbaum, Smith-Jentsch, and Behson (1998) have proposed three means by which teams can promote and facilitate their own learning to continuously improve. The focus is on the way the team (1) prepares for a learning experience, (2) manages its human resources, and (3) learns from feedback regarding how well the team is performing.

Prepractice conditions.   Cannon-Bowers, Rhodenizer, Salas, and Bowers (1998) have described a framework for understanding prepractice conditions and their impact on learning and retention. They highlight strategies for preparing team members to learn from practice experiences, including providing advice concerning where trainees should focus their attention during training, building skills of team members on metacognitive strategies, and providing prebriefing and preparatory information. For example, a prebrief can be held prior to task practice or performance during which the team prepares for the upcoming activity. Prebriefs provide the team leader and members an opportunity to set both individual and team-level goals, discuss strategies, clarify roles and responsibilities, and focus on potential problems to be encountered. They can be used to explicate the linkages between individual roles and those of their team members. Additionally, specific strategies can be developed for a variety of likely contingencies, allowing team members to form common expectations of how each other will respond.

In practice, a prebrief begins with an emphasis on the objective to improve team processes. Teamwork issues such as how to communicate effectively and how to provide support for others are highlighted and discussed. Team members are then reminded of the goals that they have set from previous practice sessions on achieving greater team cooperation and coordination. Then, team members are told that it is their responsibility to share learning experiences and critique team performance once the practice exercise is completed. Although, as the name implies, prebriefs are generally conducted prior to a practice or performance episode, the team can also capitalize on low-workload periods to engage in such preparatory activities. For example, Orasanu & Salas (1993) found that a distinguishing factor between high and low performing aircraft crews was the extent to which they utilized low-workload periods to discuss how they would handle potential emergency situations.

Team resource management.   Salas and his colleagues contend that Crew Resource Management (CRM) is a useful framework for developing teamwork skills. CRM has been defined as a set of teamwork competencies that allow the team to cope with situational demands that would overwhelm any individual team member (Salas, Prince, Bowers, Stout, Oser, & Cannon-Bowers, 1999). They have developed a methodology for designing CRM training programs. Program development begins with the identification of the mission requirements and procedures. This is followed by an assessment of the coordination demands (i.e., specific tasks requiring teamwork). These tasks are then linked to theories of team performance to derive the specific competencies to be trained. Each competency is translated into a training objective that can be empirically evaluated. The next step is to determine the instructional delivery method (i.e., lecture, video). Scenarios or exercises are then developed to provide trainees opportunities to practice each competency. These exercises also provide a means for assessing whether the targeted behaviors are demonstrated sufficiently. Based upon this assessment, constructive feedback is provided concerning effective and ineffective behaviors. Finally, the training is evaluated to determine its effectiveness in increasing the targeted competencies on the job.

Recent evaluations of CRM training programs have provided encouraging results regarding their effectiveness. CRM training has been shown to lead to as much as a 20% increase in teamwork behaviors in teams trained under this method (Salas et al., 1999). For example, the researchers found that CRM training led to increases in positive attitudes toward teamwork, knowledge of teamwork principles, and demonstration of teamwork competencies in a simulated mission. The increase in exhibited teamwork behaviors was particularly large in high-workload conditions as compared with a control group. Moreover, CRM training was found to be effective for both new aviators and those with previous experience performing their tasks as a team. Additionally, aviators who occupied different positions within their teams benefited from the same training program.

Posttraining review.   Upon completion of the practice or performance episode, a postaction review can be utilized to review and critique individual and team performance, as well as summarize lessons learned that can guide future performance. A central component of the postaction review is the provision of both individual and group-level feedback.

Feedback focuses team members on critical aspects of the task and provides a means of regulating progress toward a goal (e.g., Bandura, 1991). The effectiveness of postaction reviews is affected by the climate in the team. There must be a climate of openness and trust so that team members can feel comfortable admitting mistakes and confusing situations that occurred during performance. One means of building such a climate is for all team members to provide a self-critique early in the postaction review.

Challenge Education and Adventure Learning

This learning perspective involves the use of intact teams exposed to difficult or unfamiliar physical and mental challenges in an outdoor (and sometimes indoor) environment. The focus is on individual and team problem-solving challenges (Wagner, Baldwin, & Rowland, 1991). The goals of these activities are for a team of participants to explore strategies for enhancing teamwork, building trust, developing support networks, and incorporating risk management strategies into team decision making. At a personal level, the courses can help individuals acquire skills in taking initiative, making decisions, and setting personal improvement goals. The interventions include such activities as ropes courses, rock climbing, rappelling, sailing, rafting, and wilderness exploration (Thiagarajan, 1999).

Challenge education provides the opportunity to try new activities; time for personal reflection as to what has occurred during those activities; and a structured, facilitated session with all team members to share insights. Figure 8.1 presents a diagram of the layout for a challenge exercise called "canyon crossing" (see Snow, 1997). The exercise requires a team to solve a problem under time pressure. The task is to move the team from one side of an impassable area to the other side by constructing a bridge using the material shown

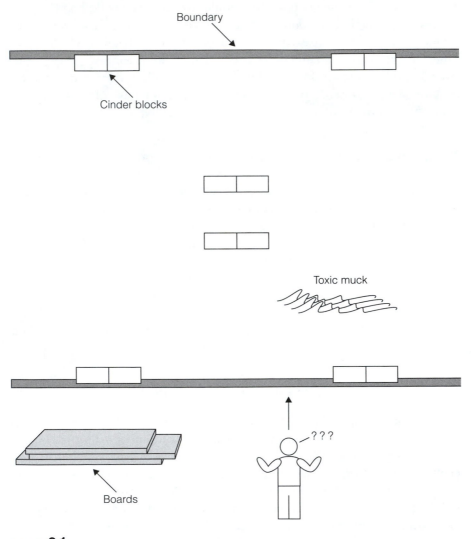

FIGURE 8.1

Canyon crossing exercise.

Source: From *Indoor/Outdoor Team-Building Games for Trainers,* by H. Snow. Copyright 1997 by McGraw-Hill. Reprinted by permission.

in the diagram (two long wooden planks, one smaller wooden plank, six cinder blocks, and rope). The team has twenty minutes to build the bridge, cross it, and bring the boards used to construct the bridge over to the other side so that hostile enemies cannot follow it. The exercise requires good planning and quick execution. After the exercise, participants and the facilitator can discuss issues such as who took over the leadership role and why, how well the team cooperated, how time pressure affected teamwork, and some of the effective and ineffective attributes of teamwork that were displayed by the team.

There are four main reasons why challenge education or adventure learning can be effective. First, it requires participants to solve challenges with their co-workers that parallel or are metaphors for problems and tasks faced on the job. An assumption is that the knowledge and skills gained from these activities can be transferred to improve team performance in the actual work setting. Second, exercises require participants to use cognitive, behavioral, physical, and emotional resources to solve problems. This can lead to a better understanding of moving beyond a reliance on rational decision-making processes and getting out of the box to be more creative. Third, these learning experiences also provide an opportunity for participants to discuss individual behaviors and group problem-solving processes that contribute to as well as constrain team effectiveness. The structured exercises provide a common base from which all team members can generate lessons learned to improve team effectiveness back on the job. Finally, these activities end with the development of personal and team action plans. These plans are intended to motivate team members to transfer the insights discovered and new behaviors that have been demonstrated to improving team performance in the work environment.

Despite its popularity, evidence regarding the effectiveness of challenge education and adventure learning is limited. Much of the support for these learning experiences is based on positive reactions from participants ("I really gained a lot from this experience") and a few studies that have looked at changes in self-concept and self-perceptions. For example, Leenders and Henderson (1991) examined field notes written by students and guides during an eight-day university credit course in canoeing and wilderness living. The analysis of this data revealed enhanced self-insight and feelings of well being from a number of the students on the trip. On the other hand, a recent empirical study questions the impact of adventure learning. Kemp (1998) examined change in self-esteem of sixty-one college students undergoing a fifteen-week college course on group dynamics that incorporated a variety of adventure learning activities. A control group only studied group dynamics from lecture and discussion sessions. Results showed no significant change in self-esteem for either group.

In addition, there are case studies that have evaluated success. These evaluations tend to be more favorable to the effects of challenge education and adventure learning. For example, Thiagarajan (1999) discussed a case in which participants in a challenge education course noted in the debriefing that they had a better understanding of big picture issues and principles of knowledge management and that they intended to transfer knowledge by developing strategies for maintaining a better knowledge management system on the job. A debriefing session held three weeks after completion of the course found that participants reported that appropriate behaviors were being applied and obstacles being minimized as a function of the training experience. In another example, Kugath (1997) reported on twenty-four families that participated in an intensive eight-hour adventure program that included rock climbing, whitewater rafting, and team-oriented games. Questionnaire data indicated that there were changes in parents' perceptions of family cohesiveness but not for enhanced problem solving or general functioning as a family. Interviews with eleven families one month after the experience confirmed that parents and children reported positive changes in family cohesiveness and that powerful memories of the program persisted.

Unfortunately, these case examples are not adequate for determining the extent to which challenge education and adventure learning lead to enhanced effectiveness of work teams (e.g., Wagner, Baldwin, & Rowland, 1991). Most of the studies are not conducted on actual workteams. What is needed are studies that focus on demonstrable changes in behavior of team members and improvements in team effectiveness on the job that can be linked to specific experiences obtained through challenge education.

Action Learning

Adult learning theory highlights the important role of learners as active participants in their own learning process. Action learning approaches have been developed to allow participants to reflect, experiment, and learn from experiences that have implications for enhancing team effectiveness. The action learning approach emphasizes that much learning occurs by dealing directly with work-related issues during a formal training session. The focus of the training is to understand and solve complex, real-life problems.

Action learning consists of six components (Marquardt, 1999). First, action learning focuses on an important problem or challenge that a team must meet. A problem is defined as occurring when the aims of a system do not meet the reality of the system. For example, an organization may be experiencing higher levels of safety-related injuries than is desirable. Second, a core group of diverse people must be identified to approach the problem from multiple perspectives and fresh viewpoints. The group might be an intact workteam or a group of experts drawn from various functions and levels in the organization. Third, the team must take a problem-solving approach. A problem-solving approach uses data to generate knowledge that leads to action plans for improvement. This problem-solving approach requires team members to interpret the data to come to a shared understanding of the problem and then diagnose the root causes of the major factors that have led to the problem. Then action plans can be based on the analysis of the root causes and what factors are more amenable to change and more likely to lead to a solution. Fourth, the team must have the power to take action and implement an improvement plan. Fifth, the team must have a commitment to learning throughout the process of problem solving. There needs to be equal emphasis on accomplishing the task of solving a problem and the learning and development of the team members that can be diffused throughout the organization. For learning to occur, the team needs the time to reflect on its experiences and draw out lessons learned for improving team process and for generalizing the learning to other activities in the organization. Finally, a sixth characteristic of action learning is the use of a facilitator to help the team balance the dual tasks of problem solving and learning. Marquardt notes that a facilitator can help the team reflect on how members communicate with one another, how they give each other feedback, how the process is following their plan, and how their assumptions might be affecting their beliefs about the problem and subsequent action plans that are generated or accepted as legitimate avenues for improvement.

Table 8.6 presents an example of an action learning approach in a small parts manufacturing company that produces gears and sprockets. The overall quality problem as identified by employees at the company was clear. A team was created that consisted of operators, the quality coordinator, manufacturing engineers, and purchasing agents. The team was trained in basic problem-solving methods including how to conduct root cause analysis. In addition, the members had already been trained in statistical process control and other methods for analyzing data. For this project, the team utilized a cause-effect

---

TABLE 8.6   **ACTION LEARNING AT A SMALL PARTS MANUFACTURER**

We quoted and received an order for a part from a new customer. The customer called for two counterbores with unusual dimensions for our normal machining operations. We were under delivery pressure from the customer. We proceeded with production per standard operation procedures. During the final inspection, we found that approximately 35% of the parts were nonconforming to the specifications desired by the customer. We sorted out the poor quality parts and inspected those that were marginal and made decisions as to what we could ship to meet the deadline. We chalked up the errors to bad machining by the operator. Two weeks later we were trying to ship for the next scheduled delivery. We encountered a similar rejection rate. A department leader tried to troubleshoot the job and found that it was impossible to do a high-quality job given the type of information given to the operators. Thus far, we have scrapped several hundred dollars' worth of material and have compromised our quality by shipping parts that do not completely meet product specifications. Everybody is very frustrated. It is time to create a team to examine this quality problem.

Source: From *Great Lakes Industry Employee Training Manual.* Courtesy of Great Lakes Industry, Inc., Jackson, MI.

analysis that helped the team to identify and organize the factors that led to the recurring quality problem. The team mapped out a list of factors that included quality issues between groups or departments within the company, contextual factors, information and communication impediments relevant to this project, and operator factors. The team generated twenty-nine factors that led to the quality problem and then prioritized the factors in terms of which were the most critical. For example, the key internal quality problems identified were that the design of the tooling on the machine was not correct, the metal being used was warped during earlier heat treating of the metal (done off-site), the sequence of operations were difficult and unfamiliar to most operators, the order was not reviewed properly to discover and solve engineering problems prior to giving the job to the operator, and that there was a lack of recognition that the parts being produced were not complying with the specifications. The team then generated a list of possible solutions including getting more tolerance from the customer, resequencing how the job would be completed, training operators on inspection methods, and doing heat treatment within the company to maintain high quality. After coming to consensus on the solutions, the team members divided up the implementation tasks (e.g., one team member focused on simplifying inspection techniques while another created a team to resequence the production operations for this part). The next time the part was ordered by the customer, the results showed a dramatic improvement in quality and on-time delivery.

The problem was addressed and learning did occur. Throughout this problem-solving process, team members were encouraged to discuss lessons learned from this experience and how to generalize this learning to other new product situations as well as to more common ones. Team members also focused on how well they were working together as a team (e.g., engineering and sales had rarely worked with operators on the floor). Based on these experiences, a common problem-solving model was developed for future situations. In addition, new procedures for how to deal with new and complex products were developed that included the creation of product teams to examine the product specifications prior to the job going to the operator. The product team included a diverse set of employees including engineering, operations, quality, and leaders.

As can be seen in this example, the main goal of action learning is the creation of creative ideas and innovative strategies that lead to solving an existing problem. Solving problems can increase feelings of personal and team accomplishment while reducing frustration. The action learning model can also increase participants' self-awareness of skill strengths and weaknesses as well as create a more positive group dynamic such as increased team cohesiveness. Although there is good agreement on what makes for an effective action learning process, the data on the effectiveness of this approach is limited to anecdotal evidence and case study like the one in Table 8.6. Nevertheless, it is clear that many companies have moved to an action learning approach where training and learning go hand in hand with problem solving and improved job performance.

DEVELOPING LEADERS

The changing nature of the workplace and workforce (see Chapter 1) highlights the need for effective leadership. Leaders have to structure activities that enhance productivity at a time when jobs are becoming increasingly complex and national and international competition is becoming more intense. The increase in service-sector jobs and the move to team-based work systems require managers to work more with people. The changing expectations of a more educated workforce toward increased responsibility and empowerment places pressure on leaders to think out of the box and be more creative in the utilization of human resources. All of this makes training for leadership and people skills even more important.

Leadership development programs have exploded over the last decade to become a multibillion-dollar business in the United States (Fulmer & Vicere, 1996). It is clear that the movement to team-based work systems, total quality management, and to a global perspective requires leaders to have broad skills in initiating and facilitating organizational effectiveness. To meet these challenges, organizations are not only emphasizing formal training but are also more involved in setting up special opportunities for learning and development to enhance the leadership capabilities of high-potential employees and of the organization as a whole (McCauley, 1999). In this section, we highlight five types of leadership development interventions. The interventions differ in their emphasis on self-development, learning from structured and unstructured on-the-job experiences, and adapting to the changing nature of the workplace and workforce.

Business Simulations

Business simulations allow leaders to experience events that are as close to the real experience as possible (Thiagarajan, 1999). A survey by Faria (1989) found that business simulations are a widely used technique. Simulations continue to be a popular approach to training leaders. For example, the American Red Cross (1999) has developed a simulation to train its leaders on emergency operations. Although a manager may only work in one area of operations, there are twenty-three areas or functions that must coordinate action during an emergency operation. Data from training needs assessments highlighted recurring issues such as needs for more effective information sharing among emergency field operations teams, better coordination of limited resources, and smoother transitions from a localized response to a nationwide network of emergency response personnel and resources. A simulation designed to focus on these issues was developed that featured scenarios requiring the participants to make decisions and take actions (e.g., how to staff facilities, place volunteers, assist clients) that have identifiable consequences.

Business simulations are a direct outgrowth of war games used to train officers in combat techniques. One military war game developed in 1798 used a map with 3600 squares, each representing a distinctive topographical feature, on which pieces representing troops and cavalry were moved (Raser, 1969). After visiting the Naval War College in 1956, members of the American Management Association developed the first application of war games to business situations. It is estimated that more than 30,000 executives participated in the large number of simulations that were developed in the following five years (Stewart, 1962). As Thornton and Cleveland (1990) note, leadership simulations have become extremely diverse in terms of a large number of aspects including complexity of the issues addressed, the number of participants, and the complexity of the tasks. They range from simple situations for individuals to complex simulations for teams of leaders that differ in organizational level. The main difference today is the power of the computer and CD-ROMs to incorporate much more information, complexity, and dynamism into simulations compared with early attempts that were basically board games.

The early business games were nearly all designed to teach basic business skills such as how to allocate resources to tasks, how to keep manufacturing costs low, and how to market products. More recent simulations have focused on building specific leadership skills such as situational awareness, coordination skills, communication and interpersonal skills, problem solving, and decision making. One of the most carefully developed and evaluated simulation efforts is known as Looking Glass, Inc. (McCall & Lombardo, 1982). The purpose of this simulation (which has been continually updated) is management development, both as individual members and as members of a team. It involves capturing communication and group dynamics in a way that permits managers to learn both by doing and by the feedback provided at the end of the exercises. A brief description of Looking Glass follows:

> Looking Glass, Inc., is a hypothetical medium-sized glass-manufacturing corporation. For a simulation, Looking Glass is quite realistic. Complete with annual report, plausible financial data, and a variety of glass products, the simulation creates the aura of an authentic organization. Participants are placed in an office-like setting, complete with telephones and an interoffice mail system. The positions actually filled in the simulation are the top management of the corporation, including four levels ranging from president to plant manager. The company consists of three divisions whose environments vary according to the degree of

change, with one division's environment being relatively placid, another turbulent, and the third a mixture of the two. Lasting six hours, the simulation is intended to be a typical day in the life of the company. It begins by placing each participant face to face with an in-basket full of memoranda. Together with background information common to all participants, this information, which differs somewhat from division to division, level to level, and position to position, constitutes the stimulus. Participants spend the rest of the day responding to these interlocking sets of stimuli, acting and interacting as they choose. Contained in the collective in-baskets of the twenty participants are more than 150 different problems that participating managers might attend to. The problems vary in importance, and they also vary, realistically, in how apparent or hidden they are to the one or more individuals who ought to be concerned about them. Also true to life, the number of problems far exceeds the time available to deal with them. (Kaplan, Lombardo, & Mazique, 1983, p. 29)

Simulations like Looking Glass offer a number of potential advantages, including a risk-free experience across a variety of situations that allow for opportunities to practice skills. In addition, simulations are dynamic as decisions made by participants have consequences. This allows participants to see more clearly the linkage between actions and the effects of those actions on others. These characteristics can have a powerful impact on learning. For example, Kaplan et al. (1983) described the performance of one group of seventeen managers from the same organization using Looking Glass. The feedback focused on the fact that team members spent most of their time alone at their desk and that the group wrote many more memos than the typical group. In addition, the managers did not choose well between high- and low-priority items. Based on this feedback, the team identified strategies that they needed to enact in their workplace to support greater teamwork and organization.

While the content validity of many simulations like Looking Glass is typically high, there is limited evaluation data on the success of simulations on improving learning and training transfer. The evaluation data available on simulations is typically reactions from leaders based on case analyses. For example, Fripp (1996) reports that 90% of participants thought a business simulation game was a very useful method for learning about how the various parts of the business interrelated, how the team of leaders could work more effectively, and how leaders can make more effective decisions. More recently, Thiagarajan (1999) reported the success of a simulation focused on customer service issues through a game called Triangles that requires participants to move through three stages of planning, manufacturing, and selling. He reports that more than 7000 individuals have completed the Triangles simulation and that these individuals have reported greater insight into the factors that inhibit a customer focus in their organizations. In one of the few empirical studies of business simulations, Pool, Heriges, Crase, and Blackburn (1992) found that participants given personal feedback on their learning styles and a training module on the characteristics of effective leaders prior to the Looking Glass simulation outperformed those who worked on the simulation with no initial feedback or training. This highlights once again the important role of preparation in the learning process. Expectations that this is to be a learning experience with clear training objectives must be conveyed before the simulation begins. Participants must also have a mastery orientation toward the simulation experience and be prepared to discuss lessons gained that have implications for learning and development.

Clearly, there is a lack of empirical research on what is actually learned through the simulation and then transferred to new behaviors on the job. It is difficult to know how effective business simulations are for making a difference in on-the-job behaviors and for improving team and organizational effectiveness. As noted by Tannenbaum and Yukl (1992), there is little evidence to indicate that these kinds of simulations result in any long-term improvement in management effectiveness. Although the impact of business simulations is open to question, researchers have noted a number of possible inhibitors to learning and transfer with business simulations. First, in some simulated games, participants may become so involved in the exciting and at times competitive aspects of the game that they lose sight of the principles and the evaluation of consequences that are its most important aspects. Instead, participants can become more concerned with beating the system and one another. Second, business simulations can lead participants to learn particular solutions to particular problems rather than learning more generalizable underlying principles and concepts. Leaders may then see a similar problem in the workplace and apply the solution implemented in the business game only to find out that the solution has been inappropriately applied in the real organizational setting. Third, Hsu (1989) points out that most games are designed to achieve learning related to problem-solving and interpersonal skills, yet that is not typically what is evaluated. He eloquently notes, "A violin practice lesson should not be judged by its musical beauty but by how much effort need be invested in fingering, bowing, and expression before the piece can be played for the audience to enjoy" (p. 429). Thus, the heavy emphasis on who wins the game or makes the most money can become a distraction in uncovering the characteristics of games that might work in effecting changes in key behaviors. After all, it is the key behaviors that should be learned in order for anything to transfer into the work situation.

Behavioral Role Modeling and Applied Learning

For over two decades, the technique that has generated much interest in leadership development has been behavioral role modeling. This approach is based on Bandura's (1977, 1991) social learning theory, which stresses the use of observing, modeling, and vicarious reinforcement as steps for modifying human behavior. This learning theory was originally discussed in Chapter 4. Bandura's theory focuses on the acquisition of novel responses through observational learning and includes a number of subprocesses that are important parts of the observational learning process:

1. The attentional processes relate to the ability of the observer to attend to and differentiate between cues. Some factors that can influence these attentional characteristics include variables like model characteristics and the ease with which modeling conditions can be discriminated. Greater modeling will occur when behavior is demonstrated in a clear and detailed manner by trusted models.
2. The retentional processes have been characterized as the capability required to remember the stimuli over a period of time. This factor is likely to be affected positively by covert and overt rehearsal and negatively by factors like interference from previously learned material.
3. The motor reproduction processes refer to the physical abilities needed to acquire and perform the behavior portrayed by the model. Most of the constraints related to this process refer to physical abilities. Thus, without considerable amounts of practice and skill, an observer might not be able to imitate the behavior of a skilled craftsperson, such as a carpenter, even if the behavior had been modeled appropriately.
4. The incentive and motivational processes are defined as the reinforcement conditions existing at the time the observed behavior is performed. Reinforcement is not a necessary condition for the learning of models' responses but is important in getting people to actually exhibit the behavior that has been learned.

In 1974 A. Goldstein and Sorcher published a book called *Changing Supervisory Behavior,* which adapted many of the principles of Bandura's social learning theory into a training approach. Their goal was to improve interpersonal and related supervisory skills. These authors criticized other approaches to training managers as focusing on changing attitudes and not directly on improving behaviors to enhance job performance. They argued that training programs typically tell managers that it is important to be good communicators, with which almost everyone agrees (and probably knows before coming into the training program). However, the programs do not teach the manager how to become a good communicator. In contrast, the A. Goldstein and Scorcher approach consists of providing trainees key behaviors found to be effective in particular situations and then showing the trainees numerous and vivid models performing those specific behaviors. Trainees are then given opportunities to practice the key behaviors demonstrated by a model and receive feedback on the extent to which the behaviors were displayed and what steps can be taken in the next practice trial to further refine the behaviors exhibited by the trainee.

Early empirical studies showed promise for the vitality of the approach (e.g., see Kraut, 1976) for improving leadership behaviors. Since then, a number of carefully carried-out empirical research efforts have been reported. One of the best behavioral role-modeling evaluation studies (discussed in Chapter 6 as one of the best training evaluation studies) was reported by Latham and Saari (1979). Their study involved 100 first-line supervisors who would receive training. Because it was not possible to train everyone at once, they randomly selected 40 supervisors and randomly assigned 20 of them to a training condition and the other 20 to a control group.

The training modules were designed to increase the effectiveness of first-line supervisors in working with their employees. The topics included orienting a new employee, motivating a poor performer, correcting poor work habits, handling a complaining employee, and overcoming resistance to change. Each session followed the same procedure of introducing the topic and key behaviors for the topic, presenting a film of a supervisor effectively handling a situation, group discussion of the effectiveness of the model in demonstrating desired behaviors, practice in role-playing the desired behaviors, and feedback from the class on effectiveness of each trainee in demonstrating desired behaviors.

During the practice sessions involving role playing, one trainee took the role of the supervisor, and another trainee had the role of the employee. The trainees did not use prepared scripts. Instead, they were asked to recreate an incident that had occurred during the past year that was relevant to the training topic for that week. During the session, the key behaviors emphasized in the film were posted so that the person playing the role of supervisor could make use of the principles. An example of the learning points for one program—handling a complaining employee—is presented in Table 8.7.

Trainees playing the role of supervisor had no idea what the employee role player would do. The supervisor role player simply responded as best he or she could using the learning points and information gained from watching the role models in the film carry out the learning points. Two trainers were present at all sessions, with the first trainer supervising the role-playing practice. The second trainer worked with the group to teach it how to provide constructive feedback that would enhance the confidence and self-esteem of the person receiving feedback. At the end of each session, trainees received printed versions of the key behaviors and were sent back to their jobs with instructions to use the supervisory skills they had gained. At the next session, trainees reported their experiences. In situations where the supervisors had difficulty, they were asked to report it to the class. Then they role-played the situation, with the class providing feedback on desired behaviors and the supervisor again practicing the appropriate behaviors. Latham and Saari (1979) also note

TABLE 8.7	BEHAVIORAL LEARNING POINTS FOR REDUCING CONFLICT

- Avoid responding with hostility or defensiveness,
- Ask for and listen openly to the employee's complaint,
- Restate the complaint for thorough understanding,
- Recognize and acknowledge his or her viewpoint,
- If necessary, state your position nondefensively, and
- State a specific date for a followup meeting.

Source: From "The Application of Social Learning Theory to Training Supervisors through Behavioral Modeling," by G. P. Latham and L. M. Saari. In *Journal of Applied Psychology*, 1979, *64*, pp. 239–246. Copyright 1979 by The American Psychological Association. Reprinted by permission.

that some of the learning points for some of the programs did not fit their specific situation, and so the points were revised by the trainees and the investigators. Latham and Saari also provided training for the supervisors of the trainees to ensure that the trainees would be rewarded for their new on-the-job behaviors.

Besides carefully designing a training program, Latham and Saari (1979) evaluated the results using reaction, learning, behavioral, and job-performance measures:

1. The reaction measures were collected immediately after training and consisted of items such as whether the training was helpful for performing the job better and for interacting more effectively with employees. These indicators showed positive results. A followup eight months after training had been completed also indicated that there was no difference in response immediately after training and eight months later.

2. The learning measure consisted of a situational test with eighty-five questions developed from critical incidents found in the job analysis. An example of one situational question is as follows:

   You have spoken with this worker several times about the fact that he doesn't keep his long hair confined under his hard hat. This constitutes a safety violation. You are walking through the plant and you just noticed that he again does not have his hair properly confined. What would you do? (Latham & Saari, 1979, p. 243)

   Trainees were asked how they would handle each situation. A scoring response was developed based on the training program for each situation before the test was administered to the trainees. The test also contained items for behavioral situations that were not covered in the training program so that trainees had to generalize what they had learned to new situations. The data indicate that the mean score for the training group was significantly higher than the score for the control group.

3. The behavioral measure consisted of trainees rating the tape-recorded behaviors of supervisors resolving supervisor-employee problems. These were based on scripts that had been developed to reflect job situations and use of learning points as presented in the training programs. The performance of the trained group was superior to that of the control group.

4. The job-performance measure consisted of ratings by the supervisors of the trainees on rating scales based on a job analysis that produced critical incidents depicting effective and ineffective supervisory behavior. The investigators found no difference in the ratings between the training and control group prior to training. Posttest measures indicate that the training group performed significantly better than the control group.

As a final step, Latham and Saari (1979) trained the control group. After their training was complete, all differences on all four measures between the control group, which was now trained, and the original training group disappeared. This kind of careful implementation and evaluation in a real work environment serves as a model for what can be accomplished with some thoughtful effort.

Since the Latham and Saari study, a number of studies (for example, Meyer & Raich, 1983; Sorcher & Spence, 1982) have found similar results. Also, in a review of the training literature examining the effectiveness of managerial techniques, Burke and Day (1986) found that behavioral role modeling is one of the more effective training methods. A meta-analysis was conducted for eighty-eight published and unpublished field studies evaluating the effects of behavior modeling training on various criteria (Taylor, 1994). The researcher found large impacts of behavioral modeling training on improving trainee knowledge and skills and more modest effects on job performance and workgroup effectiveness criteria.

Research on behavioral role modeling has also been concerned with issues exploring how to make behavioral modeling training programs more effective. A series of studies by Decker (see Decker & Nathan, 1985, for a summary) found that a small group of observers (one or two) should be present during a behavioral rehearsal and that videotaped feedback presented with the trainer's critique is more effective than the trainer's critique without videotape. A field study by Hogan, Hakel, and Decker (1986) compared trainee-generated key behaviors to trainer-provided key behaviors. The underlying rationale was that allowing individuals to generate their own key learning behaviors would facilitate the integration of the information in each one's cognitive framework.

Trainee-generated codes were found to result in significantly superior performance, although it is not clear that all trainees are capable of producing their own codes. Baldwin (1992) examined the traditional wisdom of showing trainees only positive models by comparing this condition with trainees given both positive and negative models. In the mixed modeling condition, trainees viewed a videotape showing a person following the key behaviors correctly as well as seeing another videotape of a person not following the key behaviors. Results indicated that those given both positive and negative models were more likely to generalize from the training and perform more effectively in a transfer setting than the group of trainees shown only the positive models. Finally, May and Kahnweiler (2000) used a pretest-posttest control group design to examine the impact of a mastery-oriented practice protocol during a behavioral modeling program for improving interpersonal skills. The mastery-oriented practice group was exposed to a progressive part-task role-play practice of the component skill sets followed by guided whole-task role-play practice (see Chapter 4 for a discussion of these issues). Traditional behavioral modeling programs use the whole-task training method. The results indicated that the mastery-oriented practice protocol led to higher retention rates and higher scores on a simulated case than trainees given the traditional behavioral modeling training program. Transfer measures, though, showed no difference between the two conditions.

These research studies show what can be done when efforts are expended to evaluate the effectiveness of a training method like behavioral modeling. They also demonstrate how research can lead to an understanding of why and in what ways a training method can be maximally effective.

Assessment Centers and Multirater Feedback

The assessment center is a structured off-the-job approach to measuring knowledge and skills found to be relevant to leadership effectiveness. The term *assessment center* refers to a standardized set of simulated activities and testing components that trainees are asked to complete under standardized conditions. The assessments can be paper-and-pencil tests such as personality and ability tests, worktask simulations such as an in-basket exercise (where trainees must deal with a number of memos and situations), individual interviews, and situational exercises (Klimoski, 1997). These situational exercises are usually leaderless group discussions in which trainees are asked to work on an issue or problem without any group structure. From this unstructured setting, one can observe the leadership and organizational skills of the participants as they emerge during the exercise. The original intent of assessment centers was to identify individuals with management potential for selection purposes. Although a large percentage of companies continue to use assessment centers for selection purposes, survey data now shows that 69% of companies using assessment centers focus on development (Kudish, Rotolo, Avis, Fallon, Roberts, Rollier, & Thibodeaux, 1998).

Typically, trainees are assessed in groups of six or seven by a highly trained group of assessors. They might be assessed on anywhere from ten to fifteen dimensions, such as oral communication skill, organization and planning ability, and decision making. Several days are spent on developmental activities, which include training sessions and feedback to participants. Feedback is typically delivered face to face with the trainee on trainee actions during the assessment center, what strengths and areas in need of improvement were uncovered, and developmental opportunities that are available for performance improvement (Spychalski, Quiñones, Gaugler, & Pohley, 1997). A formal feedback report might be written for the trainee or a report summarizing strengths and weaknesses across individuals might be generated for use by the organization. Figure 8.2 presents an example of an assessment chart that compares developmental needs of assessees across the eight factors assessed in the center. Such information can be useful as needs assessment information to develop new training programs in areas where a number of assessees were found to have developmental needs or where focused improvement strategies could be developed for each individual. Action plans on how to improve behaviors on the job are typically completed by trainees after the feedback session.

In addition to the experiences within the assessment center, a majority of developmental centers include *360-degree* or *multirater feedback* (Kudish et al., 1998). With multirater feedback, ratings on core competencies (many of the same competencies evaluated in the assessment center) are gathered from supervisors, peers, and subordinates. Self-ratings and customer ratings might also be obtained. For example, in one large automobile supplier company, raters were asked to provide their evaluations of the effectiveness of the leader on specific items relevant to the core competencies of vision and strategist, motivator, change manager, performance manager, coach and guide, communicator, team builder, and relational partner. Feedback reports comparing results at the item and core competency level across rater groups was provided to encourage the leader to do an honest self-diagnosis of strengths and areas in need of improvement (Borman & Bracken, 1997). Perhaps a leader is consistently rated as low on the motivator competency and especially in the areas of "celebrating small gains" and "provides me with the freedom to accomplish a project." By being confronted with this reality, the leader may set in motion developmental efforts. Rather than being a self-directed effort, facilitators are often used to help the leader interpret the data from the various rater groups and to aid in the translation of the new insights gained to actionable steps the leader can take to improve behaviors on the job.

There are a few studies that have examined the developmental impact of assessment centers on leaders. Schmitt, Ford, and Stults (1986) examined

Competency Factors

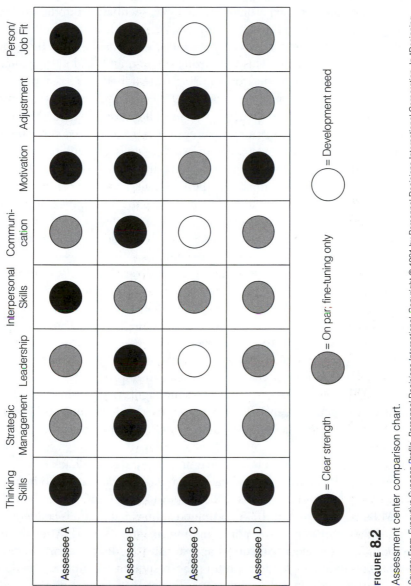

FIGURE 8.2

Assessment center comparison chart.

Source: From *Executive Success Profile, Personnel Decisions International.* Copyright © 1991 by Personnel Decisions International Corporation. In "Designing the Individual Assessment Process," by M. H. Frisch. In *Individual Psychological Assessment* edited by R. Jeanneret and R. Silzer. Copyright © 1998 by Jossey-Bass. Reprinted by permission.

changes in self-perceived skills as a function of attending a leadership assessment center. Participants provided self-ratings on eight skills before and after completing an assessment center. Results indicated that there were significant changes in self-perceived skills on five of the eight skill ratings. This change was in evidence prior to the participants receiving feedback from the assessors as to their performance in the assessment center. It is likely that feedback has an unfreezing effect on participants as they are sensitized to their own strengths and shortcomings. This unfreezing effect might lead participants to be more open to developmental ideas arising from a feedback session.

More recently, Jones and Whitmore (1995) evaluated assessment centers as interventions for leadership development. They examined the extent to which feedback from an assessment center of a large insurance company led managers to take action to develop the knowledge, skills, and abilities required for managerial success. Results indicated that participants who scored best in the center were more likely to accept the feedback from the center as accurate. Center ratings were found to be unrelated to developmental activity. Nevertheless, the percentage of developmental activities followed by participants were found to be related to subsequent promotions. The finding that participants who performed poorer in the center see the ratings as inaccurate and the assessment process as less fair has been documented elsewhere (e.g., see Iles & Robertson, 1997). This result poses a critical challenge in the use of assessment centers for development because poorer performers are the ones for whom following developmental suggestions could lead to the greatest gains in performance. Nevertheless, it has been noted that developmental assessment centers that are followed by an emphasis on more skill training, special assignments, and additional coaching can lead to improved performance on the job (Engelbracht & Fischer, 1995). This highlights once again that in order for transfer to occur, organizational support mechanisms must be in place to develop skills identified in the assessment center process as needing improvement.

On the other hand, there is evidence that multirater feedback—in particular upward feedback from subordinates—can lead to performance improvements on the job. Smither and his associates (Smither, London, Vasilopoulos, Reilly, Millsap, & Salvemini, 1995) examined subordinate ratings collected for more than 200 managers at two points in time six months apart. After the first rating period, the managers received an extensive feedback report including the data and guidelines for interpreting the results of the upward feedback process. Results indicated that managerial behavior improved by the second rating period. Atwater, Rousch, and Fischthal (1995) examined 978 cadet leaders in the U.S. Naval Academy and ratings obtained from subordinates over three different time periods. They found that after receiving feedback reports based on subordinate ratings, leaders improved their behaviors, with the greatest gain coming between the first and second rating periods. Johnson and Ferstl (1999) examined results for over 1800 managers and found that leaders who overrated themselves relative to their subordinate ratings were more likely to improve their behaviors than leaders who underrated themselves in comparison to subordinate ratings. Finally, Walker and Smither (1999) conducted a five-year study of upward feedback with 252 managers. They found that there were significant improvements in upward feedback ratings over the five-year period. Most interestingly, a more detailed analysis found that those managers who met with their subordinates to discuss their feedback report were more likely to improve their behaviors than those who did not meet with their subordinates. There is clearly a need for research that examines participant reactions and subsequent developmental activities based on both assessment center ratings and ratings from multirater feedback. It would seem that information from both sources (assessment center and multirater) that provides consistent information about areas for improvement should have a powerful effect on participants.

Experience-Centered Learning

Experience-centered learning focuses on the importance of job activities that evoke continuous learning and improvement. Experience-centered learning is based on the assumption that challenges in the job itself can stimulate learning. From this perspective, opportunities for experience-centered learning must be created for individuals in their job assignments to develop critical competencies for success. Leaders who have been questioned as to what factors had the greatest impact on developing their managerial competencies most often pointed to direct work experience followed by mentoring or tutoring by more senior leaders. Learning from formal training programs was seen as having much less impact on developing leadership competencies (e.g., McCall, Lombardo, & Morrison, 1988). This section focuses on the research on job challenge and the issue of mentoring.

Job assignments and challenge.   According to London (1989), there are two types of learning situations: incremental and frame-breaking. Incremental learning situations are those that provide time to clarify role expectations and flexibility for self-paced learning. Fundamental competencies are thus gained in a fairly linear fashion. Frame-breaking learning experiences place individuals in difficult positions without much initial preparation. Such situations require the acquisition of a large number of new skills in order to be successful. Frame-breaking requires individual investment with a high potential for learning, but also a high risk for failure.

The Center for Creative Leadership (CCL) has completed a number of studies examining the linkage of work experience, learning, and performance. Frame-breaking situations found to have major implications for enhancing learning include features such as having to handle responsibilities that are much broader than previous ones, fixing problems created by others, developing new directions for a workgroup, and handling pressures from external stakeholder groups (McCauley, Ruderman, Ohlott, & Morrow, 1994). Table 8.8 presents examples of these types of job challenges. Exposure to these types of challenges has been found to be related to increases in on-the-job learning.

| TABLE 8.8 | COMPONENTS OF A DEVELOPMENTAL JOB |

Experiencing a Job Transition

Unfamiliar Responsibilities	You must handle responsibilities that are new or very different from previous ones you have handled.

Creating Change

New Directions	You are responsible for starting something new in the organization or making strategic changes in the business.
Inherited Problems	You have to fix problems created by a predecessor or existing when you took the job.
Problems with Employees	Your employees lack adequate experience, are incompetent, or are resistant to change.

Managing at High Levels of Responsibility

High Stakes	Clear deadlines, pressure from senior managers, high visibility, and responsibility for key decisions make success or failure in your job clearly evident.
Scope and Scale	The sheer size of your job is large, and you have responsibility for multiple functions, groups, products, or services.

Managing Boundaries

External Pressure	You manage the interface with important groups outside the organization, such as customers, unions, or government agencies.
Influence Without Authority	Doing your job requires influencing peers, higher management, or other key people over whom you have no direct authority.

Dealing with Diversity

Work Across Cultures	You must work with people from different cultures or with institutions in other countries.
Workgroup Diversity	You are responsible for the work of people of both genders and different racial and ethnic backgrounds.

Based on this type of research, McCauley (1999) reports that CCL is currently developing tools to help leaders get the most out of their job experiences. The tools focus on how leaders can (1) take advantage of the learning opportunities in their current job, and (2) make job assignments part of a development planning process. Leaders complete a standardized questionnaire called the Developmental Challenge Profile (DCP). The questionnaire asks leaders to report the extent to which their current job provides challenges in areas such as unfamiliar responsibilities, new directions, inherited problems, problem employees, high-stakes projects, working against high external pressures, influencing others without having formal authority, working across cultures, and dealing with workgroup diversity (McCauley, 1999). Leaders can compare their learning challenges and what they have learned from these experiences with a normative database of leaders who have approached similar challenges. Leaders are prompted to examine this data in terms of how they might improve what and how they learn on the job. The questionnaire data can also be used to look forward to how the leader can enhance opportunities for challenging job assignments. The leader and facilitator can examine areas of low challenge in their current job and create a developmental plan to increase job challenges that might lead to improved learning on the job. In addition to individual development, the data from the questionnaire can be examined across leaders in an organization to more systematically evaluate what types of challenges leaders are or are not obtaining. This process can help organizations do a better job of identifying key work assignments that the organization can use for more effectively developing leaders. As noted by McCauley, the challenge for research is to investigate the extent to which this developmental tool and process changes how leaders view their job, how developmental job assignments are sought, and whether there is an increase in on-the-job learning that leads to improved leadership effectiveness.

Mentoring.   Individuals can also gain enhanced leadership competencies from learning partners (tutors) or mentors whose role is to work with and coach less experienced leaders. These mentors are at an organizational level above the less experienced leader or protégé but are not their supervisor. The goal of the mentoring process is to enhance skills in a focused, effective, and efficient manner so as to shorten the time it takes to become proficient and to avoid costly trial-and-error approaches to learning (Murray, 1999). Douglas and McCauley (1997) found that about 20% of companies with at least 500 employees have formal mentoring programs in place. These organizations use this type of program for a variety of purposes, including the socialization of new managers, preparation of leaders identified as having high potential, development of women and minority group members for leadership positions, and the continued development of senior executives.

Mentors typically fill three roles for a protégé. One role is to create a supportive environment where the protégé feels comfortable talking about work-related issues or problems (Noe, 1988). In this role, the mentor can help the protégé not to become discouraged when things go wrong and can offer counseling about how to handle difficult situations. Mentors can also provide the protégé with insights, encouragement, and recognition for successes in order to build the protégé's sense of competence. A second role is one of being improvement-oriented. The mentor provides feedback to the protégé as to how to learn and improve his or her performance on the job (McCauley & Douglas, 1998). A third role is more career focused in which the mentor provides the protégé with challenging work assignments and increases the protégé's exposure and visibility to top management (Yukl, 1998). In this way, the mentor helps the protégé to be better prepared to handle future promotions and assignments.

Research shows that mentoring can be an effective method for enhancing learning and performance on the job. For example, research has found that mentoring relationships are related to career promotions and increased compensation for managers. Ostroff and Kozlowski (1993) found that pairing mentors with newcomers led to a quicker socialization process than those newcomers not paired with a mentor. Chao, Walz, and Gardner (1992) found that protégés who received more career-related support reported higher levels of job satisfaction, enhanced feelings of socialization into the organization, and greater salary levels. They also found some evidence that naturally occurring or informal mentoring led to greater outcomes for the protégé than formally prescribed programs where protégés were matched with a mentor.

Research supports the conventional wisdom of linking individuals with mentors who are interested in developing others and have the coaching skills needed to affect change in others. Quality mentoring relations facilitate career advancement and job satisfaction of protégés and may also have a positive impact on the mentors who learn new skills or competencies from the experience. Yet, there is little research on the specific ways mentors aid in the development of leadership competencies.

Global Leadership

Future leaders will have to be very skilled individuals. Not only will they have to deal with the traditional issues of managing others, but they will also have to perform these activities at a time when jobs are becoming increasingly complex. The workforce is becoming more diverse. In addition, national and international competition is becoming increasingly intense. More and more organizations are crossing international lines. The increase in multinational companies requires leaders to coordinate efforts with leaders in other countries. Enhanced technologies allow virtual international teams to be formed to deal with global organizational issues (Townscend, DeMarie, & Hendrickson, 1998) such as how to standardize work processes across multiple organizations within the same multinational firm. The teams may be made up of employees located anywhere in the world. In addition to working with people in other cultures, many leaders must also have the competencies to succeed in overseas work assignments. In all of these cases, organizations need to develop leaders who can (1) enhance the contributions of a diverse workforce, (2) adapt to the demands of international assignments, and (3) address the new reality of global roles and responsibilities.

Diversity training. The increasing diversification of the workforce has led to an emphasis on how to more effectively utilize the human resources of the organization. As the pool of available employees is becoming less white and less male, leaders are driven to find ways to integrate this new mix of employees within the organizational culture and to eliminate inequities in the organization. Given how important training can be in inculcating organizational norms and values, it is not surprising that organizations are now turning toward training to propel desired cultural changes relevant to diversity issues (Ford & Fisher, 1997). Training leaders (and all employees for that matter) is often seen as a key method for eliminating artificial barriers to individual development.

Diversity training is big business with many large- and small-sized companies conducting some type of diversity training program. Training objectives can focus on increasing awareness, knowledge, understanding, and attitude change or skill enhancement. Many diversity programs focus on raising leader awareness of diversity issues. Training at this level consists primarily of the dissemination of factual information about the law, the examination of the concept of diversity, the relationship of a diverse workforce to organizational effectiveness, and the identification of factors that can influence attitudes and behaviors toward others. Typically, individuals are asked to complete questionnaires on perceived similarities and differences between groups of employees, typical communication styles, and attributions of success and failures of minority group members. Group discussion then focuses on increasing awareness of how the responses on the questionnaire indicate how individuals might discriminate against, judge, or isolate others. It is assumed that this heightened awareness leads to behavioral changes on the job.

A second set of training programs focus more directly on attitude change and increased understanding through a fuller understanding of diversity issues and how actions impact others. For example, Morrison (1992) discussed a program in which traditional managers were told how racial and gender difference can affect the organizational experience and career of a nontraditional manager. The goal was to break down stereotypes. Many of these programs use videotapes and role plays to go beyond simple awareness to a greater understanding of the negative emotional and performance effects of stereotypes, values, and behaviors on minority group members. Participants might role-play situations to more fully examine the impact of what is communicated on others.

A third set of diversity training programs directly address the enhancement of leadership skills. The training often focuses on improving coaching and mentoring skills, providing methods for effective performance feedback, and teaching techniques for resolving interpersonal conflicts. Other programs emphasize the importance of communicating more effectively with one another. The training emphasizes the way in which messages are received by various people and practice in how to communicate in a way that is appropriate to the situation (Tung, 1993). As one example of this approach, Sorcher and Spence (1982) used behavioral modeling methods to train both white supervisors and black production workers on appropriate interaction behaviors for use with one another. The research results suggested that the program reduced tensions and increased comfort levels in the work environment.

In general, there are few systematic research studies that have examined the impact of diversity training on the subsequent behaviors of leaders. Research has mainly identified positive and negative reactions of the trainees to diversity training. For example, some researchers have focused on the extent to which individuals feel threatened by programs that highlight biases and discrimination and that focus on supporting and promoting women and minorities (Kram & Hall, 1997). There is also concern that conflict between ethnic groups may increase as differences are reinforced in diversity awareness seminars. Therefore, there is great need for research that not only helps to understand these reactions but then links them to valued organizational outcomes. In addition, while training can be a key leverage point for changing norms and behaviors, there are various ways organizations can increase the value of diversity. For example, organizations can develop minority advisory boards that make recommendations to top executives on workplace climate issues, revamp what is rewarded in the organization, and develop formal mentoring relationships (Cox, 1993). The more these types of organizational change initiatives that complement diversity training interventions are enacted, the more likely it is that the knowledge and skills gained in training will transfer to the job.

Preparing the international assignee.   More managers are being asked to complete assignments in other countries to become well rounded and internationally centered rather than focused on parochial interests. Unfortunately, failure rates of leaders and top executives working in another culture are high (estimates range from 30% to 50%) with each failure costing upwards of $500,000 per executive (Triandis, 1994). Part of this failure rate has been attributed to the minimal amount of training and preparation given to leaders prior to departing to the host country.

Ronen (1989) reviewed the literature concerning training and the international assignee and offered the following propositions:

1. Often international assignees (IAs) have good track records in their assignments before being sent overseas. The main cause of failure, therefore, is not technical knowledge but rather factors such as difficulty in adjusting for either the IA or the family members of the IA.
2. Reports indicate that a manager's relational abilities (for example, interpersonal skills) account for the difference between success and failure.
3. IAs with previous overseas experience are more likely to succeed. This appears to be the case even when the previous experience was in a country different from their present assignment. The socialization experiences seem to help create a better adaptation process.

Ronen (1989) also offers a list of the attributes (Table 8.9) that his analysis of the literature suggests make a difference between success and failure. In discussing the enormous training implications, he notes that the manager given an assignment in a different country must possess the "patience of a diplomat, the zeal of a missionary, and the linguistic skill of a U.N. interpreter" (p. 418).

To meet these training challenges, a variety of intercultural training interventions have been developed to help participants reduce culture shock, establish good interpersonal relationships with others, and improve task effectiveness when working in other cultures (Triandis, Kurowski, & Gelfand, 1994). For example, culture assimilators have been developed to help people learn to make attributions similar to those made by individuals in the host culture (e.g., Albert, 1983). Scenarios are created that highlight cultural differences in the host culture from those of the leader's cultural perspective. Leaders then read each scenario and choose the attribution that makes sense in the situation. Correct answers lead to complete analysis that explains cultural difference and why the correct attribution is most likely to be used in that culture (Triandis, 1994). Studies that have been completed indicate that the cultural assimilator training can lead to enhanced learning about a culture and reduces concerns about interacting with members of the host country (Albert, 1983; Brislin, Cushner, Cherrie, & Yong, 1986).

Another type of training program includes pairing leaders with a member of the host country for a period of time to learn more about the culture prior to living overseas. Other training that is similar to diversity training focuses on heightening self-awareness and insight such as learning to appreciate strengths and differences between cultures.

TABLE
8.9   ATTRIBUTES OF SUCCESS IN OVERSEAS ASSIGNMENT

Perseverance	Technical skills and knowledge	Youthfulness
Empathy		Imagination
Courtesy and tact	Managerial ability	Resourcefulness
Respect	Organizational ability	Creativity
Interest in nationals	Administrative skills	Responsibility
Flexibility	High motivation	Alertness
Adaptability	Overseas experience	Desire to go abroad
Patience	Display of respect	Interest in foreign cultures
Tolerance	Listening skills	Intellectual curiosity
Initiative and energy	Confidence	Belief in mission and job
Openness	Frankness	Willingness to change
Nonjudgmentalness	Kindness	Spouse's positive opinion
Sincerity and integrity	Communication skills	Adaptability of spouse and family
Emotional stability	Ability to deal with stress	
Nonethnocentrism	Tolerance for ambiguity	Willingness of spouse to live abroad
Positive self-image	Political sensitivity	
Independence	Integrity	Stable marriage
Outgoingness and extraversion	Dependability	
	Industriousness	
Experience in company	Variety of outside interests	

Source: From "Training the International Assignee," by S. Ronen. In *Training and Development in Organizations* (pp. 417–453), edited by I. L. Goldstein and Associates, 1989. Copyright 1989 by Jossey-Bass, Inc. Reprinted by permission.

In general, studies show that cross-cultural training is effective (Black & Mendenhall, 1990) and can reduce failure rates in overseas assignments. Nevertheless, as noted by Triandis (1994), few studies have been published, most studies do not include experimental designs with randomization of assignment to training and control conditions, and most studies use self-reports of success (from the host country or leader) rather than more objective indicators of success. In a recent review of cross-cultural training, Bhawuk and Brislin (2000) recommend the use of more varied criteria beyond reactions to the training and pencil-and-paper knowledge measures for evaluating the effectiveness of training efforts. The expanded view of criteria includes a measure of intercultural sensitivity and the determination of an individual's "category width." Individuals high on intercultural sensitivity are more openminded concerning the differences they encounter in other cultures. Individuals with a broad category width tend to place more discrepant things into the same category.

Research indicates that those who score higher on the intercultural sensitivity questionnaire and those who have greater category width were more likely to complete their overseas tasks successfully.

Developing global leaders.   The world is becoming smaller as the marketplace becomes increasingly global in scope. A global organization is defined as one where the elements of production are dispersed across many nations (Greider, 1997). A key strategy of global organizations is to produce products in low-wage countries while hoping to sell the products in high-wage countries (Dalton, 1998). Global management is becoming increasingly viewed as a key competitive advantage for firms as they enter the international markets (Florkowski, 1997).

The role demands for leaders in a global organization are multifaceted. These roles could include motivating multicultural teams, managing information across multiple time zones, maintaining a variety of relationships (alliances, joint ventures, licensing arrangements) across countries that have different laws and standards, finding ways to customize products to meet the needs of a variety of markets and customers, and negotiating in different business environments and cultures (de Merode, 1997). The characteristics of effective global leaders include many of the same competencies that one would look for from an effective leader. These include great communication and relationship skills and high levels of business knowledge, cognitive complexity, and emotional energy and drive (e.g., Wills & Barham, 1994). Others have noted the need for global managers to also be open to new experiences, flexible, sensitive to cultural differences, and to act with integrity (Spreitzer, McCall, & Mahoney, 1997).

Dalton (1998) describes a variety of learning experiences that can lead to a more global management perspective. These experiences include long-distance multicountry projects, an expatriate assignment, managing a major multicountry project, and having global responsibility for a product. This global responsibility would include the long-term management of a product throughout the business cycle from design to production to marketing.

The question of increasing globalization also has important implications for training methods within multinational companies. As noted by Hoppe (1998), off-the-shelf training programs built on U.S. cultural assumptions may not be appropriate for people from other cultures. In particular, most U.S. leadership development programs are based on assumptions of what competencies are critical to leadership effectiveness and how developmental activities should be structured. For example, U.S. managers tend to prefer to face the data from 360-degree or multirater feedback head-on even when it is negative as opposed to reactions by managers in Japan and South Korea (Dorfman, Howell, Hibino, Lee, Tate, & Bautista, 1997). The authors found that organizational commitment remained high for the U.S. managers after the

360-degree intervention, whereas it had a negative impact on managers in the other cultures. This type of research shows the challenges for training leaders in the age of globalization and workforce diversity.

CONCLUSIONS

This chapter has highlighted the tremendous variety of training methods that are available to impart knowledge, skills, and attitudes to trainees. The methods range from formally structured training opportunities to more informal, less structured learning experiences. The methods described also show the blurring of the distinction of what is considered training as opposed to performance enhancement. Performance support systems, for example, allow for individuals to learn on the job as well as providing on-line performance support. The discussion shows that formal training is just one way individuals learn and develop in organizations.

The methods were organized into those that typically are used to improve employee, team, and leader capabilities. Clearly, training methods discussed under one category can be quite relevant for another category of trainees. For example, newcomer orientation can occur for leaders brought in from outside the organization as well as for new employees. Enterprise training can be targeted for leaders as well as for employees. In addition, experiences such as assessment centers, multirater feedback, and diversity training do not have to be limited to leadership positions. Action learning cannot only help intact teams work more effectively together but can also be used to help train employees or leaders to work more effectively together. In addition, there are similarities across training methods. For example, on-the-job training can be structured to stretch the development of employees just as structured job assignments can stretch and challenge leaders.

Regardless, the review shows the exciting opportunities available to those interested in training and learning in work organizations. There has been a large increase in the number and types of training programs available. In addition, organizations are taking learning more seriously as a key to competitive advantage. There is some way to go, though, in evaluating the effectiveness of various training methods and learning activities. Some training methods such as behavioral modeling have impressive evidence supporting their effectiveness, whereas other methods such as enterprise training have limited data on effectiveness. The importance of conducting systematic needs assessment to correctly target training as well as the need to emphasize methods for facilitating training transfer remains.

The last chapter of this book focuses on expanding our notions of learning beyond the individual to viewing learning from a broader systems perspective.

This includes the increased emphasis on building knowledge or continuous learning organizations. From this perspective, the development of an organization's human resources is viewed as a key to competitive advantage in our increasingly global economy. In addition, Chapter 9 presents attempts to deal with today's serious social problems. Thus, there are sections devoted to training and fair employment practices, training the hard-core unemployed, and outplacement training for those who have been affected by organizational downsizing.

InfoTrac College Edition

For additional readings, go to http: www.infotrac-college.com/wadsworth and enter a search term related to your interest. The following key terms will pull up several related articles.

Action Learning	Cross-Training
Adventure Learning	Diversity Training
Apprenticeship	Employee Orientation
Assessment Centers	On-the-Job Training
Behavioral Modeling	Performance Support
Business Simulations	Team Training
Cross-Cultural Training	360° Feedback/Multirater Feedback

LEARNING SYSTEMS

We have stressed that training must be a systematic approach to learning and development to improve performance in another environment. Taking a systematic approach to training means that training is intentional—it is conducted to meet some identified need in the organization. The instructional design model presented in this book highlights the steps to effective training. In this model, systematic training efforts lead to learning and development— the building of expertise. Changes in knowledge, skills, and attitudes can lead to meaningful changes in work performance and thus improve individual effectiveness.

This chapter moves beyond the focus on individual learners and looks at training from a broader, more macro perspective. Building up from our focus on the effectiveness of independent training programs and their impact on individual employees, we now take a larger perspective that considers a wide range of issues of organizational competitiveness and societal goals. We have introduced and discussed some organizational and societal issues in earlier chapters. Many of the topics we address in this chapter were introduced in Chapter 1 in "Implications for Future Training Systems." We have also discussed the importance of organizational climate and the work environment in Chapter 3 on needs assessment and Chapter 4 on factors impacting learning and transfer. In addition, we have discussed in previous chapters the notion that an individual training program is nested within a larger training system that includes a variety of training programs, methods, instructors, delivery mechanisms, and evaluation techniques. The current chapter focuses on and integrates these issues, exploring a systems perspective to training and learning.

A SYSTEMS PERSPECTIVE

An emerging organizational behavior literature on levels of analysis mirrors applied interests in moving beyond the examination of factors impacting individual effectiveness. A levels perspective, an extension of the general systems paradigm, posits that events should be viewed within their larger context. This means that activities at one level cannot be considered in isolation from influences at other levels. Individuals are part of groups of workers, departments and functions are embedded within an organization, and organizations are embedded within societies.

Businesses are spending a greater amount of money on training and development of their own workforce as people are increasingly seen as the primary source of enduring competitive advantage. Government agencies are also increasing the amount of money and attention to training and development of youths, employees, and displaced workers to more fully utilize their talents in the workforce. The growing complexity of the changes occurring in the workplace such as team-based work systems, the focus on quality and customer service, and the infusion of new technology all require a highly trained workforce that is prepared to deal with the changing realities of the workplace. Training is now viewed not only as an important factor in improving individual effectiveness but also from a broader perspective as a key lever for improving organizational performance and even the effectiveness of the society as a whole.

An implication of a systems perspective for training is that events can have a cascading effect down the various levels of analysis. For example, government policies such as protecting individuals with disabilities can impact organizational practices regarding employee training and development. How organizations value learning can impact the effectiveness of departments within that organization. Team goals and structure within departments can impact how much opportunity individuals have to obtain new knowledge and skills. In addition, effects can be upward in their influence across levels of analysis. Individuals can be active learners who help drive team effectiveness. Departments can experiment and move forward on improvement strategies that lead to the department becoming the benchmark for change throughout the organization. Organizations can lobby government agencies for help in increasing the pool of qualified applicants by funding such projects as school-to-work transition or the retraining of displaced workers.

Figure 9.1 presents an application of the systems framework to training effectiveness for improved safety and health in the workplace (Ford & Fisher, 1994). This framework illustrates how a systems perspective can be applied to a particular training setting. The framework is based on two key systems dimensions: (1) stakeholder interests and (2) organizational level. Stakeholder interests focus attention on the common and competing interests of groups regarding (in this case) safety and health. Three possible stakeholders include employers (management), employees (who may or may not be represented by a union), and government agencies (such as the U.S. Department of Labor). The stakeholder framework highlights the interests of each group. Given

Stakeholders

Organizational Level	Employer	Employee	Government
Strategic Planning	Intended Strategy	Emergent Strategy	Social Policy
	Commitment to Safety (value of employees and balance of production and safety)	Representation on Safety Issues	Balancing Employer and Employee Rights
Personnel Policy	Safety Policies and Procedures	Participation in Setting Policies	Safety Rules and Regulations
	Administration of Safety Training Programs	Participation in Development and Implementation of Safety Training	Mandated and Non-mandated Training Programs and Training Guidelines
Shop Floor	Supervisory Support for Safety	Group Norms about Safety	Enforcement Procedures and Inspections
	Implementation of Personnel Policies	Dispute Resolution about Safety Issues	Grievance Procedures and Employee Rights for a Safe Working Environment

FIGURE **9.1**

A multiple level, multiple stakeholder approach to training effectiveness.

Source: From "The Transfer of Safety Training in Work Organizations: A Systems Perspective to Continuous Learning," by J. K. Ford and S. Fisher. In *Occupational Safety and Health Training, Occupational Medicine: State of the Art Reviews,* 1994, *9,* pp. 241–260, edited by M. Colligan. Copyright 1994 by Hanley Belfus, Inc. Reprinted by permission.

different interests, these groups must resolve conflicts as well as pursue common concerns. The resolution of these overlapping and competing interests affects training efforts.

The organizational level focuses attention on the degree of emphasis on training and development throughout the organization. Three levels highlighted in Figure 9.1 are the strategic, personnel, and shop floor. The strategic level is where basic decisions are made. In this case, decisions might involve such things as how to organize work and how to balance longer term training and development concerns with shorter term production needs. The personnel level focuses on policy formation, the development of procedures, and the delivery of training. The shop-floor level includes the ongoing day-to-day worker-supervisory relationship, including the rewards that support or inhibit desired (e.g., safe) work behaviors.

The systems perspective presented in Figure 9.1 shows that the way one issue—safety and health training—is addressed in an organization is a complex interplay between stakeholder interests and organizational levels. The framework is relevant to any type of training such as enhancing customer service or improving total quality. The strength of this framework is threefold. First, it integrates traditional training issues that have typically focused on the shop-floor level with a broader framework incorporating organizational and societal issues. Second, the systems perspective adds an additional outcome of effectiveness to traditional, individually based learning and transfer outcomes. System effectiveness outcomes include the development of an organizational strategy that supports continuous learning and improvement over time. Third, the framework focuses on issues such as the development of common goals, the resolution of conflict across stakeholders, and alignment of organizational levels regarding training and development activities.

There are a number of training models that examine the factors impacting how successful training is in improving individual effectiveness on the job. As we saw in Chapter 8, there are also emerging models of team and leadership training and development. Fewer models exist, though, for training from a broader perspective at the organizational or societal levels. Nevertheless, interest in the broader, more macro issues in training and development are increasing in scope and depth. In this chapter, we turn our attention to a discussion of organizational and societal issues related to training, examples of how these issues are being addressed in organizations, and current research regarding the effectiveness of these types of efforts. The first section focuses on efforts in organizations to move beyond viewing training as a series of courses to administer to viewing training as a key component in a systematic effort to become a learning organization. The second section of this chapter focuses on systematic approaches to training that help meet dual societal goals of developing and maintaining a competitive workforce in our global economy and enhancing the quality of life for individuals within our society.

TRAINING AND THE LEARNING ORGANIZATION

Kapp (1999) contends that the only sustainable advantage an organization will have in the future is its ability to learn faster than its competitors. Similarly, Rousseau (1997) notes that to survive and thrive firms will need to learn at an increasingly rapid rate. The success of new learning initiatives such as team-based work systems relies on the development of individuals, the coordinated efforts of team members, and the support across organizational levels and stakeholders. This integrated approach to learning and development is viewed by management experts as the key to organizational competitiveness (Senge, 1990). Organizations have become quite interested in how to build learning capabilities in the workforce on an ongoing basis. This more macro perspective views the building of "intellectual capital" (Stewart, 1997) and the institution-alization of learning within the organization as a key strategic weapon for improving competitiveness and for delivering effective services.

As noted by Baldwin, Danielson, and Wiggenhorn (1997), organizations have traditionally equated learning with the development of training depart-ments and training programs focused on building specific work skills such as how to use a lathe to transform steel into a gear for a farm tractor. A learning organization perspective, though, focuses on any activity that might help the individual, team, and organization to continuously improve and develop. Thus, the goal of a learning organization is to encourage everyone in the organiza-tion—employees, line managers, supervisors, and technical personnel—to become actively engaged in expanding their skills and improving organiza-tional effectiveness. Learning becomes an everyday part of the job rather than being confined to formal training sessions in classrooms. Employees learn skills of others in their work unit, teach other employees in areas of expertise, and learn from one another on a day-to-day basis.

Thus, while learning and development are clearly rooted in individuals, organizations can attempt to create a positive learning environment. A positive learning environment occurs when individuals know how their job fits in the larger system. Individuals are assigned tasks that stretch and challenge them, mistakes are tolerated during learning, constraints to learning are minimized, new ideas are valued and encouraged, and policies and procedures support the effective use of training. Tannenbaum (1997) has developed a Learning Envi-ronment Survey to measure these types of concepts relevant to a learning organization. Table 9.1 presents example items from this survey. In a study of more than 500 people in seven organizations, he found evidence that organi-zations with stronger learning environments seemed to demonstrate greater levels of organizational effectiveness.

Fundamental Characteristics of a Learning Organization

Clearly, creating a learning organization requires a heavy investment in train-ing. This investment is closely tied to the strategic goals of the organization. For example, the vision for Saturn was to create a new type of assembly process with an emphasis on decentralized decision making and problem solv-ing and imbedding the responsibility for quality control with production teams. Saturn Corporation's target to help meet this vision was that all employees should spend 5% of their time in training once production had begun. At startup, technicians received about 300 hours of training and skilled tradespeople received about 500 hours of training in areas such as safety, qual-ity control, finance, interpersonal skills, technical job skills, and business knowledge (Meister, 1994).

TABLE 9.1	LEARNING ENVIRONMENT SURVEY

All scales used a 7-point response format with 1 = strongly disagree, 4 = neither agree nor disagree; 7 = strongly agree.

My organization typically:

- Provides people with opportunities to learn new things.
- Assigns people to positions to stretch them.
- Tolerates mistakes when someone is first learning a new task or skill.
- Views new problems and work challenges as opportunities to develop people's skills.
- Monitors to see that people continue to develop and learn throughout their career.
- Expects everyone, not just management, to solve problems and offer solutions.
- Provides paid release time for employee development purposes.
- Rewards employees for using what they have learned in training on their job.

In my organization:

- Supervisors and co-workers help reschedule work so that employees can attend training.
- Supervisors provide constructive feedback when someone tries something new on the job.
- Supervisors offer people opportunities to use new skills they learned in training.
- Training is considered an important part of career development.
- The successful people go to training.
- It is acceptable to question others about why things are done a certain way.

Source: From "Enhancing Continuous Learning: Diagnostic Findings from Multiple Companies," by S. I. Tannenbaum. In *Human Resource Management,* 1997, *36,* pp. 437–452. Copyright 1997 by Human Resource Management, Inc. Reprinted by permission of John Wiley & Sons, Inc.

Becoming a learning organization, though, goes beyond extensive training efforts. As noted by Confessore and Kops (1998), a key characteristic of a learning organization is the ability of its employees to find or make opportunities to learn from whatever situation is presented. As noted by Argyris and Schoen (1996), learning necessitates a facility for "discontinuous information processing" and the capability to deploy knowledge and demonstrable skills in novel ways and flexible combinations. Thus, the backbone of any effort to develop a learning organization is an emphasis on problem solving and innovation.

Problem-solving and innovation skills include the ability to identify the gap between the aims of an improvement effort and the reality of the current state of the system. This gap analysis leads to the investigation of the root causes of the gap and the identification of improvement options. A learning organization also has members who make choices about which improvement option has the greatest potential to add value to the organization and evaluate the effectiveness of the improvement effort.

An effective problem-solving process must begin with the collection of data. Fulmer, Gibbs, and Keys (1998) contend that there are four types of tools for generating data: (1) maintenance tools (employee suggestion systems, self-directed work teams, statistical process control, benchmarking), (2) crossover tools (transferring innovations to other departments, process reengineering, and task forces), (3) utility tools (customer surveys, external advisory groups), and (4) anticipatory tools (strategic planning, scenario analysis, joint ventures, impact analysis). Data represents the point of departure in the learning process—the more focused and targeted the data, the more focused and targeted the learning. However, data by itself is not knowledge within an organization. Data must be interpreted. The interpretation of data leads to hypotheses and theories that might account for the patterns or trends observed. When it is possible to make sense of the data, knowledge about organizational operations has been generated and can be shared among organizational members.

Shared knowledge is not enough to achieve learning that drives change. First, a consensus must emerge among people about the meaning of the data. For example, fluctuations in quality may or may not be seen as an immediate problem that needs to be addressed. Second, action is required if this collective power is to be tapped. Actions might include experiments or pilot tests. Actions might be policy changes or the redeployment of resources. Once taken, actions call for new rounds of data collection in the form of feedback, monitoring, evaluation, and follow-through. The new data then calls for additional interpretation and adjustments to the knowledge base, guiding further action. Learning and long-lasting change can be achieved through a never-ending cycle of action steps, guided by knowledge and rooted in data.

Models for Becoming a Learning Organization

The core principles of continuous learning provide a framework for guiding practice. In addition, there are numerous models of learning organizations to benchmark, and there are now professional societies that focus exclusively on understanding and facilitating the move toward becoming a learning organization. For example, there are a number of centers for organizational learning on the web, and the Society of Organizational Learning (SoL) from MIT now publishes a journal on learning organizations called *Reflections*. An examination of these centers for organizational learning and our own experiences with organizations reveal that there are many different paths to becoming a learning organization. Three different models of continuous learning are provided next to give some indication of the breadth and depth of this type of change initiative.

Building internal capability.   A wood products company developed a new plant with a vision of a team-based work system with empowered workers and an emphasis on training and continuous improvement. This vision has been achieved, in part, through the systematic application of the train-the-trainer model and a skill-based pay-for-knowledge reward system.

The plant produces particle board and has over 200 employees with production workers divided into four work teams. From the beginning, the plant built its human resource system around the train-the-trainer concept. This is a core driver in the context of a team-based, pay-for-knowledge work system. Workers train one another in technical skills as part of a pay-for-knowledge mastery program, where training mainly occurs on the job. Workers are also the lead trainers around group process and personal development training. Management emphasizes that both developmental and technical training are critical to the plant running effectively. Major portions of the technical and developmental training are focused on improving quality and customer satisfaction.

Managers, including the human resources manager, are all involved in designing the business plan for the plant. Once the plan has been established, all employees become involved in its operationalization. Training needs linked to the plan are identified both formally and informally through a number of mechanisms—from employee attitude surveys to task forces and improvement teams. Most significantly, the plans come from the teams themselves. Both management and operators initiate training and participate in decisions regarding training. With all the training that occurs, trying to maintain continuous production and schedule training is a challenge for the plant. Training is therefore a complex, decentralized function.

The training philosophy is well-articulated in the plant's mission, which reads (in part):

> Training will develop the skills and knowledge necessary to operate the mill efficiently and will contribute to individual and organizational growth.

The train-the-trainer focus of learning is especially clear in the context of the plant's commitment to quality. The quality statement of the plant states:

> We are committed to providing the necessary education and training for continuous improvement.

In explaining the strategic importance of the train-the-trainer, skill-based pay approach, the plant manager highlighted his belief that building internal capability is the only way to adapt to changing customer needs. For example, customers are increasingly looking for small runs of specialty products, which demands increased flexibility on the shop floor.

At the core of the train-the-trainer system is a training philosophy entitled LUTI—Learn, Use, Teach, and Inspect. This philosophy stresses that each person who receives training should learn the material well enough to use it and then be able to teach it to others. Employees are encouraged to teach training seminars on topics for which they have become masters or experts. Managers prefer to use in-house, expert employees as trainers rather than bringing in outside professionals. They contend that it is more effective to have insiders teach and train because they can serve as constant reminders for maintaining the skills and information learned.

Most of the technical training at the plant is currently conducted on the job due to the pay-for-knowledge mastery program. This program serves as the major driver for technical training at the plant. Individuals are cross trained and taught how to master various production processes by other experienced masters. The mastery program allows individuals and teams to set goals for what needs to be learned and how it will be learned. In fact, training manuals used to familiarize new production workers with the various production processes are written by masters of those functions.

Mastery can be obtained on any of thirteen production processes, with pay increases accompanying each acquired mastery level. Mastery involves assessing an individual's technical, operating, safety and membership (team/interpersonal) skills. To become a master at a production process, an individual must first pass a written exam about safety and the production process to be mastered. Then the employee creates an individual development plan in conjunction with the team to specify the knowledge and skills needed, how they will be learned, and the time frame for acquisition.

The individual is then trained on the job by other masters of that function. It is the team's responsibility to prepare employees for mastery. When individuals feel they are adequately prepared, a mastery board consisting of two managers, a team leader, and three peers is convened. The board administers an oral exam that places equal emphasis on membership (interpersonal) and on technical skills. Individuals must maintain mastery of each process even if additional mastery levels are acquired.

To support the pay-for-knowledge mastery program, all employees are trained in peer performance appraisal. The eight-hour sessions train people in how to give appropriate feedback to one another. This is a critical skill to the teams' interactions and the pay-for-knowledge system. In a system premised on the train-the-trainer model, the ability of workers to give one another accurate feedback is essential.

Not all training is developed initially in-house. For example, a consultant was brought in to help train managers and team leaders in starting an employee assistance program. Once these sessions were complete, workers began to offer the training. Similarly, leaders attended corporate-wide training on management skills, finance and business strategies, leadership, health management, and customer service. When these individuals returned, they trained others in the plant.

There are a wide range of training activities that take place around technical and developmental skills. Woven throughout all of the training is a core philosophy centered on a commitment to building internal capability as a core organizational strategy, which is designed to enable the plant to adapt to ever-changing business realities. This strategy has not only led to enhanced effectiveness in terms of productivity but has also allowed for a smooth transition into more customized work to meet customer changing needs.

A focus on total quality.   Since 1989, one of the authors of this book has been involved with Great Lakes Industries, a small manufacturing company in Jackson, Michigan. The company has totally reinvented itself over the past ten years from a traditional assembly-line system to a learning-based organization structured around a cellular manufacturing process. The cellular manufacturing philosophy involves the development of a team-based work system where employees are owners of a manufacturing process that leads to a finished product.

This change effort began with the creation of an overall vision and underlying values that the organization wanted to pursue and create. The vision and values were generated by a team of employees and management. The vision included the following components: (1) to remain competitive, we must continually improve quality, productivity, and profitability; (2) everyone in the company will have access to business knowledge and understand the company's financial performance and share in the long-term success; and (3) the focus must be on meeting and exceeding customer needs and maintaining long-term relationships with valued customers. The underlying values by which the vision would be accomplished were identified as: (1) the operative principle is one of teamwork, involvement, empowerment, and responsibility among its members; (2) interactions among members will embody a climate of trust, mutual respect, and open communication; and (3) we will be characterized by continuous learning that integrates problem solving, technical updating, and people skills.

There were a number of interventions to move the organization toward its vision and values of becoming a learning organization. One intervention was to use group technology to achieve high-quality standards in planning, design, and production. Group technology involves grouping like problems to exploit similarities in product and processes in efforts to simplify and control the quality of work. Second, the manufacturing process was reorganized around manufacturing cells that operate as discrete, focused factories within the company. All aspects of cell operation, production, and quality are controlled by the teams of people who operate and set them up. Third, the focus was on building and designing quality at the source. The primary responsibility for quality belonged to the operators and cell team members. To make it right the first time, the operator was given the resources, responsibilities, and tools to do the job.

The move to group technology, manufacturing cells, and quality at the source was accomplished through the shared efforts of management and line workers. Company-wide teams were created to operationalize the vision by developing a prototype for the plant, evaluating its success, and developing procedures for generalizing from the pilot program to the development of other manufacturing cells. Cross-cell teams were formed to develop guidelines for safety procedures, quality, machine maintenance, and tooling. Other teams were formed to develop a standardized set of procedures on how to operate the various machines (hobs, lathes, drills, broaching) in the factory. Within each cell team, weekly meetings were held to review quality and safety concerns and to consider ways to continuously improve cell processes.

In addition, an emphasis was given to providing workers with extensive information on the company's financial situation so that employees could see the bigger picture around the change effort. Much effort and resources were also devoted to employee training. External consultants provided training in areas such as teamwork, running effective team meetings, improving internal and external customer relations, as well as enhancing problem solving and seeking root causes to problems so that continuous improvements could be made. Consultants also developed train-the-trainer systems in which technical experts within the company were provided with skills on how to teach others within the organization to work effectively in manufacturing cells. In addition, internal technical training and cooperative educational programs have been utilized to improve skills in areas such as statistical process control, group technology, quality at the source, print reading, gauge usage, and geometric tolerance.

The change effort, in essence, has rested on the pillars of systems thinking, worker participation, and learning. Rather than being solely the transformation part of the manufacturing process (e.g., drilling a hole into a piece of steel all day), each employee and team has become a minisystem within the larger system. Each cell or minisystem is in charge of its inputs (e.g., determining what jobs to run), transformation (taking raw material and transforming it into a product), outputs (preparing output for shipping directly to the customer), and feedback (checking quality). Cell members are empowered to set up the machines in their cell in whatever way makes sense and to calculate their own cycle times for getting the work done. Cells are able to review customer orders, schedule their own work to meet customer needs, do their own maintenance, make purchases to improve cell operations, and improve daily operations.

One key component for enhancing effectiveness was the standardization of work procedures. Another key component was extensive training and education of members in areas such as statistical process control, blueprint reading, advanced machine processes, machine setup, basic maintenance issues, problem-solving skills, teambuilding, how to run effective team meetings, and internal and external customer relations. The change initiative to becoming a learning organization has been quite successful. Over the course of ten years, the company has made dramatic improvements in quality and on-time delivery. Profits are up and employee bonuses are growing as they are learning and continuously improving.

Corporate universities.   Some corporations have begun a process of making lifelong investments in their workforce. One strategy is promoting continuous learning through the development of corporate universities. The idea behind a corporate university approach is to (1) build a competency-based training curriculum for all jobs, (2) provide all employees with a common shared vision of the company and its values, (3) extend training to customers and suppliers, and (4) serve as a learning laboratory for experimenting with new approaches to learning and effective action planning (Meister, 1994).

Motorola University is one of a number of companies that are benchmarks for the concept of corporate universities. Motorola has a campus setting at each major company site worldwide and is heavily engaged in web and distance learning technologies to provide immediate access to new knowledge and information. The idea of a Motorola University started in 1980 as a program developed outside the traditional human resources department. While traditional approaches to training continued, the vision of Motorola University was geared toward addressing special business needs such as retraining or updating workers and redefining jobs roles and responsibilities (Baldwin, Danielson, & Wiggenhorn, 1997). The focus was on the necessity for organizational change, participation in solution generation, and developing new and more effective systems to push the standards of manufacturing. For example, a key initial success was the development of a two-week course that brought together manufacturing, product development, and marketing managers to discuss the product development cycle at Motorola. Based on the coordinated efforts of these teams, the production development cycle was reduced from a three- to seven-year cycle to an eighteen-month cycle. Thus, Motorola University was founded with a focus not on effective training but rather on "what organizational excellence means in a changing business environment" (Baldwin et al., 1997).

The Motorola University concept requires employees worldwide to complete a certain number of training hours focusing on Motorola products and services. For example, Motorola created a cross-functional team that built a curriculum for operators who wanted to develop the skills needed to become a technician as well as a curriculum to update the skill needs of current technicians. This effort led to the creation of a career path for those with the desire to pursue additional skills as well as upgrading current skill levels. The project team conducted an extensive training needs analysis, including the identification of key knowledge and skills, the development of training objectives for developing and upgrading skills, and the creation of a curriculum for entry-level and advanced technicians to build those key skills. Motorola also partnered with a local community college to develop a two-year associate degree in applied science in areas such as electromechanical process technology. The curriculum included up to 256 hours for developing process skills such as interpersonal, mentoring, and communication skills as well as up to 256 hours of job-specific competencies that covered the more basic technical skills of the job. Table 9.2 provides examples of coursework including requirements for 40 hours of interpersonal skills, 16 hours of communication skills, and 192 hours of technical skills for entry-level technicians.

| TABLE 9.2 | EXAMPLE COURSES FOR TRAINING ENTRY-LEVEL TECHNICIANS AT MOTOROLA |

Grade-Level Attributes
(256 Hours of Institutional Course Work)

Interpersonal Skills (40 Hrs.)
Take any combination of courses totaling a minimum of 40 hours.

Subject Code	Hours	Course Title
MGT 106	16	Effective Interactions w/ Employees
MGT 330	16	Interaction
HRD 104	16	Understanding People
HRD 108	4	Effective Listening
TCH 203	8	Managing Team Conflict
TCH 330	16	Interaction for Technicians
WFD 101	6	Understanding the Diverse Workforce
WFD 303	4	Preventing Sexual Harassment
WFD 340	8	Female/Male Communication Strategies
WFD 510	32	Efficacy Seminar for Nonexempt Women
WFD 580	32	Efficacy Seminar for Men

Communication Skills (16 Hrs.) (Written—Verbal—Nonverbal)
Take any combination of courses totaling a minimum of 16 hours.

Subject Code	Hours	Course Title
HRD 108	4	Effective Listening
HRD 300	16	Problem Analysis and Decision Making
MGT 201	16	Effective Presentations
PDE 512	16	Technical Writing
PDE 540	16	Basic Business Communications Skills
PGM 413	24	How to Write Winning Proposals
PRD 102	18	Reading Refinement for Nonexempt

Area of Technical Concentration for Type 1 Technician (192 Hrs.)
Take any combination of courses totaling a minimum of 192 hours.

Subject Code	Hours	Course Title
EDN 003	24	Ion Implantation Technology
EDN 005	24	Ion Implantation Basic
EDN 040	20	RF Fundamentals
EDN 041	24	ENI RF Generators (Advanced)
EDN 045	70	Vacuum Technology
EDN 047	16	Metalization
EDN 049	16	Diffusion/Oxidation
EDN 051	8	Basic Plasma Etching
EDN 053	8	Wet Etch
EDN 055	16	Chemical Vapor Deposition . . .
ENG 147	24	Plasma Etching

Area of Technical Concentration for Type 1 Technician (192 Hrs.)
Take any combination of courses totaling a minimum of 192 hours.

Subject Code	Hours	Course Title
MFG 460	24	Intro to Programming Robots
MFG 465	16	Intro to Machine Vision
ELE 221	64 MCC	Linear Solid-State Devices
ELE 241	64 MCC	Microprocessor Concepts
ELE 243	48 MCC	Microprocessor Applications
GTC 181	48 MCC	Introduction to Fluid Power
GTC 209	48 MCC	Automated Manufacturing (Intro to PLC)
GTC 272	48 MCC	Sequential Process Control (PLC/Robot)

Source: From "Competency Modeling at Motorola," by J. Grey, S. Simpson, J. Kennedy, and S. Tou. In David Dubois (Ed.), The Competency Case Book, copyright 1998. Published by HRD Press, Inc., Amherst, MA, 800-822-2801, www.hrdpress .com. Reprinted by permission.

Training is also available to suppliers and customers. As the champion for this initiative noted, "the university's role, which parallels the changing competency requirements of individuals within the organization, is to raise the level of inquiry within the company through a diversely structured dialogue with customers, experts, and industry representatives (suppliers, regulators, policy makers, and special interest groups), (Baldwin, et al., 1997). Thus, the training programs focus attention to knowledge processes and what knowledge is essential and significant to the work of the organization (Galvin, 1997). Another emphasis is on stimulating creative thinking such as investing energy into reinterpreting familiar concepts.

In addition to the fixed campus locations, Motorola University is also branching out to web-based training systems to allow for individual flexibility. Motorola has developed a training information system to help employees track their own training hours (Bianchini & Sipla, 1998). The system also frees training coordinators from administrative duties so they can focus on improving training and learning. Motorola University has also created a new institute to develop educational delivery systems for satellite, Internet, and virtual reality technologies.

Challenges to Becoming a Learning Organization

The three preceding examples show some of the possible paths to becoming a learning organization. Case studies such as these support the notion that organizations with strong learning environments are demonstrating greater organizational effectiveness. For example, Kapp (1999) cites a Pittsburgh-based manufacturer that embraced the concepts of a learning organization and achieved a market share improvement of 70%. Motorola, whom *Fortune* characterized as the "gold standard" of corporate training, estimates that for every dollar spent on problem solving and statistical process control training, $30 are returned to the corporation.

These examples represent success stories, yet there are also a number of attempts to become a learning organization that have led to failure. An underlying dilemma for organizations is how to maintain efficient daily operations that satisfy a variety of organizational stakeholders while allocating time, resources, and energy toward addressing critical systems issues to create a learning organization. It takes a number of years for a transformation to a learning organization to unfold into a "top-management supported, long-range effort to improve an organization's problem-solving and renewal process, particularly through a more effective and collaborative diagnosis and management of organizational culture" (French & Bell, 1999).

The move to a learning organization does present a number of challenges, as it requires a major change in organizational norms. Schein (1997) talks about the clash of three cultures in organizations—operator, engineering, and executive—that often create barriers to success. As noted by Schein, these three cultures do not understand each other very well and often fundamentally work against one another—especially when there are attempts to transform an organization. The operator culture is focused on the effective use of human resources and the production and delivery of goods and services. The engineering culture is focused on effectively designing processes and systems that efficiently manage the organization's work and reduce the need for reliance on human resources. The executive culture is primarily concerned with enhancing the financial status of the organization and setting up elaborate strategic management systems and establishing routines to increase consistency throughout the organization.

Schein describes a number of examples of clashes across these groups. One example of the conflict between operators/engineers with the executive culture occurred within a large automotive company that worked with the MIT Organizational Learning Center to develop the capacity for learning. An innovative cross-level and cross-function team was created and, through a number of organizational development experiences, became a cohesive and productive group. They focused on early identification of manufacturing problems to avoid later effects that would require costly complex redesigns. For example, changing the chassis design might increase weight, which might require a different tire design that in turn might cause more internal noise. By revealing problems early, the team was attempting to view the whole car more systematically and speed up redesign.

However, a pileup of early problems identified by the group led management to become concerned that the team was out of control. Rather than acknowledging that the team was in a learning and transformational process, they ordered the team to get itself back under control. The team realized that management did not understand the value of early problem identification and continued to use their new learning, assuming that the ultimate results would be successful. The team was able to complete the design well ahead of schedule with lower costs. Nevertheless, the members of the executive level never understood the reasons for these successes and gave themselves credit for having gotten the team under control. The team was not seen as innovative, the learning that could have been gained and diffused in the organization was lost, and the team was disbanded.

This example shows the difficulties of becoming a learning organization. A systems perspective highlights the complexity of dealing with the common and competing interests of various stakeholder groups and the issues of integrating activities across the various levels in an organization. Only through sustained leadership and the efforts of the employees to make this happen can a learning organization become a reality.

TRAINING AND SOCIETAL CONCERNS

The increasing scope and complexity of changes occurring in the workplace require a well-prepared and highly trained workforce. Progressive organizations, like those moving toward a learning approach, have devoted considerable resources to training workers to be better prepared to deal with the changing realities of the workplace.

These organizational realities have a number of implications for the society within which the organizations are embedded. Organizations need highly qualified individuals that are not only motivated but can become part of a continuously learning organization. This reflects a need to examine the education and training system in the United States and the world of work within which individuals must be able to function successfully and gainfully. These broad societal issues that have important implications for training and learning are (1) increasing the readiness of individuals to enter the workforce, (2) enhancing fair employment practices once individuals enter the workforce, and (3) retraining individuals to either maintain their current employment or to obtain gainful employment after being displaced.

Increasing Workforce Readiness

There is a widening monetary gap between the highly educated, highly skilled and the less educated, lower skilled workers in our society. This gap has led to efforts to deal with issues of increasing the readiness of individuals to join the workforce. For example, the U.S. Department of Education estimated that twenty-seven million Americans are functional illiterates who could not read, write, or calculate at levels required to perform basic daily living tasks (Torrence & Torrence, 1987). The results of the largest assessment of American adults' literacy skills—the National Adult Literacy Survey (NALS) estimated that about 21% of the adult population (about forty million Americans over the age of sixteen) had only rudimentary reading and writing skills to function in society (Kirsch, Jungeblut, Jenkins, & Kolstad, 1993). The results were reported in terms of five levels of literacy proficiency from Level 1, the ability to do simple activities such as picking out a key fact in a brief newspaper article, to Level 5, reading about and then explaining how interest on a home equity loan is calculated (Smith & Reder, 1998). Only about 3% of the sample were able to perform at the highest level. Analyses by level indicated that about one-half of adults assessed were at the two lowest levels of literacy proficiency. Literacy levels were found to be correlated with educational attainment, median weekly wages of adults employed full time, and with racial and ethnic group membership—with African Americans, Native Americans, and Hispanics more likely than whites to perform at the two lowest levels (Kirsch et al., 1993).

A number of programs from the federal, state, and local governments as well as private foundations have been developed to address the issues of literacy and basic skill needs of Americans. The total federal investment in adult education and literacy (including state grants) was $456.2 million for 1997, whereas state and local funding totaled $830 million (Johnson & Hartman, 1998). As one example, the U.S. Department of Education provided competitive grants to states in 1997 that totaled $4.7 million for literacy and basic skills training in correctional facilities.

Over the last thirty years, the focus on increasing workforce readiness has concentrated on the problems of inner-city youth—at-risk youths. Osterman (1995) noted that this focus on the inner city has been broadened in the 1990s to include all noncollege-bound young people. These broader efforts have focused on easing the transition from school to work. This section first describes the issues of basic skills training for at-risk youths and then moves to the broader discussion of the training of noncollege-bound individuals to prepare them for the workplace.

Training and education for at-risk youths.   The civil disorders of the 1960s prompted a reconsideration of our poverty-ridden communities and the problem of unemployment (Report of the National Advisory Commission on Civil Disorders, 1968). Many of the members of these communities were considered hard-core unemployed (HCU) or at-risk youths; that is, they were individuals who were not regular members of the workforce, lacked a high school diploma, and lacked basic reading and writing skills.

The possibilities for success of interventions to improve basic literacy or foundation skills of reading and writing has mainly come from research in and experiences with low-aptitude youth training programs in the military (Sticht, 1997). For example, Sticht, Armstrong, Hickey, and Caylor (1987) presented data describing the success of their programs in terms of retention rates, numbers of people completing high school equivalency degrees, performance in the military, and other similar criteria. The training program was based on a functional literacy approach that emphasized the development of basic skills within the context of the job. In addition, the authors report on other training support schemes, including revision of training materials to match trainee aptitudes. Nevertheless, Sticht (1997), in reviewing seventy-five years of military research on literacy training, warns that improvements in basic literacy require a very extensive and expensive effort to reform the educational system and a similar effort to develop an adult workforce readiness educational system.

Besides the basic literacy issue, the challenges due to the increase in workplace technology and the subsequent demands for a skilled workforce are becoming even more serious. In addition to basic literacy skills, workforce readiness includes the need for at-risk youths to develop basic work skills (e.g., issues such as punctuality, reliability, interpersonal skills) and job-specific skills (e.g., training to become a mechanic). A vast number of programs and techniques have been applied to the problems of basic work skills and job-specific skills. Yet, researchers have noted that training programs focusing on literacy, basic skills, and job-specific skills have not provided at-risk youths with adequate preparation for the realities of work.

Efforts have moved to a more total person approach that includes not only training but also job placement services, counseling, and attention. In one of these initial efforts, Nester (1971) examined a program that included the arrangement for special tutoring, baby-sitters, a variety of incentives to motivate trainees, and counseling to resolve personal problems that make it difficult to learn or to keep a job. Nester found evidence that graduates from this intensive approach were more likely to find and retain jobs than a sample of individuals not receiving these intensive services. Since then, a more holistic perspective to the education and training of at-risk youths has been undertaken.

The nation's largest and most comprehensive residential educational and job-training program for at-risk youths aged 16 to 24 is the Job Corps. Job Corps is a public-private partnership administered by the U.S. Department of Labor that focuses on a free enterprise answer to skill training for disadvantaged youth. Since 1964, the program has provided more than 1.7 million disadvantaged young people with an integrated approach to academic, vocational, and social skills training needed to gain independence and obtain quality jobs. For example, the Pittsburgh Job Corps Center (one of 118 centers in the country) currently places students in educational classes and helps them earn a GED (General Educational Development) diploma. In addition, enrichment programs are offered in a social skills development program in which students learn how to complete a resume and how to conduct themselves in a job interview. Using up-to-date equipment, the Job Corps Center also offers training in content areas such as auto repair, building maintenance, business office technology, carpentry, food service, health occupations, heavy equipment operating, and transportation.

Programs such as Job Corps have become even more important given the Welfare Reform Act of 1996, which holds states accountable for moving individuals from the welfare rolls to obtaining a job. An evaluation of the states in 1998 found that 35% of welfare recipients met the requirements of the Act— to have a job, to be actively seeking work, or to be pursuing basic education and training. In 1999, Leavitt in the *USA Today* declared that welfare to work successes were found in all fifty states, with Oregon, Montana, and Wisconsin in the lead.

Despite some successes, one challenge for federal and state agencies is to work with businesses to identify job opportunities for welfare recipients. The government has put into place a Workforce Development System that offers state and local agencies resources to help employers identify, recruit, certify, hire, and retrain new workers. The system also provides assistance with assessment tools, child care, transportation, and local contacts to help keep people in the jobs.

A second challenge is to provide the training and developmental programs to impart the skills welfare recipients need to become gainfully employed. The Worker Training and Assistance Program (WTAP) is one such program designed to help people on welfare to transition into jobs. The WTAP includes thirty-four individual training modules organized around four topics: (1) orientation, (2) workplace skills, (3) transition skills, and (4) managerial skills. The modules are broad enough to allow the user to tailor the curricula to the specific needs of the individual. The program also has a training component for managers so they may become familiar with the goals of the WTAP and more knowledgeable about the support services available to their newly hired employees.

Despite some successes, the majority of the evaluations of programs completed in the 1960s, 1970s, and 1980s to aid the HCU and at-risk youths have generally found disappointing results (Betsey, Hollister, Jr., & Papageorgiou, 1985). For example, a Job Start program was begun to provide intensive education and skill training to high school dropouts in thirteen sites across the country. An extensive evaluation effort including random assignment to condition found that educational achievements were obtained but that these achievements did not translate into employment gains (Auspos, Cave, Doolittle, & Hoerz, 1989). This limited success is troubling as the problem with disadvantaged or at-risk youth remains serious. For example, in the last decade of economic growth, the jobless rate for African American teenagers seeking employment has been two and three times the national unemployment rate.

The changing landscape of training and educational programs for at-risk youths highlights three critical challenges to designers and promoters of these types of programs. One challenge is to better understand the factors that determine success of these instructional programs. The training and educational programs might include a number of factors like job placement, counseling, health needs, basic skills, and advanced skills. Not only do we need more research on effective strategies for imparting these knowledge and skills, but we also need a better idea of how to sequence these various aspects to develop people and build toward expertise that is valued in the workplace. A second challenge is the development of a strategic evaluation approach to examine program success. Too often programs are put into place without much effort toward evaluation strategies, or the evaluation strategies emphasize answering the question of whether the program works. Although this overall goal needs to be evaluated, a more critical need is to take the instructional–systems design model seriously and link the evaluation data to reassessing training needs and redesigning programs in a systematic way so as to lead to the continuous improvement of program design and implementation. A third challenge concerns the work environment. It is clear that these training and educational programs must be considered in the context of the environments in which they operate. Unless employers are willing to take a chance with at-risk youth and provide real opportunities for success on the job, the programs cannot succeed. The transfer of training and education to the workplace is a serious concern relevant to at-risk youths.

Facilitating school-to-work transition.   As noted by Hanson (1999), programs to help at-risk youths are now being applied broadly as the centerpiece of education and educational reform. Frustrations with the quality of education have merged with the perception that the United States has done little to prepare individuals for the workplace in comparison with countries such as Germany and Japan (Kochan & Osterman, 1996). Researchers cite as support for this the fact that the market value of a high school diploma is falling. Recent data shows that high school graduates have a higher rate of unemployment (18.4%) than youths who have enrolled in college either part time (13.2%) or full time (10.3%; Hardy, 1999). In addition, about a half million youths left school in the 1997–1998 academic year without graduating and had an unemployment rate of 28.2%.

There has been a flurry of government-sponsored activities for providing better vocational training to young people. The Secretary's Commission on Achieving Necessary Skills (SCANS) is a national project that started in 1990 at the request of the Secretary of Labor to research human resource requirements for a high-performance economy. The SCANS commission contends that more than half of the people leaving high school do not have the knowledge or foundation required to find and hold a good job. Although it is difficult to find direct support for this contention, Osterman (1995) examined data from 11,406 young people from the National Longitudinal Survey of Youth and found that one third of the men and women at the beginning of their thirties were in a job that had lasted for less than a year.

To address the issue of school to work, SCANS reviewed existing skill lists and interviewed employers, educators, labor leaders, policy makers, and workers in fifty occupations to identify competencies common across a broad range of occupations. SCANS (1991) concluded that high school students need to learn not only basic academic skills but also workplace know-how skills to be successful in a high-performance economy. Its report defined workplace competencies (resources, interpersonal skills, information, systems, technology) and foundation skills (basic reading and writing skills, thinking skills, and personal qualities such as responsibility, self-esteem, sociability, self-management, and integrity) necessary for worker success. It also made recommendations about how these competencies and skills could be embedded into schools and workplaces. Table 9.3 presents a list of competencies and skills and their definitions.

In 1992, American College Testing (ACT) was awarded a contract by the U.S. Departments of Labor and Education to conduct a National Job Analysis study to provide further empirical support for the SCANS framework. In addition, ACT was charged with establishing relationships between the workplace competencies and basic foundation skills, linking core job behaviors with high-performance practices, identifying the knowledge and skills required for acquiring and using the competencies, and developing tests or assessment instruments to measure an individual's level of competency for the work competencies and foundation skills (see Nash & Korte, 1997, for a summary of this effort).

One product from this effort is an extensive testing and assessment process called WorkKeys (McLarty & Vansickle, 1997). It focuses on (1) basic

TABLE

9.3

SCANS: FIVE COMPETENCIES

Resources: Identifies, organizes, plans, and allocates resources.

a. *Time:* Selects goal-relevant activities, ranks them, allocates time, and prepares and fol-lows schedules.

b. *Money:* Uses or prepares budgets, makes forecasts, keeps records, and makes adjust-ments to meet objectives.

c. *Material and facilities:* Acquires, stores, allocates, and uses materials or space effi-ciently.

d. *Human resources:* Assesses skills and distributes work accordingly, evaluates perfor-mance and provides feedback.

Interpersonal: Works with others.

a. *Participates as member of a team:* Contributes to group effort.

b. *Teaches others new skills.*

c. *Serves clients/customers:* Works to satisfy customers' expectations.

d. *Exercises leadership:* Communicates ideas to justify position, persuades and convinces others, responsibly challenges existing procedures and policies.

e. *Negotiates:* Works toward agreements involving exchange of resources, resolves diver-gent interests.

f. *Works with diversity:* Works well with men and women from diverse backgrounds.

Information: Acquires and uses information.

a. *Acquires and evaluates information.*

b. *Organizes and maintains information.*

c. *Interprets and communicates information.*

d. *Uses computers to process information.*

Systems: Understands complex interrelationships.

a. *Understands systems:* Knows how social, organizational, and technological systems work and operates effectively with them.

b. *Monitors and corrects performance:* Distinguishes trends, predicts impacts on system operations, diagnoses deviations in systems' performance and corrects malfunctions.

c. *Improves or designs systems:* Suggests modifications to existing systems and develops new or alternative systems to improve performance.

Technology: Works with a variety of technologies.

a. *Selects technology:* Chooses procedures, tools, or equipment, including computers and related technologies.

b. *Applies technology to task:* Understands overall intent and proper procedures for setup and operation of equipment.

c. *Maintains and troubleshoots equipment:* Prevents, identifies, or solves problems with equipment, including computers and other technologies.

Source: From "What Work Requires of Schools," by Secretary's Commission on Achieving Necessary Skills, U.S. Department of Labor, 1991, Washington, DC: U.S. Government Printing Office.

communication skills of listening, reading for information, and writing; (2) problem-solving skills such as applied mathematics, applied technology, locating information, and observation; and (3) interpersonal skills such as teamwork. For example, the teamwork assessment measures an individual's skill in choosing behaviors and/or actions that simultaneously support relationships within the team and lead toward the accomplishment of work tasks. Individuals must recognize the goals of a team and identify ways to accomplish those goals in increasingly complex situations, such as those where needed resources are not readily available. The assessment is administered via videotape and contains twelve teamwork scenarios each accompanied by three multiple-choice questions. Individuals are asked to identify the most appropriate teamwork response to a specific workplace situation. The assessment contains four levels of complexity. Level three, the lowest, assesses a minimal level of teamwork skills (but this is still above no skill at all). The levels build on each other, incorporating the skills assessed at lower levels, so that level six is the most complex (see McLarty & Vansickle, 1997, for a more extensive discussion of WorkKeys). Table 9.4 presents an example item concerning customer service at a convenience store. The item is one indicator of whether a person is at level six of the teamwork dimension. The correct answer to the sample item is "D" as this action contributes both to the goal of serving the customer and also to maintaining good team relationships.

The WorkKeys assessment process has some demonstrated success. For example, an extruded products company in Ohio used the WorkKeys system to identify the skills needed for a newly created production technician position. WorkKeys reports that the new selection system to test for these skills led to a decrease in training time for entry-level people from six months to two months.

This national project has also produced the SCANS 2000 Center at the Johns Hopkins University Institute for Policy Studies. The center focuses on creating a workforce development system, integrated with the community colleges and high schools, to prepare workers to compete in the international economy of the twenty-first century. Special community projects are underway in California, Florida, Maine, and Maryland. The foundations of the SCANS 2000 model for learning are as follows:

Integrated/blended—Students simultaneously acquire SCANS competencies and academic knowledge.

Project-based—Learning is embedded in the context of realistic, workplace-based projects.

Collaborative—Teachers use strategies that emphasize cooperation, teamwork, and written and oral student presentation.

Assessment-guided—Teachers and students assess progress in acquiring SCANS competencies to guide future learning steps.

TABLE 9.4	TEAMWORK ASSESSMENT

A daily newspaper is changing from an afternoon to a morning delivery schedule. This change affects every employee, from the editor to the delivery people. The paper will have a 10:00 p.m. press deadline, and the reporters will be unable to write complete stories for many evening sports events, cultural events, and community meetings. The editor has told the team of five reporters to propose a revised schedule of assignments. This schedule should take into account each reporter's area of expertise and still ensure that all important stories are covered by the deadline.

When the team meets to discuss this schedule, a major concern is how to make the evening stories as timely as possible within the new time constraints. Team members offer several suggestions regarding how to shift assignments around to accommodate the deadline. One of the reporters insists on covering only the political stories, which are his particular interest. Another reporter argues that the political reporter should help out the sports writer by preparing background material in the afternoon for the evening's sports stories. The political reporter refuses, saying that he wasn't hired to work on sports and doesn't know anything about them. The sports writer complains that the change to a morning edition is the whole problem, that coverage of evening sports events is going to be ruined, and that management doesn't know what they are doing. The cultural reporter agrees and adds that he is thinking about finding a job elsewhere. The society reporter retorts that he should do just that; she hates doing the society stories and would take the cultural assignment in a minute.

Question:

1. As a member of this team, the sportswriter can best support the team and accomplish the task by:

    A. suggesting the editor hire several part-time reporters to help cover sports stories.

    B. suggesting that all of the reporters work on background for all types of stories so that each can do final details and editing in his or her area of expertise.

    C. volunteering to tell management that the morning edition change is a mistake and should be withdrawn.

    D. suggesting they keep their current assignments and accept a one-day delay in coverage of all evening stories.

Source: Reproduced with permission from the ACT, Inc. website (www.act.org), Work Keys Assessments section. Iowa City, Iowa. No further reproduction authorized without further permission from ACT, Inc. .

Technology-intensive—Technology is employed to create realistic scenarios, deliver instruction, and as a tool to carry out project tasks (www.scans.jhu.edu).

In Baltimore, Maryland, a major initiative is underway to transform teaching and learning for middle and high school students, their parents, teachers, and future employers. The focus is on the integration of training technologies such as CD-ROM and two-way interactive video to change the current structure of the schools by permitting students to engage in more active, inquiry-based learning work. For example, there are CD-ROM modules on learning information systems design where students are asked to develop an electronic information aid for communicating health information and setting specifications for moving a paper-based system to an on-line system. As another component in the system, participants in organizations outside the educational field share expertise and experience to reduce the gap between school and work.

There has been much systematic work completed relevant to program needs assessment and curriculum design and development. Given that full-scale implementation of school-to-work curriculum has just begun, there is little empirical data on its effectiveness. In addition, criticisms of the school-to-work movement have arisen. Opponents claim that it (1) further dilutes and weakens academics through the dumbing down of the curriculum, (2) focuses on marketing students as future workers rather than developing them as people, and (3) pushes youths to choose career paths too early (Hanson, 1999; Hardy, 1999). To minimize these types of problems, Swanson and Fouad (1999) contend that school-to-work programs need to help students better understand their own needs, interests, and abilities as well as the importance of matching these with a job or career rather than simply pushing students to find a job. Krumboltz and Worthington (1999) advocate taking more of a learning perspective by helping youth define new targets for learning and identifying opportunities for success rather than focusing attention to gaining specific skills.

The issue of school-to-work transition is not just a problem at the high school level. For example, Gilliam (1988) reports on a training study designed to help individuals who could not find jobs. The startling aspect of Gilliam's study is that the group for which this training program was designed were all college graduates who were minorities and could not find employment. Issues of fairness and equal opportunity and their implications for training are described in the next section.

Ensuring Fairness and Enhancing Opportunity at Work

The issue of employment discrimination and fairness in the selection of individuals into the workplace has generated much debate in our society. There are also fairness issues surrounding training and development once individuals join the workforce (Hartel, 1994). From this fairness perspective, all employees must be given equal access and opportunity to training, mentoring, and other development activities to avoid disparate treatment in the workplace. Fairness issues are often codified in the form of laws, principles, and guidelines that form the foundation for the evolving concept of fairness and employment practices.

In 1964 President Lyndon Johnson signed the Civil Rights Act into law. One section of that act, Title VII, has had a dramatic effect on employers, employees, job applicants, labor unions, lawyers, and industrial-organizational psychologists. Title VII makes it illegal for employers to discriminate on the basis of race, color, religion, sex, or national origin. The categories of the aged and handicapped, while not initially included, have been added later in other legislative action. The 1964 Act established the Equal Employment Opportunities Commission (EEOC) as an enforcement agency for fair employment practices. Since that time, numerous events have affected practices in this area. In 1972 an amendment to Title VII broadened its coverage to include employers with fifteen or more employees, state and government agencies, and educational institutions. The amendment also extended the authority of the EEOC to bring court actions against organizations. The EEOC published a set of guidelines in 1970; the EEOC, the Civil Service Commission, the Department of Labor, and the Department of Justice published a new set of guidelines in 1978, all of which have had effects on personnel practices. Also, the Society for Industrial and Organizational Psychology published the *Principles for the Validation and Use of Personnel Selection Procedures* (1987) to help clarify and develop guidelines for the field. Various court actions ranging from district court decisions to those of the United States Supreme Court have added to the complexity.

In 1991 a new civil rights bill was passed. In part, the bill was in response to a number of Court decisions that many people felt were making it difficult for employees to pursue fair employment issues. Thus, one Court decision (*Wards Cove Packing Co.* v. *Antonio,* 1989) had made it the responsibility of an employee, rather than employer, to show the organization used practices adversely affecting women and minorities without any "business necessity." In instances where it is shown that an organization's personnel practices adversely affect women and minorities, the 1991 Civil Rights Act returns the burden of proof to employers to show that their practices are job-related and consistent with business necessity.

Equal employment laws have traditionally focused attention on the selection of people into work organizations. Nevertheless, training issues embedded in fair employment practices are increasingly important in a knowledge-driven workforce. As people from protected classes have successfully entered the job market, the issues have shifted somewhat from employment opportunities to career opportunities. For example, the 1991 Civil Rights Act makes it clear that all phases of employment discrimination, not just tests involving entry into a job, are covered by the law. Bartlett (1978), in an insightful analysis, lists some of the kinds of decisions involving training programs that are likely to be areas of litigation. Some of the decisions listed include using training as a job prerequisite, using training performance as a criteria for another job, and using training as a basis for advancement or increased compensation.

Bartlett's 1978 prognosis turned out to be fairly accurate. Russell (1984) has carefully detailed many court cases involving these types of training issues. For example, in cases involving a drug company and a bank company, the court ruled that the companies pay plans were inadequate because the training programs had a number of violations. They excluded women, and advancement from the training program to a fully qualified employment opportunity was sporadic. More recently, there has been an emphasis on the fairness in training and developmental opportunities for women in managerial positions. In addition, with the passage of the Americans with Disabilities Act (ADA) in 1990, there has been increased attention to training and development issues relevant to individuals with disabilities. These two areas are discussed next.

Glass ceiling effect.   Barriers to advancement and increased compensation for women and minorities in the workplace have been described as the "glass ceiling effect" (Federal Glass Ceiling Commission, 1995). The glass ceiling refers to any artificial barrier that limits promotion and developmental opportunities or crowds women and minorities into staff positions and managerial positions that are removed from the essential core of the business. The Commission cites that whereas over 50% of all masters degrees are awarded to women, over 97% of top-level executives in Fortune 1000 companies remain white males.

The scope of these difficulties was first detailed in a U.S. Department of Labor report that examined the employment and promotion practices of nine Fortune 500 firms (Sugawara, 1991). The study found that this seemingly invisible barrier often blocks women and minorities from advancement into management. In addition, the study found that barriers exist at a much lower level of management than originally thought. The extent to which this type of problem affects training programs is made clear in a study by the General Accounting Office (Swoboda, 1991), which found that nearly one out of five federally sponsored training programs under the Job Training Partnership Act (JTPA) discriminates against women and blacks in the type of training opportunities made available. In these cases, minorities and women are more likely to be provided with training consistent with lower placement levels. Given these developments, court cases concerning opportunities for promotions have become more frequent. One target of litigation are programs that determine who is given the opportunity to attend a training program so they can be selected for promotion to a managerial job. Those personnel decisions are subject to the same laws as personnel decisions for entry into the job market.

A recent audit by the Department of Labor's Office of Federal Contract Compliance concluded that over half of the companies that do business with the government have problems relevant to tracking affirmative action and developmental actions within their organization. In a recent court case with Washington, Texaco, Inc., Texaco agreed to pay $3.1 million to 186 female employees who received less than their male counterparts in the "largest glass ceiling settlement" ever reached. In the settlement, Texaco agreed to expand opportunities for women and to analyze its pay scales (Galvin, 1999).

Also recently, Lyness and Thompson (1997) examined the glass ceiling effect at the top-executive level. They looked at women who had broken through the glass ceiling at the middle-management level and were now in the ranks of the upper management. They compared career and work experiences of a matched sample of women and men in the financial services field. They found that while compensation levels were comparable, women in the sample had less authority, received fewer stock options, and had less international mobility than men. They suggest that the results imply a more subtle, second higher level glass ceiling.

While there are some researchers who challenge how widespread the glass ceiling effect is (e.g., Furchtgott-Roth & Stolba, 1999), it is clear that the effect is worth more study and enhanced monitoring in organizations (Heneman, Waldeck, & Cushnie, 1997). For example, the 1998 Census of Women Board Directors of Fortune 500 companies demonstrates that women are gaining some ground but still hold only 11.1% of board seats (compared with 8.3% in 1993) and represent just 5.3% of corporate officers (Catalyst, 1998). Minority women are even less well represented compared with white women, holding less than 1.4% of total board seats.

Arvey, Azevedo, Ostgaard, and Raghuram (1997) contend that a possible cause of the glass ceiling is that the white male culture at top levels of organizations are indifferent or even hostile to the advancement of women and minorities. Even organizations that actively recruit and promote women and minorities often fail to make the work culture hospitable to them (Sharpe, 1994). The U.S. Department of Labor contends that the major cause of the glass ceiling effect is that organizations do not hold managers and executives accountable to issues of fair employment practices. In addition, there are closed internal markets in organizations where women and minorities are less likely to be made aware of job openings, and there is a lack of training and development opportunities for improving qualifications and chances for promotion (Federal Glass Ceiling Commission, 1995).

One suggestion for avoiding the glass ceiling effect is to fast track women and minority employees by giving special training and developmental opportunities, providing mentors, and giving assignments to pivotal jobs that provide core experience and boost retention of women and minorities (Arvey et al., 1997). As an example, Xerox has studied its managerial positions, identified pivotal jobs, and set goals for putting women and minorities in those positions and developing their talents (Sessa, 1992). Procter & Gamble has an orientation program called "On Boarding" specifically for women entering the organization, which is designed to develop an awareness of issues of working within the existing organizational culture (Cox, 1993). Workshops have also been created for supervisors and managers to better understand how perceptions of events can impact important managerial decisions such as promotions and career progressions of minority group members (Alderfer, 1992). To encourage organizations to take these types of proactive steps, the U.S. Department of Labor offers the Exemplar Voluntary Efforts (EVE) Awards for federal contractors who are working to shatter the glass ceiling.

Americans with Disabilities Act. Fair employment laws have also focused on disabled workers. The Americans with Disabilities Act of 1990 (ADA) makes it unlawful to discriminate in employment against a qualified individual with a disability. For example, the Act prohibits discrimination in recruitment, hiring, promotions, training, pay, social activities, and other privileges of employment (U.S. Department of Justice, Civil Rights Division, 1996). Although this act is quite complex and the implications of its application to the workplace are still unfolding, several important points are apparent. The key provision in the Act is providing individuals with reasonable accommodation. Reasonable accommodation is any change or adjustment to a job or work environment that permits a qualified applicant or employee with a disability to participate in the job application process, to perform the essential functions of the job, or to enjoy benefits and privileges of employment equal to those enjoyed by employees without disabilities. For example, reasonable accommodation may include:

- acquiring or modifying equipment or devices,
- job restructuring,
- part-time or modified work schedules,
- reassignment to a vacant position,
- adjusting or modifying examinations, training materials, or policies,
- providing readers and interpreters, and
- making the workplace readily accessible to and usable by people with disabilities. (U.S. Equal Employment Opportunity Commission, 1991, p. 4)

It is a violation of the ADA to fail to provide reasonable accommodation unless it causes undue hardship to the operation of the business. Undue hardship means that the accommodation would require significant difficulty or expense. Factors used in making this judgment in each individual case involve an assessment of the cost of the accommodation, the employer's size and financial resources, and the nature and structure of the operation. It is important to note that this act applies to individuals; thus, different individuals with different disabilities must be considered separately in terms of reasonable accommodation.

ADA provisions have had a major impact on structural changes (e.g., barrier-free access to the work site) in the workplace to accommodate the needs of employees and customers with disabilities. The impact of the ADA provisions on training practices in work organizations is more slowly emerging. As noted by Reyna and Sims (1995), training professionals must consider how to integrate disabled employees when planning and implementing their training programs. It is important for disabled employees to have equal opportunities to participate in training to improve job performance and advance their careers. Reyna and Sims present a checklist of policy, training and instruction, and physical barrier issues that need to be considered to address the provisions of the ADA. Example items from that checklist are given in Table 9.5. An examination of the checklist shows that training opportunities may need to be modified to provide for reasonable accommodation for different people. For example, reasonable accommodation might mean ensuring that the trainee can physically enter the training classroom while using a wheelchair or modifying the size of a desk so that an individual can reach a computer keyboard. It might also include efforts to address visual and hearing impairments such as developing training manuals in Braille or providing an interpreter for training lectures. Trainers might also allow the individual trainee with a disability to suggest how he or she might best be accommodated in the learning process (Fischer, 1994).

In addition, the ADA has emphasized the need for organizations to be more proactive in addressing the needs of disabled customers as well as the assimilation of workers who are disabled. One focus of ADA with implications for training has been a push for service organizations to provide training to employees on how to interact with and accommodate the needs of disabled individuals. For example, KinderCare entered a settlement agreement with

---

TABLE 9.5   **EXAMPLE OF THE IMPLICATIONS OF ADA FOR JOB TRAINING**

Policy and Sensitivity Issues

1. Is training for individuals in need of accommodation provided similarly from that provided others?   ☐ **Yes**   ☐ **No**

2. Have modifications been made to policies, practices, or procedures to address training-related accommodations for individuals with disabilities?   ☐ **Yes**   ☐ **No**

3. Are modifications made to training policies, practices, or procedures when you are providing training to individuals with disabilities?   ☐ **Yes**   ☐ **No**

4. Do you have a policy concerning "reasonable accommodations"?   ☐ **Yes**   ☐ **No**

5. Do you have a procedure to document decisions not to train disabled employees because of "undue hardship"?   ☐ **Yes**   ☐ **No**

6. Is someone responsible and accountable in your company for ensuring that disabled employees have fair opportunities for training and advancement?   ☐ **Yes**   ☐ **No**

7. Are individuals with disabilities provided equal opportunities to become trainers or participants on advisory boards for policies and procedures?   ☐ **Yes**   ☐ **No**

8. Have your managers and supervisors or other responsible parties been informed of the ADA and accommodation policies?   ☐ **Yes**   ☐ **No**

(Continued)

TABLE

9.5　**CONTINUED**

Training and Instruction Issues

9. Are training accommodations offered to individuals with disabilities in the most integrated setting appropriate to the needs of the individuals? ☐ **Yes** ☐ **No**

10. Do your training eligibility criteria screen in, not out, individuals with disabilities? ☐ **Yes** ☐ **No**

11. Are employees with disabilities provided with external training opportunities the same as those who are not disabled? ☐ **Yes** ☐ **No**

12. Does your training group consult or seek advice from advisory groups on adult education and instructing the disabled? ☐ **Yes** ☐ **No**

13. Does the training format (e.g., lecture, role plays, experiential exercises) accommodate disabled individuals in the training classroom for equal participation and learning time? ☐ **Yes** ☐ **No**

14. Is external training monitored for appropriateness of training materials and accessibility? ☐ **Yes** ☐ **No**

15. Does your company solicit input from the employee or special interest groups in making reasonable accommodations to training curriculums, material, or presentation medium? ☐ **Yes** ☐ **No**

16. Are architectural barriers and communication barriers that are structural in nature—including permanent, temporary, or movable structures such as furniture and equipment— removed from training facilities? ☐ **Yes** ☐ **No**

Physical Barriers

17. Has new training facility construction with first occupancy after January 16, 1993, been designed to be usable by individuals with disabilities? ☐ **Yes** ☐ **No**

18. Are other benefits and privileges such as meals, rest rooms, transportation, and/or overnight accommodations free from barriers that may prohibit or discourage a disabled employee from enjoying the benefits of training? ☐ **Yes** ☐ **No**

19. Have training rooms been redesigned in such a way as to allow an individual in a wheelchair to sit anywhere in the room as a nondisabled employee may choose? ☐ **Yes** ☐ **No**

20. Does your company solicit input from the employee or special interest groups in making reasonable accommodations in the training room (e.g., architectural, training materials format)? ☐ **Yes** ☐ **No**

the U.S. Department of Justice (1996) to accept children with diabetes into its child care program. As part of the agreement, KinderCare agreed to undergo a three-year employee training program on a wide range of disability-related issues including skills in how to do simple finger pricks, blood glucose monitoring, and providing appropriate care in response to low blood sugar levels. In addition, KinderCare agreed that its personnel would receive sensitivity training such as how to integrate children with disabilities into the regular program and how to communicate with children and parents with disabilities. In another case, Marriott agreed as part of a settlement to provide employees with training on how to address the needs of customers with various kinds of disabilities.

Retraining Workers Given Changing Markets

The U.S. workforce is aging along with the baby boomers with workers fifty-five and older, comprising one of the fastest growing segments of the workforce (Sterns & McDaniel, 1995). By 2030, more than a third of the population will be over the age of fifty-five (Papalia, Camp, & Feldman, 1996). This growth has implications not only for training and retraining but also for career progression. In addition, corporate downsizing has displaced a number of highly skilled blue- and white-collar employees. Although displaced workers are found across the age range, it is clear that the older worker is particularly at risk when it comes to reemployment opportunities (Sterns & Camp, 1998).

Training the older worker.   Most age discrimination cases are based on the premise that older workers cannot perform as well on the job and cannot acquire new skills in a timely manner. For example, the Office of Technology Assessment (1990) reported a case of a television company that trained their newer, younger workers on a change in technology from film to videotape. The older workers sued when they were disproportionately affected by a layoff because they had not received the training. These factors plus poorly designed training interventions for older workers will need to be overcome if older employees are going to be given opportunities in tomorrow's job market.

It is important to note that stereotypes about older workers persist despite research that does not support such beliefs. For example, a meta-analysis that integrated the results of ninety-six studies found that age and performance were generally unrelated across all types of performance measures (McEvoy & Cascio, 1989). Any differences found tended to be related to performance where there were high demands for speed and accuracy of movement. However, for the most part, the demands of most jobs were not extreme enough for ability differences to show up. In addition, there is evidence that well-practiced skills such as those of an airline pilot show little if any age decline and that older workers are more likely to have high levels of job satisfaction and job involvement.

Sterns and Doverspike (1989) note that many older trainees are highly motivated to learn but may fear failure in competition with younger, more recently educated trainees. Training programs can address these issues through programs that enhance an individual's self-efficacy. To achieve this goal, they suggest that

1. Training should be organized so that the material is job-relevant, gives positive feedback, and encourages the self-confidence of the trainee.
2. Training must ensure complete task mastery of previous components before moving on to the next step.
3. Where possible, training should build on elements that are familiar to the trainees from past learning and jobs.
4. Systems should be designed to organize information systems so memory requirements are limited.
5. Paced or time-pressured situations should be eliminated.

Of course, it should be noted that most of these training principles would be beneficial in any training program including those for entry-level workers and at-risk youths. However, they appear to be particularly pertinent for training older workers.

Training displaced workers.   Displaced workers are defined as persons aged twenty years or older who have lost or left jobs because their organization closed or moved, there was insufficient work for them to do, or their position or shift was abolished (http://stats.bls.gov/news.release/disp.nws.htm). The U.S. Bureau of Labor Statistics for the Department of Labor estimates that a total of 3.6 million workers were displaced between January 1995 and December 1997 from jobs that were held for at least three years. An additional 4.4 million people were displaced who had worked with their employer for less than three years. Relevant to the total labor base, the displacement has been disproportionately high for manufacturing jobs. In addition, Gardner (1995) found that job displacement among workers aged fifty-five to sixty-four had increased from the lowest of any age group to the highest. Reemployment rates for older workers were also found to be lower than for other age groups. Couch (1998) examined data from 204 job-displaced workers from ages fifty-one to sixty. The results indicated that even if reemployed quickly, the older worker faced long-term earning losses (a 30% reduction due in part to a drop in seniority), including reductions in the rate of retirement savings. Couch also found that the older displaced worker was more at risk to lose medical insurance as 27% were now on their spouse's health insurance plan. These data indicate that even when the economy is in relatively good shape and there is low unemployment in society in general, a number of people are losing jobs. The need for retraining and reintroduction to the workforce is clear.

A key government program to help displaced workers is the Job Training Partnership Act (JTPA). Applicants for the training program take assessments to determine their interests and abilities. The focus is on customization of a program plan for each individual. For example, one individual may be taking only a couple of college night courses to update skills in preparation for a new job while another might set up a program at the area college that can last up to two years and lead to a major career change. Title III of JTPA is called the Economic Dislocation and Worker Adjustment Assistance. It provides funds to state and local agencies so they can help dislocated workers find quality jobs. The benefits and reemployment services available to displaced workers vary from state to state.

In addition, Congress enacted The Worker Adjustment and Retraining Notification (WARN) Act, which requires notification to states about plant closures and mass layoffs so that a rapid response can be implemented. States may set up labor management committees to coordinate efforts to retain companies and make available outreach activities such as testing and counseling, labor market information, job search and placement, and supportive services such as child care, transportation allowances, and relocation assistance. States may also provide basic and remedial education, specific job skills training, entrepreneurial training, and literacy or language training (www.wdsc.org/layoff/title3.htm).

Other countries have taken a more proactive stance regarding the older displaced worker. For example, in Australia, there is a government campaign to promote the benefits of employing and retaining older workers as part of a productive workforce. Payroll tax incentives are available to employers who take on long-term unemployed older people. In addition, there is a government pilot program where older people act as mentors and advisors in fields such as business skills.

Research has documented the heavy price individuals and their families can pay when a job loss occurs. Affective consequences include depression and other mental health problems. Behavioral consequences can include antisocial behaviors, substance abuse, and increased violence in the home. Research has also highlighted ways to decrease the potential negative implications of job loss. For example, a recent longitudinal study found that individuals who thought they were given full explanations of why and how termination decisions were made were more likely to perceive the layoff as fair regardless of whether they were reemployed (Wanberg, Bunce, & Gavin, 1999). Perceptions of fairness were linked to more positive affective reactions.

Organizations are also beginning to see the benefits of helping those who are being displaced through layoffs. Many organizations have attempted to ameliorate the problems associated with downsizing by providing outplacement

services for their employees. The outplacement services can range from simply providing a place for employees to seek out employment opportunities
(long distance phone calling to employers, copying resumes, etc.) to more full
blown services to impart job search skills, outplacement counseling, and
retraining opportunities to aid in the reemployment effort.

Tang and Crofford (1999) report on a case study of the closing of a General Electric compressor facility. The outplacement service included two
weeks' pay for each year of tenure, one year of medical benefits, preferential
hiring at other GE facilities, employee assistance through an outplacement
center, and up to $5000 for retraining. Survey results of one section of the
facility found that 45% of the employees intended to fully utilize the education and retraining benefits while 67% stated they would use the outplacement center. The researchers also cite two Goodyear Tire and Rubber
Company plants where the company invested $300,000 in outplacement
counseling. Analyses revealed a return on this investment as the company
saved $4300 in supplemental unemployment benefits for each of the 1200
hourly workers who found employment within twenty-four weeks of termination. This amounted to estimated savings of $4 million.

Since 1982, the Institute for Social Research at the University of Michigan has conducted a program of research on the problems facing the unemployed and their families. In addition, the Institute has developed, implemented, and evaluated an intervention process called the JOBS program. The
goals of the JOBS program are to promote reemployment and enhance coping skills. The JOBS program consists of five half-day sessions held over a
one- to two-week period. The sessions focus on "effective job search strategies, improving participant job search skills and increasing the self-esteem,
confidence, and motivation of participants to engage in and persist in job
search activities until they become reemployed" (Price, Friedland, Choi, &
Caplan, 1998, pp. 202). The results of rigorous evaluation studies are quite
encouraging. The positive impact of the JOBS program has been documented
and replicated in randomized experimental trials that show the program
returns the unemployed to new jobs quickly and at a high rate of pay
(Vinokur, van Ryn, Gramlich, & Price, 1991), while at the same time reducing stress and mental health problems (Vinokur, Schul, Vuori, & Price, 2000).
In addition, Vinokur and Schul (1999) found that the JOBS program can help
minimize the adverse effects of a subsequent job loss. The researchers attribute much of the program's success to the fact that individuals in the JOBS
program gain an enhanced sense of control or mastery over the job search
process rather than feeling they have no control (van Ryn & Vinokur, 1992;
Vinokur & Schul, 1999). The success of the JOBS program has led to collaborative efforts in countries as diverse as Finland, Israel, and China (Price et
al., 1998). The diffusion of this innovation requires the involvement of multi-

ple stakeholder groups in each country in the design, implementation, and evaluation of these efforts.

CONCLUSIONS

This chapter has focused on training from a broader systems perspective. From this perspective, training programs can be viewed as being nested within a larger training system that includes a variety of training programs, methods, instructors, and evaluation strategies. Similarly, this system of training programs is embedded within a larger organizational system. The larger organizational system conveys information regarding the importance of training and continuous learning through strategic decisions about resource allocation, the reward and promotion system within the organization, and through the way policies, procedures, and learning approaches are implemented on a day-to-day basis in the workplace.

The chapter has also emphasized the need to move beyond the focus on enhancing individual effectiveness in a job to include effectiveness across organizational and societal levels of analysis. The increasing scope and complexity of changes occurring in the workplace, such as team-based work systems, the focus on quality, and flexible manufacturing systems, places a premium on a highly skilled workforce. Progressive organizations have devoted considerable resources to training workers to be better prepared to deal with the changing realities of the workplace. From this larger systems perspective, training cannot be viewed as an isolated accessory to organizational life but as an integral part of enhancing team and organizational effectiveness.

This chapter has also focused on the problems of the knowledge and skill gap within our society. The supply of highly skilled and talented individuals has not been able to keep up with the demands of the expanding and globally competitive job market. There is clearly a role for training and learning approaches for enhancing the likelihood that youths can be gainfully employed, that employees are treated fairly, and that displaced workers find new employment. The government, educational systems, and private sector have all been involved in this effort.

For people involved in training research and practice, the movement to viewing training within a larger learning system presents both a great opportunity and a great challenge. Although it is clear that there is a growing knowledge base, many issues still remain unresolved. The demands of society, work organizations, and the emerging number of researchers and practitioners interested in training and learning systems makes for exciting possibilities. We hope that this book stimulates efforts for improving our understanding of learning and the factors that impact training effectiveness.

INFOTRAC COLLEGE EDITION

For additional readings, go to http: www.infotrac-college.com/wadsworth and enter a search term related to your interest. The following key terms will pull up several related articles.

Corporate Universities   Retraining
Glass Ceiling   Total Quality Management
Knowledge Management   Workforce Readiness
Learning Organization

REFERENCES

Abate, C. W., Bahr, H. A., & Brabbs, J. M. (1998, July/August). Embedded simulation for the Army after next. *Armor,* Fort Knox, KY.

Adams, J. S. (1965). Injustice in social exchange. In L. Berkowitz (Ed.), *Advances in experimental social psychology,* vol. 2. New York: Academic Press.

Albert, R. (1983). The intercultural sensitizer or cultural assimilator: A cognitive approach. In D. Landis & R. Brislin (Eds.), *Handbook of intercultural training,* vol. 2, New York: Pergammon Press.

Alden, J., & Kirkhorn, J. (1996). Case studies. In R. L. Craig (Ed.), *The ASTD Training and Development Handbook* (4th ed.). New York: McGraw-Hill.

Alderfer, C. (1992). Changing race relations embedded in organization: Report on a long-term project with the XYZ corporation. In S. E. Jackson (Ed.), *Diversity in the work-place: Human resource initiatives.* New York: Guilford Press.

Aleven, V., & Ashley, K. D. (1997). Teaching case-based argumentation through a model and examples: Empirical evaluation of an intelligent learning environment. In B. duBoulay & R. Mizoguchi (Eds.), *Artificial intelligence in education.* Burke, VA: IOS Press.

Alliger, G. M., & Janek, E. A. (1989). Kirkpatrick's levels of training criteria: Thirty years later. *Personnel Psychology, 42,* 331–342.

Alliger, G. M., Tannenbaum, S. I., Bennett, W., Traver, H., & Shotland, A. (1997). A meta analysis of the relations among training criteria. *Personnel Psychology, 50,* 341–358.

American Red Cross. (1999). *Building leadership skills through a board game–based sim-ulation to create shared mental models of the organization's critical systems.* Alexan-dria, VA: American Red Cross Disaster Services.

American Society of Training and Development National HRD Executive Survey. (1998). *Information technology training: 1998 second quarter survey report.* Available: www.astd.org/virtual_community/research/nhrd_executive_survey_1998it.html.

Anderson, J. R. (1987). Skill acquisition: Compilation of weak-method problem solutions. *Psychological Review, 94,* 192–210.

Anderson, J. R. (1990). Analysis of student performance with the LISP tutor. In N. Fredericksen, R. Glaser, A. Lesgold, & M. G. Shafton (Eds.), *Diagnostic monitoring of skill and knowledge acquisition.* Hillsdale, NJ: Erlbaum.

Anderson, J. R. (1996). ACT: A simple theory of complex cognition. *American Psychologist, 51,* 355–365.

Annett, J. (1991). Skill acquisition. In J. E. Morrison (Ed.), *Training for performance: Principles of applied human learning.* New York: Wiley.

Apprentice Aerospace Ground Equipment Mechanic, Plan of Instruction, Chanute Technical Training Center (POI C3A BR42335 000), 1987.

Arcand, J., & Trevail, R. (1995). Analysis of the potential for applying performance support systems to the trucking industry. Laval, Quebec, Canada: Center for Information Technology Innovation.

Argyris, C. (1980). Some limitations of the case method: Experiences in a management development program. *Academy of Management Review, 5,* 291–298.

Argyris, C. (1999). *On organizational learning* (2nd ed.). Malden, MA: Blackwell.

Argyris, C., & Schoen, D. A. (1996). *Organizational learning.* Reading, MA: Addison-Wesley.

Arvey, R. D., Azevedo, R. E., Ostgaard, D. J., & Raghuram, S. (1997). The implications of a diverse labor market on human resource planning. In E. Kossek & S. Lobel (Eds.), *Managing diversity: Human resource strategies for transforming the workplace.* Cambridge, MA: Blackwell.

Arvey, R. D., & Cole, D. A. (1989). Evaluating change due to training. In I. L. Goldstein (Ed.), *Training and development in organizations.* San Francisco: Jossey-Bass.

Ashe, C., & Buell, D. (1998). Telecommunications and effective distance learning telecourse design. *Performance Improvement Quarterly, 11*(3), 6–15.

Atwater, L., Rousch, P., & Fischthal, A. (1995). The influence of upward feedback on self and follower ratings of leadership. *Personnel Psychology, 48,* 34–59.

Auspos, P., Cave, G., Doolittle, F., & Hoerz, G. (1989). *Implementing Job-Start: A demonstration for school dropouts in the JTPA system.* New York: MDRC.

Austin, J. T., & Villanova, P. (1992). The criterion problem: 1917–1992. *Journal of Applied Psychology, 77,* 836–874.

Baldwin, T. P. (1992). Effects of alternative modeling strategies on outcomes of interpersonal skills training. *Personnel Psychology, 77,* 147–154.

Baldwin, T. P. (1997). On-the-job training. In L. Peters, C. Greer, & S. Youngblood (Eds.), *The Blackwell encyclopedic dictionary of human resource management.* Malden, MA: Blackwell.

Baldwin, T. P. (1997). Role playing. In L. Peters, C. Greer, & S. Youngblood (Eds.), *The Blackwell encyclopedic dictionary of human resource management.* Malden, MA: Blackwell.

Baldwin, T. P., Danielson, C., & Wiggenhorn, W. (1997). The evolution of learning strategies in organizations: From employee development to business redefinition. *Academy of Management Executive, 11,* 47–58.

Baldwin, T. P., & Ford, J. K. (1988). Transfer of training: A review and directions for future research. *Personnel Psychology, 41,* 63–105.

Baldwin, T. P., & Magjuka, R. J. (1997). Organizational context and training effectiveness. In J. K. Ford & Associates (Eds.), *Improving training effectiveness in work organizations.* Mahwah, NJ: LEA.

Baldwin, T. P., Magjuka, R. J., & Loher, B. T. (1991). The perils of participation: Effects of choice of training on trainee motivation and learning. *Personnel Psychology, 44,* 51–65.

Bandura, A. (1977). *Social learning theory.* Englewood Cliffs, NJ: Prentice Hall.

Bandura, A. (1986). *Social foundations of thought and action: A social cognitive theory.* Englewood Cliffs, NJ: Prentice Hall.

Bandura, A. (1991). Social cognitive theory of self-regulation. *Organizational Behavior and Human Decision Processes, 50,* 248–287.

Banker, R. D, Field, J. M., Schroeder, R. G., & Sinha, K. K. (1996). Impact of work teams on manufacturing performance: A longitudinal field study. *Academy of Management Journal, 39,* 867–890.

Barbazette, J. (1999). Employee orientation. In D. G. Landon, K. S. Whiteside, & M. M. McKenna (Eds.), *Intervention resource guide: 50 performance improvement tools.* San Francisco: Jossey-Bass.

Bartlett, C. J. (1978). Equal employment opportunity issues in training. *Human Factors, 20,* 179–188.

Bartlett, C. J. (1982). *Teaching scale developed for Division of Behavioral and Social Sciences.* College Park, MD: University of Maryland.

Bass, B. M., & Vaughan, J. A. (1966). *Training in industry: The management of learning.* Belmont, CA: Wadsworth.

Bassi, L. J., Cheney, S., & Van Buren, M. E. (1997). Training industry trends. Available: http://www.astd.org/virtual_comm_trends/training_trends_td1197.htm.

Bassi, L. J., & Van Buren, M. E. (1998). The 1998 ASTD State of the Industry Report. *Training and Development, 52,* 21–43.

Bassi, L. J., & Van Buren, M. E. (1999). Sharpening the leading edge. *Training and Development, 53*(1), 23–33.

Becker, S. W. (1970). The parable of the pill. *Administrative Science Quarterly, 15,* 94–96.

Bennett, H. L. (1983). Remembering drink orders: The memory skills of cocktail waitresses. *Human Learning: Journal of Practical Research and Applications, 2,* 157–169.

Bennis, W. (1969). *Organization development: Its nature, origins, and prospects.* Reading, MA: Addison-Wesley.

Benyon, D., & Murray, D. (1993). Adaptive systems: From intelligent tutoring to autonomous agents. *Knowledge-Based Systems, 6,* 197–219.

Betsey, C., Hollister, Jr., R. G., & Papageorgiou, M. R. (Eds.). *Youth Employment and Training Programs: The YEDPA Years.* Washington, DC: National Research Council.

Bhawuk, D. P. S., & Brislin, R. W. (2000). Cross-cultural training: A review. *Applied Psychology: An International Review, 49,* 162–191.

Bianchini, E., & Sipla, R. (1998). Motorola Web empowers its organization. *Enterprise Systems Journal, 13*(10), 58–61.

Bina, M., & Newkirk, J. (1999). Competencies at the Rock: Creating a competency-based integrated human resources system for Prudential-HealthCare Group—Western Operations. In D. DuBois (Ed.), *The competency case book.* Amherst, MA: HRD Press.

Binner, P., Welsh, K., Barone, N., Summers, M., & Dean, R. (1997). The impact of remote-site group size on student satisfaction and relative performance in interactive telecourses. *American Journal of Distance Education, 11*(1), 23–33.

Bjork, R. A. (1995). Personal communication.

Black, J. S., & Mendenhall, M. (1990). Cross-cultural training effectiveness: A review and theoretical framework for future research. *Academy of Management Review, 15,* 113–136.

Blickensderfer, E., Cannon-Bowers, J. A., & Salas, E. (1998). Cross-training and team performance. In J. A. Cannon-Bowers & E. Salas (Eds.), *Making decisions under stress: Implications for individual and team training.* Washington, DC: APA.

Bloom, C., Linton, F., & Bell, B. (1997). Using evaluation in the design of an intelligent tutoring system. *Journal of Interactive Learning Research, 8,* 235–276.

Blum, M. L., & Naylor, J. C. (1968). *Industrial psychology: Its theoretical and social foundations.* New York: Harper & Row.

Borich, G. D. (1989). *Air Force instructor evaluation enhancement: Effective teaching behaviors and assessment procedures* (AFHRL-TP-88-55). Brooks AFB, TX: Training Systems Division.

Borman, W., & Bracken, D. W. (1997). 360 degree appraisals. In L. Peters, C. Greer, & S. Youngblood (Eds.), *The Blackwell encyclopedic dictionary of human resource management.* Malden, MA: Blackwell.

Boudreau, J. W. (1984). Decision theory contributions to HRM theory and practice. *Industrial Relations, 13,* 198–217.

Braddock, D. (1999). Occupational employment projections to 2008. *Monthly Labor Review, 132,* (11), 51–77.

Brinkerhoff, R. O., & Montesino, M. U. (1995). Partnership for training transfer: Lessons from a corporate study. *Human Resource Development Quarterly, 6,* 263–274.

Brislin, R. W., Cushner, K., Cherrie, C., & Yong, M. (1986). *Intercultural interaction: A practical guide.* Beverly Hills, CA: Sage.

Brittain, J., & Sitkin, S. (1989). Facts, figures, and organizational decisions: Carter racing and quantitative analysis in the organizational behavior classroom. *Organizational Behavior Teaching Review, 14,* 62–81.

Brockner, J., & Lee, R. J. (1995). Career development in downsizing organizations: A self-affirmation analysis. In M. London (Ed.), *Employees, careers, and job creation: Developing growth-oriented human resource strategies and programs.* San Francisco: Jossey-Bass.

Brown, A. L., & Palincsar, A. M. (1984). Reciprocal teaching of comprehension-fostering and monitoring activities. *Cognition and Instruction, 1,* 175–177.

Brown, A. L., & Palincsar, A. M. (1989). Guided, cooperative learning and individual knowledge acquisition. In L. B. Resnick (Ed.), *Knowing and learning: Essays in honor of Robert Glaser.* Hillsdale, NJ: Erlbaum.

Brown, K. G. (2000, April). *Learner choices in learner-controlled training: The influence of goal orientation and learning self-efficacy in web-based training.* Presented at the Society of Industrial and Organizational Psychology Conference, New Orleans.

Brown, K. G., & Ford, J. K. (1998). *Evaluation of a web-based training program.* Technical Report for the National Center for Manufacturing Sciences, Ann Arbor, MI.

Brown, K. G., Milner, K., & Ford, J. K. (1998). *The design of asynchronous distance learning courses.* Technical Report for the National Center for Manufacturing Sciences, Ann Arbor, MI.

Brown, K. G., Werner, M. N., Johnson, L. A., & Dunne, J. T. (1999, April). *Formative evaluation in Industrial/Organization Psychology: Further attempts to broaden training evaluation.* Presented at a symposium on Training Evaluation: Advances and New Directions for Research and Practice. Society of Industrial and Organizational Psychology, Atlanta.

Bunker, K. A., & Cohen, S. L. (1977). The rigors of training evaluation: A discussion and field demonstration. *Personnel Psychology, 30*(4), 525–541.

Burke, L. A., & Baldwin, T. P. (1999). Workforce training transfer: A study of the effect of relapse prevention training and transfer climate. *Human Resource Management, 38,* 227–242.

Burke, M. J., & Day, R. R. (1986). A cumulative study of the effectiveness of managerial training. *Journal of Applied Psychology, 71,* 232–245.

Campbell, D. T., & Stanley, J. C. (1963). *Experimental and quasi-experimental designs for research.* Chicago: Rand McNally.

Campbell, J. P. (1971). Personnel training and development. *Annual Review of Psychology.* Palo Alto, CA: Annual Reviews.

Campbell, J. P. (1988). Training design for performance improvement. In J. P. Campbell & R. J. Campbell (Eds.), *Productivity in organizations.* San Francisco: Jossey-Bass.

Campbell, J. P. (1989). The agenda for training theory and research. In I. L. Goldstein (Ed.), *Training and development in organizations.* San Francisco: Jossey-Bass.

Campbell, J. P., Dunnette, M. D., Lawler, III, E. E., & Weick, Jr., K. E. (1970). *Managerial behavior, performance, and effectiveness.* New York: McGraw Hill.

Campbell, J. P., McCloy, R. A., Oppler, S. H., & Sager, C. E. (1993). A theory of performance. In N. Schmitt, W. C. Borman & Associates (Eds.). *Personnel selection.* San Francisco: Jossey-Bass.

Campion, M. A., & Campion, J. E. (1987). Evaluation of an interview skills training program in a natural field setting. *Personnel Psychology, 40,* 675–691.

Cannon-Bowers, J. A., Burns, J. J., Salas, E., & Pruitt, J. S. (1998). Advanced technology in scenario-based training. In J. Cannon-Bowers & E. Salas (Eds.), *Making decisions under stress.* Washington, DC: American Psychological Association.

Cannon-Bowers, J. A., Rhodenizer, L., Salas, E., & Bowers, C. (1998). A framework for understanding prepractice conditions and their impact on learning. *Personnel Psychology, 51,* 291–320.

Cannon-Bowers, J. A., Salas, E., Blickensderfer, E., & Bowers, C. A. (1998). The impact of cross-training and workload on team functioning: A replication and extension of initial findings. *Human Factors, 40,* 92–101.

Cannon-Bowers, J. A., Tannenbaum, S. I., Salas, E., & Volpe, C. E. (1995). Defining competencies and establishing team training requirements. In R. A. Guzzo & E. Salas (Eds.), *Team effectiveness and decision making in organizations.* San Francisco: Jossey-Bass.

Cantor, J. A. (1991). The auto industry's new model: Car companies and community colleges collaborate to provide high-technology training. *Vocational Education Journal, 66,* 26–29.

Carbonell, J. R. (1970). AI in CAI: An artificial intelligence approach to computer-assisted instruction. *IEEE Transactions on Man-Machine Systems, 11,* 190–202.

Cascio, W. F. (1989). Using utility analysis to assess training outcomes. In I. L. Goldstein (Ed.), *Training and development in organizations.* San Francisco: Jossey-Bass.

Cascio, W. F. (1994). *Public investments in training: Perspectives on macro-level structural issues and micro-level delivery systems.* Philadelphia, PA: National Center on the Educational Quality of the Workforce, University of Pennsylvania.

Cascio, W. F., & Zammuto, R. F. (1987). *Societal trends and staffing policies.* Denver: University of Colorado.

Catalyst. (1998). *Advancing women in business: The Catalyst guide.* San Francisco: Jossey-Bass.

Chandrasekaran, R. (1998). U.S. to train workers for tech jobs. *Washington Post,* January 12, A1, A7.

Chao, G. T. (1997). Unstructured training and development: The role of organizational socialization. In J. K. Ford & Associates (Eds.), *Improving training effectiveness in work organizations.* Mahwah, NJ: LEA.

Chao, G. T., O'Leary-Kelly, A. M., Wolf, S., Klein, H. J., & Gardner, P. D. (1994). Organizational socialization: Its content and consequences. *Journal of Applied Psychology, 79,* 730–746.

Chao, G. T., Walz, P. M., & Gardner, P. D. (1992). Formal and informal mentorships: A comparison on mentoring functions and contrast with non-mentored counterparts. *Personnel Psychology, 45,* 619–636.

Chea, T. (2000). Panel urges bigger pool for tech jobs. *Washington Post,* July 14, E1, E10.

Clement, R. W. (1982). Testing the hierarchy theory of training evaluation: An expanded role for trainee reactions. *Public Personnel Management Journal, 11,* 176–184.

Cochran, N. (1978). Grandma Moses and the corruption of data. *Evaluation Quarterly, 2,* 363–375.

Cohen, S. L. (1991). The challange of training in the nineties. *Training and Development, 45,* 30–35.

Collins, A. M., Adams, M. J., & Pew, R. W. (1978). Effectiveness of an interactive map display in tutoring geography. *Journal of Educational Psychology, 70,* 1–7.

Colquitt, J. A., LePine, J. A., Noe, R. A. (2000). Trainee attributes and attitudes revisited: A meta-analytic structural equation modeling analysis of research on training motivation. *Journal of Applied Psychology, 85,* 678–706.

Confessore, S. J., & Kops, W. J. (1998). Self-directed learning and the learning organization: Examining the connection between the individual and the learning environment. *Human Resource Development Quarterly, 9,* 365–375.

Cook, M. F. (1992). Orientation. In M. F. Cook (Ed.), *The AMA handbook for employee recruitment and retention.* New York: AMACOM.

Cook, T. D., & Campbell, D. T. (1976). The design and conduct of quasi-experiments and true experiments in field settings. In M. D. Dunnette (Ed.), *Handbook of industrial and organizational psychology.* Chicago: Rand McNally.

Cook, T. D., & Campbell, D. T. (1979). *Quasi-experimentation: Design and analysis issues for field settings.* Chicago: Rand McNally.

Cook, T. D., Campbell, D. T., & Peracchio, L. (1990). Quasi-experimentation. In M. D. Dunnette & L. M. Hough (Eds.). *Handbook of industrial and organizational psychology.* Palo Alto, CA: Consulting Psychologists Press.

Couch, K. A. (1998). Late life displacement. *The Gerontologist, 38,* 7–17.

Cox, T. H. (1993). *Cultural diversity in organizations: Theory, research, and practice.* San Francisco: Berrett-Koehler.

Cox, T. H., & Blake, S. (1994). Managing cultural diversity: Implications for organizational competitiveness. In R. A. Noe, J. R. Hollenbeck, B. Gerhart, & P. M. Wright (Eds.), *Readings in human resource management.* Homewood, IL: Irwin.

Cranny, C. J., & Doherty, M. E. (1988). Importance ratings in job analysis: Notes on the misinterpretation of factor analysis. *Journal of Applied Psychology, 73,* 320–322.

Cronbach, L. J. (1957). The two disciplines of scientific psychology. *American Psychologist, 12,* 671–684.

Cronbach, L. J. (1967). How can instruction be adapted to individual differences? In R. M. Gagné (Ed.), *Learning and individual differences.* Columbus, OH: Charles E. Merrill.

Cronbach, L. J., & Snow, R. E. (1969). *Individual differences in learning ability as a function of instructional variables.* Final report, School of Education, Stanford University (Contract No. OEC-4-6061269-1217), U.S. Office of Education.

Crosby, P. (1988). *The eternally successful organization.* New York: McGraw-Hill.

Cullen, J. G., Sawzin, S. A., Sisson, G. R., & Swanson, R. A. (1978). Cost effectiveness: A model for assessing the training investment. *Training and Development Journal, 32,* 24–29.

Cutcher-Gershenfeld, J., & Ford, J. K. (1993). Worker training in Michigan: A framework for public policy. In T. Bynum & P. Grummon (Eds.), *Policy choices.* E. Lansing, MI: Michigan State University Press.

Dalton, M. A. (1998). Developing leaders for global roles. In C. D. McCauley, R. Moxley, & E. Van Velsor (Eds.), *The center for creative leadership handbook of leadership development.* San Francisco: Jossey-Bass.

Dean, P. J. (1998). Editorial—Leading the future of health care through distance learning technology and integrated performance curriculum. *Performance Improvement Quarterly, 11*(3), 3–5.

DeCecco, J. P. (1968). *The psychology of learning and instruction: Educational psychology.* Englewood Cliffs, NJ: Prentice Hall.

Decker, P. J., & Nathan, B. R. (1985). *Behavioral modeling training: Principles and applications.* New York: Praeger.

De Merode, J. (1997). An annotated review prepared for the Global Leadership Development Research Project. Greensboro, NC: Center for Creative Leadership.

Dennis, K. A., & Harris, D. (1998). Computer-based simulation as an adjunct to ab initio flight training. *International Journal of Aviation Psychology, 8,* 261–276.

Detweiler, M. C., & Lundy, D. H. (1995). Effects of single- and dual-task practice on acquiring dual-task skill. *Human Factors, 37,* 193–211.

Dipboye, R. L. (1996). Organizational barriers to implementing a rational model of training. In M. A. Quiñones & A. Ehrenstein (Eds.), *Training for a rapidly changing workplace.* Washington, DC: American Psychological Association.

Dorfman, P. W., Howell, J. P., Hibino, S., Less, J. K., Tate, U., & Bautista, A. (1997). Leadership in Western and Asian countries: Commonalities and differences in effective leadership processes across cultures. *Leadership Quarterly, 8,* 233–274.

Douglas, C. A., & McCauley, C. D. (1997). A survey on the use of formal developmental relationships in organizations. *Issues & Observations, 17,* 6.

Driskell, J. E., Willis, R. P., & Cooper, C. (1992). Effect of overlearning on retention. *Journal of Applied Psychology, 77,* 615–622.

Drucker, P. F. (1995). The age of social transformation. *Atlantic Monthly, 274*(5), 53–80.

Druckman, D., & Bjork, R. A. (1994). *Learning, remembering, and believing.* Washington, DC: National Academy Press.

DuBois, D. A., Shalin, V. L., Levi, K. R., & Borman, W. C. (1998). A cognitively-oriented approach to task analysis. *Training Research Journal, 3,* 103–142.

DuBois, D. D. (1999). Competency modeling. In D. G. Landon, K. S. Whiteside, & M. M. McKenna (Eds.), *Intervention resource guide: 50 performance improvement tools:* San Francisco: Jossey-Bass.

Duke, A. P., & Ree, M. J. (1996). Better candidates fly fewer training hours: Another time testing pays off. *Journal of Selection and Assessment, 4,* 115–121.

Eden, D. (1990). *Pygmalion in management.* Lexington, MA: Lexington Books.

Eden, D., & Aviram, A. (1993). Self-efficacy training to speed reemployment: Helping people to help themselves. *Journal of Applied Psychology, 78,* 353–360.

Eden, D., & Ravid, G. (1982). Pygmalion versus self-expectancy: Effects of instructor and self-expectancy on trainee performance. *Organizational Behavior and Human Performance, 30,* 351–364.

Eden, D., & Shani, A. B. (1982). Pygmalion goes to boot camp: Expectancy leadership and trainee performance. *Journal of Applied Psychology, 67,* 194–199.

Edgerton, H. A. (1958). *The relationship of method of instruction to trainee aptitude pattern.* (Technical Report, Contract Nornr 1042 [00]). New York: Richardson, Bellows, Henry, & Co.

Ellis, J. A., & Wulfeck, W. H. (1978). *The instructional quality inventory: IV: Job performance aid.* In NPRDC SR 79-5, Navy Personnel Research and Development Center.

Engelbracht, A. S., & Fischer, A. H. (1995). The managerial performance implications of a developmental assessment center process. *Human Relations, 48,* 1–18.

Faria, A. J. (1989). Business gaming: Current usage levels. *Journal of Management Development, 8,* 59–65.

Feldman, D. (1989). Socialization, resocialization, and training: Reframing the research agenda. In I. L. Goldstein (Ed.), *Training and development in organizations* (pp. 376–416). San Francisco: Jossey-Bass.

Feur, D. (1987). Domino's pizza: Training for fast times. *Training, 24,* 25–30.

Filipczak, B. (1996). Training on the intranets: The hope and the hype. *Training,* 24–32.

Fischer, R. J. (1994). The Americans with Disabilities Act: Implications for measurement. *Educational Measurement: Issues and Practice,* Fall, 17–37.

Fisher, C. D. (1997). Organizational socialization. In L. Peters, C. Greer, & S. Youngblood (Eds.), *The Blackwell encyclopedic dictionary of human resource management.* Malden, MA: Blackwell.

Fisk, A. D., & Schneider, W. (1981). Controlled and automatic processing during tasks requiring sustained attention: A new approach to vigilance. *Human Factors, 23,* 737–750.

Fister, S. (1999). Tech trends. *Training, 36*(8), 24–26.

Fleishman, E. A., Harris, E. F., & Burtt, H. E. (1955). Leadership and supervision in industry. *Bureau of Educational Research, Report No. 33.* The Ohio State University.

Fleishman, E. A., & Mumford, M. D. (1989). Individual attributes and training performance. In I. L. Goldstein (Ed.)., *Training and development in organizations.* San Francisco: Jossey-Bass.

Florkowski, G. W. (1997). Diversity within multinational firms. In E. Kossek & S. Lobel (Eds.), *Managing diversity.* Cambridge, MA: Blackwell.

Ford, J. K. (in press). Employee training. In A. E. Kazdin & Associates (Eds.), *Encyclopedia of psychology.* Washington, DC: APA Books.

Ford, J. K., & Fisher, S. (1994). The transfer of safety training in work organizations: A systems perspective to continuous learning. In M. Colligan (Ed.), *Occupational safety and health training, occupational medicine: State of the art reviews, 9,* 241–260.

Ford, J. K., & Fisher, S. (1997). The role of training in a changing workplace and workforce: New perspectives and approaches. In E. Kossek & S. Lobel (Eds.), *Managing diversity.* Cambridge, MA: Blackwell.

Ford, J. K., & Kraiger, K. (1995). The application of cognitive constructs and principles to the instructional systems model of training: Implications for needs assessment, design and transfer. In C. L. Cooper & I. T. Robertson (Eds.), *International review of industrial and organizational psychology.* Chichester, UK: John Wiley.

Ford, J. K., Major, D. A, Seaton, F. W., & Felber, H. K. (1993). Effects of organizational, training system, and individual characteristics on training director scanning practices. *Human Resources Development Quarterly, 4,* 333–365.

Ford, J. K., Quiñones, M. A., Sego, D. J., & Sorra, J. S. (1992). Factors affecting the opportunity to perform trained tasks on the job. *Personnel Psychology, 45,* 511–527.

Ford, J. K., & Schmidt, A. (2000). Emergency response training: Strategies for enhancing real-world performance. *Journal of Hazardous Material, 75,* 195–215.

Ford, J. K., Smith, E. M., Sego, D. J., & Quiñones, M. A. (1993). Impact of task experience and individual factors on training-emphasis ratings. *Journal of Applied Psychology, 78,* 583–590.

Ford, J. K., Smith, E. M., Weissbein, D., Gully, S., & Salas, E. (1998). Relationships of goal orientation, metacognitive activity, and practice strategies with learning outcomes and transfer. *Journal of Applied Psychology, 83,* 218–232.

Ford, J. K., & Wasson, D. (1997). Correspondence method. In L. Peters, C. Greer, & S. Youngblood (Eds.), *The Blackwell encyclopedic dictionary of human resource management.* Malden, MA: Blackwell.

Ford, J. K., & Weissbein, D. (1997). Transfer of training: An updated review and analysis. *Performance Improvement Quarterly, 10,* 2–41.

Ford, J. K., & Wroten, S. P. (1984). Introducing new methods for conducting training evaluation and for linking training evaluation to program redesign. *Personnel Psychology, 37,* 651–665.

Fowlkes, J., Dwyer, D. J., Oser, R. L., & Salas, E. (1998). Event-based approach to training (EBAT). *International Journal of Aviation Psychology, 8,* 209–222.

Frayne, C. A., & Latham, G. P. (1987). The application of social learning theory to employee self management of attendance. *Journal of Applied Psychology, 72,* 387–392.

French, W. L., & Bell, C. H. (1999). *Organizational development* (6th ed.). Englewood Cliffs, NJ: Prentice Hall.

Fripp, J. (1996). *Learning through simulations.* New York: McGraw-Hill.

Frisch, M. H. (1998). Designing the individual assessment process. In R. Jeanneret & R. Silzer (Eds.), *Individual psychological assessment.* San Francisco: Jossey-Bass.

Fullerton, H. N., Jr. (1999). Labor force projections to 2008: Steady growth and changing composition. *Monthly Labor Review, 132* (11), 19–32.

Fulmer, R. M., Gibbs, P., & Keys, J. B. (1998). The second generation learning organizations: New tools for sustaining competitive advantage. *Organizational Dynamics, 27,* 33–42.

Fulmer, R. M., & Vicere, A. (1996). *Strategic leadership development: Crafting competitiveness.* Oxford: Capstone.

Furchtgott-Roth, D., & Stolba, C. (1999). *Women's figures: An illustrated guide to the economic progress of women in America.* LaVergne, TN: AEI Press.

Gagné, R. M. (1995/1996). Learning processes and instruction. *Training Research Journal, 1,* 17–28.

Gagné, R. M., & Briggs, L. J. (1979). *Principles of instructional design.* New York: Holt, Rinehart, & Winston.

Gagné, R. M., Briggs, L. J., & Wager, W. W. (1992). *Principles of instructional design* (4th ed.). Forth Worth, TX: Harcourt Brace Jovanovich.

Gagné, R. M., & Dick, W. (1983). Instructional psychology. In *Annual review of psychology.* Palo Alto, CA: Annual Reviews.

Gail, J. E., & Hannafin, M. J. (1994). A framework for the study of hypertext. *Instructional Science, 22,* 207–232.

Gallagan, P. A. (1997). Go with the cash flow. *Training and Development, 51* (11), 19–23.

Galvin, K. (1999). Texaco to pay $3.1 million to settle sex discrimination suit. *The Legal Intelligencer,* Legal Communications, Ltd., January 7, 1999.

Galvin, R. W. (1997). Quality thinking. *Executive Excellence, 14(2),* 15–16.

Gardner, J. M. (1995). Worker displacement: A decade of change. *Monthly Labor Review, 127,* 14–23.

Gattiker, U. E. (1995). Firm and taxpayer returns from training of semiskilled employees. *Academy of Management Journal, 38,* 1152–1173.

Geber, B. (1990). Goodbye classrooms. *Training, 27,* January, 10–14.

Gery, G., & Jezsik, L. (1999). Electronic performance support systems. In D. G. Landon, K. S. Whiteside, & M. M. McKenna (Eds.), *Intervention resource guide: 50 performance improvement tools.* San Francisco: Jossey-Bass.

Gilbert, T. F. (1982). A question of performance—Part I—The probe model. *Training and Development Journal, 36,* 20–30.

Gilliam, R. (1988). *The effects of a job acquisition training program on the attitudes, behaviors, and knowledge of educated black adults.* Unpublished doctoral dissertation, University of Maryland, College Park.

Gist, M. E. (1989). The influence of training method on self-efficacy and idea generation among managers. *Personnel Psychology, 42,* 787–805.

Gist, M. E., Schwoerer, C., & Rosen, B. (1989). Effects of alternative training methods on self-efficacy and performance in computer software training. *Journal of Applied Psychology, 74,* 884–891.

Gist, M. E., Stevens, C. K., & Bavetta, A. G. (1991). Effects of self-efficacy and post-training intervention in the acquisition and maintenance of complex interpersonal skills. *Personnel Psychology, 44,* 837–861.

Gitomer, D. H. (1988). Individual differences in technical trouble shooting. *Human Performance, 1,* 111–131.

Glaser, E. M., & Taylor, S. H. (1973). Factors influencing the success of applied research. *American Psychologist, 28*(2), 140–460.

Glaser, R. (1990). The reemergence of learning theory within instructional research. *American Psychologist, 45,* 29–39.

Goettl, B. P., & Shute, V. J. (1996). Analysis of part-task training using the backward-transfer technique. *Journal of Experimental Psychology: Applied, 2,* 227–249.

Gold, S. C. (1998). The design of an ITS-based business simulation: A new epistemology for learning. *Simulation and Gaming, 29,* 462–474.

Goldstein, A. P., & Sorcher, M. (1974). *Changing supervisor behavior.* New York: Pergamon Press.

Goldstein, I. L. (1978). The pursuit of validity in the evaluation of training programs. *Human Factors, 20,* 131–144.

Goldstein, I. L. (1980). Training in work organizations. In *Annual review of psychology.* Palo Alto, CA: Annual Reviews.

Goldstein, I. L., & Bartlett, C. J. (1977). *Validation of a training program for police officers.* Unpublished data, College Park: University of Maryland.

Goldstein, I. L., Braverman, E. P., & Goldstein, H. W. (1991). Needs assessment. In K. Wexley (Ed.), *Developing human resources.* Washington, DC: BNA Books.

Goldstein, I. L., & Gilliam, P. (1990). Training system issues in the year 2000. *American Psychologist, 45,* 134–143.

Goldstein, I. L., & Goldstein, H. W. (1990). Training as an approach for organizations to the challenge of human resource issues in the year 2000. *Journal of Occupational Change Management, 3,* 30–43.

Goldstein, I. L., Macey, W. H., & Prien, E. P. (1981). Needs assessment approaches for training development. In H. Meltzer & W. R. Nord (Eds.), *Making organizations humane and productive.* New York: Wiley.

Goldstein, I. L., & Thayer, P. W. (1987, April). Panel discussion on facilitators and inhibitors of the training transfer process. Presented at Society for Industrial and Organizational Psychology, Atlanta.

Goldstein, I. L., Zedeck, S., & Schneider, B. (1993). An exploration of the job analysis-content validity process. In N. Schmitt & W. C. Borman (Eds.), *Personnel selection in organizations*. San Franciso: Jossey-Bass.

Golembiewski, R. T., & Carrigan, S. B. (1970). Planned change in organization style based on the laboratory approach. *Administrative Science Quarterly, 15,* 79–93.

Goodyear, P. (1995). Asynchronous peer interaction in distance education: The evolution of goals, practices, and technology. *Training Research Journal, 1,* 71–102.

Gordon, M. E., & Cohen, S. L. (1973). Training behavior as a predictor of trainability. *Personnel Psychology, 26,* 261–272.

Gott, S. P. (1995). *Tutoring for transfer of technical competence* (AL/HR-TP-1995-0002), Armstrong Laboratory, Brooks AFB, TX. Human Resources Directorate.

Greider, W. (1997). *One world, ready or not: The manic logic of global capitalism.* New York: Simon & Schuster.

Grey, J., Simpson, S., Kennedy, J., & Tou, S. (1998). Competency modeling at Motorola. In D. D. DuBois (Ed.), *The competency case book.* Amherst, MA: HRD Press, Inc.

Griffith, C. (1998). Building a resilient work force. *Training, 35,* 54–60.

Grove, D. A., & Ostroff, C. (1991). Program evaluation. In K. Wexley & J. Hinrichs (Eds.), *Developing human resources.* Washington, DC: BNA Books.

Guion, R. M. (1961). Criterion measurement and personnel judgments. *Personnel Psychology, 14,* 141–149.

Gunther-Mohr, C. (1997). Virtual reality training takes off. *Training and Development,* 47–48.

Haccoun, R. R. & Hamtriaux, T. (1994). Optimizing knowledge tests for inferring learning acquisition levels in single group training evaluation designs: The internal referencing strategy. *Personnel Psychology, 47,* 593–604.

Hall, E. M., Gott, S. P., & Pokony, R. A. (1995). *A procedural guide to cognitive task analysis: The PARI methodology.* Technical Report No. AL/HR-TR-1955-0108. Brooks AFB, TX: AFMC.

Hall, E. R., & Freda, J. S. (1982). *A comparison of individualized and conventional instruction in Navy technical training.* Technical Report No. 117. Orlando, FL: Training Analysis and Evaluation Group.

Hannafin, K. M., & Hannafin, M. J. (1995). The ecology of distance learning environments. *Training Research Journal, 1,* 49–69.

Hannafin, M. J., Hannafin, K. M., Hooper, S. R., Rieber, L. P., & Kini, A. S. (1996). Research on and research with emerging technologies. In D. H. Jonassen (Ed.), *Handbook of research for education communications and technology.* New York: Macmillan.

Hanson, L. S. (1999). Beyond school to work: Continuing contributions of theory and practice to career development of youth. *Career Development Quarterly, 47,* 353–358.

Hardy, L. (1999). Curriculum based on "school to work." *Education Digest, 64,* 8–14.

Harmon, S. W., & Kenney, P. J. (1994). Virtual reality training environments: Contexts and concerns. *Educational Media International, 31*(4), 228–237.

Hartel, C. E. (1994). Vantage 2000: Diversity mentoring, uplifting downsizing, techno-commuting, and other vantage points. *Industrial-Organizational Psychologist, 31*, 87–89.

Hawkridge, D. (1999). Distance learning: International comparisons. *Performance Improvement Quarterly, 12*(2), 9–20.

Heneman, R. L, Waldeck, N. E., & Cushnie, M. (1997). Diversity considerations in staffing decision-making. In E. Kossek & S. Lobel (Eds.), *Managing diversity.* Cambridge, MA: Blackwell.

Hicks, W. D., & Klimoski, R. J. (1987). Entry into training programs and its effects on training outcomes: A field experiment. *Academy of Management Journal, 30*, 542–552.

Hill, T., Smith, N. D., Mann, N. F. (1987). Toll of efficacy expectations in predicting the decision to use advanced technologies: The case of computers. *Journal of Applied Psychology, 72*, 307–313.

Hogan, P. H., Hakel, M. D., & Decker, P. J. (1986). Effects of trainee-generated versus trainer-provided rule codes on generalization in behavior modeling training. *Journal of Applied Psychology, 71*, 469–473.

Holding, D. H. (1965). *Principles of training.* London: Pergamon Press.

HOPE in Focus (2000, spring). CAT emerges as national technology research center. Focus: Hope: Detroit.

Hoppe, M. H. (1998). Cross-cultural issues in leadership development. In C. D. McCauley, R. Moxley, and E. Van Velsor (Eds.), *The center for creative leadership handbook of leadership development.* San Francisco: Jossey-Bass.

Howard, A. (1995). Rethinking the psychology of work. In A. Howard, (Ed.), *The changing nature of work.* San Francisco: Jossey-Bass.

Howell, W. C., & Cooke, N. J. (1989). Training the human information processor: A review of cognitive models. In I. L. Goldstein (Ed.), *Training in development and organizations.* San Francisco: Jossey-Bass.

Hsu, E. (1989). Role-event gaming simulation in management education. *Simulation and Games, 20*, 409–438.

Iles, P. A., & Robertson, I. T. (1997). The impact of personal selection procedures on candidates. In N. Anderson & P. Herriot (Eds.), *International handbook of selection and assessment.* Chichester, England: John Wiley.

Ilgen, D. R. (1999). Teams embedded in organizations. *American Psychologist, 54*, 129–138.

Ilgen, D. R., Fisher, C. D., & Taylor, M. S. (1979). Consequences of individual feedback on behavior in organizations. *Journal of Applied Psychology, 64*, 349–371.

Ilgen, D. R., & Klein, H. W. (1989). Individual motivation and performance: Cognitive influences on effort and choice. In J. P. Campbell & R. J. Campbell (Eds.), *Productivity in organizations.* San Francisco: Jossey-Bass.

Iverson, R. D., & Roy, P. (1994). A causal model of behavioral commitment: Evidence from a study of Australian blue-collar employees. *Journal of Management, 20,* 15–41.

Ives, W. (1990). Soft skills in high tech: Computerizing the development of interpersonal skills. *Information Delivery Systems,* March/April.

Jackson, S. E., Schuler, R. S., & Rivero, J. C. (1989). Organizational characteristics as predictors of personnel practices. *Personnel Psychology, 42,* 727–786.

Jacobs, R. L., Jones, M. J., & Neil, S. (1992). A case study in forecasting the financial benefits of unstructured and structured on-the-job training. *Human Resource Development Quarterly, 3,* 133–139.

Jentsch, F., & Bowers, C. A. (1998). Evidence for the validity of PC-based simulations in studying aircrew coordination. *International Journal of Aviation Psychology, 8,* 243–260.

Johnson, A., & Hartman, A. (1998). Adult education and literacy public policy: What it is and how it is shaped. In M. C. Smith (Ed.), *Literacy for the twenty-first century.* Westport, CT: Praeger.

Johnson, J. W., & Ferstl, K. L. (1999). The effects of interrater and self-other agreement on performance improvement following upward feedback. *Personnel Psychology, 52,* 271–304.

Johnston, R. (1995, June). The effectiveness of instructional technology: A review of the research. *Proceedings of the Virtual Reality in Medicine and Developers' Exposition.* Cambridge, MA: Virtual Reality Solutions, Inc.

Jones, R. G., & Whitmore, M. D. (1995). Evaluating developmental assessment centers as interventions. *Personnel Psychology, 48,* 377–388.

Kanfer, R. (1991). The role of motivation theory in industrial and organizational psychology. In M. D. Dunnette & L. M. Hough (Eds.), *Handbook of industrial and organizational psychology.* Palo Alto, CA: Consulting Psychologists Press.

Kanfer, R. & Ackerman, P. L. (1989). Motivation and cognitive abilities: An integrative/aptitude-treatment interaction approach to skill acquisition. *Journal of Applied Psychology, 74,* 657–690.

Kaplan, R. E., Lombardo, M. M., & Mazique, M. S. (1983). *A mirror for managers: Using simulation to develop management teams.* Technical Report No. 13. Greensboro, NC: Center for Creative Leadership.

Kapp, K. M. (1999). Transforming your manufacturing organization into a learning organization. *Hospital Material Management Quarterly, 20,* 46–54.

Katzenbach, J. R., & Smith, D. K. (1993). *The wisdom of teams: Creating the high-performance organization.* Boston: Harvard Business School Press.

Kavanagh, M. J., Gueutal, H. G., & Tannenbaum, S. I. (1990). *Human resource information systems: Application and development.* Boston: PWS-Kent.

Keegan, D. (1993). Theoretical principles of distance education. In O. Peters (Ed.), *Distance education in a postindustrial society.* New York: Routledge.

Kemp, T. (1998). Panacea or poison? Building self-esteem through adventure experiences. *Proceedings of the International Adventure Therapy Conference* (1st, Perth, Australia, July).

Kim, J. S. (1984). Effect of behavior versus outcome goal-setting and feedback on employee satisfaction and behavior. *Academy of Management Journal, 27,* 139–149.

King, P. H. (1966). *A summary of research in training for advisory roles in other cultures by the behavioral sciences laboratory* (AMRL-TR-66-131). Wright-Patterson AFB, OH: Aerospace Medical Research Laboratories.

Kirkpatrick, D. L. (1959, 1960). Techniques for evaluating training programs. *Journal of the American Society of Training Directors, 13,* 3–9, 21–26; *14,* 13–18, 28–32.

Kirkpatrick, D. L. (1994). *Evaluating training programs: The four levels.* San Francisco: Berrett-Koehler.

Kirsch, I. S., Jungeblut, A., Jenkins, L., & Kolstad, A. (1993). *Adult literacy in America: A first look at the results of the National Adult Literacy Survey.* Washington, DC: National Center for Education Statistics.

Klein, H. J., & Weaver, N. A. (2000). The effectiveness of an organizational-level orientation training program in the socialization of new hires. *Personnel Psychology, 53,* 47–66.

Klein, K. J., & Hall, R. J. (1988). Innovations in human resource management: Strategies for the future. In J. Hage (Ed.), *Future of organizations.* Lexington, MA: Lexington.

Klimoski, R. (1997). Assessment centers. In L. Peters, C. Greer, & S. Youngblood (Eds.), *The Blackwell encyclopedic dictionary of human resource management.* Malden, MA: Blackwell.

Knowles, M. S. (1990). *The adult learner: A neglected species* (4th ed.). Houston: Gulf Publishing.

Kochan, T., & Osterman, P. (1996). *Human resource development and training: Is there too little in the U.S.?* Prepared for the American Council on Competitiveness. Cambridge, MA: Harvard Business School Press.

Komaki, J., Heinzmann, A. T., & Lawson, L. (1980). Effect of training and feedback: Component analysis of a behavioral safety program. *Journal of Applied Psychology, 65,* 261–270.

Koonce, R. (1997). The Motorola story: An interview. *Training and Development, 51*(8), 26–27.

Kossek, E. E., Roberts, K., Fisher, S., & DeMarr, B. (1998). Career self-management: A quasi-experimental assessment of the effects of a training intervention. *Personnel Psychology, 51,* 935–962.

Kozlowski, S. W. J., Gully, S. M., Nason, E. R., & Smith, E. M. (1999). Developing adaptive teams: A theory of compilation and performance across levels and time. In D. R. Ilgen & E. D. Pulakos (Eds.), *The changing nature of work performance: Implications for staffing, personnel actions, and development.* San Francisco: Jossey-Bass.

Kozlowski, S. W. J., & Hults, B. M. (1987). An exploration of climates for technical updating and performance. *Personnel Psychology, 40,* 539–563.

Kraiger, K., Salas, E., & Cannon-Bowers, J. A. (1995). Measuring knowledge organization as a method of assessing learning during training. *Human Factors, 37,* 804–816.

Kraiger, K., Ford, J. K., & Salas, E. (1993). Application of cognitive, skill-based, and affective theories of learning outcomes to new methods of training evaluation. *Journal of Applied Psychology, 78,* 311–328.

Kram, K. E., & Hall, D. T. (1997). Mentoring in a context of diversity and turbulence. In E. Kossek & S. Lobel (Eds.), *Managing diversity.* Cambridge, MA: Blackwell.

Kramer, A. F., Larish, J. F., & Strayer, D. L. (1995). Training for attentional control in dual-task settings: A comparison of young and old adults. *Journal of Experimental Psychology: Applied, 1,* 50–76.

Kraut, A. I. (1975). Prediction of managerial success by peer and training-staff ratings. *Journal of Applied Psychology, 60,* 14–19.

Kraut, A. I. (1976). Developing managerial skills via modeling techniques: Some positive research findings—A symposium. *Personnel Psychology, 29,* 325–328.

Krendl, K. A., Hare, W. H., Reid, K. A., & Warren, R. (1996). Learning by any other name: Communication research traditions in learning and media. In D. H. Jonassen (Ed.), *Handbook of research for education communications and technology.* New York: Macmillan.

Krumboltz, J. D., & Worthington, R. L. (1999). The school-to-work transition from a learning theory perspective. *Career Development Quarterly, 47,* 312–325.

Kudish, J. D., Rotolo, C. T., Avis, J. M., Fallon, J. D., Roberts, F. E., Rollier, T. J., & Thibodeaux, H. F. III. (1998). *A preliminary look at assessment center practices worldwide: What's hot and what's not.* Paper presented at the 26th annual meeting of the International Congress on Assessment Center Methods, Pittsburgh, PA.

Kugath, S. D. (1997). The effects of family participation in an outdoor adventure program. *Proceedings of the International Conference on Outdoor Recreation.* ERRIC Documentation Reproduction Service (ED417050) (http://ericae.net/ericdb/ED417050.htm).

Kulik, J. A. (1994). Meta-analytic studies of findings on computer-based instruction. In E. L. Baker & H. F. O'Neil (Eds.), *Technology assessment in education and training.* Hillsdale, NJ: LEA.

Landy, F. J., & Vasey, J. (1991). Job analysis: The composition of SME samples. *Personnel Psychology, 44,* 27–50.

Latham, G. P., & Frayne, C. A. (1989). Self-management training for increased job attendance: A follow-up and replication. *Journal of Applied Psychology, 74,* 411–416.

Latham, G. P., & Saari, L. M. (1979). The application of social learning theory to training supervisors through behavioral modeling. *Journal of Applied Psychology, 64,* 239–246.

Latham, G. P., & Wexley, K. N. (1981). *Increasing productivity through performance appraisal.* Reading, MA: Addison-Wesley.

Ledvinka, J., & Scarpello, V. G. (1991). *Federal regulation of personnel and human resource management.* Boston: PWS-Kent.

Leenders, G., & Henderson, B. (1991). Dialogue of new directions: The spiritual heart of adventure learning. *Journal of Experiential Education, 14*(2), 32–38.

Leonhardt, D. (1997). Minneapolis shows the way. *Business Week,* September 1, 70.

Levine, M. (1974). Scientific method and the adversary model: Some preliminary thoughts. *American Psychologist, 29,* 661–667.

Linn, M. (1996). Cognition and distance learning. *Journal of the American Society for Information Science, 47*(11), 826–842.

Locke, E. A., & Latham, G. P. (1990). *A theory of goal setting and task performance.* Englewood Cliffs, NJ: Prentice Hall.

Locke, E. A., Shaw, K. N., Saari, L. M., & Latham, G. P. (1981). Goal setting and task performance. *Psychological Bulletin, 90,* 125–152.

Loftin, R. B. (1996). Hands across the Atlantic. *Virtual Reality Special Report* (March/April), 39–42.

Loftin, R. B., & Kenney, P. J. (1999). The use of virtual environments for training the Hubble space telescope flight team. Available: http://www.vetl.uh.edu/Hubble/vir-tel.html.

London, M. (1989). *Managing the training enterprise.* San Francisco: Jossey-Bass.

London, M. (1991). Practice in training and development. In D. W. Bray (Ed.), *Working with organizations.* New York: Guilford.

Lorge, I. (1930). *Influence of regularly interpolated time intervals upon subsequent learning.* Teachers College Contributions to Education, No. 438. New York: Teachers College Press, Columbia University.

Lowman, R. L. (1991). Ethical human resource practice in organizational settings. In D. W. Bray (Ed.), *Working with organizations.* New York: Guilford.

Luthans, F., & Kreitner, R. (1985). *Organizational behavior modification and beyond.* Glenview, IL: Scott, Foresman.

Luthans, F., Paul, R., & Baker, D. (1981). An experimental analysis of the impact of contingent reinforcement on salespersons' performance behavior. *Journal of Applied Psychology, 66,* 314–323.

Lyness, K. S., & Thompson, D. E. (1997). Above the glass ceiling? A comparison of matched samples of female and male executives. *Journal of Applied Psychology, 82,* 359–375.

Mabe, P. A. III, & West, S. G. (1982). Validity of self-evaluation of ability: A review and meta-analysis. *Journal of Applied Psychology, 67,* 280–296.

Mager, R. F. (1975). *Preparing instructional objectives.* Belmont, CA: Fearon Publishers.

Mager, R. F. (1984). *Preparing instructional objectives* (2nd ed.). Belmont, CA: Pitman Learning.

Maier, N. R. F., & Zerfoss, L. R. (1952). MRP: A technique for training large groups of supervisors and its potential use in social research. *Human Relations, 5,* 177–186.

Marquardt, M. J. (1999). *Action learning in action.* Palo Alto, CA: Davies-Black.

Martin, J. (1996). *Cybercorp: The new business revolution.* New York: AMACOM.

Martocchio, J. J. (1992). Microcomputer usage as an opportunity. The influence of context in employee training. *Personnel Psychology, 45,* 529–552.

Marx, R. D. (in press). Transfer is personal: Equipping trainees with self-management and relapse prevention strategies. *Advances in Developing Human Resources*.

Marx, R. D. (1982). Relapse prevention for managerial training: A model for maintenance of behavior change. *Academy of Management Review, 7,* 433–441.

Marx, R. D., & Hamilton, E. E. (1991). Beyond skill building: A multiple perspective view of personnel training. *Issues and Trends in Business Economics, 7,* 24–32.

Mathieu, J., & Martineau, J. W. (1997). Individual and situational influences in training motivation. In J. K. Ford & Associates (Eds.), *Improving training effectiveness in work organizations.* Mahwah, NJ: LEA.

Mathieu, J. E., & Leonard, R. L., Jr. (1987). Applying utility concepts to a training program in supervisory skills: A time-based approach. *Academy of Management Journal, 30,* 316–335.

Mathieu, J. E., Tannenbaum, S. I., & Salas, E. (1992). Influences of individual and situational characteristics on measures of training effectiveness. *Academy of Management Journal, 35,* 828–847.

May, G. L., & Kahnweiler, W. M. (2000). The effect of mastery practice design on learning and transfer in behavior modeling training. *Personnel Psychology, 53,* 353–374.

Mayer, R. E. (1975). Different problem-solving competencies established in learning computer programming with and without meaningful models. *Journal of Educational Psychology, 65,* 725–734.

Mayer, R. E. (1989). Models for understanding. *Review of Educational Research, 59,* 43–64.

Mayer, R. E., & Bromage, B. K. (1980). Differential recall protocols for technical texts due to advance organizers. *Journal of Educational Psychology, 72,* 209–225.

McCall, M. W., & Lombardo, M. M. (1982). Using simulation for leadership and management research: Through the looking glass. *Management Science, 28,* 533–549.

McCall, M. W., Lombardo, M. M., & Morrison, A. M. (1988). *The lessons of experience: How successful executives develop on the job.* Lexington, MA: Lexington Books.

McCauley, C. D. (1999, April). *The Job Challenge Profile: Participant Workbook.* San Francisco: Jossey-Bass.

McCauley, C. D., & Douglas, C. A. (1998). Developmental relationships. In C. D. McCauley, R. Moxley, and E. Van Velsor (Eds.), *The center for creative leadership handbook of leadership development.* San Francisco: Jossey-Bass.

McCauley, C. D., Ruderman, M. N., Ohlott, P. O., & Morrow, J. E. (1994). Assessing the developmental components of managerial jobs. *Journal of Applied Psychology, 79,* 544–560.

McEvoy, G. M., & Cascio, W. F. (1989). Cumulative evidence of the relationship between employee age and job performance. *Journal of Applied Psychology, 74,* 11–17.

McEnery, J., & McEnery, J. M. (1987). Self-rating in management training need assessment: A neglected opportunity. *Journal of Occupational Psychology, 60,* 49–60.

McGehee, W., & Thayer, P. W. (1961). *Training in business and industry.* New York: Wiley.

McIsaac, M. S. (1999). Distance learning: The U.S. version. *Performance Improvement Quarterly, 12*(2), 21–35.

McLarty, J. R., & Vansickle, T. R. (1997). Assessing employability skills: The WorkKeys system. In H. F. O'Neil (Ed.), *Workforce readiness: Competencies and assessment.* Mahwah, NJ: Lawrence Erlbaum.

Meister, J. C. (1994). *Corporate quality universities: Lessons in building a world-class work force.* New York: Irwin.

Melton, R. H., & Grimsley, K. D. (1998). Work climate warmer for women. *Washington Post,* March 23, A1, A8, A10.

Meyer, H. H., & Raich, M. W. (1983). An objective evaluation of a behavioral modeling training program. *Personnel Psychology, 36,* 755–762.

Michalak, D. F. (1981). The neglected half of training. *Training and Development Journal, 35,* 22–28.

Miner, J. B. (1963). Evidence regarding the value of a management course based on behavioral science subject matter. *Journal of Business of the University of Chicago, 36,* 325–335.

Mirabal, T. E. (1978). Forecasting future training costs. *Training Developmental Journal, 32*(7), 78–87.

Mirabile, R. J. (1997). Everything you want to know about competency modeling. *Training and Development, 74*(8), 73–77.

Miron, D., & McClelland, D. C. (1979). The impact of achievement motivation training on small businesses. *California Management Review, 21,* 13–28.

Mitchell, T. R. (1982). Motivation: New directions for theory, research, and practice. *Academy of Management Review, 7,* 80–88.

Morgan, R. B., & Casper, W. (2000). Examining the factor structure of participant reactions to training: A multi-dimensional approach. *Human Resources Development Quarterly, 11,* 301–317.

Morgan, R. M., & Hawkridge, D. G. (1999). Guest Editorial—Global distance learning. *Performance Improvement Quarterly, 12*(2), 6–8.

Morrison, A. M. (1992). *The new leaders: Guidelines on leadership diversity in America.* San Francisco: Jossey-Bass.

Morrow, C. C., Jarrett, M. Q., & Rupinski, M. T. (1997). An investigation of the effect and economic utility of corporate-wide training. *Personnel Psychology, 50,* 91–119.

Mumford, M. D., Weeks, J. L., Harding, F. D., & Fleishman, E. A. (1987). Measuring occupational difficulty: A construct validation against training criteria. *Journal of Applied Psychology, 72,* 578–587.

Murray, B., & Raffaele, G. C. (1997). Single-site, results-level evaluation of quality awareness training. *Human Resource Development Quarterly, 8,* 229–245.

Murray, M. (1999). Mentoring/coaching. In D. G. Landon, K. S. Whiteside, & M. M. McKenna (Eds.), *Intervention resource guide: 50 performance improvement tools.* San Francisco: Jossey-Bass.

Nash, A. N., Muczyk, J. P., & Vettori, F. L. (1971). The relative practical effectiveness of programmed instruction. *Personnel Psychology, 24,* 397–418.

Nash, B. E., & Korte, R. C. (1997). Validation of SCANS competencies by a national job analysis study (pp. 77–102) . In H. F. O'Neil (Ed.), *Workforce readiness: Competencies and assessment.* Mahwah, NJ: Lawrence Erlbaum.

National Center on the Educational Quality of the Workplace. (1995). *Education in the Workforce.* Philadelphia, PA: University of Pennsylvania.

Naylor, J. C. (1962, February). *Parameters affecting the relative efficiency of part and whole practice methods: A review of the literature* (Technical Report No. 950-1). United States Naval Training Devices Center.

Naylor, J. C., Pritchard, R. D., & Ilgen, D. R. (1980). *A theory of behavior in organizations.* Orlando, FL: Academic.

Nester, O. W. (1971). *Training the hard core: One experience.* Pittsburgh Technical Institute Report. Undated. Review of work also appearing in *Training and Development Journal, 25,* 16–19.

Newman, D. (1985). *The pursuit of validity in training: An application.* Ph.D. dissertation, University of Maryland, College Park.

Noe, R. A. (1986). Trainee attributes and attitudes: Neglected influences on training effectiveness. *Academy of Management Review, 4,* 736–749.

Noe, R. A. (1988). An investigation of the determinants of successful assigned mentoring relationships. *Personnel Psychology, 41,* 457–479.

Noe, R. A. (1999). *Employee training and development.* New York: McGraw-Hill.

Noe, R. A., & Schmitt, N. (1986). The influence of trainee attitudes on training effectiveness: Test of a model. *Personnel Psychology, 39,* 497–523.

Noe, R. A., Wilk, S., Mullen, E., & Wanek, J. (1997). Employee development: Construct validation issues. In J. K. Ford & Associates (Eds.), *Improving training effectiveness in work organizations.* Mahwah, NJ: LEA.

Offerman, L. R., & Gowing, M. K. (1990). Organizations of the future: Changes and challenges. *American Psychologist, 45,* 95–108.

Office of Technology Assessment. (1990). *Worker training: Competing in the new international economy.* Report No. OTA-ITE-457. Washington, DC: U.S. Government Printing Office.

O'Leary, V. E. (1972). The Hawthorne effect in reverse: Effects of training and practice on individual and group performance. *Journal of Applied Psychology, 56,* 491–494.

Olson, C. A. (1994, December). *Who receives formal firm-sponsored training in the U.S.?* Madison, WI: National Center for the Workplace, University of Wisconsin.

Orasanu, J., & Salas, E. (1993). Team decision making in complex environments. In G. Klein, J. M. Orasanu, & R. Calderwood (Eds.), *Decision making in action: Models and methods.* Norwood, NJ: Ablex.

Orey, M. (1993, April). *Three years of intelligent tutoring evaluation: A summary of findings.* Paper presented at the annual meeting of the American Educational Research Association, Atlanta.

Osterman, P. (1995). Skill, training, and work organization in American establishments. *Industrial Relations, 34,* 125–146.

Ostroff, C. (1991). Training effectiveness measures and scoring schemes. *Personnel Psychology, 44,* 353–374.

Ostroff, C., & Ford, J. K. (1989). Assessing training needs: Critical levels of analysis. In I. L. Goldstein (Ed.), *Training and development in organizations.* San Francisco: Jossey-Bass.

Ostroff, C., & Kozlowski, S. W. J. (1993). The role of mentoring in the information-gathering processes of newcomers during early organizational socialization. *Journal of Vocational Behavior, 42,* 170–183.

Overmyer-Day, L., & Benson, G. (1996). Training success stories. *Training and Development, 50* (6), 24–29.

Panell, R. C., & Laabs, G. J. (1979). Construction of a criterion-referenced, diagnostic test for an individual instruction program. *Journal of Applied Psychology, 64,* 255–261.

Papalia, D. E., Camp, C. J., & Feldman, R. (1996). *Adult development and aging.* New York: McGraw-Hill.

Pedalino, E., & Gamboa, V. U. (1974). Behavior modification and absenteeism: Intervention in one industrial setting. *Journal of Applied Psychology, 59,* 694–698.

Pfister, G. (1975). Outcomes of laboratory training for police officers. *Journal of Social Issues, 31,* 115–121.

Phillips, D. (1991). Terror at zero feet: A crew's simulated brush with disaster. *Washington Post,* January 1, A3.

Pinto, P. R., & Walker, J. W. (1978). What do training and development professionals really do? *Training and Development Journal, 28,* 58–64.

Pool, S. L., Heriges, S. W., Crase, J. K., & Blackburn, M. S. (1992, March). *Individualized feedback versus group training: Effects on performance, learning, and transfer.* Southeastern Psychological Association Annual Meeting, Knoxville, TN.

Price, R. H., Friedland, D. S., Choi, J. N., & Caplan, R. D. (1998). Job-loss and work transitions in a time of global economic change. In X. B. Arriaga & S. Oskamp (Eds.), *Addressing community problems: Research and intervention.* Thousand Oaks, CA: Sage.

Prien, E. P. (1977). The function of job analysis in content validation. *Personnel Psychology, 30,* 167–174.

Prien, E. P., Goldstein, I. L., & Macey, W. H. (1985). *Multi-method job analysis: Methodology and applications.* Unpublished paper.

Prien, E. P., Goldstein, I. L., & Macey, W. H. (1987). Multidomain job analysis: Procedures and applications in human resource management and development. *Training and Development Journal, 41,* 68–72.

Pritchard, R. D. (1969). Equity theory: A review and critique. *Organizational Behavior and Human Performance, 4,* 176–211.

Quiñones, M. A. (1997). Contextual influences on training effectiveness. In M. A. Quiñones & A. Ehrenstein (Eds.), *Training for a rapidly changing workplace.* Washington, DC: American Psychological Association.

Quiñones, M. A., & Ehrenstein, A. (1997). *Training for a rapidly changing workplace.* Washington, DC: American Psychological Association.

Quiñones, M. A., Ford, J. K., Sego, D. J., & Smith, E. (1996). The effects of individual and transfer environment characteristics on the opportunity to perform trained tasks. *Training Research Journal, 1,* 29–48.

Ralphs, L. T., & Stephen, E. (1986). HRD in the Fortune 500. *Training and Development Journal, 40,* 69–76.

Raser, J. R. (1969). *Simulation and society: An exploration of scientific gaming.* Boston: Allyn & Bacon.

Raybould, B. (1996). Performance support engineering: An emerging development methodology for enabling organizational learning. *Performance Improvement Quarterly, 8,* 7–22.

Raynor, J. O., & Rubin, I. S. (1971). Effects of achievement motivation and future orientation on level of performance. *Journal of Personality and Social Psychology, 17,* 36–41.

Ree, M. J., Carretta, T. R., & Teachout, M. S. (1995). Role of ability and prior job knowledge in complex training performance. *Journal of Applied Psychology, 80,* 721–730.

Reeves , T. C. (1992). Evaluating interactive multimedia. *Educational Technology, 32,* 47–53.

Reich, R. B. (1991). *The work of nations: Preparing ourselves for 21st century capitalism.* New York: Knopf.

Reilly, R. R., & Israelski, E. W. (1988). Development and validation of minicourses in the telecommunications industry. *Journal of Applied Psychology, 73,* 721–726.

Reilly, R. R., & Manese, W. R. (1979). The validation of a minicourse for telephone company switching technicians. *Personnel Psychology, 32,* 83–90.

Report of the National Advisory Commission on Civil Disorders. (1968). New York: Bantam Books.

Reyna, M., & Sims, R. R. (1995). ADA and its implications for job training. In J. G. Veres & R. R. Sims (Eds.), *Human resource management and the Americans with Disabilities Act.* Westport, CT: Quorum Books.

Rickel, J., & Johnson, W. L. (1999). Animated agents for procedural training in virtual reality: Perception, cognition, and motor control. *Applied Artificial Intelligence, 12,* 343–382.

Robertson, I. T., & Downs, S. (1989). Work sample tests of trainability: A meta-analysis. *Journal of Applied Psychology, 74,* 402–410.

Robinson, D. G., & Robinson, J. C. (1995). *Performance consulting: Moving beyond training.* San Francisco: Berrett-Koehler.

Rogers, W., Maurer, T., Salas, E., & Fisk, A. (1997). Task analysis and cognitive theory: Controlled and automatic processing task analytic methodology. In J. K. Ford & Associates (Eds.), *Improving training effectiveness in work organizations.* Mahwah, NJ: LEA.

Rogers, W. A., Fisk, A. D., Mead, S. E., Walker, N., & Cabrera, W. F. (1996). Training older adults to use automatic teller machines. *Human Factors, 38,* 425–431.

Ronen, S. (1989). Training the international assignee. In I. L. Goldstein (Ed.), *Training and development in organizations.* San Francisco: Jossey-Bass.

Rothwell, W. J. (1999). On-the-job training. In D. G. Landon, K. S. Whiteside, & M. M. McKenna (Eds.), *Intervention resource guide: 50 performance improvement tools.* San Francisco: Jossey-Bass.

Rothwell, W. J., & Kolb, J. A. (1999). Major workforce and workplace trends influencing the training and development field in the USA. *International Journal of Training and Development, 3,* 44–53.

Rotter, J. B. (1966). Generalized expectancies for internal vs. external locus of control of reinforcement. *Psychological Monographs, 80,* 1–69.

Rouillier, J. Z., & Goldstein, I. L. (1993). The relationship between organizational transfer climate and positive transfer of training. *Human Resource Development Quarterly, 4,* 377–390.

Rousseau, D. M. (1997). Organizational behavior in the new organizational era. *Annual Review of Psychology, 48,* 515–546.

Rubinsky, S., & Smith, N. (1973). Safety training by accident simulation. *Journal of Applied Psychology, 57,* 68–73.

Russell, J. S. (1984). A review of fair employment cases in the field of training. *Personnel Psychology, 37,* 261–276.

Russell, J. S., Terborg, J. R., & Powers, M. L. (1985). Organizational performance and organizational level training and support. *Personnel Psychology, 38,* 849–863.

Ryman, D. H., & Biersner, R. J. (1975). Attitudes predictive of diving training success. *Personnel Psychology, 28,* 181–188.

Saari, L. M., Johnson, T. R., McLaughlin, S. D., & Zimmerle, D. M. (1988). A survey of management training and education practices in U.S. companies. *Personnel Psychology, 41,* 731–743.

Sackett, P. R., & Mullen, E. J. (1993). Beyond formal experimental design: Towards an expanded view of the training evaluation process. *Personnel Psychology, 46,* 613–628.

Salas, E., Bowers, C., & Rhodenizer, L. (1998). It is not how much you have but how you use it: Toward a rational use of simulation to support aviation training. *International Journal of Aviation Psychology, 8,* 197–209.

Salas, E., & Cannon-Bowers, J. A. (in press). The science of training: A decade of progress. *Annual review of psychology.* Palo Alto, CA: Annual Reviews.

Salas, E., Cannon-Bowers, J. A., & Kozlowski, S. W. J. (1997). The science and practice of training—Current trends and emerging themes. In J. K. Ford & Associates (Eds.), *Improving training effectiveness in work organizations,* Mahwah, NJ: LEA.

Salas, E., Dickinson, T. L., Converse, S. A., & Tannenbaum, S. I. (1992). Toward an understanding of team performance and training. In R. W. Swezey & E. Salas (Eds.), *Teams: Their training and performance.* Norwood, NJ: ABLEX.

Salas, E., Prince, C., Bowers, C. A., Stout, R. J., Oser, R. L., & Cannon-Bowers, J. A. (1999). A methodology for enhancing crew resource management training. *Human Factors, 41,* 161–172.

Salvendy, G., & Pilitsis, J. (1980). The development and validation of an analytical training program for medical suturing. *Human Factors, 22,* 153–170.

Sanders, P., & Vanouzas, J. N. (1983). Socialization to learning. *Training and Development Journal, 37,* 14–21.

Saretsky, G. (1972). The OEO P.C. experiment and the John Henry effect. *Phi Delta Kappan, 53,* 579–581.

Sawyer, C. R., Pain, R. F., Van Cott, H., & Banks, W. W. (1982). Nuclear control room modifications and the role of transfer of training principles: A review of issues and research. (NUREG/CR-2828, EGG-2211). Idaho Falls, ID: Idaho National Engineering Laboratory.

Schaafstal, A., Schraagen, J. M., & van Berlo, M. (2000). Cognitive task analysis and innovation of training: The case of structured troubleshooting. *Human Factors, 42,* 75–86.

Schein, E. (1995). *Career survival: Strategic job/role planning,* San Diego: Pfeiffer & Company.

Schein, E. (1997). Three cultures of management: The key to organizational learning. *Sloan Management Review, 38,* 9–20.

Schendel, J. D., & Hagman, J. D. (1982). On sustaining procedural skills over a prolonged retention interval. *Journal of Applied Psychology, 67,* 605–610.

Schmidt, R. A., & Wulf, G. (1997). Continuous concurrent feedback degrades skill learning: Implications for training and simulation. *Human Factors, 39,* 509–525.

Schmitt, N., & Cohen, S. A. (1989). Internal analysis of task ratings by job incumbents. *Journal of Applied Psychology, 74,* 96–104.

Schmitt, N., Ford, J. K., & Stults, D. M. (1986). Changes in self-perceived ability as a function of performance in an assessment center. *Journal of Occupational Psychology, 59,* 327–335.

Schneider, B., & Konz, A. M. (1989). Strategic job analysis. *Human Resources Management, 28,* 51–63.

Schuler, R. S. (1994). Repositioning the human resource function. In R. A. Noe, J. R. Hollenbeck, B. Gerhart, & P. M. Wright (Eds.). *Readings in human resource management.* Homewood, IL: Irwin.

Secretary's Commission on Achieving Necessary Skills. (1991). *What work requires of schools: SCANS report for America 2000.* U.S. Department of Labor. Washington, DC: U.S. Government Printing Office.

Senge, P. (1990). *The fifth discipline.* New York: Doubleday.

Sessa, V. I. (1992). Managing diversity at the Xerox Corporation: Balanced workforce goal and caucus groups. In S. E. Jackson (Ed.), *Diversity in the workplace: Human resource initiatives.* New York: Guilford Press.

Sharpe, R. (1994). The waiting game: Women make strides but men stay firmly in top company jobs. *Wall Street Journal,* March 29.

Shiffrin, R. M., & Schneider, W. (1977). Controlled and automatic human information processing: II. Perceptual learning, automatic attending, and a general theory. *Psychological Review, 84,* 127–190.

Siegel, A. I. (1983). The miniature job training and evaluation approach: Additional findings. *Personnel Psychology, 36,* 41–56.

Skarlicki, D. P., & Latham, G. P. (1997). Leadership training in organizational justice to increase citizenship behavior within a labor union: A replication. *Personnel Psychology, 50,* 617–631.

Skinner, B. F. (1954). Science of learning and the art of teaching. *Harvard Educational Review, 24,* 86–97.

Smith, E. A. (1990). Theory and practice in training videos: An exploration. *Human Resource Development Quarterly, 1,* 409–412.

Smith, E., Ford, J. K., & Kozlowski, S. W. J. (1997). Building adaptive expertise: Implications for training design. In M. A. Quiñones & A. Ehrenstein (Eds.), *Training for the 21st century: Applications of psychological research.* Washington, DC: American Psychological Association.

Smith, M. C., & Reder, S. (1998). Introduction: Adult literacy research and the National Adult Literacy Survey. In M. C. Smith (Ed.), *Literacy for the twenty-first century.* Westport, CT: Praeger.

Smither, J. W., London, M., Vasilopoulos, N. L., Reilly, R. R., Millsap, R. E., & Salvemini, N. (1995). An examination of the effects of an upward feedback program over time. *Personnel Psychology, 48,* 1–34.

Snow, H. (1997). *Indoor/outdoor team-building games for trainers.* New York: McGraw-Hill.

Snow, R. E., & Lohman, D. F. (1984). Toward a theory of cognitive aptitude for learning from instruction. *Journal of Educational Psychology, 76,* 347–376.

Society for Industrial and Organizational Psychology. (1987). *Principles for the validation and use of personnel selection procedures* (3rd ed.). College Park, MD: Author.

Sorcher, M., & Spence, R. (1982). The interface project: Behavior modeling as social technology in South Africa. *Personnel Psychology, 35,* 557–581.

Spencer, L. M., & Spencer, S. M. (1993). *Competence at work.* New York: Wiley.

Spreitzer, G., McCall, M. W., & Mahoney, J. D. (1997). Early identification of international executive potential. *Journal of Applied Psychology, 82,* 6–29.

Spychalski, A. C., Quiñones, M. A., Gaugler, B., & Pohley, K. (1997). A survey of assessment center practices in organizations in the United States. *Personnel Psychology, 50,* 71–90.

Stamps, D. (1999). Enterprise training: This changes everything. *Training, 36,* 40–48.

Steadham, S. V. (1980). Learning to select a needs assessment strategy. *Training and Development Journal, 30,* 55–61.

Steele-Johnson, D., & Hyde, B. G. (1997). Advanced technologies in training: Intelligent tutoring system and virtual reality. In J. K. Ford & Associates (Eds.), *Improving the effectiveness in work organizations.* Mahwah, NJ: LEA.

Stern, D., Finkelstein, N., Stone, J., Latting, J., & Dornsife, C. (1994). *Research on school-to-work transition programs in the United States* (NCRVE Report No. MDS-771). Berkeley: University of California, National Center for Research in Vocational Education.

Sterns, H. L., & Camp, C. J. (1998). Applied gerontology. *Applied Psychology: An International Review, 47,* 175–198.

Sterns, H. L., & Doverspike, D. (1989). Aging and the training and learning process. In I. L. Goldstein (Ed.), *Training and development in organizations.* San Francisco: Jossey-Bass.

Sterns, H. L., & McDaniel, M. A. (1995). Industrial gerontology. In G. Maddox (Ed.), *The encyclopedia of aging* (2nd ed.). New York: Springer.

Stevens, C. K., & Gist, M. E. (1997). Effects of self-efficacy and goal orientation training on negotiation skill maintenance: What are the mechanisms? *Personnel Psychology, 50,* 955–978.

Stewart, L. (1962). Management games today. In J. M. Kibbee, C. J. Kraft, & B. Nanus (Eds.), *Management games.* New York: Reinhold.

Stewart, T. (1997). *Intellectual capital: The new wealth of organizations.* New York: Currency.

Sticht, T. G. (1997). Assessing foundation skills for work. In H. F. O'Neil (Ed.), *Workforce readiness.* Mahwah, N.J.: LEA

Sticht, T. G., Armstrong, W. B., Hickey, D. T., & Caylor, J. S. (1987). *Cast off youth.* New York: Praeger.

Stone, R. J. (1993). VR and cyberspace: From science fiction to science fact. *Information Services and Use, 11,* 283–300.

Sugawara, S. (1991). Study: Firms holding back women and minorities. *Washington Post,* August 9, B1-3.

Swanson, J. L., & Fouad, N. A. (1999). Applying theories of person-environment fit to the transition from school to work. *Career Development Quarterly, 47,* 337–347.

Swezey, R. W. (1981). *Individual performance assessment: An approach to criterion-referenced test development.* Reston, VA: Reston Publishing Co.

Swezey, R. W. (1983). Application of a transfer of training model to training device assessment. *Journal of Educational Technology Systems, 11,* 225–238.

Swoboda, F. (1991). GAO finds job training discrimination. *Washington Post,* July 17, A21.

Tang, T. L-P., & Crofford, A. B. (1999). The anticipation of plant closing: Employee reactions. *Journal of Social Psychology, 139,* 44–48.

Tannenbaum, S. I. (1997). Enhancing continuous learning: Diagnostic findings from multiple companies. *Human Resource Management, 36,* 437–452.

Tannenbaum, S. I., Mathieu, J. E., Salas, E., & Cannon-Bowers, J. A. (1991). Meeting trainees' expectations: The influence of training fulfillment on the development of commitment, self-efficacy, and motivation. *Journal of Applied Psychology, 76,* 759–769.

Tannenbaum, S. I., Smith-Jentsch, K. A., & Behson, S. J. (1998). Training team leaders to facilitate team learning and performance. In J. A. Cannon-Bowers & E. Salas (Eds.), *Making decisions under stress: implications for individual and team training.* Washington, DC: APA.

Tannenbaum, S. I., & Yukl, G. (1992). Training and development in work organizations. *Annual review of psychology.* Palo Alto, CA: Annual Reviews.

Taylor, P. (1994, May). *The effectiveness of behavior modeling training in organizations.* Presented at the 4th International Human Resources Management Conference, Queensland, Australia.

Teachout, M. S., Sego, D. J., & Ford, J. K. (1997/1998). An integrated approach to summative evaluation for facilitating training course improvement. *Training Research Journal, 3,* 169–184.

Teahan, J. E. (1976). Role playing and group experiences to facilitate attitude and value changes among black and white police officers. *Journal of Social Issues, 31,* 35–45.

Tesoro, F. (1998). Implementing an ROI measurement process at Dell Computer. *Performance Improvement Quarterly, 11,* 103–114.

Tessmer, M. (1995). Formative multimedia evaluation. *Training Research Journal, 1,* 127–149.

Thayer, P. W. (1997). A rapidly changing world: Some implications for training systems in the year 2001 and beyond. In M. A. Quiñones & A. Ehrenstein (Eds.), *Training for a rapidly changing workplace.* Washington, DC: American Psychological Association.

Thayer, P. W., & Teachout, M. S. (1995). *A climate for transfer model* (Technical Report No. AL/HR-TP-1995-0035). Human Resources Directorate, Brooks AFB, Texas.

Thiagarajan, S. (1999). Challenge education. In D. G. Landon, K. S. Whiteside, & M. M. McKenna (Eds.), *Intervention resource guide: 50 performance improvement tools.* San Francisco: Jossey-Bass.

Thorndike, E. L. (1927). The law of effect. *American Journal of Psychology, 39,* 212–222.

Thornton, G. C., & Cleveland, J. N. (1990). Developing managerial talent through simulation. *American Psychologist, 45,* 190–199.

Threlkeld, R., & Brzoska, K. (1994). Research in distance education. In B. Willis (Ed.), *Distance education: Strategies and tools.* Englewood Cliffs, NJ: Educational Technology Publications.

Time. (1988). The literacy gap. December 19, 56–57.

Torrence, D. R., & Torrence, J. (1987). Training in the face of illiteracy: *Training and Development Journal, 41,* 44–48.

Townscend, A. M., DeMarie, S., & Hendrickson, A. R. (1998). Virtual teams: Technology and the workplace of the future. *Academy of Management Executive, 12,* 17–29.

Tracey, J. B., Tannenbaum, S. I., & Kavanagh, M. J. (1995). Applying trained skills on the job: The importance of the work environment. *Journal of Applied Psychology, 80,* 239–252.

Triandis, H. C. (1994). Cross-cultural industrial and organizational psychology. In M. D. Dunnette & L. Hough (Eds.), *Handbook of industrial and organizational psychology* (vol. 4, pp. 103–172). Palo Alto, CA: Consulting Psychologists Press.

Triandis, H. C., Kurowski, L. L., & Gelfand, M. J. (1994). Workplace diversity. In M. D. Dunnette & L. Hough (Eds.), *Handbook of industrial and organizational psychology,* vol. 4. Palo Alto, CA: Consulting Psychologists Press.

Trowbridge, M. A., & Cason, H. (1932). An experimental study of Thorndike's theory of learning. *Journal of General Psychology, 7,* 245–260.

Tung, R. L. (1993). Managing cross-national and intra-national diversity. *Human Resource Management, 32,* 461–477.

USA Today. (1999). *Welfare to work success reported in all 50 states.* (P. Leavitt). August 2.

U.S. Department of Justice. (1996). Enforcing the ADA: A status report from the Department of Justice. KinderCare Settlement Agreement. Available: http://www.usdoj.gov/crt/ada/kinder1.htm.

U.S. Department of Justice, Civil Rights Division. (1996). *A guide to disability rights laws.* Washington, DC: U.S. Government Printing Office.

U.S. Department of Labor, Commission on Achieving Necessary Skills (SCANS). (1991). *What work requires of schools.* Washington, DC: U.S. Government Printing Office.

U.S. Department of Labor. (March 1995). Glass Ceiling Commission: *Good for business: Making full use of the nation's human capital.* Washington, DC: author.

U.S. Department of Labor's Employment and Training Administration. (1998). O°NET. Washington, DC: U.S. Government Printing Office.

U.S. Equal Employment Opportunity Commission. (1991). *The Americans with Disabilities Act: Your responsibilities as an employer.* Report No. EEOC-BK-17.

U.S. Merit Systems Protection Board. (1995). *Leadership for change.* Washington, DC: U.S. Government Printing Office.

Van Ryn, M., & Vinokur, A. D. (1992). How did it work? An examination of the mechanisms through which an intervention for the unemployed promoted job search behavior. *American Journal of Community Psychology, 20,* 577–597.

Vicente, K. (1999). *Cognitive work analysis: Toward safe, productive, and healthy computer-based work.* Mahwah, NJ: LEA.

Vinokur, A. D., & Schul, Y. (1999). Mastery and inoculation against setbacks as active ingredients in the JOBS intervention for the unemployed. *Journal of Consulting and Clinical Psychology, 65,* 867–877.

Vinokur, A. D., Schul, Y., Vuori, J., & Price, R. H. (2000). Two years after a job loss: Long-term impact of the JOBS program on reemployment and mental health. *Journal of Health Psychology, 5,* 32–47.

Vinokur, A. D., van Ryn, M., Gramlich, E., & Price, R. H. (1991). Long-term follow-up and benefit cost analysis of the JOBS program: A preventive intervention for the unemployed. *Journal of Applied Psychology, 76,* 213–129.

Vobejda, B. (1987). The new cutting edge in factories. *Washington Post,* April 14, A14.

Volet, S. E. (1991). Modeling and coaching of relevant metacognitive strategies for enhancing university students' learning. *Learning and Instruction, 1,* 319–328.

Volpe, C. E., Cannon-Bowers, J. A, Salas, E., & Spector, P. E. (1996). The impact of cross training on team functioning: An empirical investigation. *Human Factors, 38,* 87–100.

Vroom, V. H. (1964). *Work and motivation.* New York: Wiley.

Wagner, R. J., Baldwin, T. P., & Rowland, C. C. (1991). Outdoor training: Revolution or fad? *Training and Development Journal, 45,* 50–57.

Walker, A. G., & Smither, J. W. (1999). A five-year study of upward feedback: What managers do with their results matters. *Personnel Psychology, 52,* 393–423.

Walker, N., & Fisk, A. D. (1995). Human Factors goes to the gridiron. *Ergonomics in Design,* July, 8–13.

Wall, T. D., & Jackson, P. R. (1995). New manufacturing initiatives shopfloor design. In A. Howard (Ed.), *The changing nature of work.* San Francisco: Jossey-Bass.

Wanberg, C. R., Bunce, L. W., & Gavin, M. B. (1999). Perceived fairness of layoffs among individuals who have been laid off: A longitudinal study. *Personnel Psychology, 52,* 59–84.

Wanous, J. P. (1980). *Organizational entry: Recruitment, selection, orientation, and socialization of newcomers.* Reading, MA: Addison-Wesley.

Wanous, J. P. (1992). *Organizational entry: Recruitment, selection, orientation, and socialization of newcomers* (2nd ed.). Reading, MA: Addison-Wesley.

Wards Cove Packing Co. v. Antonio, 109 S. Ct. 2115 (1989).

Warr, P., & Bruce, D. (1995). Trainee characteristics and the outcomes of open learning. *Personnel Psychology, 48,* 347–375.

Washington Post. (1996). First police retraining class finishes with mixed grades. April 1, A1, 12–13.

Washington Post. (2000). Skilled-workers visa cap is reached early. March 18, A12.

Waterman, R. H., Waterman, J. A., & Collard, B. A. (1994). Toward a career resilient workforce. *Harvard Business Review, 72,* July-August, 87–95.

Watkins, K. E. (1990). Tacit beliefs of human resource developers: Producing unintended consequences. *Human Resource Development Quarterly, 1,* 263–275.

Webster, J., & Hackley, P. (1997). Teaching effectiveness in technology-mediated distance learning. *Academy of Management Journal, 40*(6), 1282–1309.

Weiss, H. M. (1990). Learning theory and industrial psychology. In M. D. Dunnette & L. M. Hough (Eds.), *Handbook of industrial and organizational psychology.* Palo Alto, CA: Consulting Psychologists Press.

Wesley, R. J., Shebilske, W. L., & Monk, J. M. (1993). *A preliminary empirical evaluation of virtual reality as a training tool for visual-spatial tasks.* Brooks AFB, TX: Armstrong Laboratory, Air Force Material Command.

Wexley, K., & Latham, G. P. (1981). *Developing and training human resources in organizations.* Glenview, IL: Scott, Foresman.

Wherry, R. J. (1957). The past and future of criterion evaluation. *Personnel Psychology, 10,* 1–5.

Williams, T. C., Thayer, P. W., & Pond, S. B. (1991). *Test of a model of motivational influences on reactions to training and learning.* Presented at the meetings of the Society for Industrial and Organizational Psychology, St. Louis.

Wills, S., & Barham, K. (1994). Being an international manager. *European Management Journal, 12,* 49–58.

Wood, R., & Bandura, A. (1989). Social cognitive theory of organizational management. *Academy of Management Review, 14,* 361–384.

Woolf, B. (1992). AI in education. In S. Shapiro (Ed.), *Encyclopedia of artificial intelligence* (2nd ed.), New York: Wiley.

Wulfeck, W. H. II, Ellis, J. A., Richards, R. E., Wood, N. D., & Merrill, M. D. (1978). The instructional quality inventory: I. Introduction and overview. *NPRDC Technology Report 79-3.* San Diego, CA. Navy Personnel Research and Development Center.

Yang, H., Sackett, P. R., & Arvey, R. D. (1996). Statistical power and cost in training evaluation: Some new considerations. *Personnel Psychology, 49,* 651–668.

Yelon, S. (in press). *Performance-centered instruction.* E. Lansing, MI: Michigan State University Press.

Yelon, S., Reznich, C., & Sleight, D. (1997). Medical fellows tell stories of application: A grounded theory on the dynamics of transfer. *Performance Improvement Quarterly, 10,* 134–155.

Yukl, G. A. (1998). *Leadership in organizations* (4th ed.). Upper Saddle River, NJ: Prentice Hall.

Zhang, S., & Fulford, C. (1994). Are time and psychological interactivity the same thing in the distance learning television classroom? *Educational Technology, 34*(6), 58–64.

AUTHOR INDEX

SUBJECT INDEX